Fodor's
The Czech Republic & Slovakia

Reprinted from *Fodor's Eastern Europe*

Fodor's Travel Publications, Inc.
New York • Toronto • London • Sydney • Auckland

ISBN 0-679-02572-3

Fodor's The Czech Republic & Slovakia

Editor: Scott McNeely
Contributors: Mark Baker, Chris Billy, Robert Blake, Craig Cabanis, William Echikson, Anita Guerrini, Alan Levy, Jeffrey Obser, Marcy Pritchard, Linda K. Schmidt
Creative Director: Fabrizio La Rocca
Cartographer: David Lindroth
Illustrator: Karl Tanner
Cover Photograph: Kevin Galvin

Design: Vignelli Associates

Special Sales

Contents

Foreword   *v*

Highlights   *viii*

Fodor's Choice   *x*

1   Essential Information   *1*

Before You Go *2*

Government Tourist Offices *2*
Tours and Packages *2*
When to Go *4*
What to Pack *4*
Taking Money Abroad *6*
Getting Money from Home *7*
What It Will Cost *8*
Passports and Visas *8*
Customs and Duties *9*
Traveling with Cameras, Camcorders, and Laptops *10*
Staying Healthy *11*
Insurance *12*
Car Rentals *14*
Rail Passes *15*
Student and Youth Travel *16*
Traveling with Children *17*
Hints for Travelers with Disabilities *18*
Hints for Older Travelers *19*
Further Reading *20*

Arriving and Departing *21*

From North America by Plane *21*
From the United Kingdom by Plane, Car, Bus, and Train *24*

Staying in the Czech Republic and Slovakia *25*

Getting Around *25*
Telephones *26*
Dining *26*
Lodging *27*
Credit Cards *28*

2   Czech Republic   *29*

Before You Go *31*
Arriving and Departing *36*
Staying in the Czech Republic *37*
Prague *43*
Bohemia *89*
Moravia *122*

3 Slovakia
3 Slovakia *142*

Before You Go *144*
Arriving and Departing *147*
Staying in Slovakia *148*
Bratislava *153*
The High Tatras *168*
Eastern Slovakia *176*

Czech Vocabulary *190*

Index *200*

Maps

Czech Republic *xii*
Slovakia *xiii*
World Time Zones *xiv–xv*
Prague Metro *48*
Prague (Tours 1–4) *50–51*
Tour 5: Prague Castle (Pražský hrad) *70*
Prague Dining and Lodging *82–83*
Bohemia *93*
Moravia *126*
Brno *132*
Slovakia Exploring *157*
Bratislava *158*

Foreword

While every care has been taken to ensure the accuracy of the information in this guide, the passage of time will always bring change, and consequently, the publisher cannot accept responsibility for errors that may occur.

All prices and opening times quoted here are based on information supplied to us at press time. Hours and admission fees may change, however, and the prudent traveler will avoid inconvenience by calling ahead.

Fodor's wants to hear about your travel experiences, both pleasant and unpleasant. When a hotel or restaurant fails to live up to its billing, let us know and we will investigate the complaint and revise our entries where the facts warrant it.

Send your letters to the editors of Fodor's Travel Publications, 201 E. 50th Street, New York, NY 10022.

Highlights and Fodor's Choice

Highlights

The major political and economic reforms begun in the early 1990s throughout Eastern Europe are now bringing in Western stores, cafés, hotels, and restaurants. But behind the big (mostly Western) names opening up on the main shopping streets, the local small-scale private sector is beginning to blossom. Every week small state-owned shops and restaurants are auctioned off to would-be entrepreneurs, turning the corner store that used to sell dreary sweaters behind dirty windows into a neon-clad electronic-and-imported-cosmetics store, or the sleepy used bookstore into a delicatessen.

Czech Republic Following the breakup of the Czechoslovak state in 1993, the new Czech Republic continues along its path of economic and cultural revitalization, with the eventual goal of being incorporation into the European Community (EC) by the year 2000. Far from hurting the country, the Czech-Slovak split has freed officials to concentrate on pressing economic problems in Bohemia and Moravia, without having to worry about Slovakia. Chief among these problems are rising prices, falling living standards, and rising unemployment. Tourism, however, remains one of the brightest sectors of the economy, and travelers will likely be unaffected by the grim economic statistics.

One tangible impact of the country's economic reforms has been an acceleration in the pace of architectural renovations. The scaffolding that has long surrounded many of Prague's historic structures is finally being dismantled, and many hotels and even family-operated inns are installing new fixtures and applying a fresh coat of paint. One of the areas to get a face-lift over the past few years is Old Town Square (Staroměstské náměstí), one of the jewels of the "new" Prague, lined by such landmarks as the Tyn Church and the Old Town Hall.

The number of hotels keeps pace with the growing number of visitors. This is even true of Prague, which has become a major European tourist destination. At press time, Penta hotels had just opened up a new four-star facility in central Prague. Several other new projects are expected during the course of the year. The **Hotel Praha,** once Communist-party lodgings, has been taken over by the Hyatt chain and is scheduled to reopen as a luxury hotel in late 1994. Like the number of new large hotels, the number of smaller, privately owned hotels and pensions is also on the rise.

Prague's cultural life continues to thrive: New theater groups sprout up right and left, and the schedule of concerts and operas has grown each season since the revolution of 1989. The **Prague Spring Music Festival,** which even before the collapse of the communist government was one of the great events on the European calendar, promises to attract record numbers of music lovers in the next few years; it is held annually from mid-May to early June. One sad note: Prague's famous Charles Bridge is scheduled to be closed for much of 1994 for necessary repairs.

Slovakia Europe's youngest country continues to be dogged by bad press and a bit of an identity complex. Decisions to proceed on environmental megaprojects, such as new nuclear reactors and the highly controversial Gabčikovo dam on the Danube, have kept officials on the defensive for much of the past year. Moreover, the government's unwillingness to commit to a rapid program of economic reform has some wondering (only partly in jest) whether the Communists haven't secretly regained control. Visitors to this beautiful country can, however, afford to remain blithely ignorant of these political machinations.

Slovakia has retained the former Czechoslovakia's policy of encouraging tourism; visitors from the United States or United Kingdom do not need visas, although those entering Slovakia from the Czech Republic should be prepared to show a passport. In addition, Czech money is no longer valid in Slovakia (and vice versa).

Changes in the hotel and restaurant scene are far less noticeable in Slovakia than in the Czech Republic. The long-awaited Hotel Danube opened its doors in the Slovak capital, Bratislava, in 1993, bringing the number of deluxe hotels in town to two. An old Bratislava favorite, the Carlton, was closed for a much-needed face-lift in 1993; the hotel expects to reopen sometime this year. Elsewhere in the country, it's business as usual for the tourist sector. Hotel operators in the High Tatras report slower seasons than in the past, as the East bloc clientele on which they've relied for the past 40 years try out the more exotic destinations in Spain and France. Interest in the Tatras is sure to grow in the future, though, as West Europeans and Americans discover their charm and natural beauty.

Fodor's Choice

No two people will agree on what makes a perfect vacation, but it can be fun and helpful to know what others think. We hope you'll have a chance to experience some of Fodor's Choices yourself while visiting the Czech Republic and Slovakia. For detailed information on individual entries, see the relevant sections of this guidebook.

Lodging

Czech Republic   Dvořák, Karlovy Vary, Bohemia *(Very Expensive)*

Grandhotel Pupp, Karlovy Vary *(Very Expensive)*

U Pavá, Prague *(Very Expensive)*

Pension U Raka, Prague *(Expensive)*

Ruže, Český Krumlov, Bohemia *(Expensive)*

Černý Orel, Telč, Moravia *(Moderate)*

Hubertus, Valtice, Moravia *(Inexpensive)*

Slovakia   Grand Hotel, Starý Smokovec, *(Expensive)*

Grandhotel Praha, Tatranská Lomnica, *(Expensive)*

Dining

Czech Republic   U Zlaté Hrušky, Prague *(Very Expensive)*

Stodola, Konopiště, Bohemia *(Expensive)*

U Mecenáše, Prague *(Expensive)*

Lobkovická, Prague *(Expensive)*

Penguin's, Prague *(Moderate)*

Slovakia   Rybarský cech, Bratislava, *(Expensive)*

Koliba, Zochová Chata, Modra, *(Moderate)*

Castles and Churches

Czech Republic   St. Vitus Cathedral, Hradčany, Prague

Tyn Church, Staré Město, Prague

Krumlov Castle, Český Krumlov, Bohemia

St. Barbara's Cathedral, Kutná Hora, Bohemia

Villa Tugendhut, Brno, Moravia

St. Anne's Chapel, Olomouc, Moravia

Slovakia   Church and Convent of the Poor Clares, Bratislava

Červený Kameň Castle, Modra

The wood churches off the Dukla Pass road, Svidník

St. Jacob's Church, Levoča

Museums

Czech Republic National Gallery, Prague

The State Jewish Museum, Prague

Theresienstadt Memorial Museum, Terezín, Bohemia

Slovakia Šariš Icon Museum, Bardejov

Towns and Villages

Czech Republic Český Krumlov, Bohemia

Mariánské Lazně, Bohemia

Telč, Moravia

Slovakia Bardejov, High Tatra mountains

Levoča, High Tatra mountains

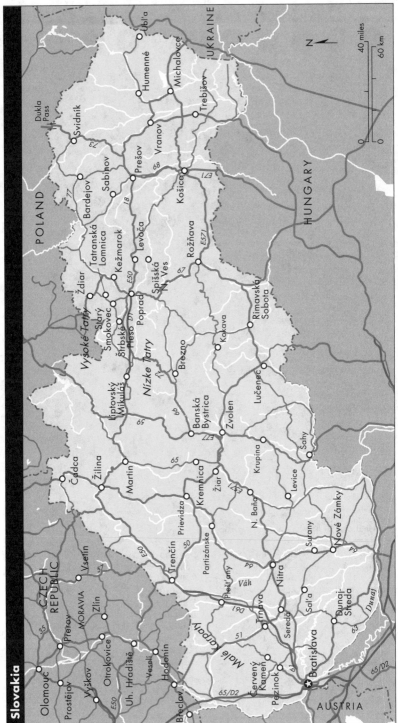

Slovakia

World Time Zones

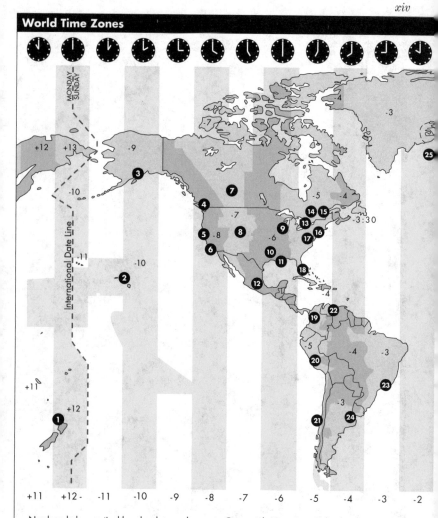

Numbers below vertical bands relate each zone to Greenwich Mean Time (0 hrs.).
Local times frequently differ from these general indications,
as indicated by light-face numbers on map.

Algiers, **29**	Berlin, **34**	Delhi, **48**	Istanbul, **40**
Anchorage, **3**	Bogotá, **19**	Denver, **8**	Jerusalem, **42**
Athens, **41**	Budapest, **37**	Djakarta, **53**	Johannesburg, **44**
Auckland, **1**	Buenos Aires, **24**	Dublin, **26**	Lima, **20**
Baghdad, **46**	Caracas, **22**	Edmonton, **7**	Lisbon, **28**
Bangkok, **50**	Chicago, **9**	Hong Kong, **56**	London (Greenwich), **27**
Beijing, **54**	Copenhagen, **33**	Honolulu, **2**	Los Angeles, **6**
	Dallas, **10**		Madrid, **38**
			Manila, **57**

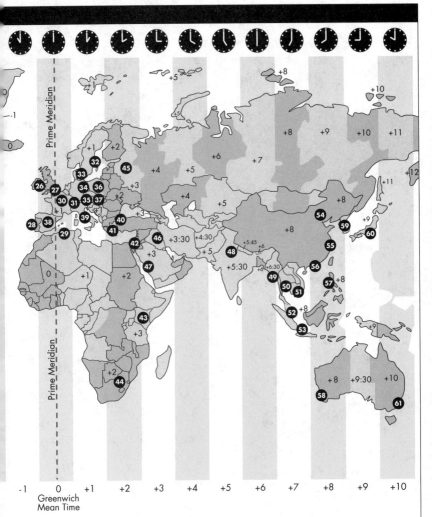

-1   0   +1   +2   +3   +4   +5   +6   +7   +8   +9   +10

Greenwich
Mean Time

Mecca, **47**
Mexico City, **12**
Miami, **18**
Montréal, **15**
Moscow, **45**
Nairobi, **43**
New Orleans, **11**
New York City, **16**

Ottawa, **14**
Paris, **30**
Perth, **58**
Reykjavík, **25**
Rio de Janeiro, **23**
Rome, **39**
Saigon (Ho Chi Minh City), **51**

San Francisco, **5**
Santiago, **21**
Seoul, **59**
Shanghai, **55**
Singapore, **52**
Stockholm, **32**
Sydney, **61**
Tokyo, **60**

Toronto, **13**
Vancouver, **4**
Vienna, **35**
Warsaw, **36**
Washington, D.C., **17**
Yangon, **49**
Zürich, **31**

1 Essential Information

Before You Go

Government Tourist Offices

In the United States Čedok (10 E. 40th St., New York, NY 10016, tel. 212/689–9720), the Czech Republic and Slovakian travel bureau, is actually a travel agent rather than a tourist information office. It will provide hotel and travel information, tickets, and reservations, but don't expect too much in the way of general information.

In Canada For information on the Czech Republic and Slovakia, call or write any U.S. office.

In the United Kingdom Čedok (17–18 Old Bond St., London W1X 4RB, tel.071/629–6058), the Czech Republic and Slovakia travel bureau, is a travel agency, not a source of general information. However, the office will provide hotel information and make reservations.

Tours and Packages

Should you buy your travel arrangements to Eastern Europe packaged or do it yourself? There are advantages either way. Buying packaged arrangements saves you money, particularly if you can find a program that includes exactly the features you want. You also get a pretty good idea of what your trip will cost from the outset. Generally, you have two options: escorted tours and independent packages. Escorted tours are most often via motorcoach, with a tour director in charge. They're ideal if you don't mind having limited free time and traveling with strangers. Your baggage is handled, your time rigorously scheduled, and most meals planned. Such tours are therefore the most hassle-free way to see a destination, as well as generally the least expensive. Independent packages allow plenty of flexibility. They generally include airline travel and hotels, with certain options available, such as sightseeing, car rental, and excursions. Such packages are usually more expensive than escorted tours, but your time is your own.

Although you can book directly through tour operators, you will pay no more to go through a travel agent, who will be able to tell you about tours and packages from a number of operators. Whatever program you ultimately choose, be sure to find out exactly what is included: taxes, tips, transfers, meals, baggage handling, ground transportation, entertainment, excursions, sports and recreation (and rental equipment if necessary). Ask about the level of hotel used, its location, the size of its rooms, the kind of beds, and its amenities, such as pool, room service, or programs for children, if these things are important to you. Find out the operator's cancellation penalties. Nearly everyone charges them, and the only way to avoid them is to buy trip-cancellation insurance (*see* Trip Insurance, *below*). Also ask about the single supplement, a surcharge assessed to solo travelers. Some operators do not make you pay it if you agree to be matched up with a roommate of the same sex, even if one is not found by departure time. Remember that a program that has features you won't use, whether for rental sporting equipment or discounted museum admissions, may not be the most cost-wise choice for you.

Fully Escorted Tours
Escorted tours are usually sold in three categories: deluxe, first-class, and tourist or budget class. The most important differences are the price, of course, and the level of accommodations. Some operators specialize in one category, and others offer a range. Most itineraries are jam-packed with sightseeing, so you see a lot in a short amount of time (usually one place per day). To judge just how fast-paced the tour is, review the itinerary carefully. If you are in a different hotel each night, you will be getting up early each day to head out, travel to your next destination, do some sightseeing, have dinner, and go to bed; then you'll start all over again. If you want some free time, make sure it's mentioned in the tour brochure; if you want to be escorted to every meal, confirm that any tour you consider does that. Also, when comparing programs, be sure to find out if the motorcoach is air-conditioned and has a rest room on board. Make your selection based on price and stops on the itinerary.

Contact **Abercrombie & Kent** (1520 Kensington Rd., Oak Brook, IL 60521, tel. 708/954–2944 or 800/323–7308) and **Maupintour** (Box 807, Lawrence, KS 66044, tel. 913/843–1211 or 800/255–4266) in the deluxe category; **British Airways** (tel. 800/247–9297), **Caravan Tours** (401 N. Michigan Ave, Suite 3325, Chicago, IL 60611, tel. 312/321–9800 or 800/227–2826), **Delta Dream Vacations** (tel. 800/872–7786), **Globus** (95–25 Queens Blvd., Rego Park, NY 11374, tel. 718/268–7000 or 800/221–0090), **Lufthansa** (tel. 800/645–3880), **Olson-Travelworld** (Box 10066, Manhattan Beach, CA 90226, tel. 310/546–8400 or 800/421–5785), and **Trafalgar Tours** (21 E. 26th St., New York, NY 10010, tel. 212/689–8977 or 800/854–0103) in the first-class category; and **Cosmos,** Globus's sister company (at the same number) in the budget category.

Independent Packages
Independent packages, which travel agents call FITs (for Foreign Independent Travel), are offered by airlines, tour operators who may also do escorted programs, and any number of other companies from large, established firms to small, new entrepreneurs.

Delta Dream Vacations, and **Orbis Travel** (*see above*) also offer independent packages, as does **Travel Bound** (599 Broadway, New York, NY 10012, tel. 212/334–1350 or 800/456–8656).

Their programs come in a range of prices based on levels of luxury and options—in hotel and airfare, sightseeing, car rental, transfers, admission to local attractions, and other extras. Note that when pricing different packages, it sometimes pays to purchase the same arrangements separately, as when a rock-bottom promotional airfare is being offered, for example. Again, base your choice on what's available for your budget for the destinations you want to visit.

Special-Interest Travel
Special-interest programs may be fully escorted or independent. Some require a certain amount of expertise, but most are for the average traveler with an interest and are usually hosted by experts in the subject matter. When the program is escorted, it enjoys the advantages and disadvantages of all escorted programs; because your fellow travelers are apt to be passionate or knowledgeable about the subject, they can prove as enjoyable a part of your travel as the destination itself. The price range is wide, but the cost is usually higher—sometimes a lot higher—than that of ordinary escorted tours and packages, because of the expert guidance and special activities.

General **Abercrombie & Kent** (*see above*) offers a variety of programs including wine-tasting, ballooning, and museum tours.

Music **Daily-Thorp** (330 W. 58th St., New York, NY 10019, tel. 212/307–1555) offers a deluxe opera-and-music tour of Europe that includes Prague.

When to Go

The tourist season generally runs from April or May through October; spring and fall combine good weather with a more bearable level of tourism. Try visiting the Giant Mountain of Bohemia or the High Tatras in Slovakia in late spring or fall; the colors are dazzling and you'll have the hotels and restaurants pretty much to yourself. Bear in mind that many attractions are closed November through March.

Prague is beautiful year-round, but avoid midsummer (especially July and August) and the Christmas and Easter holidays, when the city is choked with visitors.

Climate The following are the average daily maximum and minimum temperatures for major cities in the region.

Bratislava	**Jan.**	36F	2C	**May**	70F	21C	**Sept.**	72F	22C
		27	– 3		52	11		54	12
	Feb.	39F	4C	**June**	75F	24C	**Oct.**	59F	15C
		28	– 2		57	14		45	7
	Mar.	48F	9C	**July**	79F	26C	**Nov.**	46F	8C
		34	1		61	16		37	3
	Apr.	61F	16C	**Aug.**	79F	26C	**Dec.**	39F	4C
		43	6		61	16		32	0

Prague	**Jan.**	36F	2C	**May**	66F	19C	**Sept.**	68F	20C
		25	– 4		46	8		50	10
	Feb.	37F	3C	**June**	72F	22C	**Oct.**	55F	13C
		27	– 3		52	11		41	5
	Mar.	46F	8C	**July**	75F	24C	**Nov.**	46F	8C
		32	0		55	13		36	2
	Apr.	58F	14C	**Aug.**	73F	23C	**Dec.**	37F	3C
		39	4		55	13		28	– 2

Information Sources For current weather conditions for cities in the United States and abroad, plus the local time and helpful travel tips, call the **Weather Channel Connection** (tel. 900/932–8437; 95¢ per minute) from a touch-tone phone.

What to Pack

Clothing Don't worry about packing lots of formal clothing. Fashion was all but nonexistent under 40 years of communist rule, and Western dress of any kind is considered stylish. A sports jacket for men, and a dress or pants for women, is appropriate for an evening out. Everywhere else, you'll feel comfortable in casual corduroy or jeans.

Eastern Europe enjoys all the extremes of an inland climate, so plan accordingly. In the higher elevations winter can last until April, and even in summer the evenings will be on the cool side.

Many areas are best seen on foot, so take a pair of sturdy walking shoes and be prepared to use them. High heels will present considerable problems on the cobblestone streets of Prague. If you plan on visiting the mountains, make sure the shoes have good traction and ankle support, as some trails can be quite challenging.

Miscellaneous Many items that you take for granted at home are occasionally unavailable or of questionable quality in Eastern Europe. Take your own toiletries and personal-hygiene products with you. Women should pack tampons or sanitary napkins, which are in chronic short supply. Few places have any sports equipment for rent; an alternative to bringing your own equipment would be to buy what you need locally and take it home with you. In general, sporting goods are relatively cheap and of good quality. Bring an extra pair of eyeglasses or contact lenses. If you have a health problem that may require you to purchase a prescription drug, pack enough to last the duration of the trip, or have your doctor write a prescription using the drug's generic name, as brand names vary from country to country. And don't forget to pack a list of the addresses of offices that supply refunds for lost or stolen traveler's checks.

Electricity The electrical current in Eastern Europe is 220 volts, 50 cycles alternating current (AC); the United States runs on 110-volt, 60-cycle AC current. Unlike wall outlets in the United States, which accept plugs with two flat prongs, outlets in Eastern Europe generally take plugs with three prongs, although some older establishments, especially in Romania, may use 110 volts.

Adapters, To plug in U.S.-made appliances abroad, you'll need an adapter
Converters, plug. To reduce the voltage entering the appliance from 220 to
Transformers 110 volts, you'll also need a converter, unless it is a dual-voltage appliance made for travel. There are converters for high-wattage appliances (such as hair dryers), low-wattage items (such as electric toothbrushes and razors), and combination models. Hotels sometimes have outlets marked "For Shavers Only" near the sink; these are 110-volt outlets for low-wattage appliances; don't use them for a high-wattage appliance. If you're traveling with a laptop computer, especially an older one, you may need a transformer—a type of converter used with electronic-circuitry products. Newer laptop computers are auto-sensing, operating equally well on 110 and 220 volts (so you need only the appropriate adapter plug). When in doubt, consult your owner's manual or the manufacturer. Or get a copy of the free brochure "Foreign Electricity is No Deep Dark Secret," published by adapter-converter manufacturer Franzus (Murtha Industrial Park, Box 142, Beacon Falls, CT 06403, tel. 203/723–6664; send a stamped, self-addressed envelope when ordering).

Luggage Free baggage allowances on airlines depend on the airline, the
Regulations route, and the class of your ticket. In general, on domestic flights and on international flights between the United States and foreign destinations, you are entitled to check two bags— neither exceeding 62 inches, or 158 centimeters (length + width + height), or weighing more than 70 pounds (32 kilograms). A third piece may be brought aboard as a carryon; its total dimensions are generally limited to less than 45 inches (114 centimeters), so it will fit easily under the seat in front of you or in the overhead compartment. There are variations, so ask in advance. The single rule, a Federal Aviation Administra-

tion safety regulation that pertains to carry-on baggage on U.S. airlines, requires only that carryons be properly stowed and allows the airline to limit allowances and tailor them to different aircraft and operational conditions. Charges for excess, oversize, or overweight pieces vary, so inquire before you pack.

If you are flying between two foreign destinations, note that baggage allowances may be determined not by piece but by weight, which generally allows 88 pounds (40 kilograms) of luggage in first class, 66 pounds (30 kilograms) in business class, and 44 pounds (20 kilograms) in economy. If your flight between two cities abroad *connects* with your transatlantic or transpacific flight, the piece method still applies.

Safeguarding Your Luggage Before leaving home, itemize your bags' contents and their worth; this list will help you estimate the extent of your loss if your bags go astray. To minimize that risk, tag them inside and out with your name, address, and phone number. (If you use your home address, cover it so that potential thieves can't see it.) At check-in, make sure that the tag attached by baggage handlers bears the correct three-letter code for your destination. If your bags do not arrive with you, or if you detect damage, do not leave the airport until you've filed a written report with the airline.

Taking Money Abroad

Traveler's Checks Although you will want plenty of cash when visiting small cities or rural areas, traveler's checks are usually preferable. The most widely recognized are **American Express, Citicorp, Thomas Cook,** and **Visa,** which are sold by major commercial banks. American Express also issues *Traveler's Cheques for Two,* which can be counter-signed and used by you or your traveling companion. Some checks are free; usually the issuing company or the bank at which you make your purchase charges 1%–2% of the checks' face value as a fee. Be sure to buy a few checks in small denominations to cash toward the end of your trip, when you don't want to be left with more foreign currency than you can spend. Always record the numbers of checks as you spend them, and keep this list separate from the checks.

Currency Exchange Banks and bank-operated exchange booths at airports and railroad stations are usually the best places to change money. Hotels, stores, and privately run exchange firms typically offer less favorable rates.

Before your trip, pay attention to how the dollar is doing vis-à-vis Eastern European currencies. If the dollar is losing strength, try to pay as many travel bills as possible in advance, especially the big ones. If it is getting stronger, pay for costly items overseas, and use your credit card whenever possible—you'll come out ahead, whether the exchange rate at which your purchase is calculated is the one in effect the day the vendor's bank abroad processes the charge, or the one prevailing on the day the charge company's service center processes it at home.

To avoid lines at airport currency-exchange booths, arrive in a foreign country with a small amount of the local currency already in your pocket—a so-called tip pack. **Thomas Cook Currency Services** (630 5th Ave., New York, NY 10111, tel. 212/757–6915) supplies foreign currency by mail.

Getting Money from Home

Cash Machines Automated-teller machines (ATMs) are proliferating; many are tied to international networks such as **Cirrus** and **Plus**. You can use your bank card at ATMs away from home to withdraw money from an account and get cash advances on a credit-card account (providing your card has been programmed with a personal identification number, or PIN). Check in advance on limits on withdrawals and cash advances within specified periods. Ask whether your bank-card or credit-card PIN number will need to be reprogrammed for use in the area you'll be visiting—a possibility if the number has more than four digits. Remember that on cash advances you are charged interest from the day you get the money from ATMs as well as from tellers. And note that, although transaction fees for ATM withdrawals abroad will probably be higher than fees for withdrawals at home, Cirrus and Plus exchange rates tend to be good.

Be sure to plan ahead: Obtain ATM locations and the names of affiliated cash-machine networks before departure. There are Cirrus ATMs in both the Czech Republic and Slovakia; for specific foreign Cirrus locations, call 800/424–7787; for foreign Plus locations, consult the Plus directory at your local bank.

American Express Cardholder Services The company's **Express Cash** system lets you withdraw cash and/or traveler's checks from a worldwide network of 57,000 American Express dispensers and participating bank ATMs. You must *enroll first* (call 800/227-4669 for a form and allow two weeks for processing). Withdrawals are charged not to your card but to a designated bank account. You can withdraw up to $1,000 per seven-day period on the basic card, more if your card is gold or platinum. There is a 2% fee (minimum $2.50, maximum $10) for each cash transaction, and a 1% fee for traveler's checks (except for the platinum card), which are available only from American Express dispensers.

At AmEx offices, cardholders can also cash personal checks for up to $1,000 in any seven-day period (21 days abroad); of this $200 can be in cash, more if available, with the balance paid in traveler's checks, for which all but platinum cardholders pay a 1% fee. Higher limits apply to the gold and platinum cards.

Wiring Money You don't have to be a cardholder to send or receive an **American Express MoneyGram** for up to $10,000. To send one, go to an American Express MoneyGram agent, pay up to $1,000 with a credit card and anything over that in cash, and phone a transaction reference number to your intended recipient, who needs only to present identification and the reference number to the nearest MoneyGram agent to pick up the cash. There are MoneyGram agents in more than 60 countries (call 800/543–4080 for locations). Fees range from 5% to 10%, depending on the amount and how you pay. You can't use American Express, which is really a convenience card—only Discover, MasterCard, and Visa credit cards.

You can also use **Western Union**. To wire money, take either cash or a check to the nearest office. (Or you can call and use a credit card.) Fees are roughly 5%–10%. Western Union service to Eastern Europe is limited, generally serving only major cities. Money sent from the United States or Canada will be available for pick up at agent locations in the Czech Republic within minutes. (Note that once the money is in the system it can be picked up at *any* location. You don't have to miss your train waiting for it to arrive in City A, because if there's an agent in City B, where you're headed, you can pick it up there, too.) There are approximately 20,000 agents worldwide (call 800/325–6000 for locations).

What It Will Cost

Despite rising inflation, the Czech Republic is still generally a bargain by Western standards. Prague remains the exception, however. Hotel prices, in particular, frequently meet or exceed the U.S. and Western European average—and are higher than the standard of facilities would warrant. Nevertheless, you can still find bargain private accommodations. The prices at tourist resorts outside of the capital are lower and, in the outlying areas and off the beaten track, incredibly low. Tourists can now legally pay for hotel rooms in crowns, although some hotels will still insist on payment in "hard" (i.e., Western) currency.

Sample Costs   A cup of coffee will cost about 15 Kč.; museum entrance, 20 Kč.; a good theater seat, up to 100 Kč.; a cinema seat , 30 Kč.; a half liter (pint) of beer, 15 Kč.; a 1-mile taxi ride, 60 Kč.; a bottle of Moravian wine in a good restaurant, 100 Kč–150 Kč.; a glass (2 deciliters or 7 ounces) of wine, 25 Kč.

Passports and Visas

If your passport is lost or stolen abroad, report it immediately to the nearest embassy or consulate and to the local police. If you can provide the consular officer with the information contained in the passport, they will usually be able to issue you a new passport. For this reason, it is a good idea to keep a copy of the data page of your passport in a separate place, or to leave the passport number, date, and place of issuance with a relative or friend at home.

U.S. Citizens   A valid passport is sufficient for stays of up to 30 days in the Czech Republic and Slovakia. No visa is required to enter these countries.

Canadian Citizens   Canadian citizens are required to have a passport and visa for stays of up to 30 days. To obtain a visa, you must have a valid passport, one passport-type photo, a completed application, and the C$50 fee. For applications and further information, contact the Czech Republic embassy (541 Sussex Dr., Ottawa, Ont. K1N 6Z6, tel. 613/562–3875).

Canadian citizens are required to have a passport and visa for stays of up to 30 days in Slovakia. As with the Czech Republic, you'll need a valid passport and passport-type photo, a completed application, and the C$50 fee. For applications and information, contact the Slovakian embassy (50 Rideau Terr., Ottawa, Ont. K1M 2A1, tel. 613/749–4442).

U.K. Citizens   British citizens need a valid 10-year passport to enter the Czech Republic and Slovakia (cost £15 for a standard 32-page passport, £30 for a 94-page passport). A British Visitors Passport is not acceptable. Visas are not required.

Customs and Duties

On Arrival You may import duty-free into the Czech Republic, 250 cigarettes or the equivalent in tobacco, 1 liter of spirits, and 2 liters of wine. In addition to the above, you are permitted to import gifts valued at up to 1,000 Kčs (approximately $35) and ½ liter of perfume.

If you are bringing any valuables or foreign-made equipment from home into the country, such as cameras, it's wise to carry the original receipts with you or register the items with U.S. Customs before you leave (Form 4457). Otherwise you could end up paying duty on your return.

Returning Home
U.S. Customs Provided you've been out of the country for at least 48 hours and haven't already used the exemption, or any part of it, in the past 30 days, you may bring home $400 worth of foreign goods duty-free. So can each member of your family, regardless of age; and your exemptions may be pooled, so one of you can bring in more if another brings in less. A flat 10% duty applies to the next $1,000 of goods; above $1,400, the rate varies with the merchandise. (If the 48-hour or 30-day limits apply, your duty-free allowance drops to $25, which may not be pooled.) Please note that these are the *general* rules; more generous allowances for some items, including arts and handicrafts, are in effect for the Czech Republic, which is considered a developing country benefiting from the Generalized System of Preferences (GSP).

Travelers 21 or older may bring back 1 liter of alcohol duty-free, provided the beverage laws of the state through which they reenter the United States allow it. In addition, 100 non-Cuban cigars and 200 cigarettes are allowed, regardless of your age. Antiques and works of art more than 100 years old are duty-free.

Gifts valued at less than $50 may be mailed duty-free to state-side friends and relatives, with a limit of one package per day per addressee (do not send alcohol or tobacco products, nor perfume valued at more than $5). These gifts do not count as part of your exemption, unless you bring them home with you. Mark the package "Unsolicited Gift" and include the nature of the gift and its retail value.

For a copy of "Know Before You Go," a free brochure detailing what you may and may not bring back to the United States, rates of duty, and other pointers, contact the **U.S. Customs Service** (Box 7407, Washington, DC 20044, tel. 202/927–6724). A copy of "GSP and the Traveler" is available from the same source.

Canadian Customs Once per calendar year, when you've been out of Canada for at least seven days, you may bring in $300 worth of goods duty-free. If you've been away less than seven days but more than 48 hours, the duty-free exemption drops to $100 but can be claimed any number of times (as can a $20 duty-free exemption for absences of 24 hours or more). You cannot combine the yearly and 48-hour exemptions, use the $300 exemption only partially (to save the balance for a later trip), or pool exemptions with family members. Goods claimed under the $300 exemption may follow you by mail; those claimed under the lesser exemptions must accompany you on your return.

Alcohol and tobacco products may be included in the yearly and 48-hour exemptions but not in the 24-hour exemption. If you meet the age requirements of the province through which you reenter Canada, you may bring in, duty-free, 1.14 liters (40 imperial ounces) of wine or liquor *or* two dozen 12-ounce cans or bottles of beer or ale. If you are 16 or older, you may bring in, duty-free, 200 cigarettes, 50 cigars or cigarillos, and 400 tobacco sticks or 400 grams of manufactured tobacco.

Gifts may be mailed to friends in Canada duty-free. These do not count as part of your exemption. Each gift may be worth up to of $60—label the package "Unsolicited Gift—Value under $60." There are no limits on the number of gifts that may be sent per day or per addressee, but you can't mail alcohol or tobacco.

For more information, including details of duties on items that exceed your duty-free limit, ask the Revenue Canada Customs and Excise Department (Connaught Bldg., MacKenzie Ave., Ottawa, Ont., K1A OL5, tel. 613/957–0275) for a copy of the free brochure "I Declare/Je Déclare."

U.K. Customs From countries outside the EC, you may import duty-free 200 cigarettes, 100 cigarillos, 50 cigars or 250 grams of tobacco; 1 liter of spirits or 2 liters of fortified or sparkling wine; 2 liters of still table wine; 60 milliliters of perfume; 250 milliliters of toilet water; plus £36 worth of other goods, including gifts and souvenirs.

For further information or a copy of "A Guide for Travellers," which details standard customs procedures as well as what you may bring into the United Kingdom from abroad, contact HM Customs and Excise (New King's Beam House, 22 Upper Ground, London SE1 9PJ, tel. 071/620–1313).

Traveling with Cameras, Camcorders, and Laptops

Film and Cameras If your camera is new or if you haven't used it for a while, shoot and develop a few rolls of film before leaving home. Pack some lens tissue and an extra battery for your built-in light meter, and invest in an inexpensive skylight filter, to both protect your lens and provide some definition in hazy shots. Store film in a cool, dry place—never in the car's glove compartment or on the shelf under the rear window.

Films above ISO 400 are more sensitive to damage from airport security X-rays than others; very high speed films, ISO 1,000 and above, are exceedingly vulnerable. To protect your film, don't put it in checked luggage; carry it with you in a plastic bag and ask for a hand inspection. Such requests are honored at American airports but are up to the inspector abroad. Don't depend on a lead-lined bag to protect film in checked luggage—the airline may very well turn up the dosage of radiation to see what you've got in there. Airport metal detectors do not harm film, although you'll set off the alarm if you walk through one with a roll in your pocket. Call the Kodak Information Center (tel. 800/242–2424) for details.

Camcorders Before your trip, put new or long-unused camcorders through their paces, and practice panning and zooming. Invest in a skylight filter to protect the lens, and check the lithium battery that lights up the LCD (liquid crystal display) modes. As for the rechargeable nickel-cadmium batteries that are the camera's power source, take along an extra pair, so while you're using your camcorder you'll have one battery ready and another recharging. Most newer camcorders are equipped with the battery (which generally slides or clicks onto the camera body) and, to recharge it, with what's known as a universal or worldwide AC adapter charger (or multivoltage converter) that can be used whether the voltage is 110 or 220. All that's needed is the appropriate plug.

Videotape Unlike still-camera film, videotape is not damaged by X-rays. However, it may well be harmed by the magnetic field of a walk-through metal detector. Airport security personnel may want you to turn the camcorder on to prove that that's what it is, so make sure the battery is charged when you get to the airport. Note that although the United States, Canada, Japan, Korea, Taiwan, and other countries operate on the National Television System Committee video standard (NTSC), Eastern Europe uses PAL technology. So you will not be able to view your tapes through the local TV set or view movies bought there in your home VCR. Blank tapes bought in Eastern Europe can be used for NTSC camcorder taping, however—although you'll probably find they cost more in Eastern Europe and wish you'd brought an adequate supply along.

Laptops Security X-rays do not harm hard-disk or floppy-disk storage. Most airlines allow you to use your laptop aloft but request that you turn it off during takeoff and landing so as not to interfere with navigation equipment. Make sure the battery is charged when you arrive at the airport, because you may be asked to turn on the computer at security checkpoints to prove that it is what it appears to be. If you're a heavy computer user, consider traveling with a backup battery. For international travel, register your laptop with U.S. Customs as you leave the country, providing it's manufactured abroad (U.S.-origin items cannot be registered at U.S. Customs); when you do so, you'll get a certificate, good for as long as you own the item, containing your name and address, a description of the laptop, and its serial number, that will quash any questions that may arise on your return. If your laptop is U.S.-made, call the consulate of the country you'll be visiting to find out whether it should be registered with customs in that country upon arrival. Some travelers do this as a matter of course and ask customs officers to sign a document that specifies the total configuration of the system, computer and peripherals, and its value. In addition, before leaving home, find out about repair facilities at your destination, and don't forget any transformer or adapter plug you may need (*see* Electricity, *above*).

Staying Healthy

You may gain weight, but there are few other serious health hazards for the traveler in Eastern Europe. Tap water tastes bad but is generally drinkable; when it runs rusty out of the tap or the aroma of chlorine is overpowering, it might help to have some iodine tablets or bottled water handy. Milk may not be pasteurized and can make Westerners sick; stick to cheese to satisfy calcium cravings. Vegetarians and those on special diets may have a problem with the heavy local cuisine, which is based nearly exclusively on pork and beef. To keep your vitamin intake above the danger levels, buy fresh fruits and vegetables at seasonal street markets—regular grocery stores often don't sell them.

No vaccinations are required for entry into any of the Eastern European countries covered in this book, but selective vaccinations are recommended by IAMAT (*see below*). Those traveling in forested areas should consider vaccinating themselves against central European, or tick-borne, encephalitis. Schedule vaccinations well in advance of departure because some require several doses, and others may cause uncomfortable side effects.

To avoid problems clearing customs, diabetic travelers carrying needles and syringes should keep handy a letter from their physician confirming their need for insulin injections.

Finding a Doctor The **International Association for Medical Assistance to Travellers** (IAMAT, 417 Center St., Lewiston, NY 14092, tel. 716/754–4883; 40 Regal Rd., Guelph, Ontario N1K 1B5; 57 Voirets, 1212 Grand-Lancy, Geneva, Switzerland) publishes a worldwide directory of English-speaking physicians whose qualifications meet IAMAT standards and who have agreed to treat members for a set fee. Membership is free.

Assistance Companies Pretrip medical referrals, emergency evacuation or repatriation, 24-hour telephone hot lines for medical consultation, dispatch of medical personnel, relay of medical records, up-front cash for emergencies, and other personal and legal assistance are among the services provided by several membership organizations specializing in medical assistance to travelers. Among them are **International SOS Assistance** (Box 11568, Philadelphia, PA 19116, tel. 215/244–1500 or 800/523–8930; Box 466, Pl. Bonaventure, Montréal, Québec H5A 1C1, tel. 514/874–7674 or 800/363–0263), **Near Services** (450 Prairie Ave., Suite 101, Calumet City, IL 60409, tel. 708/868–6700 or 800/654–6700), and **Travel Assistance International** (1133 15th St. NW, Suite 400, Washington, DC 20005, tel. 202/331–1609 or 800/821–2828), part of Europ Assistance Worldwide Services, Inc. Because these companies will also sell you death-and-dismemberment, trip-cancellation, and other insurance coverage, there is some overlap with the travel-insurance policies discussed below, which may include the services of an assistance company among the insurance options or reimburse travelers for such services without providing them.

Insurance

U.S. Residents Most tour operators, travel agents, and insurance agents sell specialized health-and-accident, flight, trip-cancellation, and luggage insurance as well as comprehensive policies with some or all of these features. But before you make any purchase, review your existing health and homeowner policies to find out whether they cover expenses incurred while traveling.

Health-and-Accident Insurance Supplemental health-and-accident insurance for travelers is usually a part of comprehensive policies. Specific policy provisions vary, but they tend to address three general areas, beginning with reimbursement for medical expenses caused by illness or an accident during a trip. Such policies may reimburse anywhere from $1,000 to $150,000 worth of medical expenses; dental benefits may also be included. A second common feature is the personal-accident, or death-and-dismemberment, provision, which pays a lump sum to your beneficiaries if your die or to you if you lose one or both limbs or your eyesight. This is similar to the flight insurance described below, although it is not necessarily limited to accidents involving airplanes or even other "common carriers" (buses, trains, and ships) and can be in effect 24 hours a day. The lump sum awarded can range from $15,000 to $500,000. A third area generally addressed by these policies is medical assistance (referrals, evacuation, or repatriation and other services). Some policies reimburse travelers for the cost of such services; others may automatically enroll you as a member of a particular medical-assistance company.

Flight Insurance   This insurance, often bought as a last-minute impulse at the airport, pays a lump sum to a beneficiary when a plane crashes and the insured dies (and sometimes to a surviving passenger who loses eyesight or a limb); thus it supplements the airlines' own coverage as described in the limits-of-liability paragraphs on your ticket (up to $75,000 on international flights, $20,000 on domestic—this is generally subject to litigation). Charging an airline ticket to a major credit card often automatically signs you up for flight insurance; in this case, the coverage may also embrace travel by bus, train, and ship.

Baggage Insurance   In the event of loss, damage, or theft on international flights, airlines limit their liability to $20 per kilogram for checked baggage (roughly about $640 per 70-pound bag) and $400 per passenger for unchecked baggage. On domestic flights, the ceiling is $1,250 per passenger. Excess-valuation insurance can be bought directly from the airline at check-in but leaves your bags vulnerable on the ground.

Trip Insurance   There are two sides to this coin. **Trip-cancellation-and-interruption insurance** protects you in the event you are unable to undertake or finish your trip. **Default** or **bankruptcy insurance** protects you against a supplier's failure to deliver. Consider the former if your airline ticket, cruise, or package tour does not allow changes or cancellations. The amount of coverage to buy should equal the cost of your trip should you, a traveling companion, or a family member get sick, forcing you to stay home, plus the nondiscounted one-way airline ticket you would need to buy if you had to return home early. Read the fine print carefully; pay attention to sections defining "family member" and "preexisting medical conditions." A characteristic quirk of default policies is that they often do not cover default by travel agencies or default by a tour operator, airline, or cruise line if you bought your tour and the coverage directly from the firm in question. To reduce your need for default insurance, give preference to tours packaged by members of the United States Tour Operators Association (USTOA), which maintains a fund to reimburse clients in the event of member defaults. Even better, pay for travel arrangements with a major credit card, so that you can refuse to pay the bill if services have not been rendered—and let the card company fight your battles.

Comprehensive Policies   Companies supplying comprehensive policies with some or all of the above features include **Access America, Inc.,** underwritten by BCS Insurance Company (Box 11188, Richmond, VA 23230, tel. 800/284–8300); **Carefree Travel Insurance**, underwritten by The Hartford (Box 310, 120 Mineola Blvd., Mineola, NY 11501, tel. 516/294–0220 or 800/323–3149); **Tele-Trip** (Mutual of Omaha Plaza, Box 31762, Omaha, NE 68131, tel. 800/228–

9792), a subsidiary of Mutual of Omaha; **The Travelers Companies** (1 Tower Sq., Hartford, CT 06183, tel. 203/277–0111 or 800/243–3174); **Travel Guard International**, underwritten by Transamerica Occidental Life Companies (1145 Clark St., Stevens Point, WI 54481, tel. 715/345–0505 or 800/782–5151); and **Wallach and Company, Inc.** (107 W. Federal St., Box 480, Middleburg, VA 22117, tel. 703/687–3166 or 800/237–6615). These companies may also offer the above types of insurance separately.

U.K. Residents Most tour operators, travel agents, and insurance agents sell specialized policies covering accident, medical expenses, personal liability, trip cancellation, and loss or theft of personal property. Some policies include coverage for delayed departure and legal expenses, winter-sports, accidents, or motoring abroad. You can also purchase an annual travel-insurance policy valid for every trip you make during the year in which it's purchased (usually only trips of less than 90 days). Before you leave, make sure you will be covered if you have a preexisting medical condition or are pregnant; your insurers may not pay for routine or continuing treatment, or may require a note from your doctor certifying your fitness to travel.

For advice by phone or a free booklet, "Holiday Insurance," that sets out what to expect from a holiday-insurance policy and gives price guidelines, contact the **Association of British Insurers** (51 Gresham St., London EC2V 7HQ, tel. 071/600–3333; 30 Gordon St., Glasgow G1 3PU, tel. 041/226–3905; Scottish Provincial Bldg., Donegall Sq. W, Belfast BT1 6JE, tel. 0232/249176; call for other locations).

Car Rentals

There are no special requirements for renting a car in the Czech Republic, but be sure to shop around, as prices can differ greatly. **Avis** and **Hertz** offer Western makes for as much as $400–$600 per week. Smaller local companies, on the other hand, can rent Czechoslovak cars for as low as $130 per week.

The following rental agencies are based in Prague.

Avis. Opletalova 33, Nové Město, tel. 02/222324; Hotel Atrium, tel. 02/284–2043; airport, tel. 02/367807.
Budget. Airport, tel. 02/316–5214; Hotel Inter-Continental, tel. 02/231–9595.
Esocar. Husitská 58, Prague 3, tel. 02/691–2244.
Hertz. Airport, tel. 02/312–0717; Hotel Atrium, tel. 284–2047; Hotel Diplomat (tel. 02/312–0717).
Pragocar. Milevská 2, Prague 4, tel. 02/692–2875.
Unix. V celnici 4, Nové Město, tel. 02/233693.

Extra Charges Picking up the car in one city or country and leaving it in another will almost always entail drop-off charges or one-way service fees, which can be substantial. The cost of a collision or loss-damage waiver (*see below*) can be high, also. Automatic transmissions and air-conditioning are not universally available abroad; ask for them when you book if you want them, and check the cost before you commit yourself to the rental.

Cutting Costs If you know you will want a car for more than a day or two, you can save by planning ahead. Major international companies have programs that discount their standard rates by 15%–30% if you make the reservation before departure (anywhere from two to 14 days), rent for a minimum number of days (typically three or four), and prepay the rental. Ask about these advance-purchase schemes when you call for information. More economical rentals are those that come as part of fly/drive or other packages, even those as bare-bones as the rental plus an airline ticket (*see* Tours and Packages, *above*).

Other sources of savings are the several companies that operate as wholesalers—companies that do not own their own fleets but rent in bulk from those that do and offer advantageous rates to their customers. Rentals through such companies must be arranged and paid for before you leave the United States. Among them are **Auto Europe** (Box 1097, Camden, ME 04843, tel. 207/236–8235 or 800/223–5555, 800/458–9503 in Canada), and **Kemwel** (106 Calvert St., Harrison, NY 10528, tel. 914/835–5555 or 800/678–0678). **Foremost Euro-Car** (5430 Van Nuys Blvd., Suite 306, Van Nuys, CA 91401, tel. 818/786–1960 or 800/272–3299) leases cars in Western Europe that can be driven into Eastern Europe. You won't see these wholesalers' deals advertised; they're even better in summer, when business travel is down. Always ask whether the prices are guaranteed in U.S. dollars or foreign currency and if unlimited mileage is available. Find out about any required deposits, cancellation penalties, and drop-off charges, and confirm the cost of the CDW. Wholesalers often do not serve all Eastern European countries, and there are restrictions about travel between countries; be sure to check before you rent.

One last tip: Remember to fill the tank when you turn in the vehicle, to avoid being charged for refueling at what you'll swear is the most expensive pump in town.

Insurance and Collision Damage Waiver The standard rental contract includes liability coverage (for damage to public property, injury to pedestrians, etc.) and coverage for the car against fire, theft (not included in certain countries), and collision damage with a deductible—most commonly $2,000–$3,000, occasionally more. In case of an accident, you are responsible for the deductible amount unless you've purchased the collision damage waiver (CDW), which costs an average $12 a day, although this varies depending on what you've rented, where, and from whom.

Because this adds up quickly, you may be inclined to say "no thanks"—and that's certainly your option, although the rental agent may not tell you so. Note before you decline that deductibles are occasionally high enough that you might total a car and still be responsible for its full value. Planning ahead will help you make the right decision. By all means, find out if your own insurance covers damage to a rental car while traveling (not simply a car to drive when yours is in for repairs). Check whether charging car rentals to any of your credit cards will get you a CDW at no charge.

Rail Passes

The **European East Pass** is good for unlimited first-class travel on the national railroads of Austria, the Czech Republic, Slovakia, Hungary, and Poland. The pass allows five days of travel within a 15-day period ($169) or 10 days of travel within 30 days ($275). Apply through your travel agent or through **Rail Europe** (226–230 Westchester Ave., White Plains, NY 10604, tel.

914/682–5172 or 800/848–7245 from the East and 800/848-7245 from the West).

The **EurailPass,** valid for unlimited first-class train travel through 17 countries, including Hungary, is an excellent value if you plan to travel around the Continent, but it does not include travel to the Czech Republic, Slovakia, Poland, Bulgaria, or Romania.

Eurail passes are available for 15 days ($460), 21 days ($598), one month ($728), two months ($998), and three months ($1,260). **Eurail Saverpasses,** valid for 15 days, cost $390 per person; you must do all your traveling with at least one companion (two companions from April through September). **Eurail Youthpasses,** which cover second-class travel, cost $508 for one month, $698 for two; you must be under 26 on the first day you travel. Flexipasses allow you to travel for five, 10, or 15 days within any two-month period. You pay $298, $496, and $676 for the **Eurail Flexipass,** sold for first-class travel; and $220, $348, and $474 for the **Eurail Youth Flexipass,** available to those under 26 on their first travel day, sold for second-class travel. Apply through your travel agent or **Rail Europe.**

European citizens or anyone who has lived within the EC for longer than six months can purchase an **InterRail Pass** (£249), good for one month's travel in the Eastern European countries covered in this book. The pass works just like Eurail, except that it gives only a 50% discount on train fares within the country where it was purchased. Be prepared to prove your citizenship or six months of continuous residency. InterRail is availabe only in Europe and can be purchased through local student or budget travel offices. In Great Britain you can buy InterRail at main British Rail stations and some travel agencies.

Don't make the mistake of assuming that your rail pass guarantees you seats on the trains you want to ride. Seat reservations are required on some trains, particularly high-speed trains, and are a good idea on trains that may be crowded. You will also need reservations for overnight sleeping accommodations. Rail Europe can help you determine if you need reservations and can make them for you (about $10 each, less if you purchase them in Europe at the time of travel).

Student and Youth Travel

Travel Agencies The foremost U.S. student travel agency is **Council Travel,** a subsidiary of the nonprofit Council on International Educational Exchange. It specializes in low-cost travel arrangements, is the exclusive U.S. agent for several discount cards, and, with its sister CIEE subsidiary, **Council Charter,** is a source of airfare bargains. The Council Charter brochure and CIEE's twice-yearly *Student Travels* magazine, which details its programs, are available at the Council Travel office at CIEE headquarters (205 E. 42nd Street, New York, NY 10017, tel. 212/ 661–1450) and at 37 branches in college towns nationwide (free in person, $1 by mail). The **Educational Travel Center** (ETC, 438 N. Francis St., Madison, WI 53703, tel. 608/256–5551) also offers low-cost rail passes, domestic and international airline tickets (mostly for flights departing from Chicago), and other budgetwise travel arrangements. Other travel agencies catering to students include **Travel Management International** (TMI,

18 Prescott St., Suite 4, Cambridge, MA 02138, tel. 617/661–8187) and **Travel Cuts** (187 College St., Toronto, Ont. M5T 1P7, tel. 416/979–2406).

Discount Cards For discounts on transportation and on museum and attractions admissions, buy the **International Student Identity Card** (ISIC) if you're a bona fide student, or the **International Youth Card** (IYC) if you're under 26. In the United States the ISIC and IYC cards cost $15 each and include basic travel accident and sickness coverage. Apply to **CIEE** (*see* address *above*, tel. 212/661–1414; the application is in *Student Travels*). In Canada the cards are available for $15 each from **Travel Cuts** (*see above*). In the United Kingdom they cost £5 and £4 respectively at student unions and student travel companies, including Council Travel's London office (28A Poland St., London W1V 3DB, tel. 071/437–7767).

Hosteling An **International Youth Hostel Federation** (IYHF) membership card is the key to more than 5,300 hostel locations in 59 countries; the sex-segregated, dormitory-style sleeping quarters, including some for families, go for $7–$20 a night per person. Membership is available in the United States through **American Youth Hostels** (AYH, 733 15th St. NW, Washington, DC 20005, tel. 202/783–6161), the American link in the worldwide chain, and costs $25 for adults 18–54, $10 for those under 18, $15 for those 55 and over, and $35 for families. Volume 1 of the two-volume *Guide to Budget Accommodation* lists hostels in Europe and the Mediterranean ($13.95, including postage). IYHF membership is available in Canada through the **Canadian Hostelling Association** (CHA, 1600 James Naismith Dr., Suite 608, Gloucester, Ont. K1B 5N4, tel. 613/748–5638) for $26.75, and in the United Kingdom through the **Youth Hostel Association of England and Wales** (Trevelyan House, 8 St. Stephen's Hill, St. Albans, Herts. AL1 2DY, tel. 0727/55215) for £9.

Traveling with Children

Newsletter *Family Travel Times,* published 10 times a year by Travel With Your Children (TWYCH, 45 W. 18th St., 7th Floor Tower, New York, NY 10011, tel. 212/206–0688; annual subscription $55), covers destinations, types of vacations, and modes of travel.

Books *Traveling with Children—And Enjoying It,* by Arlene K. Butler ($11.95 plus $3 shipping per book; Globe Pequot Press, Box 833, Old Saybrook, CT 06475, tel. 800/243–0495, or 800/962–0973 in CT) helps plan your trip with children, from toddlers to teens.

Getting There On international flights, the fare for infants under two not oc-
Air Fares cupying a seat is generally 10% of the accompanying adult's fare; children ages 2–11 usually pay half to two-thirds of the adult fare. On domestic flights, children under two not occupying a seat travel free, and older children currently travel on the "lowest applicable" adult fare.

Baggage In general, infants paying 10% of the adult fare are allowed one carry-on bag, not to exceed 70 pounds or 45 inches (length + width + height). The adult baggage allowance applies for children paying half or more of the adult fare. Check with the airline for particulars, especially regarding flights between two foreign destinations, where allowances for infants may be less generous than those above.

Safety Seats The FAA recommends the use of safety seats aloft and details approved models in the free leaflet **"Child/Infant Safety Seats Recommended for Use in Aircraft"** (available from the Federal Aviation Administration, APA–200, 800 Independence Ave. SW, Washington, DC 20591, tel. 202/267–3479). Airline policy varies. U.S. carriers must allow FAA-approved models, but because these seats are strapped into a regular passenger seat, they may require that parents buy a ticket even for an infant under two who would otherwise ride free. Foreign carriers may not allow infant seats, may charge the child's rather than the infant's fare for their use, or may require you to hold your baby during takeoff and landing, thus defeating the seat's purpose.

Facilities Aloft Airlines do provide other facilities and services for children, such as children's meals and freestanding bassinets (to those sitting in seats at the bulkhead, where there's enough legroom to accommodate them). Make your request when reserving. The annual February/March issue of *Family Travel Times* gives details of the children's services of dozens of airlines ($10; *see above*). **"Kids and Teens in Flight"** (free from the U.S. Department of Transportation, tel. 202/366–2220) offers tips for children flying alone.

Lodging Young visitors to the Czech Republic will enjoy staying at one of Prague's picturesque floating "botels." For further information contact Čedok.

Baby-Sitting Ask at the hotel desk or local tourist office for information on
Services baby-sitters.

Hints for Travelers with Disabilities

Provisions for handicapped travelers in Eastern Europe are extremely limited; traveling with a nondisabled companion is probably the best solution. While many hotels, especially large American or international chains, offer some wheelchair-accessible rooms, special facilities at museums, restaurants, and on public transportation are difficult to find.

Organizations Several organizations provide travel information for people
United States with disabilities, usually for a membership fee, and some publish newsletters and bulletins. Among them are the **Information Center for Individuals with Disabilities** (Fort Point Pl., 27–43 Wormwood St., Boston, MA 02210, tel. 617/727–5540 or 800/462–5015 in MA between 11 and 4, or leave message; TDD/TTY tel. 617/345–9743); **Mobility International USA** (Box 3551, Eugene, OR 97403, voice and TDD tel. 503/343–1284), the U.S. branch of an international organization based in Britain (*see below*) and present in 30 countries; **MossRehab Hospital Travel Information Service** (1200 W. Tabor Rd., Philadelphia, PA 19141, tel. 215/456–9603, TDD tel. 215/456–9602); the **Society for the Advancement of Travel for the Handicapped** (SATH, 347 5th Ave., Suite 610, New York, NY 10016, tel. 212/447–7284, fax 212/725–8253); the **Travel Industry and Disabled Exchange** (TIDE, 5435 Donna Ave., Tarzana, CA 91356, tel. 818/368–5648); and **Travelin' Talk** (Box 3534, Clarksville, TN 37043, tel. 615/552–6670).

United Kingdom Main information sources include the **Royal Association for Disability and Rehabilitation** (RADAR, 25 Mortimer St., London W1N 8AB, tel. 071/637–5400), which publishes travel information for the disabled in Britain, and **Mobility International** (228 Borough High St., London SE1 1JX, tel. 071/403–5688), the headquarters of an international membership organization that serves as a clearinghouse of travel information for people with disabilities.

Travel Agencies and Tour Operators **Directions Unlimited** (720 N. Bedford Rd., Bedford Hills, NY 10507, tel. 914/241–1700), a travel agency, has expertise in tours and cruises for the disabled. **Evergreen Travel Service** (4114 198th St. SW, Suite 13, Lynnwood, WA 98036, tel. 206/776–1184 or 800/435–2288) operates Wings on Wheels Tours for those in wheelchairs, White Cane Tours for the blind, and tours for the deaf, and makes group and independent arrangements for travelers with any disability. **Flying Wheels Travel** (143 W. Bridge St., Box 382, Owatonna, MN 55060, tel. 800/535–6790 or 800/722–9351 in MN), a tour operator and travel agency, arranges international tours, cruises, and independent travel itineraries for people with mobility disabilities. **Nautilus**, at the same address as TIDE (*see above*), packages tours for the disabled internationally.

Publications In addition to the fact sheets, newsletters, and books mentioned above are several free publications available from the Consumer Information Center (Pueblo, CO 81009): **"New Horizons for the Air Traveler with a Disability,"** a U.S. Department of Transportation booklet describing changes resulting from the 1986 Air Carrier Access Act and those still to come from the 1990 Americans with Disabilities Act (include Department 608Y in the address), and the Airport Operators Council's *Access Travel: Airports* (Dept. 5804), which describes facilities and services for the disabled at more than 500 airports worldwide.

Twin Peaks Press (Box 129, Vancouver, WA 98666, tel. 206/694–2462 or 800/637–2256) publishes the *Directory of Travel Agencies for the Disabled* ($19.95), listing more than 370 agencies worldwide; *Travel for the Disabled* ($19.95), listing some 500 access guides and accessible places worldwide; the *Directory of Accessible Van Rentals* ($9.95) for campers and RV travelers worldwide; and *Wheelchair Vagabond* ($14.95), a collection of personal travel tips. Add $2 per book for shipping.

Hints for Older Travelers

Organizations The **American Association of Retired Persons** (AARP, 601 E St. NW, Washington, DC 20049, tel. 202/434–2277) provides independent travelers the Purchase Privilege Program, which offers discounts on hotels, car rentals, and sightseeing, and arranges group tours, cruises, and apartment living through AARP Travel Experience from American Express (400 Pinnacle Way, Suite 450, Norcross, GA 30071, tel. 800/927–0111); these can be booked through travel agents, except for the cruises, which must be booked directly (tel. 800/745–4567). AARP membership is open to those 50 and over; annual dues are $8 per person or couple.

Two other membership organizations offer discounts on lodgings, car rentals, and other travel products, along with such nontravel perks as magazines and newsletters. The **National**

Council of Senior Citizens (1331 F St. NW, Washington, DC 20004, tel. 202/347–8800) is a nonprofit advocacy group with some 5,000 local clubs across the United States; membership costs $12 per person or couple annually. **Mature Outlook** (6001 N. Clark St., Chicago, IL 60660, tel. 800/336–6330), a Sears Roebuck & Co. subsidiary with 800,000 members, charges $9.95 for an annual membership.

Note: When using any senior-citizen identification card for reduced hotel rates, mention it when booking, not when checking out. At restaurants, show your card before you're seated; discounts may be limited to certain menus, days, or hours. If you are renting a car, ask about promotional rates that might improve on your senior-citizen discount.

Educational Travel   **Elderhostel** (75 Federal St., 3rd floor, Boston, MA 02110, tel. 617/426–7788) is a nonprofit organization that has offered inexpensive study programs for people 60 and older since 1975. Programs take place at more than 1,800 educational institutions in the United States, Canada, and 45 other countries including the Czech Republic; and courses cover everything from marine science to Greek myths and cowboy poetry. Participants generally attend lectures in the morning and spend the afternoon sightseeing or on field trips; they live in dorms on the host campuses. Fees for two- to three-week international trips—including room, board, and transportation from the United States—range from $1,800 to $4,500.

Interhostel (University of New Hampshire, 6 Garrison Ave., Durham, NH 03824, tel. 800/733–9753), a more recent enterprise than Elderhostel, caters to a slightly younger clientele—that is, 50 and over—and runs programs overseas in some 25 countries. But the idea is similar: Lectures and field trips mix with sightseeing, and participants stay in dormitories at cooperating educational institutions or in modest hotels. Programs are usually two weeks in length and cost $1,500–$2,100, not including airfare from the United States.

Further Reading

The political changes in Eastern Europe have inspired a flurry of new books on the area. Patrick Brogan's *The Captive Nations: Eastern Europe 1945–1990* looks at recent revolutions and their aftermath and provides a historical background on eight countries plus the Baltic republics. J. F. Brown's contribution is *Surge to Freedom: The End of Communist Rule in Eastern Europe*, and William Echikison joins in with *Lighting the Night: Revolution in Eastern Europe*. Timothy Garton Ash writes about the transformation of Poland, Czechoslovakia, Hungary, and East Germany in the 1980s in *The Uses of Adversity: Essays on the Fate of Central Europe* and also offers a fascinating personal account in *The Magic Lantern: The Revolution of '89 Witnessed in Warsaw, Budapest, Berlin, and Prague*. For more background material on the region also consider *East Central Europe in the 19th and 20th Centuries, 1848–1945*, by Ivan T. Berend and Gyorgy Ranki.

With the increased interest in the Czech Republic in recent years, English readers now have an excellent range of both fiction and nonfiction about the country at their disposal. The most widely read Czech author of fiction in English is probably Milan Kundera, whose well-crafted tales illuminate both the foibles of human nature and the unique tribulations of life in communist Czechoslovakia in a humorous but thought-provoking way. *The Unbearable Lightness of Being* takes a look at the 1968 invasion and its aftermath through the eyes of a strained young couple. The very entertaining *Book of Laughter and Forgetting* deals in part with the importance of memory and the cruel irony of how it fades over time. The author was no doubt coming to terms with his own forgetting as he wrote the book from his Paris exile. *The Joke*, Kundera's earliest work available in English, takes a serious look at the dire consequences of humorlessness among Communists.

Josef Škvorecký, another contemporary Czechoslovak writer, lives in exile in Canada. In his widely available *The Engineer of Human Souls*, he attempts to relate his experiences in Canada to his earlier life in Czechoslovakia under Nazi and, later, communist occupation.

Franz Kafka's *The Trial* and *The Castle* will help you feel some of the dread and mystery that he and other German writers detected beneath the 1,000 golden spires of Prague. His books were actually an indictment of the bizarre bureaucracy of the Austro-Hungarian empire, though they now seem eerily prophetic of the even crueler and more arbitrary communist system that was to come. For this reason, until recently most of his works could not be purchased in his native country.

Jaroslav Hašek's hilarious classic *The Good Soldier Schweik* concerns the antics of a good-natured boob who survives World War I in the Austro-Hungarian army. Many regard Schweik as the archetypal Czech: a guileless, downtrodden fellow who somehow always manages to get by.

As for nonfiction, the best place to start is probably *Living in Truth*, an absorbing collection of 22 inspiring essays written by President Václav Havel during his years "underground" as a dissident playwright. The first essay is an open letter to the former communist president Gustav Husák, written before the 1989 revolution, concerning the erosion of public life that occurs when the populace is forced to lip-synch empty slogans. Havel's view is that a just society is one that enables its citizens to live out their lives true to their conscience. Havel's plays are also worth seeing for a better understanding of the absurdities and pressures of life under the former communist regime.

For an excellent social and historical background on the former Czechoslovakia look to David W. Paul's *Czechoslovakia: Profile of a Socialist Republic at the Crossroads of Europe* or R. W. Seton-Watson's *The History of the Czechs and the Slovaks*.

Arriving and Departing

From North America by Plane

Flights are either nonstop, direct, or connecting. A **nonstop** flight requires no change of plane and makes no stops. A **direct** flight stops at least once and can involve a change of plane, although the flight number remains the same; if the first leg is late, the second waits. This is not the case with a **connecting** flight, which involves a different plane and a different flight number.

Airports and Airlines All international flights to the Czech Republic fly into Prague's **Ruzyně Airport,** about 20 kilometers (12 miles) northwest of downtown. The airport is small and easy to negotiate.

ČSA, (Czechoslovak Airlines), the Czech and Slovak national carrier (tel. 718/656–8439), maintains direct flights to Prague twice weekly from New York's JFK, and once a week from both Los Angeles and Montréal. The airline is considering introducting daily flights.

Several other international airlines have good connections from cities in the United States and Canada to European bases and from there to Prague. **British Airways** (tel. 800/247–9297) flies daily via London; and **SwissAir** (tel. 718/995–8400), daily via Zurich.

Flying Times From New York, a nonstop flight to Prague takes 9–10 hours; with a stopover, the journey will take at least 12–13 hours. From Montréal nonstop it is 7½ hours; from Los Angeles, 16 hours.

Cutting Flight Costs The Sunday travel section of most newspapers is a good source of deals. When booking, particularly through an unfamiliar company, call the Better Business Bureau to find out whether any complaints have been registered against the company, pay with a credit card if you can, and consider trip-cancellation and default insurance (*see* Insurance, *above*).

Promotional Airfares All the less expensive fares, called promotional or discount fares, are round-trip and involve restrictions. The exact nature of the restrictions depends on the airline, the route, and the season and on whether travel is domestic or international, but you must usually buy the ticket—commonly called an APEX (advance purchase excursion) when it's for international travel—in advance (7, 14, or 21 days are usual). You must also respect certain minimum- and maximum-stay requirements (for instance, over a Saturday night or at least seven and no more than 30, 45, or 90 days), and you must be willing to pay penalties for changes. Airlines generally allow some changes for a fee. But the cheaper the fare, the more likely the ticket is nonrefundable; it would take a death in the family for the airline to give you any of your money back if you had to cancel. The cheapest fares are also subject to availability; because only a certain percentage of the plane's total seats will be sold at that price, they may go quickly.

Consolidators Consolidators or bulk-fare operators—also known as bucket shops—buy blocks of seats on scheduled flights that airlines anticipate they won't be able to sell. They pay wholesale prices, add a markup, and resell the seats to travel agents or directly to the public at prices that still undercut the airline's promotional or discount fares. You pay more than on a charter but ordinarily less than for an APEX ticket, and, even when there is not much of a price difference, the ticket usually comes without the advance-purchase restriction. Moreover, although tickets are marked nonrefundable so you can't turn them in to the airline for a full-fare refund, some consolidators sometimes give you your money back. Carefully read the fine print detailing penalties for changes and cancellations. If you doubt the reliability of a company, call the airline once you've made your booking and confirm that you do, indeed, have a reservation on the flight. The biggest U.S. consolidator, C.L. Thomson Express, sells only to travel agents. Well-established consolidators selling to the public include **UniTravel** (Box 12485, St. Louis, MO 63132, tel. 314/569–0900 or 800/325–2222); **Council Charter** (205 E. 42nd St., New York, NY 10017, tel. 212/661–0311 or 800/800–8222), a division of the Council on International Educational Exchange and a longtime charter operator now functioning more as a consolidator; and **Travac** (989 6th Ave., New York, NY 10018, tel. 212/563–3303 or 800/872–8800), also a former charterer.

Charter Flights   Charters usually have the lowest fares and the most restrictions. Departures are limited and seldom on time, and you can lose all or most of your money if you cancel. (Generally, the closer to departure you cancel, the more you lose, although sometimes you will be charged only a small fee if you supply a substitute passenger.) The charterer, on the other hand, may legally cancel the flight for any reason up to 10 days before departure; within 10 days of departure, the flight may be canceled only if it becomes physically impossible to operate it. The charterer may also revise the itinerary or increase the price after you have bought the ticket, but if the new arrangement constitutes a "major change," you have the right to a refund. Before buying a charter ticket, read the fine print for the company's refund policy and details on major changes. Money for charter flights is usually paid into a bank escrow account, the name of which should be on the contract. If you don't pay by credit card, make your check payable to the escrow account (unless you're dealing with a travel agent, in which case, his or her check should be payable to the escrow account). The Department of Transportation's Consumer Affairs Office (I–25, Washington, DC 20590, tel. 202/366–2220) can answer questions on charters and send you its "Plane Talk: Public Charter Flights" information sheet.

Charter operators may offer flights alone or with ground arrangements that constitute a charter package. Well-established charter operators include **Council Charter** (205 E. 42nd St., New York, NY 10017, tel. 212/661–0311 or 800/800–8222), now largely a consolidator, despite its name, and **Travel Charter** (1120 E. Long Lake Rd., Troy, MI 48098, tel. 313/528–3570 or 800/521–5267), with Midwestern departures. **DER Tours** (Box 1606, Des Plains, IL 60017, tel. 800/782–2424), a charterer and consolidator, sells through travel agents.

Discount Travel   Travel clubs offer their members unsold space on airplanes,
Clubs   cruise ships, and package tours at nearly the last minute and at well below the original cost. Suppliers thus receive some revenue for their "leftovers," and members get a bargain. Membership generally includes a regular bulletin or access to a toll-free telephone hot line giving details of available trips departing anywhere from three or four days to several months in the future. Packages tend to be more common than flights alone, so if airfares are your only interest, read the literature before joining. Reductions on hotels are also available. Clubs include **Discount Travel International** (114 Forrest Ave., Suite 203, Narberth, PA 19072, tel. 215/668–7184; $45 annually, single or family), **Moment's Notice** (425 Madison Ave., New York, NY 10017, tel. 212/486–0503; $45 annually, single or family), **Travelers Advantage** (CUC Travel Service, 49 Music Sq. W, Nashville, TN 37203, tel. 800/548–1116; $49 annually, single or family), and **Worldwide Discount Travel Club** (1674 Meridian

Ave., Miami Beach, FL 33139, tel. 305/534–2082; $50 annually for family, $40 single).

Enjoying the Flight Fly at night if you're able to sleep on a plane. Because the air aloft is dry, drink plenty of beverages while on board; remember that drinking alcohol contributes to jet lag, as do heavy meals. Sleepers usually prefer window seats to curl up against; restless passengers ask to be on the aisle. Bulkhead seats, in the front row of each cabin, have more legroom, but since there's no seat ahead, trays attach awkwardly to the arms of your seat, and you must stow all possessions overhead. Bulkhead seats are usually reserved for the disabled, the elderly, and people traveling with babies.

Smoking Since February 1990, smoking has been banned on all domestic flights of less than six hours duration; the ban also applies to domestic segments of international flights aboard U.S. and foreign carriers. On U.S. carriers flying to Eastern Europe and other destinations abroad, a seat in a no-smoking section must be provided for every passenger who requests one, and the section must be enlarged to accommodate such passengers if necessary as long as they have complied with the airline's deadline for check-in and seat assignment. If smoking bothers you, request a seat far from the smoking section.

Foreign airlines are exempt from these rules but do provide no-smoking sections, and some nations, including Canada as of July 1, 1993, have gone as far as to ban smoking on all domestic flights; other countries may ban smoking on flights of less than a specified duration. The International Civil Aviation Organization has set July 1, 1996, as the date to ban smoking aboard airlines worldwide, but the body has no power to enforce its decisions.

From the United Kingdom by Plane, Car, Bus, and Train

By Plane British Airways (tel. 071/897–4000) has daily nonstop service to Prague from London (with connections to major British cities); ČSA (tel. 071/255–1898) flies five times a week nonstop from London. The flight takes around three hours.

By Car The most convenient ferry ports for Prague are Hoek van Holland and Ostend. To reach Prague from either ferry port, drive first to Cologne (Köln) and then through either Dresden or Frankfurt.

By Bus There is no direct bus service from the United Kingdom to the Czech Republic; the closest you can get is Munich, and from there the train is your best bet. International Express (Coach Travel Center, 13 Lower Regent St., London SW1Y 4LR, tel. 071/439–9368) operates daily in summer, leaving London's Victoria Coach Station in mid-evening and arriving in Munich about 23 hours later.

By Train There are no direct trains from London. You can take a direct train from Paris via Frankfurt to Prague (daily) or from Berlin via Dresden to Prague (three times a day). Vienna is a good starting point for Prague, Brno, or Bratislava. There are three trains a day from Vienna's Franz Josefsbahnhof to Prague via Třeboň and Tábor (5½ hours) and two from the Südbahnhof (South Station) via Brno (5 hours).

Staying in the Czech Republic and Slovakia

Getting Around

By Plane ČSA (Czechoslovak Airlines) maintains remarkably good internal air service linking Prague with Brno, Karlovy Vary, and Ostrava, as well as with Poprad (Tatras), Piešt'any, and Košice in Slovakia. The flights, by jet or turboprop aircraft, are relatively cheap and frequent. Reservations can be made through Čedok offices abroad or ČSA in Prague (Revoluční 1, tel. 02/231–2595 or 02/235–2785).

By Train Trains come in a variety of speeds, but it's not really worth taking anything less than an express train, marked in red on the timetable. Tickets are relatively cheap; first class is considerably more spacious and comfortable and well worth the 50% more than what you'll pay for standard tickets. If you don't specify "express" when you buy your ticket, you may have to pay a supplement on the train. If you haven't bought a ticket in advance at the station, it's easy to buy one on the train for a small extra charge. On timetables, departures (*odjezd*) appear on a yellow background; arrivals (*příjezd* are on white. It is possible to book *couchettes* (sleepers) on most overnight trains, but don't expect much in the way of comfort. The European East Pass and the InterRail Pass—but not the EurailPass or Eurail Youthpass—are valid for unlimited train travel within the Czech Republic and Slovakia.

By Bus The Czech Republic and Slovakia's extremely comprehensive state-run bus service, ČSAD, is usually much quicker than the normal trains and more frequent than express trains, unless you're going to the major cities. Prices are about the same as for the train. Buy your tickets from the ticket window at the bus station or directly from the driver on the bus. Long-distance buses can be full, so you might want to book a seat in advance; Čedok will help you do this. The only drawback to traveling by bus is figuring out the timetables. They are easy to read, but beware of the small letters denoting exceptions to the time given. If in doubt, inquire at the information window or ask someone for assistance.

By Car Traveling by car is the easiest and most flexible way of seeing the Czech Republic and Slovakia. There are a few four-lane highways, but most of the roads are in reasonably good shape and traffic is usually light. The road can be poorly marked, however, so before you start out buy the excellent *Auto Atlas ČSFR* or the larger-scale *Velký Autoatlas Československá* (which also shows locations of lead-free gas pumps); both are multilingual, inexpensive, and available at any bookstore. Both countries follow the usual Continental rules of the road. A right turn on red is permitted only when indicated by a green arrow. Signposts with yellow diamonds indicate a main road where drivers have the right of way. The speed limit is 110 kph (70 mph) on four-lane highways, 90 kph (55 mph) on open roads, and 60 kph (40 mph) in built-up areas. The fine for speeding is 300 Kč., payable on the spot. Seat belts are compulsory, and drinking before driving is absolutely prohibited.

Don't rent a car if you intend to visit only Prague. Most of the city center is closed to traffic, and you'll save yourself a lot of hassle by sticking to public transportation. If you do arrive in Prague by car, bear in mind that you can park in the center of town, including on Wenceslas Square, only if you have a voucher from one of the major hotels. If you're not staying in a hotel, a good legal solution is to park the car on one of the little streets behind the Bohemian National Museum (at the top of Wenceslas Square). This neighborhood is technically not considered part of Prague's central district, and anyone can park there.

For accidents, call the emergency number (tel. 154). In case of repair problems, get in touch with the 24-hour **Autoturist Servis** (Limuzská 12, Prague 10, tel. 02/773455); in Bratislava contact the 24-hour service (07/363711). Autotourist offices throughout the Czech Republic can provide motoring information of all kinds. The Auto Atlas ČSFR has a list of emergency road-repair numbers in the various towns in both countries.

A word of caution: If you have any alcohol whatsoever in your body, *do not* drive in Eastern Europe. Penalties are fierce, and the blood-alcohol limit is practically zero.

Roads and Gasoline The main roads, usually made of macadam or concrete, are built to a fairly high standard. There are now quite substantial stretches of highway on main routes, and a lot of rebuilding is being done. Gas stations are fewer than in the West, sited at intervals of about 48 kilometers (30 miles) along main routes and on the outskirts of large towns. Very few stations are open after 9:30 PM. At least two grades of gasoline are sold in East European countries, usually 90–93 octane (regular) and 94–98 octane (super). Lead-free gasoline is available in very few gas stations. The supply of gas to filling stations is by no means regular, so that there are sometimes long lines and considerable delays. Try to get in the habit of filling your tank whenever you see a station, to avoid being stranded on a long drive.

Telephones

AT&T and **MCI** both have direct calling programs overseas. AT&T's **USADirect** service allows you to call collect or charge calls from abroad to your AT&T calling card. Either way, you pay AT&T rates and speak to an English-speaking operator. The access code to use when dialing from within the Czech Republic and Slovakia is tel. 00–420–00101. The MCI access code for the Czech Republic and Slovakia is 00–420–00112.

Dining

Eastern European cuisine, regional by nature, is suffering from an identity crisis. Until 1989, and in varying degrees, Eastern Europe suffered food shortages and rationing of even the most basic foodstuffs. In many countries, pork and potatoes became de facto replacements for the elaborate folk dishes that once graced tables from Warsaw to Sofia.

With the collapse of communism, Eastern European cuisines are on the rebound. You always could find an excellent meal in Budapest, even at the height of the Cold War; but the recent proliferation of restaurants in Budapest and throughout Eastern Europe is hopeful news, indeed. Bucharest and Sofia seem destined to lag behind, but even so, you can still find quiet eateries offering excellent, modern versions of traditional recipes.

Restaurants in Eastern Europe come in all shapes and sizes. Some remain state-owned and attached to tedious cement-block hotels. Others have sprung up in abandoned warehouses or former Communist party digs. You'll find some in the most unlikely places such as Slovakia's remote High Tatras mountains.

Restaurant standards remain high in East European capitals; in Prague, for example, you'll find everything from formal bistros to boisterous wine halls. Prices have risen dramatically since 1989, but you can still enjoy a decadent meal, even in the cities, for well under $15.

Lodging

If your experience of East European hotels is limited to capital cities such as Prague and Budapest, you may be pleasantly surprised. There are Baroque mansions-turned-guest houses and elegant high-rise resorts, not to mention bed-and-breakfast inns presided over by matronly babushkas. Now that communism is a thing of the past, there seems to be more interest in maintaining and upgrading facilities (though, inevitably, there are exceptions).

Outside major cities, hotels and inns are more rustic than elegant. Standards of service generally do not suffer, but in most rural areas the definition of luxury includes little more than a television and private bathroom. In some instances, you may have no choice but to stay in one of the cement high-rise hotels that scar skylines from Poland to the Czech Republic to Romania. It's hard to say why Communists required their hotels to be as big and impersonal as possible, but they did, and it may take a few more years to exorcise or "beautify" these ubiquitous monsters.

The good news is that room rates are reasonable in all but a handful of international chain hotels that have sprung up in Eastern Europe since 1989. During the high season it is possible to find a spacious, well-maintained double room for less than $40; in rural Eastern Europe, you may have difficulty parting with more than $20 per night for lodgings. Reservations are vital if you plan to visit Prague, Budapest, Warsaw, or most other major cities during the summer season. Reservations are a good idea but not imperative if you plan to strike out into the countryside.

Home Exchange This is obviously an inexpensive solution to the lodging problem, because house-swapping means living rent-free. You find a house, apartment, or other vacation property to exchange for your own by becoming a member of a home-exchange organization, which then sends you its annual directories listing available exchanges and includes your own listing in at least one of them. Arrangements for the actual exchange are made by the two parties to it, not by the organization. Principal clearinghouses include **Intervac U.S./International Home Exchange** (Box 590504, San Francisco, CA 94159, tel. 415/435–3497), the oldest, with thousands of foreign and domestic homes for exchange in its three annual directories; membership is $62, or $72 if you want to receive the directories but remain unlisted. The **Vacation Exchange Club** (Box 650, Key West, FL 33041, tel. 800/638–3841), also with thousands of foreign and domestic listings, publishes four annual directories plus updates; the $50 membership includes your listing in one book. **Loan-a-Home** (2 Park La., Apt. 6E, Mount Vernon, NY 10552, tel. 914/664–7640) specializes in long-term exchanges; there is no charge to list your home, but the directories cost $35 or $45 depending on the number you receive.

Credit Cards

The following credit-card abbreviations are used: AE, American Express; DC, Diner's Club; MC, MasterCard/Access/Barclays; V, Visa.

2 The Czech Republic

By Mark Baker

Mark Baker is a freelance journalist and travel writer living in Prague.

A victim of enforced obscurity throughout much of the 20th century, the Czech Republic, comprising the provinces of Bohemia and Moravia (but no longer Slovakia), is once again in the spotlight. In a world where revolution was synonymous with violence, and in a country where truth was quashed by the tanks of Eastern-Bloc socialism, in November 1989 Václav Havel's sonorous voice proclaimed the victory of the "Velvet Revolution" to enthusiastic crowds on Wenceslas Square and preached the value of "living in truth." Recording the dramatic events of the time, television cameras panned across Prague's glorious skyline and fired the world's imagination with the image of political renewal superimposed on somber Gothic and voluptuous Baroque.

Travelers have rediscovered the country, and Czechs and Moravians have rediscovered the world. Not so long ago, the visitor was unhindered by crowds of tourists but had to struggle with a creeping sensation of melancholy and neglect that threatened to eclipse the city's beauty. Combined with a truly frustrating lack of services in every branch of the tourist industry, a trip to Czechoslovakia was always an adventure in the full sense of the word.

At least on the surface, the atmosphere is changing rapidly. The stagnant "normalization" of the Husák era, which froze the city out of the developments of the late-20th century, is giving way to the dynamic and cosmopolitan. The revolution brought enthusiasm, bustle, and such conveniences as English-language newspapers, attentive hotels, and, occasionally, restaurants that will try to find you a seat even if you don't have a reservation.

The revolution inspired one other thing: nationalism. Unable to unite on a common course of economic renewal Czechs and Slovaks peacefully agreed to dissolve their 74-year-old federal state on January 1, 1993. While the division was greeted with sadness by outsiders, visitors to either country are not likely to notice much difference save for the hassle of an extra border and the need now to change money when traveling back and forth. The chapter below covers the Czech Republic and its constituent provinces of Bohemia and Moravia. Slovakia is covered in a separate country chapter.

The drab remnants of socialist reality are still omnipresent on the back roads of Bohemia and Moravia. But many of the changes made by the Communists were superficial—adding ugliness, but leaving the society's core more or less intact. The colors are less jarring, not designed to attract the moneyed eye; the fittings are as they always were, not adapted to the needs of a new world.

The experience of visiting the Czech Republic still involves stepping back in time. Even in Prague, now deluged by tourists in the summer months, the sense of history—stretching back through centuries of wars, empires, and monuments to everyday life—remains uncluttered by the trappings of modernity. The peculiar melancholy of Central Europe, less tainted now by the oppressive political realities of the postwar era, still lurks in narrow streets and forgotten corners. Crumbling facades, dilapidated palaces, and treacherous cobbled streets both shock and enchant the visitor used to a world where what remains of history has been spruced up for tourist eyes.

The strange, old-world, and at times frustratingly bureaucratic atmosphere of the Czech Republic is not all a product of the communist era. Many of the small rituals that impinge on the visitor are actually remnants of the Habsburg Empire and are also to be found, perhaps to a lesser degree, in Vienna and Budapest. The *šatná* (coatroom), for example, plays a vivid role in any visit to a restaurant or theater at any time of year other than summer. Even in the coldest weather, coats must be given with a few coins to the attendant, usually an old lady with a sharp eye for ignorant or disobedient tourists. The attendant often also plays a role in controlling the rest room; the entrance fee entitles the visitor to a small roll of paper, ceremoniously kept on the attendant's table. Another odd custom, associated with this part of the world, are the *Tabák-Trafiks*, the little stores that sell two things connected for no apparent reason: tobacco products and public-transport tickets.

Outside of the capital, for those willing to put up with the inconveniences of shabby hotels and mediocre restaurants, the sense of rediscovering a neglected world is even stronger. And the range is startling, from imperial spas, with their graceful colonnades and dilapidated villas, to the hundreds of arcaded town squares, modestly displaying the passing of time with each splendid layer of once contemporary style. Gothic towers, Renaissance facades, Baroque interiors, and aging modern supermarkets merge. Between the man-made sights, the visitor is rewarded with glorious mountain ranges and fertile rolling countryside, laced with carp ponds and forests.

The key to enjoying the country is to relax. There is no point in demanding high levels of service or quality. And for the budget-conscious traveler, this is Central Europe at its most beautiful, at prices that are several times below those of Austria and even Hungary.

Before You Go

Government Tourist Offices

Čedok, the official travel bureau for the Czech Republic and Slovakia, is actually a travel agent rather than a tourist information office. It will supply you with hotel and travel information, and book air and rail tickets for travel within either country, but don't expect too much in the way of general information.

In the United States: 10 E. 40th St., New York, NY 10016, tel. 212/689–9720. **In the United Kingdom:** 17–18 Old Bond St., London W1X 4RB, tel. 071/629–6058.

Tour Groups

U.S. Tour Operators **General Tours** (245 Fifth Ave., New York, NY 10016, tel. 212/685–1800 or 800/221–2216) combines Prague and Budapest on a nine-day tour, which features comprehensive city sightseeing plus excursions to Konopiště, Lidice, and the Danube Bend in Hungary.

Love Holidays/Uniworld (Box 16000 Ventura Blvd., Suite 1105, Encino, CA 91436, tel. 818/501–6868 or 800/733–7820) gives you Prague and the "Best of Czechoslovakia" in 10 days. The eight-day tour of Prague and the "Jewels of Bohemia" includes full-day excursions into the surrounding countryside.

For other operators that include Prague and the Czech Republic on their Eastern Europe itineraries, *see* Tour Groups in Chapter 1.

U.K. Tour Operators Čedok Tours and Holidays (17–18 Old Bond St., London W1X 4RB, tel. 071/629–6058) offers four- and eight-day packages to Prague, with optional sightseeing excursions to the countryside, and packages to the Prague Spring Music Festival.

Hamilton Travel Ltd. (6 Heddon St., London W1R 7LH, tel. 071/439–3199) offers flight/accommodation packages for one or more nights to Prague.

Page & Moy Ltd. (136–140 London Rd., Leicester LE2 1EN, tel. 0533/552251) offers a three-night package to Prague, including a city sightseeing tour and an optional visit to Karlštejn Castle.

Sovereign Cities (Groundstar House, London Road, Crawley, West Sussex RH10 2TB, tel. 0293/561444) offers three- and seven-night flight/hotel packages in the Czech Republic with optional sightseeing excursions.

Travelscene Ltd. (Travelscene House, 11–15 St. Ann's Rd., Harrow, Middlesex HA1 1AS, tel. 081/427–4445) offers three- and seven-night flight/hotel packages to Prague with optional excursions, and a seven-night, two-center holiday with Vienna.

When to Go

Prague is beautiful year-round, but avoid midsummer (especially July and August) and the Christmas and Easter holidays, when the city is overrun with tourists. Spring and fall generally combine good weather with a more bearable level of tourism. During the winter months you'll encounter few other visitors and have the opportunity to see Prague breathtakingly covered in snow; but many of the sights are closed, and it can get very cold. The same guidelines apply generally to traveling in the rest of Bohemia and Moravia, although even in high season (August), the number of visitors to these areas is far smaller than in Prague. The Giant Mountains of Bohemia come into their own in winter (December–February), when skiers from all over the country crowd the slopes and resorts. If you're not into skiing, try visiting the mountains in late spring (May or June) or fall, when the colors are dazzling and you'll have the hotels and restaurants pretty much to yourself. Bear in mind that many castles and museums are closed November through March.

Festivals and Seasonal Events

The Czech government publishes an annual "Calendar of Tourist Events" in English, available from Čedok or the Prague Information service. Čedok offices can provide you with exact dates and additional information.

March: Prague City of Music Festival
April: International Consumer Goods Fair (Brno), Jazz Festival (Kroměříž)
May: Prague Spring Music Festival, International Childrens' Film Festival (Zlín)

June: Smetana National Opera Festival (Litomyšl), International Festival of Mime (Mariánské Lázně)
July: Prague Summer Culture Festival
August: Chopin Festival (Mariánské Lázně)
August–September: Brno Folklore Festival
September: Brno Engineering Goods Fair
October: Brno International Music Festival, Karlovy Vary Film Festival, Prague Marathon, International Jazz Festival (Prague)

What to Pack

In the postcommunist Czech Republic, Western dress of any kind is considered stylish, so don't bother bringing your tuxedo. A sports jacket for men, and a dress or pants for women, is appropriate for an evening out in Prague or in the better Bohemian spa towns. Everywhere else, you'll feel comfortable in casual corduroys or jeans. Most of the country is best seen on foot, so take a pair of sturdy walking shoes and be prepared to use them. Throughout Eastern Europe, high heels present a considerable problem on cobblestone streets, and Prague is no exception. If you plan on visiting the mountains, make sure your shoes have good traction and ankle support, as some trails can be quite challenging. Many consumer goods are still in short supply. Be sure to bring any medications or special toiletries you may require. You will need an electrical adapter for small appliances; the voltage is 220, with 50 cycles.

Czech Currency

The unit of currency in the Czech Republic is the koruna, or crown (Kč.), which is divided into 100 haléř, or halers. There are (little-used) coins of 10, 20, and 50 halers; coins of 1, 2, 5, 10, and 50 Kč., and notes of 10, 20, 50, 100, 200, 500, and 1,000 Kč. The 100-Kč. notes are by far the most useful. The 1,000-Kč. note won't always be accepted for small purchases, because the proprietor may not have enough change.

Try to avoid exchanging money at hotels or private exchange booths, including the ubiquitous Čekobanka and Exact Change booths. They routinely take commissions of 8–10%. The best place to exchange is at bank counters, where the commissions average 1–3%. Although the crown is more or less convertible, you will still encounter difficulty in exchanging your money when you leave. To facilitate this process, keep your original exchange receipts so no one will think you bought your crowns on the black market. It is technically illegal to buy crowns abroad and bring them into the Czech Republic (or to take them out when you leave), although this is not strictly controlled. The black market for Western currencies is still thriving, but it's best to keep well away; such deals are strictly illegal and if caught you risk deportation. At press time (fall 1993) the official exchange rate was around 27 Kč. to the U.S. dollar and 45 Kč. to the pound sterling. There is no longer a special exchange rate for tourists.

What It Will Cost

Despite rising inflation, the Czech Republic is still generally a bargain by Western standards. Prague remains the exception, however. Hotel prices, in particular, frequently meet or exceed the U.S. and Western European average—and are higher than the standard of facilities would warrant. Nevertheless, you can still find bargain private accommodations. The prices at tourist resorts outside of the capital are lower and, in the outlying areas and off the beaten track, incredibly low. Tourists can now legally pay for hotel rooms in crowns, although some hotels will still insist on payment in "hard" (i.e., Western) currency.

Sample Costs   A cup of coffee will cost about 15 Kč.; museum entrance, 20 Kč.; a good theater seat, up to 100 Kč.; a cinema seat, 30 Kč.; a half liter (pint) of beer, 15 Kč.; a 1-mile taxi ride, 60 Kč.; a bottle of Moravian wine in a good restaurant, 100 Kč.–150 Kč.; a glass (2 deciliters or 7 ounces) of wine, 25 Kč.

Passports and Visas

American and British citizens require only a valid passport for stays up to 30 days in the Czech Republic. No visas are necessary. Canadian citizens, however, must obtain a visa (C$50) before entering the Czech Republic. For applications and information, contact the Czech embassy (541 Sussex Dr., Ottawa, Ontario K1N 6Z6, tel. 613/562–3875). U.S. citizens can receive additional information from the Czech embassy (3900 Linnean Ave. NW, Washington, DC, tel. 202/363–6315).

Customs and Duties

On Arrival   You may import duty-free into the Czech Republic 250 cigarettes or the equivalent in tobacco, one liter of spirits, two liters of wine, and ½ liter of perfume. You may also bring up to 1,000 Kč. worth of gifts and souvenirs.

If you take into the Czech Republic any valuables or foreign-made equipment from home, such as cameras, it's wise to carry the original receipts with you or register the items with U.S. Customs before you leave (Form 4457). Otherwise you could end up paying duty on your return.

On Departure   From the Czech Republic you can take out gifts and souvenirs valued up to 1,000 Kč., as well as goods bought at Tuzex hard-currency shops (keep the receipts). Crystal and some other items not bought at hard-currency shops may be subject to a tax of 100% of their retail price. Only antiques bought at Tuzex or specially appointed shops may be exported.

Language

Czech, a western-Slavic language, closely related to Slovak and Polish, is the official language of the Czech Republic. Learning English is popular among young people, but German is still the most useful language for tourists. Don't be surprised if you get a response in German to a question asked in English. If the idea of attempting Czech is daunting, you might consider bringing a German phrasebook.

Staying Healthy

The Czech Republic poses no great health risks for the short-term visitor. Tap water tastes bad but is generally drinkable. Those on special diets and vegetarians may have a problem with the heavy local cuisine, which is based nearly exclusively on pork and beef. For more information, *see* Staying Healthy in Chapter 1.

Car Rentals

There are no special requirements for renting a car in the Czech Republic, but be sure to shop around, as prices can differ greatly. **Avis** and **Hertz** offer Western makes for as much as $400–$600 per week. Smaller local companies, on the other hand, can rent Czechoslovak cars for as low as $130 per week.

The following rental agencies are based in Prague.

Avis. Opletalova 33, Nové Město, tel. 02/222324; Hotel Atrium, tel. 02/284–2043; airport, tel. 02/367807.
Budget. Airport, tel. 02/316–5214; Hotel Inter-Continental, tel. 02/231–9595.
Esocar. Husitská 58, Prague 3, tel. 02/691–2244.
Hertz. Airport, tel. 02/312–0717; Hotel Atrium, tel. 284–2047; Hotel Diplomat (tel. 02/312–0717).
Pragocar. Milevská 2, Prague 4, tel. 02/692–2875.
Unix. V celnici 4, Nové Město, tel. 02/233693.

Rail Passes

The **European East Pass** is good for unlimited first-class travel on the national railroads of Austria, the Czech Republic, Slovakia, Hungary, and Poland. The pass allows five days of travel within a 15-day period ($169) or 10 days of travel within a 30-day period ($275). Apply through your travel agent or through **Rail Europe** (226–230 Westchester Ave., White Plains, NY 10604, tel. 914/682–2999 or 800/848–7245).

The **EurailPass** and **Eurail Youthpass** are not valid for travel within the Czech Republic. The **InterRail Pass** (£249), available to European citizens only through local student or budget travel offices, is valid for one month of unlimited train travel in the Czech Republic and the other countries covered in this book. For more information, *see* Rail Passes in Chapter 1.

Student and Youth Travel

In the Czech Republic, **ČKM Youth Travel Service** (Žitná 12, Prague 1, tel. 02/205446) provides information on student hostels and travel bargains within the Czech Republic. For general information about student identity cards, work abroad programs, and youth hostelling, *see* Student and Youth Travel in Chapter 1.

Further Reading

With the increased interest in the Czech Republic in recent years, English readers now have an excellent range of both fiction and nonfiction about the country at their disposal. The most widely read Czech author of fiction in English is probably Milan Kundera, whose well-crafted tales illuminate both the foibles of human nature and the unique tribulations of life in communist Czechoslovakia in a humorous but thought-provoking way. *The Unbearable Lightness of Being* takes a look at the 1968 invasion and its aftermath through the eyes of a strained young couple. The very entertaining *Book of Laughter and Forgetting* deals in part with the importance of memory and the cruel irony of how it fades over time. The author was no doubt coming to terms with his own forgetting as he wrote the book from his Paris exile. *The Joke,* Kundera's earliest work available in English, takes a serious look at the dire consequences of humorlessness among Communists.

Josef Škvorecký, another contemporary Czechoslovak writer, lives in exile in Canada. In his widely available *The Engineer of Human Souls*, he attempts to relate his experiences in Canada to his earlier life in Czechoslovakia under Nazi and, later, communist occupation.

Franz Kafka's *The Trial* and *The Castle* will help you feel some of the dread and mystery that he and other German writers detected beneath the 1,000 golden spires of Prague. His books were actually an indictment of the bizarre bureaucracy of the Austro-Hungarian empire, though they now seem eerily prophetic of the even crueler and more arbitrary communist system that was to come. For this reason, until recently most of his works could not be purchased in his native country.

Jaroslav Hašek's hilarious classic *The Good Soldier Schweik* concerns the antics of a good-natured boob who survives World War I in the Austro-Hungarian army. Many regard Schweik as the archetypal Czech: a guileless, downtrodden fellow who somehow always manages to get by.

As for nonfiction, the best place to start is probably *Living in Truth*, an absorbing collection of 22 inspiring essays written by President Václav Havel during his years "underground" as a dissident playwright. The first essay is an open letter to the former communist president Gustav Husák, written before the 1989 revolution, concerning the erosion of public life that occurs when the populace is forced to lip-synch empty slogans. Havel's view is that a just society is one that enables its citizens to live out their lives true to their conscience. Havel's plays are also worth seeing for a better understanding of the absurdities and pressures of life under the former communist regime.

For an excellent social and historical background on the former Czechoslovakia look to David W. Paul's *Czechoslovakia: Profile of a Socialist Republic at the Crossroads of Europe* or R. W. Seton-Watson's *The History of the Czechs and the Slovaks.*

Arriving and Departing

From North America by Plane

Airports and Airlines All international flights to the Czech Republic fly into Prague's **Ruzyně Airport,** about 20 kilometers (12 miles) northwest of downtown. The airport is small and easy to negotiate.

ČSA, (Czechoslovak Airlines), the Czech and Slovak national carrier (tel. 718/656–8439), maintains direct flights to Prague twice weekly from New York's JFK, and once a week from both Los Angeles and Montreal. The airline is considering introducing daily flights.

Several other international airlines have good connections from cities in the United States and Canada to European bases and from there to Prague. **British Airways** (tel. 800/247–9297) flies daily via London; and **SwissAir** (tel. 718/995–8400), daily via Zurich.

Flying Time From New York, a nonstop flight to Prague takes 9–10 hours; with a stopover, the journey will take at least 12–13 hours. From Montreal nonstop it is 7½ hours; from Los Angeles, 16 hours.

From the United Kingdom by Plane, Car, Bus, and Train

By Plane **British Airways** (tel. 071/897–4000) has daily nonstop service to Prague from London (with connections to major British cities); ČSA (tel. 071/255–1898) flies five times a week nonstop from London. The flight takes around three hours.

By Car The most convenient ferry ports for Prague are Hoek van Holland and Ostend. To reach Prague from either ferry port, drive first to Cologne (Köln) and then through either Dresden or Frankfurt.

By Bus There is no direct bus service from the United Kingdom to the Czech Republic; the closest you can get is Munich, and from there the train is your best bet. **International Express** (Coach Travel Center, 13 Lower Regent St., London SW1Y 4LR, tel. 071/439–9368) operates daily in summer, leaving London's Victoria Coach Station in mid-evening and arriving in Munich about 23 hours later.

By Train There are no direct trains from London. You can take a direct train from Paris via Frankfurt to Prague (daily) or from Berlin via Dresden to Prague (three times a day). Vienna is a good starting point for Prague, Brno, or Bratislava. There are three trains a day from Vienna's Franz Josefsbahnhof to Prague via Třeboň and Tábor (5½ hours) and two from the Südbahnhof (South Station) via Brno (five hours).

Staying in the Czech Republic

Getting Around

By Plane ČSA (Czechoslovak Airlines) maintains a remarkably good internal air service linking Prague with Brno, Karlovy Vary, and Ostrava, as well as with Poprad (Tatras), Piešt'any, and Košice in Slovakia. The flights, by jet or turboprop aircraft, are relatively cheap and frequent. Reservations can be made through Čedok offices abroad or ČSA in Prague (Revoluční 1, tel. 02/231–2595 or 02/235–2785).

By Train Trains come in a variety of speeds, but it's not really worth taking anything less than an express train, marked in red on the timetable. Tickets are relatively cheap; first class is considerably more spacious and comfortable and well worth the 50% more than you'll pay for standard tickets. If you don't specify "express" when you buy your ticket, you may have to pay a supplement on the train. If you haven't bought a ticket in advance at the station, it's easy to buy one on the train for a small extra charge. On timetables, departures (*odjezd*) appear on a yellow background; arrivals (*příjezd*) are on white. It is possible to book *couchettes* (sleepers) on most overnight trains, but don't expect much in the way of comfort. The European East Pass and the InterRail Pass—but not the EurailPass or Eurail Youthpass—are valid for unlimited train travel within the Czech Republic.

By Bus The Czech Republic's extremely comprehensive state-run bus service, ČSAD, is usually much quicker than the normal trains and more frequent than express trains, unless you're going to the major cities. Prices are about the same as for the train. Buy your tickets from the ticket window at the bus station or directly from the driver on the bus. Long-distance buses can be full, so you might want to book a seat in advance; Čedok will help you do this. The only drawback to traveling by bus is figuring out the timetables. They are easy to read, but beware of the small letters denoting exceptions to the time given. If in doubt, inquire at the information window or ask someone for assistance.

By Car Traveling by car is the easiest and most flexible way of seeing the Czech Republic. There are few four-lane highways, but most of the roads are in reasonably good shape and traffic is usually light. The road can be poorly marked, however, so before you start out buy the excellent *Auto Atlas ČSFR* or the larger-scale *Velký Autoatlas Československá* (which also shows locations of lead-free gas pumps); both are multilingual, inexpensive, and available at any bookstore. The Czech Republic follows the usual Continental rules of the road. A right turn on red is permitted only when indicated by a green arrow. Signposts with yellow diamonds indicate a main road where drivers have the right of way. The speed limit is 110 kph (70 mph) on four-lane highways, 90 kph (55 mph) on open roads, and 60 kph (40 mph) in built-up areas. The fine for speeding is 300 Kč., payable on the spot. Seat belts are compulsory, and drinking before driving is absolutely prohibited.

Don't rent a car if you intend to visit only Prague. Most of the center of the city is closed to traffic, and you'll save yourself a lot of hassle by sticking to public transportation. If you do arrive in Prague by car, bear in mind that you can park in the center of town, including on Wenceslas Square, only if you have a voucher from one of the major hotels. If you're not staying in a hotel, a good legal solution is to park the car on one of the little streets behind the Bohemian National Museum (at the top of Wenceslas Square). This neighborhood is technically not considered part of Prague's central district, and anyone can park there.

For accidents, call the emergency number (tel. 154). In case of repair problems, get in touch with the 24-hour **Autoturist Servis** (Limuzská 12, Prague 10, tel. 02/773455). Autoturist offices throughout the Czech Republic can provide motoring information of all kinds. The Auto Atlas ČSFR has a list of emergency road-repair numbers in the various towns.

Telephones

Local Calls Coin-operated telephones take either just 1-Kč. coins, or 1-, 2-, and 5-Kč. coins. Some newer public phones operate only with a special telephone card, available from newsstands and tobacconists in denominations of 50 Kč. and 150 Kč. A call within Prague costs 1 Kč. To make a call, lift the receiver and listen for the dial tone, a series of long buzzes. Dial the number. Public phones are located in metro stations and on street corners; unfortunately, they're often out of order. Try asking in a hotel if you're stuck.

International Calls   To reach an English-speaking operator in the United States, dial tel. 00–420–00101 (AT&T) or tel. 00–420–00112 (MCI) from almost any pay phone. The operator will connect your collect or credit card call at standard AT&T or MCI rates. In Prague, the main post office (Hlavní pošta, Jindřišská ul. 14), open 24 hours, is the best place to make a direct-dial long-distance call. Otherwise, ask the receptionist at any hotel to put a call through for you, though beware: The more expensive the hotel, the more expensive the call will be.

Mail

Postal Rates   Postcards to the United States cost 6 Kč.; letters, 11 Kč.; to Great Britain a postcard is 4 Kč.; a letter, 6 Kč. Prices are due for an increase in 1994, so check with your hotel for current rates. You can buy stamps at post offices, hotels, and shops that sell postcards.

Receiving Mail   If you don't know where you'll be staying, **American Express** mail service is a great convenience, available at no charge to anyone holding an American Express credit card or carrying American Express traveler's checks. The American Express office is located on Wenceslas Square in central Prague. You can also have mail held *poste restante* at post offices in major towns, but the letters should be marked *Pošta 1* to designate the city's main post office. The *poste restante* window is No. 28 at the main post office in Prague (Jindřišská ul. 14). You will be asked for identification when you collect mail.

Tipping

To reward good service in a restaurant, round the bill up to the nearest multiple of 10 (if the bill comes to 83 Kč., for example, give the waiter 90 Kč.); 10% is considered appropriate on very large tabs. If you have difficulty communicating the amount to the waiter, just leave the money on the table. Tip porters who bring bags to your rooms 20 Kč. For room service, a 20-Kč. tip is enough. In taxis, round the bill up by 10%. Give tour guides and helpful concierges between 20 Kč. and 30 Kč. for services rendered.

Opening and Closing Times

Bank hours vary, but most are open weekdays 8–3:30, with an hour lunch break. Private exchange offices are usually open longer hours. Museums are usually open daily except Monday (or Tuesday) 9–5; some, including many castles, are open only from May through October. Stores are open weekdays 9–6; some grocery stores open at 6 AM. Department stores often stay open until 7 PM. On Saturday, most stores close at noon. Nearly all stores are closed on Sunday.

National Holidays   January 1; Easter Monday; May 1 (Labor Day); May 9 (Liberation); July 5 (Sts. Cyril and Methodius); July 6 (Jan Hus); October 28 (Independence); and December 24, 25, and 26.

Shopping

In Prague, Karlovy Vary, and elsewhere in Bohemia, look for elegant and unusual crystal and porcelain. Bohemia is also renowned for the quality and deep-red color of its garnets; keep an eye out for beautiful garnet rings and broaches, set in either gold or silver. You can also find excellent ceramics, especially in Moravia, as well as other folk artifacts, such as printed textiles, lace, hand-knit sweaters, and painted eggs. There are attractive crafts stores throughout the Czech Republic. Karlovy Vary is blessed with a variety of unique items to buy, including the strange pipelike drinking mugs used in the spas; roses; vases left to petrify in the mineral-laden water; and *Oblaten*, crispy wafers sometimes covered with chocolate. Here, you'll also find *Becherovka*, a tasty herbal aperitif that makes a nice gift to take home.

Sports and Outdoor Activities

Bicycling Czechs are avid cyclists. The flatter areas of southern Bohemia and Moravia are ideal for biking. Outside of the larger towns, quieter roads stretch out for miles. The hillier terrain of northern Bohemia makes it popular with mountain-biking enthusiasts. Not many places rent bikes, though. Inquire at Čedok or at your hotel for rental information. Alternatively, ask at the American Hospitality Center in Prague.

Boating and Sailing The country's main boating area is the enormous series of dams and reservoirs along the Vltava south of Prague. The most popular lake is Slapy, where it is possible to rent small paddleboats as well as to relax and swim on a hot day. If you have your own kayak, you can test your skills on one of the excellent rivers near Český Krumlov.

Camping There are hundreds of camping sites for tents and trailers throughout the Czech Republic, but most are open only in summer (May to mid-September). You can get a map of all the sites, with addresses, opening times, and facilities, from Čedok. Camping outside of official sites is prohibited. Some camping grounds also offer bungalows. Campsites are divided into categories A and B according to facilities, but both have hot water and toilets.

Fishing Many lakes and rivers are suitable for fishing, but you'll need both a fishing license, valid for a year, and a fishing permit, valid for a day, week, month, or year, for the particular body of water you plan to fish in. Both are available from Čedok offices. You'll have to bring your own tackle with you or buy it locally.

Golf There are very few golf courses in the Czech Republic. The best known and possibly most attractive 18-hole course is at the elegant Hotel Golf in Mariánské Lázně. You will also find smaller courses in Prague and Karlovy Vary. Ask at one of the larger hotels for details.

Hiking The Czech Republic is a hiker's paradise, with 40,000 kilometers (25,000 miles) of well-kept, marked, and signposted trails both in the mountainous regions and leading through beautiful countryside from town to town. You'll find the colored markings denoting trails on trees, fences, walls, rocks, and elsewhere. The colors correspond to the path-marking on the large-scale *Soubor turistickych* maps. The main paths are marked in red, others in blue and green; the least important trails are marked in yellow. The best areas for ambitious mountain walkers are the Beskydy mountain range (Giant Mountains) in northern Moravia and the Krkonoše range in Northern Bohemia. The rolling Šumava hills of southern Bohemia are excellent for less ambitious walkers.

Skiing The two main skiing areas in the Czech Republic are the Krkonoše range in northern Bohemia and the Šumava hills of southern Bohemia (lifts at both operate from January through March). In the former, you'll find a number of organizations renting skis—although supplies may be limited. Both places are also good for cross-country skiing.

Tennis The larger hotels can usually arrange for tennis courts if they don't have them in-house. In larger towns, ask at the Čedok office or in hotels for the address of public tennis courts.

Dining

The quality of restaurant cuisine in the Czech Republic remains uneven. Many excellent private restaurants have sprung up in Prague in recent years, but in the countryside, the food is often monotonous and of low quality. The traditional dishes—roast pork or duck with dumplings, or broiled meat with sauce—can be light and tasty when well prepared. Frequently, however, they're just tossed onto your plate with little forethought or care. The problem stems from the years of communist rule, when private restaurants were shut down and replaced by state-run establishments with standardized menus and recipes. Often in smaller towns, the hotel restaurant, sadly, is still the only dining option available.

Restaurants generally fall into three categories. A *pivnice*, or beer hall, usually offers a simple menu of goulash or pork with dumplings at very low prices. The drawback is that the food is often poorly prepared while the surroundings can be noisy and crowded (expect to share a table). More attractive (and more expensive) are the *vinárna* (wine cellars) and normal *restaurace* (restaurants), which serve a full range of dishes and are usually open only during mealtimes. Wine cellars, some occupying Romanesque basements, can be a real treat, and you should certainly seek them out. A fourth dining option, the *lahůdky* (snack bar or deli), is the quickest and cheapest option. At snack bars, typically, you order from a counter and eat standing up. Street stands sell a variety of traditional, if heavy, alternatives, including *párek* (hot dogs), *smažený sýr* (fried cheese), and *bramborák* (potato pancakes).

The increase in the number of visitors to the country has placed a strain on restaurants. To avoid disappointment, always try to book a table in advance, especially in Prague. Your hotel may be able to reserve a table better than if you call yourself. If you don't have a reservation, try showing up just before mealtime (11:30 for lunch, 5:30 for dinner).

Most places do not serve foreign wines, so wine lists usually are limited to reasonably good Moravian wines. The best varieties come from Mikulov and Znojmo in Moravia and are as follows:

White: Müller Thurgau is green when young but yellows with maturity. The wine's fine muscat bouquet and light flavor go well with fish and veal. **Neuburské,** yellow-green in color and with a dry, smoky bouquet, is delicious with roasts. **Rulandské bilé,** a semi-dry white also known by its French name, burgundy, has a flowery bouquet and full-bodied flavor. It's a good complement to poultry and veal. The dry, smooth flavor of **Ryzlink Rýnský** is best enjoyed with cold entrées and fish. **Veltlínské zelené,** distinguished by its beautiful light-green color, also goes well with cold entrées.

Red: Frankovka, fiery red and slightly acidic, is well suited to game and grilled meats. **Rulandské cervené,** cherry-red in color and flavor, is an excellent dry companion to poultry, game, and grilled meats. **Vavřinecké,** a dark, semisweet red, stands up well to red meats.

Mealtimes Lunch, usually eaten between noon and 2, is the main meal for Czechs and offers the best deal for tourists. Many restaurants put out a special luncheon menu (*denní lístek*), usually printed only in Czech, with more appetizing selections at better prices. If you don't see it, ask your waiter. Dinner is usually served from 5 until 9 or 10, but don't wait too long to eat. First of all, most Czechs eat only a light meal or cold plate of meat and cheese in the evening. Secondly, restaurant cooks frequently knock off early on slow nights, and the later you arrive, the more likely the kitchen will be closed. In general, dinner menus do not differ substantially from lunch offerings, except that the prices are higher.

Ratings Czechs don't normally go in for three-course meals, and the following prices apply only if you are having a first course, main course, and dessert (excluding wine and tip).

Category	Prague*	Other Areas*
Very Expensive	over $25	over $20
Expensive	$15–$25	$10–$20
Moderate	$7–$15	$5–$10
Inexpensive	under $7	under $5

per person, including appetizer, main course, and dessert but excluding wine and tip

Lodging

The number of hotels and pensions has increased dramatically throughout the Czech Republic, in step with the influx of tourists. Finding a suitable room should pose no problem, although it is highly recommended that you book ahead during the peak tourist season (July and August, and the Christmas and Easter holidays). Hotel prices, in general, remain high. This is especially true in Prague and in the spa towns of western Bohemia. Better value often can be found at private pensions and with individual homeowners offering rooms to let. In the outlying towns, the best strategy is to inquire at the local tourist information office or simply fan out around the town and look for room-for-rent signs on houses (usually in German: ZIMMER FREI, PRIVAT ZIMMER).

Outside of Prague and the major tourist centers, hotels tend to fall into two categories: the old-fashioned hotel on the main square, with rooms over a restaurant, no private bathrooms, and a price lower than you can imagine; or the modern, impersonal, and often ugly high rise with all the basic facilities and a reasonable price. Nevertheless, you'll rarely find a room that is not clean, and some hotels (of both varieties) can be very pleasant indeed. Hostels are understood to mean dormitory rooms and are probably best avoided. In the mountainous areas, you can often find little *chata* (chalets), where pleasant surroundings compensate for a lack of basic amenities. *Autokempink* (campsites) generally have a few bungalows.

The Czech Republic's official hotel classification, based on letters (Deluxe, A*, B*, B, C), is gradually being changed to the international star system, though it will be some time before the old system is completely replaced. These ratings correspond closely to our categories as follows: Deluxe or five-star (Very Expensive); A* or four-star (Expensive); B* or three-star (Moderate); and B or two-star (Inexpensive). We've included C hotels, some with cold water only, in our listings where accommodations are scarce. Often you can book rooms—both at hotels and in private homes—through Čedok. Otherwise, try calling or writing the hotel directly.

Ratings The prices quoted below are for double rooms during high season, generally not including breakfast. At certain periods, such as Easter or during festivals, prices can jump 15%–25%; as a rule, always ask the price before taking a room.

Category	Prague*	Other Areas*
Very Expensive	over $200	over $100
Expensive	$100–$200	$50–$100
Moderate	$50–$100	$15–$50
Inexpensive	under $50	under $15

*All prices are for a standard double room during peak season.

Prague

"We are living in the Left Bank of the '90s," wrote Alan Levy, the editor-in-chief of the *Prague Post*, for the newspaper's debut edition in 1991. With those simple words, Levy gave rise to one of the sweetest myths to grace the postrevolutionary period in Eastern Europe. Prague isn't really the modern equivalent of 1920s Paris, but the characterization isn't wholly inaccurate, either. Like all other good myths, whether grounded in fact or fantasy, the belief that something special is happening here has achieved some measure of truth through sheer repetition and force of will. By hook or by crook, Prague has become, well, quite Bohemian in its own way.

In the five years since Prague's students took to the streets to help bring down the 40-year-old communist regime, the city has enjoyed an unparalleled cultural renaissance. Much of the energy has come from planeloads of idealistic young Americans, but the enthusiasm has been shared in near-equal measure by their Czech counterparts and by the many newcomers who have arrived from all over the world. Amid Prague's cobblestone streets and gold-tipped spires, new galleries, cafés, and clubs teem with bright-eyed "expatriates" and perplexed locals who must wonder how their city came to be Eastern Europe's new Left Bank. New shops and, perhaps most noticeably, scads of new restaurants recently have opened up, expanding the city's culinary reach far beyond the traditional roast pork and dumplings. Many have something to learn yet in the way of presentation and service, but Praguers still marvel at a variety that was unthinkable only a few years ago.

The arts and theater also are thriving in the "new" Prague. Young playwrights, some writing in English, regularly stage their own works. Weekly poetry readings are standing-room-only. The city's dozen or so rock clubs are jammed nightly; bands play everything from metal and psychedelic to garage and grunge. Developments in jazz and classical have been just as daring.

All of this frenetic activity plays well against a stunning backdrop of towering churches and centuries-old bridges and alleyways. Prague achieved much of its present glory in the 14th century, during the long reign of Charles IV, king of Bohemia and Moravia, and Holy Roman Emperor. It was Charles who established a university in the city and laid out the New Town (Nové Město), charting Prague's growth.

In the 15th century, the city's development was hampered by the Hussite Wars, a series of crusades launched by the Holy Roman Empire to subdue the fiercely independent Czech noblemen. The Czechs were eventually defeated in 1620 at the Battle of White Mountain (Bílá Hora) near Prague and were ruled by the Habsburg family for the next 300 years. Under the Habsburgs, Prague became a German-speaking city and an important administrative center, but it was forced to play second fiddle to the monarchy's capital of Vienna. Much of the Lesser Town (Malá Strana), across the river, was built up at this time, becoming home to Austrian nobility and its Baroque tastes.

Prague regained its status as a national capital in 1918, with the creation of the modern Czechoslovak state, and quickly asserted itself in the interwar period as a vital cultural center. Although the city escaped World War II essentially intact, it and the rest of Czechoslovakia fell under the political and cultural domination of the Soviet Union until the 1989 popular uprisings that ended the 40-year reign of the country's pro-Soviet government. The election of dissident playwright Václav Havel to the post of national president in June 1990 set the stage for the city's renaissance, which has since proceeded at a dizzying, quite Bohemian rate.

Important Addresses and Numbers

Tourist Information

Čedok, the ubiquitous state-run travel agency, is the first stop for general tourist information and city maps. Čedok will also exchange money, arrange guided tours, and book passage on airlines, buses, and trains. You can pay for Čedok services, including booking rail tickets, with any major credit card. Note limited weekend hours. *Main office: Na příkopě 18, tel. 02/212-7111, fax 02/236-7475. Open weekdays 8:30–5, Sat. 8:30–12:30.*

The **Prague Information Service** (PIS, Staroměstské nám. 22, tel. 02/224311, fax 02/226067) is generally less helpful than Čedok but offers city maps and general tourist information. It can also exchange money and help in obtaining tickets for cultural events.

The friendly, English-speaking staff at **AVE,** located in the main train station (Hlavní nádraží, tel. 02/2362560, fax 02/ 2362956), will gladly sell you a map of Prague (cost: 10 Kč.) and answer basic questions. The organization also offers an excellent room-finding service and will change money. The office is open daily 6 AM–11 PM.

The **American Hospitality Center** (AHC, Na mustku 7, tel. 02/ 267770) is open to visitors of all nationalities and will provide maps and general tourist information from its convenient office near the bottom of Wenceslas Square. The organization also serves coffee, cold drinks, and pizza and will help secure concert and theater tickets. The office is open daily 10–6 (10–8 in summer). The affiliated **Prague Suites,** located down the street at Melantrichova 8 (tel. 02/269384, fax 02/266179), can assist in finding luxury accommodation in private apartments.

To find out what's on for the month and to get the latest tips for shopping, dining, and entertainment, consult one or both of Prague's two English-language newspapers, *The Prague Post* (weekly, 25 Kč.) and *Prognosis* (biweekly, 20 Kč.). Both have comprehensive entertainment listings and can be purchased at the AHC and most downtown newsstands. The monthly *Prague Guide*, available at newsstands and tourist offices for 25 Kč., provides a good overview of major cultural events and has comprehensive listings of restaurants, hotels, and organizations offering traveler assistance.

Embassies
U.S. Embassy. Tržiště 15, Malá Strana, tel. 02/536641.
British Embassy. Thunovská ul. 14, Malá Strana, tel. 02/ 533347.
Canadian Embassy. Mickiewiczova ul. 6, Hradčany, tel. 02/ 312–0251.

Emergencies
Police (tel. 2121). **Ambulance** (tel. 155). **Medical emergencies** tel. (02/299381; English or German). **Dentists** (tel. 02/261374 for 24-hour emergency service).

English-Language Bookstores
Part bookstore and part café, **The Globe** (Janovského 14, Prague 7, close to Vltava metro station) carries a diverse and reasonably priced selection of used and new paperbacks. **Bohemian Ventures** (Nám. Jana Palacha, open weekdays 9–6, Sat. 9–12) at the Charles University Philosophical Faculty near Staroměstská metro station stocks mostly Penguin-published titles. Street vendors on Wenceslas Square and Na příkopě carry leading foreign newspapers and periodicals. For hiking maps and auto atlases, try **Melantrich** (Na příkopě 3, Nové Město, tel. 02/26716).

Late-Night Pharmacy
The pharmacy at Na příkopě 7 (tel. 02/220081), just a few steps down from Wenceslas Square, is open 24 hours.

Travel Agencies
Thomas Cook (Václavské nám. 47, tel. 02/263106, fax 02/ 265695) and **American Express** (Václavské nám. 56, tel. 02/ 229487, fax 02/261504) can make travel arrangements, exchange money, and issue and redeem traveler's checks. American Express maintains an automatic-teller machine for use by card members. Both agencies are open weekdays 9–6; American Express is also open Saturday 9–12.

Čedok (*see* Tourist Information, *above*) is a good source for international train and bus tickets and one of the few places in town where it is possible to use a credit card for purchasing train tickets.

Two foreign agencies, **Austropa** (Revoluční 13, tel. 02/231–3661, fax 02/231–1525) and **Wolff** (Na příkopě 22, tel. 02/263568, fax 02/264820), are good sources for discounted international air tickets. Both are open weekdays 9–6 and Saturday 9–noon.

Arriving and Departing by Plane

Airports and Airlines **Ruzyně Airport** is situated 20 kilometers (12 miles) northwest of the downtown area. The airport is small but uncongested and easily negotiated.

ČSA (the Czech national carrier) offers direct flights all over the world from Ruzyně. Major airlines with offices in Prague include **Air France** (tel. 02/260155), **Alitalia** (tel. 02/231–0535), **Austrian Airlines** (tel. 02/232–2795), **British Airways** (tel. 02/232–9020), ČSA (tel. 02/2146; flight information, tel. 02/231–7395), **Delta** (tel. 02/232472), **KLM** (tel. 02/264362), **Lufthansa** (tel. 02/231–7551), **SAS** (tel. 02/228141), and **Swissair** (tel. 02/232–4707).

Between the Airport and Downtown A special ČSA shuttle bus stops at all major hotels. The bus departs two to three times an hour between 7:40 AM and 9:30 PM from the bus stop directly outside the main entrance. You can buy your ticket (cost: 60 Kč.) on the bus. Regular municipal bus service (No. 119) connects the airport and the **Dejvická** metro stop; the fare is 4 Kč. From Dejvická you can take a subway to the city center, but you must buy an additional ticket (4 Kč.). To reach Wenceslas Square, get off at the Můstek station.

Taxis offer the easiest and most convenient way of getting downtown. The trip is a straight shot down the Evropská Boulevard and takes approximately 20 minutes. The road is not usually busy, but you can reckon with an additional 10 minutes during rush hour (7–9 AM and 4–7 PM). The ride costs about 300 Kč.

Arriving and Departing By Car, Train, and Bus

By Car Prague is well served by major roads and highways from anywhere in the country. On arriving in the city, simply follow the signs to *centrum* (city center). During the day, traffic can be heavy, especially on the approach to Wenceslas Square. Pay particular attention to the trams, which enjoy the right of way in every situation. Note that the immediate center of Prague, including Wenceslas Square itself, is closed to private vehicles.

By Train International trains arrive at and depart from either the main station, **Hlavní nádraží**, about 500 yards east of Wencelas Square; or the suburban **Nádraží Holešovice,** situated about 2 kilometers (1½ miles) north of the city center. This is an unending source of confusion—always make certain you know which station your train is using. For train times, consult timetables in stations or get in line at the information office upstairs at the main station (tel. 02/235–3836; open weekdays 6 AM–7 PM). The Čedok office at Na příkopě 18 (tel. 02/2127111) also provides train information and issues tickets.

Wenceslas Square is a convenient 15-minute walk from the main station, or you can take the subway (line C) one stop to Muzeum. A taxi ride from the main station to the center will cost about 50 Kč. To reach the city center from Nádraží Holešovice, take the subway (line C) four stops to Muzeum.

By Bus The Czech national bus line, **ČSAD**, operates its dense network from the sprawling main bus station on Na Florenci (metro stop: Florenc, lines B or C). For information about routes and schedules call 02/221445, or consult timetables posted at the station. If the ticket windows are closed, you can usually buy a ticket from the driver.

Getting Around

To see Prague properly, there is no alternative to walking, especially since much of the city center is off-limits to automobiles. And the walking couldn't be more pleasant—most of it along the beautiful bridges and cobblestone streets of the city's historic core. Before venturing out, however, be sure you have a good map.

By Subway Prague's subway system, the metro, is clean and reliable. Trains run every day from 5 AM to midnight. *Jizdenky* (tickets) cost 4 Kč. apiece and can be bought at hotels, tobacconists, or at vending machines at station entrances. Have some 1- or 2-Kč. coins handy for the machines (5-Kč. coins don't work). Validate the tickets yourself at machines before descending the escalators; each ticket is good for 60 minutes of uninterrupted travel. Special daily and extended passes, valid for all buses, trams, and subways, can be purchased at newsstands, train stations, and Čedok offices. A one-day pass costs 30 Kč., a two-day pass 50 Kč., a three-day pass 65 Kč., and a five-day pass 100 Kč. Trains are patrolled frequently; the fine for riding without a valid ticket is 200 Kč.

By Bus and Tram Prague's extensive bus and streetcar network allows for fast, efficient travel throughout the city. Tickets are the same as those used for the metro (cost: 4 Kč.), although you validate them at machines inside the bus or streetcar. Bus and tram tickets are valid only for a particular ride; if you change to a different tram or bus, or get on the metro, you must validate a new ticket. Signal to stop the bus by pushing the button by the doors. Tram doors open automatically at all scheduled stops. Special "night trams" run every night from around midnight to 5 AM and connect the city center with outlying areas.

By Taxi Dishonest taxi drivers are the shame of the nation. Luckily, visitors do not need to rely on taxis for trips within the city center (it's usually easier to walk or take the subway). Typical scams include drivers doctoring the meter or simply failing to turn the meter on and then demanding an exorbitant sum at the end of the ride. In an honest cab, the meter will start at 6 Kč. and increase by 10 Kč. per kilometer (half-mile) or 1 Kč. per minute at rest. Most rides within town should cost no more than 80 Kč.–100 Kč. To minimize the chances of getting ripped off, avoid taxi stands in Wenceslas Square and other heavily touristed areas. The best alternative is to phone in advance for a taxi. Some reputable firms are **AAA Taxi** (tel. 02/342410), **BM Taxi** (tel. 02/256144), **Reax** (tel. 02/472–1453), and **Sedop** (tel. 02/752110). Many firms have English-speaking operators.

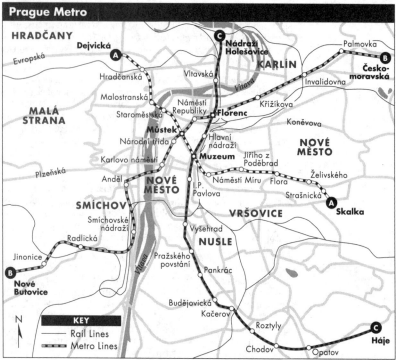

Prague Metro

Guided Tours

Čedok's (tel. 02/231–8255) three-hour Historical Prague tour (450 Kč.), offered year-round, is a combination bus-walking venture that covers all of the major sights. It departs daily at 10 AM from the Čedok office at Bilkova ulice 21 (near the InterContinental Hotel). Between May and September, Panoramic Prague (290 Kč.), an abbreviated version of the above tour, departs daily except Sunday at 11 AM and 4 PM from the Čedok office at Na příkopé 18. On Monday and Thursday Čedok also offers Old Prague on Foot, a slower-paced, four-hour walking tour that departs at 9 AM from Na příkopě 18. The price is 290 Kč.

Many private firms now offer combination bus–walking tours of the city that typically last two or three hours and cost 300 Kč.–400 Kč. For more information, inquire directly with any of the dozen operators with booths on Staroměstské nám (near the Jan Hus monument) or Náměstí Republiky (near the Obecní Dům).

Personal Guides You can contact the Čedok office at Bilkova 6 (tel. 02/231–8255) to arrange a personalized walking tour. Times and itineraries are negotiable; prices start at around 350 Kč. per hour.

Highlights for First-Time Visitors

Charles Bridge (*see* Tour 2)
Old Town Square (*see* Tour 1)
Prague Castle (*see* Tour 3)
St. Nicholas Church in Malá Strana (*see* Tour 2)
Týn Church (*see* Tour 1)

Exploring Prague

The spine of the city is the river Vltava (also known as the Moldau), which runs through the city from south to north with a single sharp curve to the east. Prague originally comprised five independent towns, represented today by its main historical districts: **Hradčany** (Castle Area), **Malá Strana** (Lesser Town), **Staré Město** (Old Town), **Nové Město** (New Town), and **Josefov** (the Jewish Quarter).

Hradčany, the seat of Czech royalty for hundreds of years, has as its center the **Pražský Hrad** (Prague Castle), which overlooks the city from its hilltop west of the Vltava. Steps lead down from Hradčany to Malá Strana, an area dense with ornate mansions built by 17th- and 18th-century nobility.

Karlův Most (Charles Bridge) connects Malá Strana with Staré Město. Just a few blocks east of the bridge is the focal point of the Old Town, **Staroměstské náměstí** (Old Town Square). Staré Město is bounded by the curving Vltava and three large commercial avenues: **Revoluční ulice** to the east, **Na příkopě** to the southeast, and **Národní třída** to the south.

Beyond lies the Nové Město; several blocks south is **Karlovo náměstí**, the city's largest square. Roughly one kilometer (half a mile) farther south is **Vyšehrad**, an ancient castle site high above the river.

On a promontory to the east of Wenceslas Square stretches **Vinohrady**, once the favored neighborhood of Czech nobility; below Vinohrady lie the crumbling neighborhoods of **Žižkov** to the north and **Nusle** to the south. On the west banks of the Vltava south and east of Hradčany lie many older residential neighborhoods and enormous parks. About 3 kilometers (2 miles) from the center in every direction, communist-era housing projects begin their unappealing sprawl.

Tour 1: The Old Town

Numbers in the margin correspond to points of interest on the Prague (Tours 1–4) map.

❶ **Václavské náměstí** (Wenceslas Square), convenient to hotels and transportation, is an appropriate place to begin a tour of the Old Town (Staré Město). A long, gently sloping boulevard rather than a square in the usual sense, Václavské náměstí is bordered at the top (the southern end) by the Czech National Museum and at the bottom by the pedestrian shopping areas of **Národní třída** and **Na příkopě**. Visitors may recognize this spot from their television sets, for it was here that some 500,000 students and citizens gathered in the heady days of November 1989 to protest the policies of the former communist regime. The government capitulated after a week of demonstrations, without a shot fired or the loss of a single life, bringing to power the first democratic government in 40 years (under playwright-president Václav Havel). Today, this peaceful transfer of power is proudly referred to as the "Velvet" or "Gentle" Revolution (*něžná revolucia*).

It was only fitting that the 1989 revolution should take place on Wenceslas Square. Throughout much of Czech history, the square has served as the focal point for popular discontent. In **❷** 1848 citizens protested Habsburg rule at the **Statue of St.**

Prague: Tours 1–4

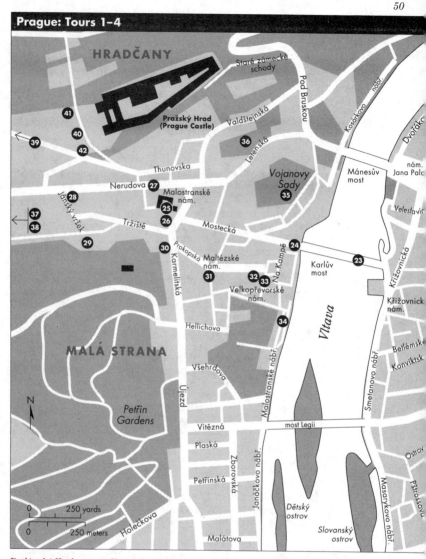

HRADČANY

Staré zámecké schody

Pod Bruskou

Kosárkovo nábř.

Dvořáko

Pražský Hrad (Prague Castle)

Valdštejnská

Thunovska

Nerudova 27

Malostranské nám.

25

26

Letenská

36

Vojanovy Sady

35

Mánesův most

nám. Jana Pala

28

37

38

Jánský vršek

Tržiště

29

30

Prokopská

Mostecká

Maltézské nám.

31

32 33

Velkopřevorské nám.

Na Kampě

24

23

Karlův most

Veleslavi

Křižovnická

Křižovnick nám.

34

Vltava

Karmelitská

Hellichova

MALÁ STRANA

Všehrdova

Újezd

Bellemsk

Konviktsk

Smetanovo nábř.

N

Petřín Gardens

Vítězná

most Legii

Ostrov

Plaská

Zborovská

Janáčkovo nábř.

Dětský ostrov

Petřínská

Slovanský ostrov

Masarykovo nábř.

Pstrossov

0   250 yards

0   250 meters

Haleckova

Malátova

Betlémská Kaple, **17**
Bretfeld Palác, **28**
Chrám Sv. Mikuláše, **26**
Clam-Gallas Palota, **15**
Hotel Europa, **4**
Hradčanské Náměstí, **40**
Jan Hus Monument, **11**
Kampa Island, **34**
Karlův Most (Charles Bridge), **23**
Kostel Sv. Jiljí, **16**

Kostel Sv. Martina ve Zdi, **18**
Kostel Sv. Mikuláše, **13**
Lennon Peace Wall, **33**
Loreto Church, **39**
Maislova Synagóga, **22**
Malá Strana Bridge Towers, **24**
Malé Náměstí, **14**
Malostranské Náměstí, **25**
Maltézské Náměstí, **31**
Náměstí Republiky, **7**

Národní Galérie, **41**
Národní Muzeum, **3**
Nerudova Ulice, **27**
Pohořelec, **37**
Schönbornský Palác, **29**
Schwarzenberg Palota, **42**
Sixt House, **8**
Staroměstská Radnice, **12**
Staroměstské Náměstí (Old Town Square), **9**

Staronová Synagóga, **20**
Starý Židovský Hřbitov, **21**
Statue of St. Wenceslas, **2**
Stavovské Divadlo, **5**
Strahovský Klášter, **38**
Týn Church, **10**
Václavské Náměstí (Wenceslas Square), **1**
Velkopřevorské Náměstí, **32**

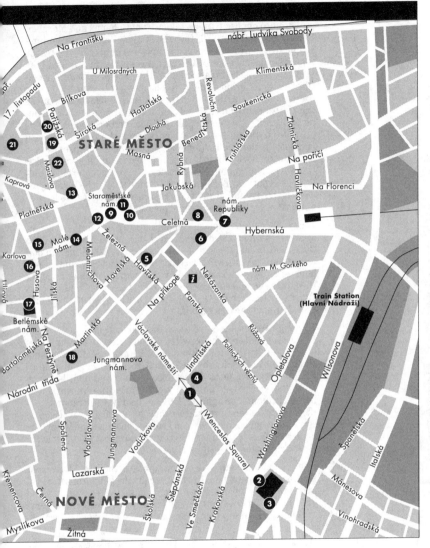

Vojanovy Sady, **35**
Vrtbovský Palác, **30**
Vysoká Synagóga, **19**
Zahrada
Valdštejnského
Paláca, **36**
Živnostenská Banka, **6**

Wenceslas in front of the National Museum. In 1939 residents gathered to oppose Hitler's takeover of Bohemia and Moravia. It was here also, in 1969, that the student Jan Palach set himself on fire to protest the bloody invasion of his country by the Soviet Union and other Warsaw Pact countries in August of the previous year. The invasion ended the "Prague Spring," a cultural and political movement emphasizing free expression that was supported by Alexander Dubček, the popular leader at the time. Although Dubček never intended to dismantle communist authority completely, his political and economic reforms proved too daring for fellow comrades in the rest of Eastern Europe. In the months following the invasion, conservatives loyal to the Soviet Union were installed in all influential positions. The subsequent two decades ushered in a period of cultural stagnation. Thousands of residents left the country or went underground; many more resigned themselves to lives of minimal expectations and small pleasures.

Today, Wenceslas Square comprises Prague's liveliest street scene. Don't miss the dense maze of arcades tucked away from the street in buildings that line both sides. You'll find an odd assortment of cafés, discos, ice cream parlors, and movie houses, all seemingly unfazed by the passage of time. At night the square changes character somewhat as dance music pours out from the crowded discos and leather-jacketed cronies crowd around the taxi stands.

Although Wenceslas Square was first laid out by Charles IV in 1348 as the center of the New Town (Nové Město), few buildings of architectural merit line the square today. Even the imposing ❸ structure of the **Národní Muzeum** (Czech National Museum), designed by Prague architect Josef Schulz and built between 1885 and 1890, does not really come into its own until it is bathed in nighttime lighting. During the day, the grandiose edifice seems an inappropriate venue for a musty collection of stones and bones, minerals, and coins. This museum is only for dedicated fans of the genre! *Václavské nám. 68, tel. 02/269451. Admission: 20 Kč. Open Wed.–Mon. 9–5.*

❹ One eye-catching building on the square is the **Hotel Europa** at No. 25, a riot of art nouveau that recalls the glamorous world of turn-of-the-century Prague. Don't miss the elegant stained glass and mosaics of the café and restaurant. The terrace, serving drinks in the summer, is an excellent spot for people-watching.

To begin the approach to the Old Town proper, walk past the tall, art-deco, Koruna complex (once an enormous fast-food joint, now an office complex) and turn onto the handsome pedestrian zone called **Na příkopě**. The name means "at the moat," harking back to the time when the street was indeed a moat separating the Old Town on the left from the New Town on the right. Today Na příkopě is prime shopping territory, its smaller boutiques considered far more elegant than the motley collection of stores on Wenceslas Square. But don't expect much real elegance here: After 40 years of communist orthodoxy in the fashion world, it will be many years before the boutiques really can match Western European standards.

Turn left onto Havířská ulice and follow this small alley to the glittering green-and-cream splendor of the newly renovated ❺ **Stavovské Divadlo** (Estates Theater). Built in the 1780s in the classical style and reopened in 1991 after years of renovation, the handsome theater was for many years a beacon of Czech-language culture in a city long dominated by German. It is probably best known as the site of the world premiere of Mozart's opera *Don Giovanni* in October 1787, with the composer himself in the conducting role. Prague audiences were quick to acknowledge Mozart's genius. The opera was an instant hit here, though it flopped nearly everywhere else in Europe. Mozart wrote most of the opera's second act in Prague at the Villa Bertramka, where he was a frequent guest (*see* Off the Beaten Track, *below*).

Return to Na příkopě, turn left, and continue to the end of the street. On weekdays between 8 AM and 5 PM, it's well worth taking a peek at the stunning interior of the **Živnostenská banka** (Merchants' Bank) at No. 20. The style, a tasteful example of 19th-century exuberance, reflected the city's growing prosperity at the time. Ignore the guards and walk up the decorated stairs to the beautiful main banking room (note, however, that taking photos is forbidden).

Na příkopě ends abruptly at the **Náměstí Republiky** (Republic Square), an important New Town transportation hub (with a metro stop) but a square that has never really come together as a vital public space, perhaps because of its jarring architectural eclecticism. Taken one by one, each building is interesting in its own right, but the ensemble is less than the sum of the parts. The severe Depression-era facade of the **Česka Národní banka** (Czech National Bank, Na příkopě 30) makes the building look more like a fortress than the nation's central bank.

Close by stands the stately **Prašná brána** (Powder Tower), its festive Gothic spires looming above the square. Construction of the tower, one of the city's 13 original gates, was begun by King Vladislav II of Jagiello in 1475. At the time, the kings of Bohemia maintained their royal residence next door (on the site of the current Obecní dům, the Municipal House), and the tower was intended to be the grandest gate of all. But Vladislav was Polish and thus heartily disliked by the rebellious Czech citizens of Prague. Nine years after he assumed power, fearing for his life, he moved the royal court across the river to Prague Castle. Work on the tower was abandoned and the half-finished structure was used to store gunpowder—hence its odd name—until the end of the 17th century. The oldest part of the tower is the base; the golden spires were not added until the end of the last century. The climb to the top affords a striking view of the Old Town and Prague Castle in the distance. *Nám. Republiky. Admission: 20 Kč. adults, 10 Kč. students. Open Apr.–Oct., daily 9–6.*

Adjacent to the dignified Powder Tower, the **Obecní dům** (Municipal House) looks decidedly decadent. The style, mature art nouveau, recalls the lengths the Czech middle classes went to at the turn of the century to imitate Paris, then the epitome of style and glamour. Much of the interior bears the work of the art nouveau master Alfons Mucha and other leading Czech artists. Mucha decorated the main Hall of the Lord Mayor upstairs. His magical frescoes depicting Czech history are considered a masterpiece of the genre. Throughout the year some of the city's best concerts are held in its beautiful Smetana Hall, on the second floor.

Time Out The **Obecni Dům café,** usually packed with tourists, serves reasonably good coffee and cake in a resplendent setting. Ignore the slow service and enjoy the view. If you prefer a subtler elegance, head around the corner to the café at **Hotel Paříž** (U Obecního domu 1), a Jugendstil jewel tucked away on a quiet street.

Walk through the arch at the base of the Powder Tower and down the formal **Celetná ulice,** the first leg of the so-called Royal Way, in years past the traditional coronation route of the Czech kings. Monarchs favored this route primarily for its stunning entry into **Staroměstské náměstí** (Old Town Square) and because the houses along Celetná were among the city's finest, providing a suitable backdrop to the coronation procession. (Most of the facades indicate that the buildings are from the 17th or 18th century, but appearances are deceiving: Many of the houses in fact have foundations dating from the 12th century or earlier.) The pink **Sixt House** at Celetná 2 sports one of the street's most handsome, if restrained, Baroque facades. The house itself dates from the 12th century—its Romanesque vaults are still visible in the wine restaurant in the basement.

❽

❾ **Staroměstské náměstí** (Old Town Square), at the end of Celetná, is dazzling (the scaffolding that obscured many of its finest buildings during recent renovations is finally down). Long the heart of the Old Town, the square grew to its present proportions when the city's original marketplace was moved away from the river in the 12th century. Its shape and appearance have changed little over the years. During the day the square takes on a festive atmosphere as musicians vie for the favor of onlookers, hefty young men in medieval outfits mint coins, and artists display their renditions of Prague street scenes. It's worth coming back to the square at night, as well, when the unlit shadowy towers of the Týn Church (to your right as you enter the square) rise forebodingly over the glowing Baroque facades. The crowds thin out, and the ghosts of the square's stormy past return.

During the 15th century, the square was the focal point of conflict between Czech Hussites and German Catholics. In 1422 the radical Hussite preacher Jan Želivský was executed here for his part in storming the New Town's town hall. Three Catholic consuls and seven German citizens were thrown out of the window in the ensuing fray—the first of Prague's many famous "defenestrations." Within a few years, the Hussites had taken over the town, expelled the Germans, and set up their own administration.

❿ The center of their activity was the double-spired **Týn Church** (Kostel Panny Marie před Týnem), which rises over the square from behind a row of patrician houses. Construction of its twin jet-black spires, which still jar the eye, was begun by King Jiří of Poděbrad in 1461 during the heyday of the Hussites. Jiří had a gilded chalice, the symbol of the Hussites, proudly displayed on the front gable between the two towers. Following the defeat of the Hussites by the Catholic Habsburgs, the chalice was removed and eventually replaced by a Madonna. As a final blow, the chalice was melted down and made into the Madonna's glimmering halo (you still can see it by walking into the center of the square and looking up between the spires). The entrance to Týn Church is through the arcades, under the red house at No. 604. *Celetná 5. Admission: 20 Kč. Open weekdays 9–6, Sat. 9–noon, Sun. 1–6.*

Although the exterior of Týn Church is one of the best examples of Prague Gothic (in part the work of Peter Parler, architect of the Charles Bridge and St. Vitus Cathedral), much of the interior, including the tall nave, was rebuilt in the Baroque style in the 17th century. Some Gothic pieces remain, however: Look to the left of the main altar for a beautifully preserved set of early Gothic carvings. The main altar itself was painted by Karel Škréta, a luminary of the Czech Baroque. Before leaving the church, look for the grave marker (tucked away to the right of the main altar) of the great Danish astronomer Tycho de Brahe, who came to Prague as "Imperial Mathematicus" in 1599 under Rudolf II. As a scientist, Tycho had a place in history that is assured: Johannes Kepler (another resident of the Prague court) used Tycho's observations to formulate his laws of planetary motion. But it is myth that has endeared Tycho to the hearts of Prague residents: The robust Dane, who was apparently fond of duels, lost part of his nose in one (take a closer look at the marker). He quickly had a wax nose fashioned for everyday use but preferred to parade around on holidays and festive occasions sporting a bright silver one instead.

To the immediate left of Týn Church is **U Zvonů** (No. 13), a Baroque structure that has been stripped down to its original Gothic elements. It occasionally hosts concerts and art exhibitions. The exhibitions change frequently, and it's worth stopping by to see what's on.

A short walk away stands the dazzling pink-and-ocher **Palác Kinských** (Kinský Palace), built in 1765 and considered one of Prague's finest late-Baroque structures. With its exaggerated pink overlay and numerous statues, the facade looks extreme when contrasted with the more staid Baroque elements of other nearby buildings. The palace once housed a German school (where Franz Kafka was a student for nine misery-laden years) and presently contains the National Gallery's graphics collection. The main exhibition room is on the second floor; exhibits change every few months and are usually worth seeing. It was from this building that communist leader Klement Gottwald, flanked by his comrade Clementis, first addressed the crowds after seizing power in February 1948—an event recounted in the first chapter of Milan Kundera's novel *The Book of Laughter and Forgetting. Staroměstské nám. 12. Admission: 10 Kč. adults, 5 Kč. children and students. Open Tues.–Sun. 10–6.*

At this end of the square, you can't help but notice the expressive **Jan Hus monument.** Few memorials have elicited as much controversy as this one, which was dedicated in July 1915, exactly 500 years after Hus was burned at the stake in Constance, Germany. Some maintain that the monument's Secessionist style (the inscription seems to come right from turn-of-the-century Vienna) clashes with the Gothic and Baroque of the square. Others dispute the romantic depiction of Hus, who appears here in flowing garb as tall and bearded. The real Hus, historians maintain, was short and had a baby face. Still, no one can take issue with the influence of this fiery preacher, whose ability to transform doctrinal disputes, both literally and metaphorically, into the language of the common man made him into a religious and national symbol for the Czechs.

12 Opposite the Týn Church is the Gothic **Staroměstská radnice** (Old Town Hall), which gives the square its sense of importance. As you walk toward the building from the Hus monument, look for the 27 white crosses on the ground just in front of the Town Hall. These mark the spot where 27 Bohemian noblemen were killed by the Habsburgs in 1621 during the dark days following the defeat of the Czechs at the Battle of White Mountain. The grotesque spectacle, designed to quash any further national or religious opposition, took some five hours to complete, as the men were put to the sword or hanged, one by one.

The Town Hall has served as the center of administration for the Old Town since 1338, when King Johann of Luxembourg first granted the city council the right to a permanent location. Walk around the structure to the left and you'll see that it's actually a series of houses jutting into the square; they were purchased over the years and successively added to the complex. The most interesting is the **U Minuty,** the corner building to the left of the clock tower, with its 16th-century Renaissance sgraffito of Biblical and classical motifs.

The impressive 200-foot **Town Hall tower** was first built in the 14th century and given its current late-Gothic appearance around 1500 by the master Matyáš Rejsek. For a rare view of the Old Town and its maze of crooked streets and alleyways, climb to the top of the tower. The climb is not strenuous, but steep stairs at the top unfortunately prevent the disabled from enjoying the view. Enter through the door to the left of the tower.

As the hour approaches, join the crowds milling below the tower's 15th-century **Astronomical Clock** for a brief but spooky spectacle taken straight from the Middle Ages. Just before the hour, look to the upper part of the clock, where a skeleton begins by tolling a death knell and turning an hour-glass upside down. The 12 apostles parade momentarily, and then a cockerel flaps its wings and crows, piercing the air as the hour finally strikes, solemnly. To the right of the skeleton, the dreaded Turk nods his head, seemingly hinting at another invasion like those of the 16th and 17th centuries. Immediately after the hour, guided tours in English and German (German only during winter) of the Town Hall depart inside from the main desk. However, the only notables inside are the fine Renaissance ceilings and Gothic Council Room. *Staroměstské nám. Admission to hall: 20 Kč. adults, 10 Kč. children and students; admission to tower: 10 Kč. adults, 5 Kč. children and students. Hall open daily 9–6; tower open daily 10–6.*

Time Out   Staroměstské náměstí is a convenient spot for refreshments. **Tchibo,** at No. 6, has tasty sandwiches and excellent coffee, and an outdoor terrace in season.

Walk north along the edge of the small park beside the Town **13** Hall to reach the Baroque **Kostel svatého Mikuláše** (Church of St. Nicholas), not to be confused with the Lesser Town's St. Nicholas Church, on the other side of the river (*see* Tour 2, *below*). Though both churches were designed in the 18th century by Prague's own master of the late Baroque, Kilian Ignaz Dientzenhofer, this St. Nicholas is probably less successful than its namesake across town in capturing the style's lyric exuberance. Still, Dientzenhofer utilized the limited space to create a structure that neither dominates nor retreats from the imposing square. The interior is compact, with a beautiful but small chandelier and an enormous black organ that seems to overwhelm the rear of the church. The church often hosts afternoon concerts.

Franz Kafka's birthplace is just to the left of St. Nicholas on U radnice. A small plaque can be found on the side of the house. For years, this memorial to Kafka's birth (July 3, 1883) was the only public acknowledgement of the writer's stature in world literature, reflecting the traditionally ambiguous attitude of the Czechoslovak government to his work. The Communists were always too uncomfortable with Kafka's themes of bureaucracy and alienation to sing his praises too loudly, if at all. As a German and a Jew, moreover, Kafka could easily be dismissed as standing outside of the mainstream of Czech literature. Following the 1989 revolution, however, Kafka's popularity has soared, and his works are now widely available in Czech. A fascinating little museum has been set up in the house of his birth. *U radnice 5. Admission: 20 Kč. Open daily 10–7.*

Continue southwest from Old Town Square until you come to
⑭ **Malé náměstí** (Small Square), a nearly perfect ensemble of facades dating from the Middle Ages. Note the Renaissance iron fountain dating from 1560, in the center of the square. The sgraffito on the house at No. 3 is not as old as it looks (1890), but here and there you can find authentic Gothic portals and Renaissance sgraffito that betray the square's true age.

Look for tiny **Karlova ulice,** which begins in the southwest corner of Malé náměstí, and take another quick right to stay on it (watch the signs—this medieval street seems designed to confound the visitor). The character of Karlova ulice has changed in recent years to meet the growing number of tourists. Galleries and gift shops now occupy almost every storefront. But the cobblestones, narrow alleys, and crumbling gables still make it easy to imagine what life was like 400 years ago.

Turn left at the T-intersection where Karlova seems to end in front of the Středočeská Galérie, and continue left down the quieter Husova třída (if you want to go on directly to Tour 3, veer to the right for the Charles Bridge and the other side of the river). Fans of unbridled Baroque—the kind more common to Vienna than to Prague—may want to pause first and inspect
⑮ the exotic **Clam–Gallas palota** (Clam-Gallas Palace) at Husova 20. You'll recognize it easily: Look for the Titans in the doorway holding up what must be a very heavy Baroque facade. The palace dates from 1713 and is the work of Johann Bernhard Fischer von Erlach, the famed Viennese virtuoso of the day. Enter the building (push past the guard as if you know what you're doing) for a glimpse of the finely carved staircase, the work of the master himself, and of the Italian frescoes featuring Apollo that surround it. The Gallas family was prominent in the 18th century but has long since died out. The building now houses the municipal archives and is rarely open for visitors.

Return to the T-intersection and continue down Husova. For a glimpse of a less successful Baroque reconstruction, take a
⑯ close look at the **Kostel svatého Jiljí** (Church of St. Giles), across from No. 7, another important outpost of Czech Protestantism

in the 16th century. The exterior is powerful Gothic, including the buttresses and a characteristic portal; the interior, surprisingly, is Baroque, dating from the 17th century.

Continue walking along Husova třída to Na Perštýně, and turn right at tiny Betlémská ulice. The alley opens up onto a quiet square of the same name (Betlémské náměstí) and upon the **⑰** most revered of all Hussite churches in Prague, the **Betlémská kaple** (Bethlehem Chapel). The church's elegant simplicity is in stark contrast to the diverting Gothic and Baroque of the rest of the city. The original structure dates from the end of the 14th century, and Hus himself was a regular preacher here from 1402 until his death, in 1415. After the Thirty Years' War the church fell into the hands of the Jesuits and was finally demolished in 1786. Excavations carried out after World War I uncovered the original portal and three windows, and the entire church was reconstructed in the 1950s. Although little remains of the first church, some remnants of Hus's teachings can still be read on the inside walls. *Betlémské nám. 5. Admission free. Open Apr.–Sept., daily 9–6; Oct.–Mar., daily 9–5.*

Return to Na Perštýně, and continue walking to the right. As you near the backs of the buildings of the busy **Národní třída** (National Boulevard), turn left at Martinská ulice. At the end **⑱** of the street, the forlorn but majestic church **Kostel svatého Martina ve zdi** (St. Martin-in-the-Wall) stands like a postwar ruin. It's difficult to believe that this forgotten church, with a NO PARKING sign blocking its main portal, once played a major role in the development of Protestant practices. Still, it was here in 1414 that Holy Communion was first given to the Bohemian laity with both bread and the wine, in offence to the Catholic custom of the time, which dictated that only bread was to be offered to the masses, with wine reserved for the priests and clergy. From then on, the chalice came to symbolize the Hussite movement.

Walk around the church to the left and through a little archway of apartments onto the bustling Národní třída. To the left, a five-minute walk away, lies Wenceslas Square and the starting point of the tour.

Time Out Turn right instead of left onto Národní třída and head to the newly renovated **Café Slavia** (Národní třída 1, open daily 9–11), long considered one of Prague's most "literary" cafés. Enjoy the fine view of Prague Castle while sipping a coffee.

Tour 2: The Jewish Ghetto

Leave Staroměstské Náměsti (Old Town Square) via the handsome Pařížská, and head north in the direction of the river and the Hotel Inter-Continental to reach **Josefov,** the Jewish ghetto. The buildings and houses along the Pařížská date from the end of the 19th century, and their elegant facades reflect the prosperity of the Czech middle classes at the time. Here and there you can spot the influence of the Viennese Jugendstil, with its emphasis on mosaics, geometric forms, and gold inlay. The look is fresh against the busier 19th-century revival facades of most of the other structures.

The festive atmosphere, however, changes suddenly as you enter the area of the ghetto. The buildings are lower here, and older; the mood is hushed. Sadly, little of the old ghetto remains. The Jews had survived centuries of discrimination, but two unrelated events of modern times have left the ghetto little more than a collection of museums. Around 1900, city officials decided for hygienic purposes to raze the ghetto and pave over its crooked streets. Only the synagogues, the town hall, and a few other buildings survived this early attempt at urban renewal. The second event was the Holocaust. Under Nazi occupation, a staggering percentage of Prague's Jews were deported or murdered in concentration camps. And of the 35,000 Jews living in the ghetto before World War II, only about 1,200 returned to resettle the neighborhood after the war.

The treasures and artifacts of the ghetto are now the property of the **Státní Židovské muzeum** (State Jewish Museum), a complex comprising the Old Jewish Cemetery and the collections of the remaining individual synagogues. The holdings are vast, thanks, ironically, to Adolf Hitler, who had planned to open a museum here documenting the life and practices of what he had hoped would be an "extinct" people. The cemetery and most of the synagogues are open to the public. Each synagogue specializes in certain artifacts, and you can buy tickets for all the **⑲** buildings at the **Vysoká synagóga** (High Synagogue), which features rich Torah mantles and silver. *Červená ulice (enter at No. 101). Tel. 02/231–0681. Admission: 20 Kč. adults, 10 Kč. students. Open Sun.–Fri. 10–12:30 and 1–6 (until 5 in winter).*

Adjacent to the High Synagogue, at Maislova 18, is the **Židovská radnice** (Jewish Town Hall), now home to the Jewish Community Center. The hall was the creation of Mordecai Maisel, an influential Jewish leader at the end of the 16th century. It was restored in the 18th century and given its clock and bell tower at that time. A second clock, with Hebrew numbers, turns to the left. The building also houses Prague's only kosher restaurant, Shalom.

⑳ The **Staronová synagóga** (Old-New Synagogue) across the street at Červená 2 is the oldest standing synagogue in Europe. Dating from the middle of the 13th century, it is also one of the most important works of early Gothic in Prague. The odd name recalls the legend that the synagogue was built on the site of an ancient Jewish temple and that stones from the temple were used to build the present structure. The synagogue has not only survived fires and the razing of the ghetto at the end of the last century but also emerged from the Nazi occupation intact and is still in active use. The oldest part of the synagogue is the entrance, with its vault supported by two pillars. The grille at the center of the hall dates from the 15th century. Note that men are required to cover their heads inside, and that during services men and women sit apart.

Continue along Červená ulice, which becomes the little street U **starého hřbitova** (At the Old Cemetery) beyond Maislova ulice. At the bend in the road lies the Jewish ghetto's most astonish-**㉑** ing sight, the **Starý židovský Hřbitov** (Old Jewish Cemetery). From the 14th century to 1787, all Jews living in Prague found their final resting place in this tiny, melancholy space, not far from the busy city. Some 12,000 graves in all are piled atop one another in 12 layers. Walk the paths amid the gravestones. The relief symbols represent the name or profession of the deceased. The oldest marked grave belongs to the poet Avigdor Kara, who died in 1439. The best-known marker is probably that of Jehuda ben Bezalel, the famed Rabbi Loew, who is credited with having created the mythical Golem in 1573. Even today, small scraps of paper bearing wishes are stuffed into the cracks of the rabbi's tomb in the hope that he will grant them. Loew's grave lies just a few steps from the entrance, near the western wall of the cemetery.

Just to the right of the cemetery entrance is the **Obřadní síň** (Ceremony Hall), which houses a moving exhibition of drawings made by children held at the Nazi concentration camp at Terezín (Theresienstadt), in northern Bohemia. In the early years of the war, the Nazis used the camp for propaganda purposes to demonstrate their "humanity" toward the Jews, and prisoners were given relative freedom to lead "normal" lives. Transports to death camps in Poland began in earnest in the final months of the war, however, and many thousands of Terezín prisoners, including many of these children, eventually perished . *U starého hřbitov. Admission to cemetery and Ceremony Hall: 20 Kč. adults, 10 Kč. children and students. Cemetery and hall open Sun.–Fri. 9–5 (until 4:30 in winter).*

Further testimony to the appalling crimes perpetrated against the Jews during World War II can be seen in the **Pinkasova synagóga** (Pinkas Synagogue), a handsome Gothic structure whose foundation dates from the 11th century. The names of 77,297 Bohemian and Moravian Jews murdered by the Nazis were inscribed in rows on the walls inside. Many of the names, sadly, were destroyed by water damage over the years. Enter the synagogue from Široká street on the other side of the cemetery. *Admission: 20 Kč. adults, 10 Kč. students. Open Sun.–Fri. 10–12:30 and 1–6 (until 5 in winter).*

Time Out **U Rudolfa** (Maislova 5) specializes in grilled meats, prepared before your eyes. Time your visit for off hours, however; the tiny restaurant fills up quickly. If there's no room, **U Golema** (Maislova 8) offers a strange mixture of Jewish, but not kosher, delicacies, including tasty Elixir Soup.

Return to Maislova ulice via U starého hřbitova, and turn right in the direction of the Old Town once again, crossing Široká ㉒ ulice. Look in at the **Maislova synagóga** (Maisel Synagogue), which houses an enormous collection of silver articles of worship confiscated by the Nazis from synagogues throughout Central Europe. Here you'll find the State Jewish Museum's finest collection of Torah wrappers and mantles, silver pointers, breastplates and spice boxes, candle holders (the eight-branched Hanukkiah and the seven-branched menorah), and Levite washing sets. *Maislova 10. Admission: 20 Kč. adults, 10 Kč. students. Open Sun.–Fri. 10–12:30 and 1–6 (until 5 in winter).*

Tour 3: Charles Bridge and Malá Strana

Prague's **Malá Strana** (the so-called Lesser Quarter, or Little Town) is not for the methodical tourist. Its charm lies in the tiny lanes, the sudden blasts of bombastic architecture, and the soul-stirring views that emerge for a second before disappearing behind the sloping roofs. The area is at its best in the evening, when the softer light hides the crumbling facades and brings you into a world of glimmering beauty.

❷③ Begin the tour on the Old Town side of **Karlův most** (the Charles Bridge), which you can reach by foot in about 10 minutes from the Old Town Square. The view from the foot of the bridge is nothing short of breathtaking, encompassing the towers and domes of Malá Strana and the soaring spires of the St. Vitus Cathedral to the northwest. This heavenly vision, one of the most beautiful in Europe, changes subtly in perspective as you walk across the bridge, attended by the host of Baroque saints that decorates the bridge's peaceful Gothic stones. At night its drama is spellbinding: St. Vitus Cathedral lit in a ghostly green, the castle in monumental yellow, and the church of St. Nicholas in a voluptuous pink, all viewed through the menacing silhouettes of the bowed statues and the Gothic towers (if you do nothing else in Prague, you must visit the Charles Bridge at night). During the day, the pedestrian bridge buzzes with activity. Street musicians vie with artisans hawking jewelry, paintings, and glass for the hearts and wallets of the passing multitude. At night, the crowds thin out a little, the musicians multiply, and the bridge becomes a long block party—nearly everyone brings a bottle.

When the Přemyslide princes set up residence in Prague in the 10th century, there was a ford across the Vltava at this point, a vital link along one of Europe's major trading routes. After several wooden bridges and the first stone bridge had washed away in floods, Charles IV appointed a 27-year-old German, Peter Parler, architect of St. Vitus Cathedral, to build a new structure in 1357. After 1620, following the defeat of Czech Protestants by Catholic Habsburgs at the Battle of White Mountain, the bridge and its adornment became caught up in the Catholic–Hussite (Protestant) conflict. The many Baroque statues, built by Catholics and which began to appear in the late 17th century, eventually came to symbolize the totality of the Austrian (hence Catholic) triumph. The Czech writer Milan Kundera sees the statues from this perspective: "The thousands of saints looking out from all sides, threatening you, following you, hypnotizing you, are the raging hordes of occupiers who invaded Bohemia three hundred and fifty years ago to tear the people's faith and language from their hearts."

The religious conflict is less obvious nowadays, leaving only the artistic tension between Baroque and Gothic that gives the bridge its allure. The **Old Town Bridge Tower** was where Paler began his bridge-building. The carved facades he designed for the sides of the bridge were destroyed by Swedish soldiers in 1648, at the end of the Thirty Years' War. The sculptures facing the square, however, are still intact; they depict the old gout-ridden Charles IV with his son, who later became Wenceslas IV. The climb of 138 steps is well worth the effort for the views it affords of the Old Town and, across the river, of Mala Strana and Prague Castle. *Admission: 20 Kč. adults, 10 Kč. children and students. Open Apr.–Oct., daily 9–6.*

It's worth pausing to take a closer look at some of the statues as you walk toward Malá Strana. The third on the right, a brass crucifix with Hebrew lettering in gold, was mounted on the location of a wooden cross that was destroyed in the battle with the Swedes (the golden lettering was reputedly financed by a Jew accused of defiling the cross). The eighth statue on the right, St. John of Nepomuk, is the oldest of all; it was designed by Johann Brokoff in 1683. On the left-hand side, sticking out from the bridge between the ninth and tenth statues (the latter has a wonderfully expressive vanquished Satan), stands a Roland statue. This knightly figure, bearing the coat of arms of the Old Town, once was a reminder that this part of the bridge belonged to the Old Town before Prague became a unified city in 1784. The square below is the Kampa Island, separated from the Lesser Town by an arm of the Vltava known as Čertovka (Devil's Stream) (*see below*).

In the eyes of most art historians, the most valuable statue is the twelfth, on the left. Mathias Braun's statue of St. Luitgarde depicts the blind saint kissing Christ's wounds. The most compelling grouping, however, is the second from the end on the left, a work of Ferdinand Maximilien Brokov from 1714. Here the saints are incidental; the main attraction is the Turk, his face expressing extreme boredom while guarding Christians imprisoned in the cage at his side. When the statue was erected, just 29 years after the second Turkish invasion of Vienna, it scandalized the Prague public, who smeared the statue with mud.

By now, you are almost at the end of the bridge. In front of you
24 is the striking conjunction of the two **Malá Strana Bridge Towers,** one Gothic, the other Romanesque. Together they frame the Baroque flamboyance of the St. Nicholas Church in the distance. At night this is an absolutely wondrous sight. The lower, Romanesque tower formed a part of the earlier wooden and stone bridges, its present appearance stemming from a renovation in 1591. The Gothic tower, **Mostecká Věž,** was added to the bridge a few decades after its completion. If you didn't climb the tower on the Old Town side of the bridge, it's worth scrambling up the wooden stairs inside this tower for the views over the roofs of the Malá Strana and of the Old Town across the river. *Mostecká ul. Admission: 20 Kč. adults, 10 Kč. children and students. Open Apr.–Oct., daily 9–6.*

Walk under the gateway of the towers into the little uphill street called **Mostecká ulice.** You have now entered the **Malá Strana** (Lesser Quarter), established in 1257 and for years home to the merchants and craftsmen who served the royal court. Follow Mostecká ulice up to the rectangular
25 **Malostranské náměstí** (Lesser Quarter Square), now the district's traffic hub rather than its heart. The arcaded houses on the left, dating from the 16th and 17th centuries, exhibit a mix of Baroque and Renaissance elements. The beautiful blue building at No. 10, on the far side of the square, houses one of Prague's best restaurants, U Mecenáše (*see* Dining, *below*).

26 On the left side of the square stands **Chrám svatého Mikuláše** (St. Nicholas Church). With its dynamic curves, this church is one of the purest and most ambitious examples of High Baroque. The celebrated architect Christoph Dientzenhofer began the Jesuit church in 1704 on the site of one of the more active Hussite churches of 15th-century Prague. Work on the building was taken over by his son Kilian Ignaz Dientzenhofer, who built the dome and presbytery; Anselmo Lurago completed the whole in 1755 by adding the bell tower. The juxtaposition of the broad, full-bodied dome with the slender bell tower is one of the many striking architectural contrasts that mark the Prague skyline. Inside, the vast pink-and-green space is impossible to take in with a single glance; every corner bristles with movement, guiding the eye first to the dramatic statues, then to the hectic frescoes, and on to the shining faux-marble pillars. Many of the statues are the work of Ignaz Platzer; they constitute his last blaze of success. When the centralizing and secularizing reforms of Joseph II toward the end of the 18th century brought an end to the flamboyant Baroque era, Platzer's workshop was forced to declare bankruptcy. *Malostranské nám. Admission: 20 Kč. adults, 10 Kč. children and students. Open daily 9–4 (until 5 or 6 in summer).*

㉗ From Malostranské náměsti, turn left onto **Nerudova ulice,** named for the 19th-century Czech journalist and poet Jan Neruda (after whom Chilean poet Pablo Neruda renamed himself). This steep little street used to be the last leg of the Royal Way, walked by the king before his coronation, and it is still the best way to get to the castle (*see* Tour 4, *below*). Until Joseph II's administrative reforms in the late 18th century, house-numbering was unknown in Prague. Each house bore a name, depicted on the facade, and these are particularly prominent on Nerudova ulice. House No. 6, **U červeného orla** (At the Red Eagle), proudly displays a faded painting of a red eagle. Number 12 is known as **U tří housliček** (At the Three Violins). In the early 18th century, three generations of the Edlinger violin-making family lived here. Joseph II's scheme numbered each house according to its position in Prague's separate "towns" (here, Malá Strana), rather than according to its sequence on the street. The red plates record these original house numbers; the blue ones are the numbers used in addresses today.

Time Out Nerudova ulice is filled with little restaurants and snack bars and offers something for everyone. U zeleného čaje at No. 19 (tel. 02/231–5750) is a fragrant little tea room, offering fruit and herbal teas as well as light salads and sweets. U Kocoura at No. 2 is a traditional pub that hasn't caved in to touristic niceties.

Two palaces break the unity of the burghers' houses on Nerudova ulice. Both were designed by the adventurous Baroque architect Giovanni Santini, one of the Italian builders most in demand by wealthy nobles of the early 18th century. The **Morzin Palace,** on the left at No. 5, is now the Romanian embassy. The fascinating facade, with an allegory of night and day, was created in 1713 and is the work of F. M. Brokov of Charles Bridge statue fame. Across the street at No. 20 is the **Thun-Hohenstein Palace,** now the Italian embassy. The gateway with two enormous eagles (the emblem of the Kolovrat family, who owned the building at the time) is the work of the other great Charles Bridge statue-builder, Mathias Braun. Santini himself lived at No. 14, the so-called **Valkoun House.**

While you're at this end of the street, it's worth taking a quick **㉘** look at the Rococo **Bretfeld palác** (Bretfeld Palace), No. 33, on the corner of Nerudova ulice and Janský vršek. The relief of St. Nicholas on the facade is the work of Ignaz Platzer, but the building is valued more for its historical associations than for its architecture: This is where Mozart, his lyricist partner Lorenzo da Ponte, and the aging but still infamous philanderer and music-lover Casanova stayed at the time of the world premiere of *Don Giovanni* in 1787. The Malá Strana recently gained a new connection with Mozart when its streets were used to represent 18th-century Vienna in the filming of Miloš Forman's *Amadeus.*

Go back down a few houses until you come to the archway at No. 13, more or less opposite the Santini **Kostel Panny Marie ustavičné pomoci u Kajetánů** (Church of Our Lady of Perpetual Help at the Theatines). The archway, marked *Restaurace*, hides one of the many winding passageways that give the Malá Strana its enchantingly ghostly character at night. Follow the dog-leg curve downhill, past two restaurants, vine-covered walls, and some broken-down houses. The alleyway really comes into its own only in the dark, the dim lighting hiding the grime and highlighting the mystery.

29 You emerge from the passageway at the top of **Tržiště ulice,** opposite the **Schönbornský palác** (Schönborn Palace). Franz Kafka had an apartment in this building from March through August 1917, after moving out from Zlatá ulička (Golden Lane) (*see* Tour 3). The U.S. embassy now occupies this prime location. If you look through the gates, you can see the beautiful formal gardens rising up to the Petřin hill; they are unfortunately not open to the public.

30 Follow Tržiště downhill until you come to the main road, **Karmelitská ulice.** Here on your right is No. 25, an unobtrusive door hiding the entranceway to the intimate **Vrtbovský palác** (Vrtba Palace and Gardens). Walk through the courtyard between the two Renaissance houses, the one to the left built in 1575, the one to the right in 1591. The owner of the latter house was one of the 27 Bohemian nobles executed by the Habsburgs in 1621 (*see* Tour 1). The house was given as confiscated property to Count Sezima of Vrtba, who bought the neighboring property and turned the buildings into a late-Renaissance palace. The *Vrtbovská zahrada* (Vrtba Gardens) boasts one of the best views over the Malá Strana rooftops and is a fascinating oasis from the tourist beat. Unfortunately, the gardens are perpetually closed for renovation, even though there is no sign of work in progress. The powerful stone figure of Atlas that caps the entranceway dates from 1720 and is the work of Mathias Braun. *Karmelitská ul. 25.*

Continue walking along Karmelitská until you reach the comfortably ramshackle **Kostel Panny Marie Vítězné** (Church of Our Lady of Victories), the unlikely home of one of Prague's best-known religious artifacts, the Pražské Ježulatko (Infant Jesus of Prague). Originally brought to Prague from Spain in the 16th century, this tiny porcelain doll (now bathed in neon lighting straight out of Las Vegas) is renowned worldwide for showering miracles on anyone willing to kneel before it and pray. Nuns from a nearby convent arrive at dawn each day to change the infant's clothes; pieces of the doll's extensive wardrobe have been sent by believers from around the world. *Karmalitská 9a. Admission free.*

31 Cross over Karmelitská and walk down tiny **Prokopská ulice,** opposite the Vrtba Palace. On the left is the former Baroque **Church of St. Procopius,** now oddly adapted into an apartment block. At the end of the lane, you emerge onto the peaceful **Maltézské náměstí** (Maltese Square), named for the Knights of Malta. In the middle of the square is a sculpture depicting John the Baptist. This work, by Ferdinand Brokov, was erected in 1715 to commemorate the end of a plague. The relief on the far side shows Salome engrossed in her dance of the seven veils while John is being decapitated. There are two intricately decorated palaces on this square, to the right the Rococo Turba

Palace, now the Japanese embassy, and at the bottom, the Nostitz Palace, the Dutch embassy.

32 Follow Lázeňská street to the **Velkopřevorské náměstí** (Grand Priory Square). The palace fronting the square is considered one of the finest Baroque buildings in the Malá Strana, though it is now part of the Maltese embassy and no longer open to the public. Opposite the palace is the flamboyant orange-and-white stucco facade of the Buquoy Palace, built in 1719 by Giovanni Santini and the present home of the French embassy. From the street you can glimpse an enormous twinkling chandelier through the window, but this is about all you'll get to see of the elegant interior.

Across from this pompous display of Baroque finery stands the **33** **Lennon Peace Wall,** a peculiar monument to the passive rebellion of Czech youth against the strictures of the former communist regime. Under the Communists, Western rock music was officially discouraged, and students adopted the former Beatle as a symbol of resistance. Paintings of John Lennon and lyrics from his songs in Czech and English began to appear on the wall sometime in the 1980s. Even today, long after the Communists have departed, new graffiti still turns up regularly. It's not clear how long the police or the owners of the wall will continue to tolerate the massive amounts of writing (which has started to spread to other walls around the neighborhood), but the volume of writing suggests that the Lennon myth continues to endure.

At the lower end of the square, a tiny bridge takes you across **34** the Čertovka tributary to **Kampa Island.** The name Čertovka translates as Devil's Stream and reputedly refers to a cranky old lady who once lived on Maltese Square (given the river's present filthy state, however, the name is ironically appropriate). A right turn around the corner brings you to the foot of **Kampa Gardens,** whose unusually well kept lawns are one of the few places in Prague where sitting on the grass is openly tolerated. If it's a warm day, spread out a blanket and bask for a while in the sunshine. The row of benches that lines the river to the left also is also a popular spot to contemplate the city. At night this stretch along the river is especially romantic.

Make your way north toward the Charles Bridge by following either Na Kampě or the network of small streets running parallel to the river. Walk underneath the Charles Bridge and onto the street named U lužického semináře. This area is known as the Venice of Prague. The house at No. 1 is the inn U tří Pštrosů (The Three Ostriches), one of Prague's oldest and most charming hotels. The original building stems from the 16th century, when one of the early owners was a supplier of ostrich feathers to the royal court. The top floors and curlicue gables were early Baroque additions from the 17th century. The inn was the site of the first coffeehouse in Prague, opened by the Armenian Deodat Damajian in 1714.

Time Out At the corner of Na Kampě, right next to the arches of the Charles Bridge, the small standup café **Bistro Bruncvík** (No. 7) serves hot wine and coffee in winter and cold drinks in summer. Its slices of pizza also are satisfying.

Continue along this Old World street, past a small square, until **35** you reach a gate that marks the entrance to **Vojanovy sady,** once the gardens of the Monastery of the Discalced Carmelites, later taken over by the Order of the English Virgins and now part of the Ministry of Finance (entrance on Letenská). With its weeping willows, fruit trees, and benches, the park is another peaceful haven in summer. Exhibitions of modern sculptures are often held here, contrasting sharply with the two Baroque chapels and the graceful Ignaz Platzer statue of John of Nepomuk standing on a fish at the entrance. The park is surrounded by the high walls of the old monastery and new Ministry of Finance buildings, with only an occasional glimpse of a tower or spire to remind you that you're in Prague. *Open daily 8–5 (until 7 in summer).*

Continue north along U lužického semináře, bearing left along the main road briefly until the intersection with **Letenská ulice,** which veers off to the left. If you've had enough sightseeing, you can easily return to the Old Town via the metro from here (Malostranská station).

Otherwise, even though it is open only during summer, the **❸❻ Zahrada Valdštejnského paláca** (Wallenstein Gardens) merit a short visit. Albrecht von Wallenstein, onetime owner of the house and gardens, began a meteoric military career in 1624 when the Austrian emperor Ferdinand II retained him to save the empire from the Swedes and Protestants during the Thirty Years' War. Wallenstein, wealthy by marriage, offered to raise 20,000 men at his own cost and lead them personally. Ferdinand II accepted and showered Wallenstein with confiscated land and titles. Wallenstein's first acquisition was this enormous area, where in 1623, having knocked down 23 houses, a brick factory, and three gardens, he began to build his magnificent palace (*Valdštejnský palác,* now government buildings closed to the public), with its idiosyncratic high-walled gardens. Walking around the formal paths, you come across numerous statues, an unusual fountain with a woman spouting water from her breasts, and a lava-stone grotto along the wall. *Off Letenská ul. Admission free. Open May 1–Sept. 30, daily 9–7.*

From here, one option is to walk straight back down Letenská ulice to the Malostranská metro station. A more attractive route would take you up Letenská (past the U svatého Tomáše pub, where you can get wonderful dark beer), right on Tomášská ulice into Valdštejnské náměstí and down the exquisitely Baroque Valdštejnská ulice, ending up back at the Malostranské station, near the intersection with Pod Brouskou.

Tour 4: The Castle District

To the west of Prague Castle is the residential **Hradčany** (Castle District), the town that emerged in the early 14th century out of a collection of monasteries and churches. The concentration of history packed into one small area makes Prague Castle and the Castle District challenging objects for visitors not versed in the ups and downs of Bohemian kings, religious uprisings, wars, and oppression. The picturesque area surrounding Prague Castle, with its breathtaking vistas of the Old Town and Malá Strana, is ideal for just wandering; but the castle itself, with its convoluted history and architecture, is difficult to appreciate fully without investing a little more time, which is why we cover the castle on a separate tour (*see* Tour 5, *below).

Our tour of the Castle District begins on Nerudova ulice, which runs east–west a few hundred yards south of Prague Castle. At the western foot of the street, look for a flight of stone steps guarded by two saintly statues. The stairs lead up to Loretánská ulice, affording panoramic views of St. Nicholas Church and Malá Strana. At the top of the steps, turn left and walk a couple hundred yards until you come to a dusty elongated square named **Pohořelec** (Scene of Fire), the site of tragic fires in 1420, 1541, and 1741.

37

Time Out   Busy Pohořelec square is a good place to grab a quick bite before tackling the castle. **Sate Grill** at No. 3 (open daily 11–8) offers a very passable Czech interpretation of Indonesian cooking in a standup, fast-food setting. At No. 11, **Caffe Calafuria** is an agreeable spot for coffee and a pastry.

Go through the inconspicuous gateway at No. 8 and up the steps, and you'll find yourself in the courtyard of the **Strahovský klášter** (Strahov Monastery). Founded by the Premonstratensian order in 1140, the monastery remained in their hands until 1952, when the Communists abolished all religious orders and turned the entire complex into the **Památník národního písemnictví** (Museum of National Literature). The major building of interest is the **Strahov Library,** with its collection of early Czech manuscripts, the 10th-century Strahov New Testament, and the collected works of famed Danish astronomer Tycho de Brahe. Also of note is the late-18th-century **Philosophical Hall.** Engulfing its ceilings is a startling sky-blue fresco completed by the Austrian painter Franz Anton Maulbertsch in just six months. The fresco depicts an unusual cast of characters, including Socrates' nagging wife Xanthippe, Greek astronomer Thales with his trusty telescope, and a collection of Greek philosophers mingling with Descartes, Diderot, and Voltaire. *Strahovské nádvoří 132. Admission: 20 Kč. adults, 10 Kč. children and students. Open daily 9–noon and 1–5.*

38

Retrace your steps to Loretánské náměstí, which is flanked by the feminine curves of the Baroque **Loreto Church.** The church's seductive lines were a conscious move on the part of Counter-Reformation Jesuits in the 17th century who wanted to build up the cult of Mary and attract the largely Protestant Bohemians back to the church. According to legend, angels had carried Mary's house in Nazareth and dropped it in a patch of laurel trees in Ancona, Italy; known as *Loreto* (from the Latin for laurel), it immediately became a center of pilgrimage. The Prague Loreto was one of many re-creations of this scene across Europe, and it worked: Pilgrims came in droves. The graceful facade, with its voluptuous tower, was built in 1720 by Kilian Ignaz Dientzenhofer, the architect of the two St. Nicholas churches in Prague. Most spectacular of all is a small exhibition upstairs displaying the religious treasures presented to Mary in thanks for various services, including a monstrance studded with 6,500 diamonds. *Loretánské nám. 7, tel. 02/536–6228. Admission: 30 Kč. adults, 5 Kč. children and students. Open Tues.–Sun. 9–12:15 and 1–4:30.*

39

Across the road, the 29 half-pillars of the **Černínský palác** (Chernin Palace) now mask the Czech Ministry of Foreign Affairs. During World War II this ungainly palace was the seat of the occupying German government. At the bottom of Loretánsk é náměstí, a little lane trails to the left into the area known as **Nový Svět**; the name means "new world," though the district is as Old World as they come. Turn right onto the street Nový Svět. This picturesque winding little alley, with facades from the 17th and 18th centuries, once housed Prague's poorest residents; now many of the homes are used as artists' studios. The last house on the street, at No. 1, was the home of the Danish-born astronomer Tycho de Brahe. Living so close to the Loreto, so the story goes, Tycho was constantly disturbed during his nightly star-gazing by the church bells. He ended up complaining to his patron, Emperor Rudolf II, who instructed the Capuchin monks to finish their services before the first star appeared in the sky.

Continue around the corner, where you get a tantalizing view of the cathedral through the trees. Walk past the Austrian embassy to Kanovnická ulice, a winding street lined with the dignified but melancholy **Kostel svatého Jana Nepomuckého** (Church of St. John Nepomuk). At the top of the street, on the left, the rounded, Renaissance, corner house **Martinický palác** (Martinic Palace) catches the eye with its detailed sgraffito drawings.

40 Martinic Palace opens onto **Hradčanské náměstí** (Hradčany Square). With its fabulous mixture of Baroque and Renaissance housing, topped by the castle itself, the square featured prominently (ironically, disguised as Vienna) in the film *Amadeus*, directed by the exiled Czech director Miloš Forman. The house at No. 7 was the set for Mozart's residence, where the composer was haunted by the masked figure he thought was his father. Forman used the flamboyant Rococo **Arcibiskupský palác** (Archbishop's Palace), at the top of the square on the left, as the Viennese archbishop's palace. The plush interior, shown off in the film, is open to the public only on Maudy Thursday.

41 To the left of the Archbishop's Palace is an alleyway leading down to the **Národní galérie** (National Gallery), housed in the 18th-century **Šternberský palác** (Sternberg Palace). You need an hour at least to view the palace's impressive art collection—one collection in Prague you should not miss. On the first floor there's an exhibition of icons and other religious art from the 3rd through the 14th centuries. Up a second flight of steps is an entire room full of Cranachs and an assortment of paintings from Holbein, Dürer, Brueghel, Van Dyck, Canaletto, and Rubens, not to mention works by modern masters like Picasso, Matisse, Chagall, and Kokoschka. *Hradčanské nám. 15, tel. 02/ 352441 or 02/534457. Admission: 40 Kč. adults, 10 Kč. children and students. Open Tues.–Sun. 10–6.*

42 Across the square, the handsome sgraffito sweep of **Schwarzenberg palota** (Schwarzenberg Palace) beckons; this is the building you saw from the backside at the beginning of the tour. The palace was built for the Lobkowitz family between 1545 and 1563; today it houses the **Vojenské muzeum** (Military Museum), one of the largest of its kind in Europe. Of more general interest are the jousting tournaments held in the courtyard in summer. *Hradčanské nám. 2. Admission: 20 Kč. adults, 10 Kč. children and students. Open May 1–Sept. 30, Tues.–Sun. 9–4:30.*

Tour 5: Prague Castle

Numbers in the margin correspond to points of interest on the Tour 5: Prague Castle (Pražský hrad) map.

Despite its monolithic presence, **Pražský Hrad** (Prague Castle) is a collection of buildings dating from the 10th to the 20th century, all linked by internal courtyards. The most important structures are St. Vitus Cathedral, clearly visible soaring above the castle walls, and the Royal Palace, the official residence of kings and presidents and still the center of political power in the Czech Republic.

The main entrance to Prague Castle from Hradčanské náměstí is a little disappointing. Going through the wrought-iron gate, guarded at ground level by pristine Czech soldiers and from above by the ferocious **Battling Titans** (a copy of Ignaz **43** Platzer's original 18th-century statues), you enter the **První Nádvoří** (First Courtyard), built on the site of old moats and gates that once separated the castle from the surrounding buildings and thus protect the vulnerable western flank. This courtyard is one of the more recent additions to the castle, commissioned by the Habsburg empress Maria Theresa and designed by her court architect Nicolò Pacassi in the 1760s. Today it forms part of the presidential office complex. Pacassi's reconstruction was intended to unify the eclectic collection of buildings that made up the castle. From a distance, the effect is monumental. As you move farther into the castle, large parts appear to be relatively new, while in reality they cover splendid Gothic and Romanesque interiors.

44 It is worth looking closely at **Matyášova Brána** (Matthias Gate) before going through to the next courtyard. Built in 1614, the stone gate once stood alone in front of the moats and bridges that surrounded the castle. Under the Habsburgs, the gate survived by being grafted as a relief onto the palace building. As you go through the gate, notice the ceremonial white-marble entrance halls on either side. These lead up to President Václav Havel's reception rooms, which are not open to the public.

45 The **Druhé nádvoří** (Second Courtyard) was the major victim of Pacassi's attempts at imparting classical grandeur to the castle. Except for the view of the spires of St. Vitus Cathedral towering above the palace, there's little for the eye to feast upon here. Built in the late-16th and early-17th centuries, this courtyard was part of an even earlier reconstruction program commissioned by Rudolf II, under whom Prague enjoyed a period of unparalleled cultural development. Once the Prague court was established, the emperor gathered around him some of the worlds's best craftsmen, artists, and scientists, including the brilliant astronomers Johannes Kepler and Tycho de Brahe.

Rudolf also amassed a large collection of art, surveying instruments, and coins. The bulk of the collection was looted by the Swedes and Habsburgs during the Thirty Years' War or auctioned off during the 18th century, but a small part of the collection was rediscovered in unused castle rooms in the 1960s **46** and is now on display in the **Hradní galérie** (Castle Gallery), on the left side of the Second Courtyard. Apart from works by world-famous artists such as Titian, Rubens, and Tintoretto,

Tour 5: Prague Castle (Pražský hrad)

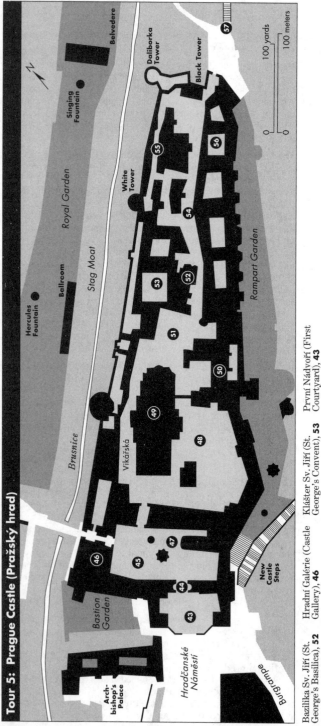

Bazilika Sv. Jiří (St. George's Basilica), **52**

Chrám Sv. Víta (St. Vitus Cathedral), **49**

Druhé Nádvoří (Second Courtyard), **45**

Hradní Galérie (Castle Gallery), **46**

Jiřská Ulice (St. George's Lane), **54**

Jiřské Náměstí (St. George's Square), **51**

Kaple Sv. Kříže (Chapel of the Holy Cross), **47**

Klášter Sv. Jiří (St. George's Convent), **53**

Královský Palác (Royal Palace), **50**

Lobkovický Palác, **56**

Matyášova Brána (Matthias Gate), **44**

První Nádvoří (First Courtyard), **43**

Staré Zámecké Schody (Old Castle Steps), **57**

Třetí Nádvoří (Third Courtyard), **48**

Zlatá Ulička (Golden Lane), **55**

look for the rarer works of Rudolf's court painters Hans von Aachen and Bartolomeo Spranger, and of the Bohemian Baroque painters Jan Kupecký and Petr Brandl. The passageway at the gallery entrance is the northern entrance to the castle and leads out over a luxurious ravine known as the **Jelení příkop** (Stag Moat). *Admission: 10 Kč. adults, 5 Kč. children and students. Open Tues.–Sun. 10–6 (until 5:30 in winter).*

The Second Courtyard also houses the religious reliquary of Charles IV inside the **Kaple svatého Kříže** (Chapel of the Holy Cross). Displays include Gothic silver busts of the major Bohemian patron saints and a collection of bones and vestments that supposedly belonged to various saints. *Admission: 10 Kč. adults, 5 Kč. children and students. Open Tues.–Sun. 9–4 (until 5 in summer).*

Through the passageway on the far wall you come to the **Třetí nádvoří** (Third Courtyard). As you enter, the graceful soaring towers of **Chrám svatého Víta** (St. Vitus Cathedral) command your attention and admiration. The Gothic cathedral, among the most beautiful in Europe, has a long and complicated history, beginning in the 10th century and continuing to its completion in 1929. If you want to hear more about the ins and outs, English-speaking guided tours of the cathedral and the Old Royal Palace (*see below*) can be arranged at the Information Office around the left side of the cathedral, past the Vikářka restaurant.

Once you enter the cathedral, pause to take in the vast but delicate beauty of the Gothic interior, glowing in the colorful light that filters through the startlingly brilliant stained-glass windows. This back half, including the western facade and the two towers you can see from outside, was not completed until 1929, following the initiative of the Union for the Completion of the Cathedral set up in the last days of the 19th century. Don't let the neo-Gothic delusion keep you from examining this new section. The six stained-glass windows to your left and right and the large rose window behind are modern masterpieces. Take a good look at the third window up on the left. The familiar art nouveau flamboyance, depicting the blessing of the 9th-century St. Cyril and St. Methodius (missionaries to the Slavs and creators of the Cyrillic alphabet), is the work of the Czech father of the style, Alfons Mucha. He achieved the subtle coloring by painting rather than staining the glass.

If you walk a little farther on, just past the entrance to your right, you will find the exquisitely ornate **Chapel of St. Wenceslas.** This square chapel, with a 14th-century tomb holding the saint's remains, is the ancient heart of the cathedral. Wenceslas (the "good king" of Christmas-carol fame) was a determined Christian in an era of widespread paganism. In 925, as prince of Bohemia, he founded a rotunda church dedicated to St. Vitus on this site. But the prince's brother, Boleslav, was impatient to take power and ambushed Wenceslas four years later near a church north of Prague. Wenceslas was originally buried in that church, but his grave produced so many miracles that he rapidly became a symbol of piety for the common people, something that greatly irritated the new Prince Boleslav. In 931 Boleslav was finally forced to honor his brother by reburying the body in the St. Vitus Rotunda. Shortly after that, Wenceslas was canonized.

The cathedral's rotunda was replaced by a Romanesque basilica in the late-11th century. Work was begun on the existing building in 1344 on the initiative of the man who was later to become Charles IV. For the first few years the chief architect was the Frenchman Mathias d'Arras, but after his death, in 1352, the work was continued by the 22-year-old German architect Peter Parler, who went on to build the Charles Bridge and many other Prague treasures.

The small door in the back of the chapel leads to the **Crown Chamber,** the repository of the Bohemian crown jewels. It remains locked with seven keys held by seven different people and definitely is not open to the public.

A little beyond the Wenceslas Chapel on the same side, a small cash desk marks the entrance to the **underground crypt** (admission: 5 Kč.), interesting primarily for the information it provides about the cathedral's history. As you descend the stairs, on the right you'll see parts of the old Romanesque basilica. A little farther on, in a niche to the left, are parts of the foundations of the rotunda. Moving around into the second room, you'll find a rather eclectic group of royal remains ensconced in new sarcophagi dating from the 1930s. In the center is Charles IV, who died in 1378. Rudolf II, patron of Renaissance Prague, is entombed at the rear. To his right is Maria Amalia, the only child of Maria Theresa to reside in Prague. Ascending the wooden steps back into the cathedral, you come to the white marble **Royal Mausoleum,** atop which lie stone statues of the first two Habsburg kings to rule in Bohemia, Ferdinand I and Maximilian II.

The cathedral's **Royal Oratory,** was used by the kings and their families when attending mass. Built in 1493, the work is a perfect example of the late-Gothic, laced on the outside with a stone network of gnarled branches very similar in pattern to the ceiling vaulting in the Old Royal Palace (*see below*). The oratory is connected to the palace by an elevated covered walkway, which you can see from outside.

From here you can't fail to catch sight of the ornate silver **sarcophagus of St. John of Nepomuk,** designed by the famous Viennese architect Fischer von Erlach. According to legend, when Nepomuk's body was exhumed in 1721 to be reinterred, the tongue was found to be still intact and pumping with blood. These strange tales sadly served a highly political purpose. The Catholic church and the Habsburgs were seeking a new folk hero to replace the protestant Jan Hus, whom they despised. The late Father Nepomuk was sainted and reburied a few years later with great ceremony in the 3,700-pound silver tomb, replete with angels and cherubim; the tongue was enshrined in its own reliquary.

The chapels around the back of the cathedral, the work of the original architect, Mathias d'Arras, are unfortunately closed to the public. Opposite the wooden relief, depicting the looting of the cathedral by Protestants in 1619, is the **Wallenstein Chapel.** Since the last century, it has housed the Gothic tombstones of its two architects, Mathias d'Arras and Peter Parler, who died in 1352 and 1399 respectively. If you look up to the balcony you can just make out the busts of these two men, designed by Parler's workshop. The other busts around the triforium depict various Czech kings.

The Hussite wars in the 15th century put an end to the first phase of the cathedral's construction. During the short era of illusory peace before the Thirty Years' War, lack of money laid to rest any idea of finishing the building, and the cathedral was closed by a wall built across from the Wenceslas Chapel. Not until the 20th century was the western side of the cathedral, with its two towers, completed according to Parler's original plans. *St. Vitus Cathedral. Admission free. Open May–Sept., Tues.–Sun. 9–5; Oct.–Apr., Tues.–Sun. 9–4.*

The contrast between the cool, dark interior of the cathedral and the brightly colored Pacassi facades of the Third Court-yard is startling. The clean lines of the courtyard are Plečnik's work from the 1930s, but the modern look is a deception. Plečnik's paving was intended to cover an underground world of wooden houses, streets, and walls dating from the 9th through 12th century that was rediscovered when the cathedral was completed. Since these are not open to the public, we are left with the modern structure (supplemented recently by an exchange office). Plečnik did add a few eclectic features to catch the eye: a granite obelisk to commemorate the fallen of the First World War, a black marble pedestal for the Gothic statue of St. George (the original is in the museum), and the peculiar golden ball topping the eagle fountain that unobtru-sively marks the entrance to the **Královský palác** (Royal Palace). There are two main points of interest inside the externally nondescript palace. The first is the **Vladislavský sál** (Vladislav Hall), the largest secular Gothic interior space in Central Europe. The enormous hall was completed in 1493 by Benedict Ried, who was to late–Bohemian Gothic what Peter Parler was to the earlier version. The room imparts a sense of space and light, softened by the sensuous lines of the vaulted ceilings and brought to a dignified close by the simple oblong form of the early Renaissance windows, a style that was just beginning to make inroads in Central Europe. In its heyday, the hall was the site of jousting tournaments, festive markets, banquets, and coronations. In more recent times, it has been used to inaugurate presidents, from the Communist Klement Gottwald in 1948 to Václav Havel in 1990.

From the front of the hall, turn right into the rooms of the **Česká kancelář** (Bohemian Chancellery). This wing was built by the same Benedict Ried only 10 years after the hall was completed, but it shows a much stronger Renaissance influence. Pass through the Renaissance portal into the last chamber of the Chancellery. This room was the site of the Second Prague Defenestration in 1618, an event that marked the beginning of the Bohemian rebellion and, ultimately, of the Thirty Years' War. This peculiarly Bohemian method of expressing protest (throwing someone out of a window) had first been used in 1419 in the New Town Hall, an event that led to the Hussite wars. Two hundred years later the same conflict was reexpressed in terms of Habsburg-backed Catholics versus Bohemian Protestants. Rudolf II had reached an uneasy agreement with the Bohemian nobles, allowing them religious freedom in exchange for financial support. But his successor, Ferdinand II, was a rabid opponent of Protestantism and disregarded Rudolf's tolerant "Letter of Majesty." Enraged, the Protestant nobles stormed the castle and Chancellery and threw two Catholic officials and their secretary, for good measure, out of the window. Legend has it that they landed on a mound of horse dung and escaped unharmed, an event that the Jesuits interpreted as a miracle. The square window in question is on the left as you come into the room.

The exit to the **Palace Courtyard** is halfway down the Vladislav Hall on the left. Before leaving, you might want to peek into some of the other rooms. At the back of the hall, a staircase leads up to a gallery of the **All Saints' Chapel.** Little remains of Peter Parler's original work, but the church contains some fine works of art. The large room to the left of the staircase is the **Stará sněmovna** (Council Chamber), where the Bohemian nobles met with the king in a kind of prototype parliament. Portraits of the Habsburg rulers line the walls. As you leave the palace, be sure to notice the gradually descending steps. This is the **Riders' Staircase** to the left of the Council Chamber; this was the entranceway for knights who came for the jousting tournaments. *Royal Palace, tel. 02/2101. Admission: 10 Kč. adults, 5 Kč. children and students. Open Tues.–Sun. 9–5 (until 4 in winter).*

51 The exit from the Royal Palace will bring you out onto **Jiřské náměstí** (St. George's Square); at its east end stands the
52 Romanesque **Bazilika svatého Jiří** (St. George's Basilica). This church was originally built in the 10th century by Prince Vratislav I, the father of Prince (and St.) Wenceslas. It was dedicated to St. George (of dragon fame), who, it was believed, would be more agreeable to the still largely pagan people. The outside was remodeled in early Baroque times, although the striking rusty-red color is in keeping with the look of the original, 10th-century structure. The interior, however, following substantial renovation, looks more or less as it did in the 12th century and is the best-preserved Romanesque relic in the country. The effect is at once barnlike and peaceful, the warm golden yellow of the stone walls and the small triplet arched windows exuding a sense of enduring harmony. The houseshaped, painted tomb at the front of the church holds the remains of the founder, Vratislav I. Up the steps, in a chapel to the right, is the tomb Paler designed for St. Ludmila, the grandmother of St. Wenceslas. *Tel. 02/2101. Admission: 10 Kč. adults, 5 Kč. children and students. Open Tues.–Sun. 9–5 (until 4 in winter).*

53 Next to the basilica on the square is the former **Klášter svatého Jiří** (St. George's Convent), which now houses the Old Bohemian Art Collection of the **Czech National Gallery.** The museum runs through the history of Czech art from the early Middle Ages, with exhibits that include religious statues, icons, and triptychs, as well as the rather more secular themes of the Mannerist school and the voluptuous work of the court painters of Rudolf II. *Tel. 02/535240 or 02/535246. Admission: 40 Kč. adults, 10 Kč. children and students. Open Tues.–Sun. 9–5:30.*

54 Walk down **Jiřská ulice** (St. George's Lane) until you come to a
55 street leading to the left. At the top is **Zlatá ulička** (Golden Lane), an enchanting collection of tiny, ancient, brightly colored houses with long, sloping roofs, crouching under the fortification wall and looking remarkably like a Disney set for *Snow White and the Seven Dwarfs.* Legend has it that these were the lodgings of the international group of alchemists whom Rudolf II brought to the court to produce gold. The truth is a little less romantic: The houses were built in the 16th century for the castle guards, who supplemented their income by practicing vari-

ous crafts outside the jurisdiction of the powerful guilds. By the early 20th century, Golden Lane had become the home of poor artists and writers. Franz Kafka, who lived at No. 22 in 1916 and 1917, described the house on first sight as "so small, so dirty, impossible to live in and lacking everything necessary." But he soon came to love the place. As he wrote to his fiancée, "Life here is something special . . . to close out the world not just by shutting the door to a room or apartment but to the whole house, to step out into the snow of the silent lane." The lane now houses tiny stores selling books, music, and crafts.

56 Return to Jiřská ulice and continue on down to **Lobkovický palác** (Lobkovitz Palace). From the beginning of the 17th century until the 1940s, this building was the residence of the powerful Catholic Lobkovitz family. It was to this house that the two defenestrated officials escaped after landing on the dung hill in 1618. In the 1970s, the building was restored to its early Baroque appearance and now houses the permanent exhibition "Monuments of the Czech National Past." If you want to get a chronological understanding of Czech history from the beginnings of the Great Moravian Empire in the 9th century to the Czech national uprising in 1848, this is your chance. Copies of the crown jewels are on display here; but it is the rich collection of illuminated Bibles, old musical instruments, coins, weapons, royal decrees, paintings, and statues that makes the museum well worth visiting. Detailed information on the exhibits is available in English. *Admission: 10 Kč. adults, 5 Kč. children and students. Open Tues.–Sun. 9–5 (until 4 in winter).*

Turn right out of the Lobkovitz Palace, and leave the castle grounds through the east gate. Take a look over the bastion on your right for one last great view of the city. From here, de-
57 scend the romantic, vine-draped **Staré zámecké schody** (Old Castle Steps), which come out just above the Malostranská metro station. A direct subway line runs from here to Wenceslas Square (Můstek station).

What to See and Do with Children

Prague's small but delightful **Zoologická zahrada** (zoo) is located north of the city in Troja, under the shadow of the Troja castle. Take the metro line C to Holešovické nábřeží and change to bus No. 112. *Admission: 30 Kč. adults, 10 Kč. children. Open May, daily 7–6; June–Sept., daily 7–7; Oct.–Apr., daily 7–3.*

An hour or two of **rowing on the Vltava** is a great way to spend a sunny afternoon in Prague. Boats are available for rent in season (May–September) on the island across from the embankment near the Národní Divadlo (National Theater) for 40 Kč. an hour.

One of the unique delights of Prague for children and adults alike is **feeding the swans** along the banks of the Vltava River, and one spot in Malá Strana is especially popular. Walk to the right from the exit of the Malostranská metro stop, and walk up the street called U lužického semináře. The riverbank is accessible to your left just before you get to the Vojanovy park on the right. The atmosphere here is festive, especially on weekends, and the views over the city are breathtaking.

There are no fewer than three **puppet theaters** in Prague, all of which perform primarily for young children. Ask at Čedok or your hotel for details of performances.

Off the Beaten Track

Kafka's Grave. Kafka's modest tombstone in the New Jewish Cemetery (Židovské hřbitovy), situated beyond Vinohrady in a rather depressing part of Prague, seems grossly inadequate to Kafka's stature but oddly in proportion to his own modest ambitions. The cemetery is usually open for visitors; guards sometimes inexplicably seal off the grounds, but you can still glimpse the grave through the gate's iron bars. Take the metro to Želivského, turn right at the main cemetery gate, and follow the wall for about 100 yards. Dr. Franz Kafka's thin, white tombstone lies at the front of section 21.

Kostel Najsvětějšího Srdca Pana (Church of the Most Sacred Heart). If you've had your fill of Romanesque, Gothic, and Baroque, take the metro to Vinohrady (Jiřího z Poděbrad station) for a look at this amazing Art Deco cathedral. Designed in 1927 by Slovenian architect Jože Plečnik, the same architect commissioned to update the Prague Castle, the church more resembles a luxury ocean liner than a place of worship. The effect was conscious; in the 1920s and '30s, the avant garde carefully imitated mammoth objects of modern technology. Plečnik used many modern elements on the inside: Notice the hanging speakers, seemingly designed to bring the word of God directly to the ears of each worshiper. You may be able to find someone at the back entrance of the church who will let you walk up the long ramp into the fascinating glass clock tower.

Letenské sady (Letna Gardens). Come to this large, shady park for an unforgettable view from on high of Prague's bridges. From the enormous cement pedestal at the center of the park, the largest statue of Stalin in Eastern Europe once beckoned to citizens on the Old Town Square far below. The statue was ripped down in the 1960s, when Stalinism was first discredited. Now the ideology-weary city fathers don't quite know what to do with the space. The room below the base is occasionally used as a venue for rock music. The walks and grass that stretch out behind the pedestal are perfect for relaxing on a warm afternoon. On sunny Sundays expatriots often meet up here to play ultimate frisbee. To get to Letna, cross the Svatopluka Čecha bridge, opposite the Hotel Inter-Continental, and climb the stairs.

Petřín. For a superb view of the city—from a mostly undiscovered, tourist-free perch—take the small funicular up through the hills of the Malá Strana to Prague's own miniature version of the Eiffel Tower. To reach the funicular, cross the Leglí bridge near the Národní Divadlo (National Theater), and walk straight ahead to the Petřín park. You can use normal public transport tickets for the funicular. Although the tower is closed to visitors, the area with the broken-down hall of mirrors and seemingly abandoned church is beautifully peaceful and well worth an afternoon's wandering. For the descent, meander on foot down through the stations of the cross on the pathways leading back to the Malá Strana. If you branch off to the left in the direction of the Strahov Monastery, you'll get one of the best views of Prague, with the castle out to the left, embracing the roofs of the Malá Strana and the Old Town far below.

Villa Bertramka. Mozart fans won't want to pass up a visit to this villa, where the great composer lived when in Prague. The small, well-organized museum is packed with memorabilia, including the program from that exciting night in 1787 when *Don Giovanni* had its world premiere in Prague. Also on hand is one of the master's pianos. Take the metro line B to the Anděl station, walk down Plzeňská ulice a few hundred yards, and take a left at Mozartova ulice. *Mozartova ul. 169, Smíchov, tel. 02/543893. Admission: 20 Kč. adults, 10 Kč. children. Open daily 10–5.*

Shopping

Despite the relative shortage of quality clothes—Prague has a long way to go before it can match the shopping meccas of Paris and Rome—Prague is a great place to pick up gifts and souvenirs. Bohemian crystal and porcelain deservedly enjoy a worldwide reputation for quality, and plenty of shops offer excellent bargains. The local market for antiques and artworks still is relatively undeveloped. In addition, the dozens of antiquarian bookshops can yield some excellent finds, particularly in German and Czech books and graphics. Another bargains is recorded music: LP and even CD prices are about half of what you would pay in the West.

Shopping Districts
The major shopping areas are **Národní třída,** running past Můstek to Na příkopě, and the area around **Staroměstské náměstí** (Old Town Square). **Pařížská ulice, Karlova ulice** (on the way to the Charles Bridge), and the area just south of **Josefov** (the Jewish Quarter) are also good places to try boutiques and antiques shops. In the Malá Strana, try **Nerudova ulice,** the street that runs up to the Castle Hill district.

Department Stores
These are generally poorly stocked, but a stroll through one may yield some interesting finds and bargains. The best are **Kotva** (Nám. Republiky 8), **Máj** (Národní třída 26), **Bílá Labut'** (Na poříčí 23), and **Krone** (Václavské nám. 21).

Street Markets
For fruits and vegetables, the best street market in central Prague is on **Havelská ulice** in the Old Town. But arrive early in the day if you want something a bit more exotic than tomatoes and cucumbers. The best market for nonfood items is the flea market in **Holešovice,** north of the city center, although there isn't really much of interest here outside of cheap tobacco and electronics products. Take metro line C to the Vltavská station, and then ride any tram that stops to the left of the metro. Exit at the first stop, and follow the crowds.

Specialty Stores
Antiques
Starožitnosti (Antiques shops) are everywhere in Prague, but you'll need a sharp eye to distinguish truly valuable pieces from merely interesting ones. Many dealers carry old glassware and vases. Antique jewelry, many pieces featuring garnets, is also popular. Remember to retain your receipts as proof of legitimate purchases, otherwise you may have difficulties bringing antiques out of the country. Comparison-shop at stores along Karlova ulice in the Old Town. Also check in and around the streets of the Jewish Ghetto for shops specializing in Jewish antiques and artifacts. **Art Program** (Nerudova ul. 28) in the Malá

Strana has an especially beautiful collection of art-deco jewelry and glassware.

Books and Prints It's hard to imagine a more beautiful bookstore than **U Karlova Mostu** (Karlova ul. 2, Staré Město, tel. 02/265672), with its impressive selection of old maps and prints, rare books, and even current copies of the *New York Review of Books*. One shop that comes close is **Antikvariát Karel Křenek** (Celetná 31, tel. 02/231–4734), near the Powder Tower in the Old Town. It stocks prints and graphics from the 1920s and '30s, in addition to a small collection of English books. The **Melantrich** (Na příkopě 3, tel. 02/267166) is a small but excellent source for high-quality art and graphics books. The store also stocks a full set of maps to most Czech cities, auto atlases, and English-language magazines and newspapers.

Crystal and Porcelain **Moser** (Na příkopě 12, tel. 02/221851), the flagship store for the world-famous Karlovy Vary glass maker, is the first address for stylish, high-quality lead crystal and china. Even if you're not in the market to buy, stop by the store simply to browse through the elegant wood-paneled salesrooms on the second floor. The staff will gladly pack goods for traveling. The two branches of the glassware store **Bohemia** (Národní třída 43; Celetná 11) carry beautiful crystal wineglasses and candle holders. If you still can not find anything, have no fear: There is a crystal shop on just about every street in central Prague.

Food Specialty food stores have been slow to catch on in Prague. **Fruits de France** (Jindřišská ul., Nové Město) stocks fresh fruits and vegetables imported directly from France at Western prices. The bakeries at the **Krone** and **Kotva** department stores (*see above*) sell surprisingly delicious breads and pastries. Both stores also have large and well-stocked basement grocery stores.

Fun Things for Children Children enjoy the beautiful watercolor and colored-chalk sets available in nearly every stationery store at rock-bottom prices. The Czechs are also master illustrators, and the books they've made for young "pre-readers" are some of the world's loveliest. The best store to browse in is **Albatros** (Na perštýně 1, tel. 02/236565), on the corner with Národní třída. Many stores also offer unique wooden toys, sure to delight any young child. For these, look in at **Obchod Vším Možným** (Nerudova 45, tel. 02/536941). For older children and teens, it's worth considering a Czech or Eastern European watch, telescope, or set of binoculars. The quality/price ratio is unbeatable.

Jewelry The **Granát** shop at Dlouhá 30 in the Old Town has a comprehensive selection of garnet jewelry, plus contemporary and traditional pieces set in gold and silver. Several shops specializing in gold jewelry line Wenceslas Square.

Musical Instruments **Dům hudebních nástrojů** (Jungmannova nám. 17, tel. 02/236–1376) carries a complete range of quality musical instruments at reasonable prices. **Melodia** (Karmelitská 20, Malá Strana) carries a complete range of Czech-made accordions and other instruments.

Sports Equipment Try the large **Dům Sportu** (Jungmannova ul. 28) for reasonably priced tennis rackets, ice skates, sleds, skis, or whatever else you need but forgot to bring. **Adidas** has an outlet at Na Příkopě 15. Department stores (*see above*) also sometimes carry middle-quality sports equipment.

Participant Sports and Fitness

Fitness Clubs The best fitness clubs in town are at the **Forum Hotel** (Kongresova ul. 1, tel. 02/410111; Vyšehrad metro station) and at the **Atrium Hotel** (Pobrežní 1, tel. 02/284–1111; Florenc metro station). Both are open to nonresidents, but call first to inquire about rates and to make an appointment.

Golf You can golf year-round at Prague's only course, located outside the city at the **Stop Motel** (Plzeňská ul. 215, tel. 02/271311). Take a taxi to the motel, or tram No. 7 to the end of the line.

Jogging The best place to jog is in the **Letenské sady,** the large park across the river from the Hotel Inter-Continental. Cross the Svatopluka Čecha bridge, climb the stairs and turn to the right for a good long run far away from the car fumes. The **Riegrový Sady,** a small park in Vinohrady behind the main train station, is also nice, but it is small and a bit out of the way.

Swimming The best public swimming pool in Prague is at the **Podolí Swimming Stadium** in Podolí, easily reached from the city center via streetcar No. 3 or 17. The indoor pool is 50 meters long, and the complex also includes two open-air pools, a sauna, and a steam bath. The pool at the **Atrium Hotel** is smaller, but the location is more convenient (*see* Fitness Clubs, *above*).

Tennis Public courts are located at the **Spartakiade Stadium** in Břevnov. Take the No. 8 tram to the end from the Hradčanská metro stop, and change to bus No. 143, 149, or 217. The **Atrium Hotel** (*see* Fitness Clubs, *above*) has two indoor courts available for public use.

Spectator Sports

Prague plays host to a wide variety of spectator sports, including world-class ice hockey, handball, tennis, and swimming. Most events, however, are held at irregular intervals. The best place to find out what's going on (and where) is the weekly sports page of *The Prague Post,* or you can inquire at your hotel or the American Hospitality Center (*see* Tourist Information in Important Addresses and Numbers, *above*).

Soccer National and international matches are played regularly at the Letna Stadium in Holešovice, behind the Letenské Sady (*see* Jogging, *above*). To reach the stadium, take tram No. 1, 25, or 26 to the Sparta stop.

Dining

Dining possibilities in Prague have increased greatly in the past year as hundreds of new places have opened to cope with the increased tourist demand. Quality and price can vary widely, though. Be wary of tourist traps; cross-check prices of foreign-language menus with Czech versions. Also ask if there is a *denní lístek* (daily menu). These menus, usually written only in Czech, generally list cheaper and often fresher selections. Note that many places have daily menus only for the midday meal.

The crush of visitors has placed tremendous strain on the more popular restaurants. The upshot is that reservations are nearly always required; this is especially true during peak tourist periods. If you don't have reservations, try arriving a little before standard meal times: 11:30 AM for lunch, or 5:30 PM for dinner.

A cheaper and quicker alternative to the sit-down establishments listed below would be to take a light meal at one of the city's growing number of street stands and fast-food places. Look for stands offering *Parky* (hot dogs) or *Smažený syr* (fried cheese). McDonald's, with several locations in the city, heads the list of Western imports. For more exotic fare, try a gyro (made from pork) at the stand on the Staromětské náměstí or the very good vegetarian fare at **Country Life** (Melantrichova ul. 15, no phone, closed Saturday). Pizza has become very popular in recent years. Go to **New York Pizza** (Martinska 2, near Národní tř., tel. 02/268134) for some of the city's best. The German coffeemaker Tchibo has teamed up with a local bakery and now offers tasty sandwiches and excellent coffee at convenient locations on the Staromětské náměstí and at the top of Wenceslas Square.

Highly recommended restaurants in each price category are indicated by a star ★.

Very Expensive **Parnas.** This is the first choice for visiting dignitaries and ★ businesspeople blessed with expense accounts. Creative, freshly prepared cuisine, more nouvelle than Bohemian, is served in an opulent 1920s setting. Window seats afford stunning views of Prague Castle. Parnas has a small, mostly Czech vintage wine list and a fine selection of appetizers (try the smoked salmon) and desserts (the chocolate mousse is a must). *Smetanovo nábřeží 2, Nové Město, tel. 02/261250. Reservations advised. Jacket and tie required. AE, DC, MC, V. No lunch.*

★ **U Mecenáše.** A fetching Renaissance inn from the 17th century, with dark, highbacked benches in the front room and cozy, elegant sofas and chairs in back, this is the place to splurge: From the aperitifs to the steaks and the cognac (swirled lovingly in oversized glasses), the presentation is seamless. *Malostranské nám. 10, Malá Strana, tel. 02/533881. Reservations advised. Jacket and tie required. AE, DC, MC, V.*

U Zlaté Hrušky. At this bustling bistro perched on one of Prague's prettiest cobblestone streets, slide into one of the cozy dark-wood booths and let the cheerful staff advise on wines and specials. Duck and carp are house favorites. After dinner, stroll to the castle for an unforgettable panorama. *Nový Svět 3, Hradčany, tel. 02/531133. Reservations required. Jacket and tie required. AE, DC, MC, V.*

V Zátiší. White walls and casual grace accentuate the subtle flavors of smoked salmon, plaice, beef Wellington, and other non-Czech specialties. Order the house *Rulandské červené*, a fruity Moravian red wine that meets the exacting standards of the food. In behavior unusual for the city, the benign waiters fairly fall over each other to serve diners. *Liliová 1, Betlémské nám., Staré Město, tel. 02/265107. Reservations advised. Dress: casual but neat. AE, DC, MC, V.*

Expensive **Lobkovická.** This dignified *vinárna* (wine hall) set inside a ★ 17th-century town palace serves some of Prague's most imaginative dishes. Chicken breast with crabmeat and curry sauce is an excellent main dish and typical of the kitchen's innovative approach to sauces and spice. Deep-red carpeting sets the perfect mood for enjoying bottles of Moravian wine brought from the musty depths of the restaurant's wine cellar. *Vlašská 17,*

American Express offers Travelers Cheques built for two.

American Express® Cheques *for Two*. The first Travelers Cheques that allow either of you to use them because both of you have signed them. And only one of you needs to be present to purchase them.

Cheques *for Two* are accepted anywhere regular American Express Travelers Cheques are, which is just about everywhere. So stop by your bank, AAA* or any American Express Travel Service Office and ask for Cheques *for Two.*

AMERICAN EXPRESS **Travelers Cheques** ®

Malá Strana, tel. 02/530185. Reservations advised. Jacket and tie required. AE, DC, MC, V.

U Cedru. This intimate Lebanese restaurant, crowded with diplomats who know where to find the real thing, has an excellent range of Middle Eastern appetizers and main courses. For a moderately priced meal, try several appetizers—humus and garlic yogurt, perhaps—instead of a main course. *Na Hutích, Prague 6, tel. 02/3122974. Reservations advised. Dress: casual but neat. AE, DC, MC, V.*

U Zlatého Rožně. This is a dark cellar-restaurant where fresh salmon and other seafood draw reserved throngs of diplomats and their retinues. The romantic setting is marred somewhat by kitschy marine memorabilia, but no one comes for the decor. Try the herring appetizers, followed by poached salmon with baked potato, or plaice with baked brie and croquettes. The baked-apple dessert is one of the city's best. *Cs. Armady 22, Prague 6, tel. 02/312–1032. Reservations advised. Dress: casual but neat. AE, DC, MC, V.*

Moderate **Indický.** Vegetarians will find some relief from the tyranny of a meat-dominated culture in this quiet little Indian restaurant just off Wenceslas Square. Mild vegetable curries and vegetable rice dishes (plus, for meat eaters, an array of chicken and pork dishes) are accompanied by remarkably good *nan* bread. The cheerful decor, tastefully complemented by Indian paintings and quiet music, creates a pleasant atmosphere, comfortable for those dining alone. If the restaurant is full, try the more casual snack bar next door. The service is less attentive, but the food is the same. *Štěpánská ul. 61, Nové Město, tel. 02/261936. Reservations advised. Dress: casual but neat. No credit cards.*

Myslivna. The name means "hunting lodge," and the cooks at this far-flung neighborhood eatery certainly know their way around venison, quail, and boar. Attentive staff can advise on wines: Try Vavřinecké, a hearty red that holds its own with any beast. The stuffed quail and the leg of venison with walnuts both get high marks. A cab from the city center to Myslivna should cost under 300Kč. *Jagellonska 21, Prague 3, tel. 02/6270209. Reservations advised. Dress: casual but neat. AE, V.*

★ **Penguin's.** The emphasis at this popular eatery is on classic Czech and international dishes, served in an elegant mauve and matte-black setting. Try any of the steaks or the chicken breast with potatoes; the vegetable dishes are the freshest in town. The penguin in the name refers to the Pittsburgh variety, of hockey fame—the owner's favorite team. *Zborovská 5, Prague 5, tel. 02/545660. Reservations advised. Dress: casual but neat. No credit cards.*

Pezinok. Slovak cooking is hard to find, and this cozy wine restaurant is still the best in town. Heavy furnishings and subdued lighting add an oddly formal touch. Order à la carte (the set menus are overpriced) and choose from homemade sausages or *halušky*, boiled noodles served with a tangy sheep's cheese. The restaurant's full-bodied wines come from the Slovak town for which the restaurant was named. *Purkyňova 4, Nové Město, tel. 02/291996. Reservations advised. Dress: casual but neat. AE, DC, MC, V.*

Inexpensive **Demínka.** This spacious 19th-century café offers some respite
★ from Prague's throngs of tourists. It's a perfect place to have coffee and write a letter. Try the cheap and tasty *Smažený sýr* (fried cheese) or the hearty goulash soup. A small sandwich or

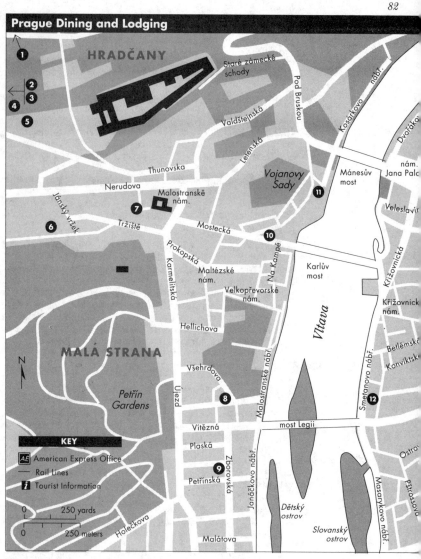

Prague Dining and Lodging

Dining
U Cedru, **2**
Demínka, **28**
Indický, **26**
U Koleje, **30**
V Krakoské, **27**
Lobkovická, **6**
U Mecenáše, **7**
Myslivna, **31**

Parnas, **12**
Penguin's, **9**
Pezinok, **24**
V. Zátiši, **13**
U Zlaté Hrušky, **4**
U Zlatého Rožně, **3**
U Zlatého Tygra, **14**
Na Zvonařce, **29**

Lodging
Apollo, **15**
Axa, **19**
City Hotel Moráň, **25**
Diplomat, **1**
Harmony, **18**
Hybernia, **22**
Kampa, **8**

Meteor Plaza, **21**
Opera, **17**
Palace, **23**
Paříž, **20**
U Páva, **11**
Pension Louda, **16**
Pension U Raka, **5**
Tří Pštrosů, **10**

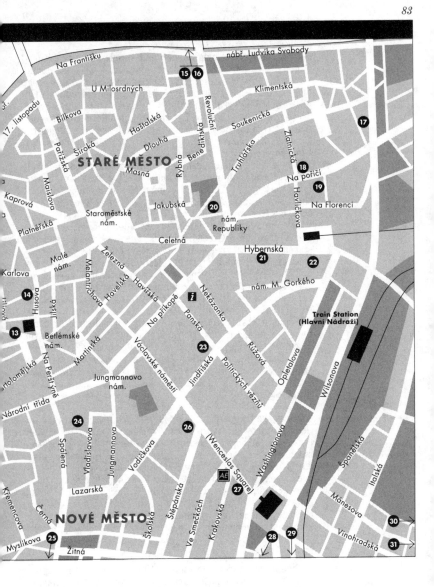

schnitzel at Demínka makes a fine afternoon snack. *Škrétova 1, Prague 2, tel. 02/228595. No credit cards.*

Na Zvonařce. This bright beer hall supplements traditional Czech dishes—mostly pork, beer, and pork—with some innovative Czech and international choices, all at unbeatably cheap prices. Noteworthy entrées include juicy fried chicken and English roast beef; fruit dumplings for dessert are a rare treat. The service may be slow, but that simply allows time to commune with a tankard of ale on the outside terrace during the summer. *Šafaříkova 1, Prague 2, tel. 02/691–1311. Reservations advised. No credit cards.*

★ **U Koleje.** This popular, laid-back pub is suitable for the whole family. Besides offering excellent beers, U Koleje serves satisfying pork and beef dishes. During peak hours you may have to share a table. *Slavíkova 24, Prague 2, tel. 02/6274163. Reservations advised. No credit cards.*

U Zlatého Tygra. This impossibly crowded pub is the last of a breed of authentic Czech beer halls. The heavy smoke and cold stares from locals preclude a long stay, but don't be deterred from enjoying fine beer and typical pub stables like the ham-and-cheese plate. Befitting a traditional beer hall, the service is surly and reservations are unheard of, and the doors do not open until 3 PM. *Husova 17, Staré Město, tel. 02/265219. No credit cards. Closed Sun.*

V Krakovské. At this clean, proper pub that is close to the major tourist sights, the food is traditional and hearty; this is the place to try Bohemian duck, washed down with a dark beer from Domažlice in western Bohemia. *Krakovská 20, Nové Město, tel. 02/261537. Reservations advised. No credit cards.*

Lodging

Visitors are frequently disappointed by the city's lodging options. Hotel owners were quick to raise prices after 1989, when tourists first began flocking to Prague, but they have been much, much slower in raising their facilities to Western standards. In most of the Very Expensive and Expensive hotels, you can expect to find a restaurant and an exchange bureau on or near the premises. Bills are paid in Czech crowns, though some hotels still insist that you pay in hard (that is, Western) currency; be certain to inquire *before* making a reservation. During the summer season reservations are absolutely imperative; the remainder of the year they are sincerely recommended.

A cheaper and often more interesting alternative to Prague's generally mediocre hotels are private rooms and apartments. Prague is full of travel agencies offering such accommodations; the only drawback is that you may have to sacrifice a little privacy. The best room-finding service is probably **AVE** (tel. 02/236–2560, fax 02/236–2956), with offices in the main train station (Hlavní nádraží) and at Holešovice station (Nádraží Holešovice). Both offices are open daily from 7 AM to 10:30 PM. Prices start at around $15 per person per night. Insist on a room in the city center, however, or you may find yourself in a dreary, far-flung suburb. Other helpful room-finding agencies include **Hello Ltd.** (Senovázné nám. 3, Nové Město, tel. 02/224283), **City of Prague Accommodation Service** (Haštalské nám., Staré Město, tel. 02/231–0202, fax 02/231–4076; open daily 8–8, until 10 in summer), and **Prague Suites Accommodation Service**

(Melantrichova 8, Staré Město). If all else fails, just take a walk through the Old Town: The number of places advertising "Accommodation" (often written in German as *Unterkunft* or *Zimmer Frei*) is astounding.

Highly recommended lodgings in each price category are indicated by a star ★.

Very Expensive

Diplomat. This sprawling complex opened in 1990 and is still regarded as the best business hotel in town. Even though it's in the suburbs, the Diplomat is convenient to the airport and, via the metro, to the city center. The modern rooms may not exude much character, but they are tastefully furnished and quite comfortable. The hotel staff are competent and many are bilingual. Guests have access to a pool, sauna, and fitness center. *Evropská 15, Prague 6, tel. 02/331–4111, fax 02/331–4215. 387 rooms with bath. Facilities: restaurant, bar, nightclub, pool, fitness center, sauna, conference room. AE, DC, MC, V.*

Palace. For the well-heeled, this is Prague's most coveted address—an art-nouveau town palace perched on a busy corner only a block from the very central Wenceslas Square. Renovated in 1989, the hotel's spacious, well-appointed rooms, each with a private white marble bathroom, are fitted in velvety pinks and greens cribbed straight from an Alfons Mucha print. Two rooms are set aside for disabled travelers. The ground-floor buffet boasts the city's finest salad bar. *Panská 12, Nové Město, tel. 02/235–9394, fax 02/235–9373. 125 rooms with bath. Facilities: 2 restaurants, café, bar, snack bar, satellite TV, minibars. AE, DC, MC, V.*

Paříž. The smallish rooms hardly justify the high price, yet the hotel's unique art-nouveau facade and its excellent location near the Old Town's Powder Tower keep the occupancy rate near 99%. (The apathetic staff sours the mood only slightly.) Ask for a room away from the deceptively peaceful street. *U Obecního domů 1, Staré Město, tel. 02/236–0820, fax 02/236–7448. 86 rooms with bath. Facilities: restaurant, café. AE, DC, MC, V.*

★ **Pension U Raka.** This private guest house offers the peace and coziness of an Alpine lodge, plus a superb location on the ancient, winding streets of Nový Svět, just behind the Loretan Church and a five-minute walk from Prague Castle. The dark wood building has only five rooms, but if you can get a reservation (try at least a month in advance), you will gain a wonderful base for exploring Prague. *Černínská ul. 10/93, tel. 02/351453, fax 02/353074. 5 rooms. No credit cards.*

Expensive

City Hotel Morán. This 19th-century town house was tastefully renovated in 1992; now the lobby and public areas are bright and inviting, made over in an updated Jugendstil style. The modern if slightly bland rooms are a cut above the Prague standard for convenience and cleanliness; ask for one on the sixth floor for a good view of Prague Castle. A hearty Sunday brunch is served in the ground-floor restaurant. *Na Moráni 15, Prague 2, tel. 02/294251, fax 02/297533. 53 rooms, most with bath. Facilities: restaurant, bar. AE, DC, MC, V.*

Meteor Plaza. This popular Old Town hotel, operated by the Best Western chain, combines the best of New World convenience and Old World charm (Empress Maria Theresa's son, Joseph, stayed here when he was passing through in the 18th century). The setting is ideal: a newly renovated, Baroque building that is only five minutes by foot from downtown. There is a good, if touristy, in-house wine cellar. *Hybernska 6, Nové Město, tel. 02/235–8517, fax 02/224715. 86 rooms with bath. Facilities: restaurant, business center, terrace. AE, DC, MC, V.*

Tří Pštrosů. The location could not be better—a romantic corner in the Malá Strana only a stone's throw from the river and the Charles Bridge. The airy rooms, dating back 300 years, still have their original oak-beamed ceilings and antique furniture; many also have views over the river. An excellent in-house restaurant serves traditional Czech dishes to guests and nonguests alike. *Dražického nám. 12, Malá Strana, tel. 02/536151, fax 02/536155. 18 rooms with bath. Facilities: restaurant. AE, DC, MC, V.*

★ **U Páva.** This newly renovated, neoclassical inn, set on a quiet gas-lit street in Malá Strana, offers upstairs suites that afford an unforgettable view of Prague Castle. Best of all, the U Páva is small and intimate—the perfect escape for those who've had their fill of cement high-rise resorts. The staff is courteous and helpful while the reception and public areas are elegant and discreet. *U lužického semináře 106, Malá Strana, tel. 02/532251, fax 02/533379. 11 rooms with bath. Facilities: restaurant, wine bar. AE, DC, MC, V.*

Moderate **Axa.** Funky and functional, this modernist high rise, built in 1932, was a mainstay of the budget-hotel crowd until a recent reconstruction forced substantial price hikes. The rooms, now with color television sets and modern plumbing, are certainly improved; however, the lobby and public areas look decidedly tacky, with plastic flowers and glaring lights. *Na poříčí 40, tel. 02/232–4467, fax 02/232–2172. 133 rooms, most with bath. Facilities: restaurant, bar, nightclub. No credit cards.*

Harmony. This is one of the newly renovated, formerly state-owned standbys. The stern 1930s facade clashes with the bright, "nouveau riche" 1990s interior, but cheerful receptionists and big, clean rooms compensate for the aesthetic flaws. Ask for a room away from the bustle of one of Prague's busiest streets. *Na poříčí 31, tel. 02/232–0016, fax 02/231–0009. 60 rooms with bath. Facilities: restaurant, snack bar. AE, DC, MC, V.*

★ **Kampa.** This early Baroque armory turned hotel is tucked away on a leafy corner just south of Malá Strana. The rooms are clean, if sparse, though the bucolic setting makes up for any discomforts. Note the late-Gothic vaulting in the massive dining room. *Všehrdova 16, Prague 1, tel. 02/539045, fax 02/532815. 85 rooms with bath. Facilities: restaurant, café. AE, DC, MC, V.*

Opera. Once the hospice of choice for divas performing at the nearby State Theater, the Opera greatly declined under the Communists. New owners, however, are working hard to restore the hotel's former luster. Until then, the clean (but smallish) rooms, friendly staff, and fin-de-siècle charm are still reason enough to recommend it. *Těšnov 13, tel. 02/231–5609, fax 02/231–1477. 66 rooms with bath. Facilities: restaurant, snack bar. AE, DC, MC, V.*

Inexpensive **Apollo.** This is a standard, no-frills, square-box hotel where clean rooms come at a fair price. Its primary flaw is its location, roughly 20 minutes by metro or bus from the city center. *Kubišova 23, tel. 02/842108, fax 02/845776. Metro Holešovice, then tram No. 5 or 17 to Hercovka. 32 rooms with bath or shower. No credit cards.*

Hybernia. The dull appearance of this train-station flophouse hardly suggests that it is actually a respectably clean, secure hotel. The rooms are of the two-bed-and-a-table variety but are perfectly adequate for short stays. The location, next to Masarykovo train station and a short walk from the main station, is excellent for the money. *Hybernska 24, tel. 02/220431, fax 02/222204. 70 rooms, some with bath. Facilities: restaurant, bar, lounge. No credit cards.*

★ **Pension Louda.** The friendly owners of this family-run guest house, set in a suburb roughly 20 minutes by tram from the city center, go out of their way to make you feel welcome. The large, spotless rooms are an unbelievable bargain, and the hilltop location offers a stunning view of greater Prague. *Kubišova 10, Prague 8; tel. 02/843302. Take tram No. 5 or 17 (Hercovka station) from metro Holešovice. 9 rooms. No credit cards.*

The Arts and Nightlife

The Arts Prague's cultural flair is legendary, though performances are usually booked far in advance by all sorts of Praguers. The concierge at your hotel may be able to reserve tickets for you. Otherwise, for the cheapest tickets, go directly to the theater box office a few days in advance or immediately before a performance. **Bohemia Ticket International** (Na příkopě 16, tel. 02/228738, and Wenceslas Square 25, tel. 02/260333) sells tickets for major cultural events at semi-inflated prices. Tickets also can be purchased at **American Express** (*see* Important Addresses and Numbers, *above*).

For details of cultural events look to the English-language newspapers *The Prague Post* and *Prognosis*, or to the monthly English-language *Prague Guide*, available at hotels and tourist offices.

Film If a film was made in the United States or Britain, the chances are good that it will be shown with Czech subtitles rather than dubbed. (Film titles, however, are usually translated into Czech, so your only clue as to the movie's country of origin may be the poster used in advertisements.) Popular cinemas include **Alfa** (Václavské nám. 26, tel. 02/220724), **Blaník** (Václavské nám. 56, tel. 02/235–2162), **Hvězda** (Václavské nám. 38, tel. 02/229187), **Paříž** (Václavské nám. 22), **Sevastopol** (Na příkopě 31, tel. 02/264328), and **Svetozor** (Vodičkova ul. 39, tel. 02/263616). Prague's English-language newspapers carry film reviews and full timetables.

Music Classical concerts are held all over the city throughout the year. The best venues are the resplendent art-nouveau **Obecní dům** (Smetana Hall, Nám. Republiky 5, tel. 02/232–5858), home of the Prague Symphony Orchestra, and **Dvořák Hall** (in the Rudolfinum, nám. Jana Palacha), home of the Czech Philharmonic. Performances also are held regularly in the **National Gallery** in Prague Castle, in the **gardens** below the castle (where the music comes with a view), and at the **National Museum** on Wenceslas Square. Concerts at the **Villa Bertramka** (Mozartova 169, Smíchov, tel. 02/543893) emphasize the music of Mozart and his contemporaries (*see* Off the Beaten Track, *above*).

Fans of organ music will be delighted by the number of recitals held in Prague's historic halls and churches. Popular programs are offered at **St. Vitus Cathedral** in Hradčany, **U Křížovníků** near the Charles Bridge, the **Church of St. Nicholas** in Malá

Strana, and **St. James's Church** on Malá Štupartská in the Old Town, where the organ plays amid a complement of Baroque statuary.

Opera and Ballet The Czech Republic has a strong operatic tradition, and performances at the **Národní divadlo** (National Theater, Národní třída 2, tel. 02/205364) and the **Statní Opera Praha** (State Opera House, Wilsonova 4, tel. 02/265353), at the top of Wenceslas Square, can be excellent. Operas are usually sung in Czech, and the repertoire is heavy on the national composers Janáček, Dvořák, and Smetana. The historic **Stavovské divadlo** (Estates' Theater, Ovocný tř. 6, Staré Město, tel. 02/265353), where *Don Giovanni* debuted in the 18th century, plays host to a mix of operas and dramatic works. The National and State theaters also occasionally have ballets.

Theater Most dramatic works are performed in Czech. For those who find the Czech language a vast mystery, try the excellent **Black Theater** mime group, based at Václav Havel's old theater, the **Divadlo na Zábradlí** (Theater on the Balustrade, Anenské nám. 5, Staré Město, tel. 02/236–0449). Performances usually begin at 7 or 7:30. Several English-language theater groups operate sporadically in Prague during the tourist season; pick up a copy of *The Prague Post* or *Prognosis* for complete listings.

Nightlife Bars or lounges are not traditional Prague fixtures; social life,
Pubs, Bars, of the drinking variety, usually takes place in pubs (*pivnici*),
and Lounges which are liberally sprinkled throughout the city's neighborhoods. Tourists are welcome to join in the evening ritual of sitting around large tables and talking, smoking, and drinking beer in enormous quantities. Before venturing in, however, it's best to familiarize yourself with a few points of pub etiquette: First, always ask before sitting down if a chair is free. To order a beer (*pivo*), do not wave the waiter down or shout across the room; he will usually assume you want beer and bring it over to you without asking. He will also bring subsequent rounds to the table without asking. To refuse, just shake your head or say no thanks. At the end of the evening, usually around 10:30 or 11:00, the waiter will come to tally up the bill. Some of the most popular pubs in the city center include **U Medvídků** (Na Perštýně 7, tel. 02/235–8904), **U Vejvodů** (Jilská 4, tel. 02/220686), and **U Zlatého Tygra** (Husova ul. 17, no phone). All can get impossibly crowded.

An alternative to Prague's pubs are the few American-style bars that have sprung up in the past year. **Jo's Bar** (Malostranské nám. 7), one of the best and a haven for younger expats, serves bottled beer, mixed drinks, and good Mexican food. The major hotels also run their own bars and nightclubs. The **Piano Bar** (Hotel Palace, Panská ul. 12) is the most pleasant of the lot; jacket and tie are suggested.

Cabaret A multimedia extravaganza with actors, mime, and film is performed at **Laterna Magika** (Národní třída 4, Nové Město, tel. 02/266260). Tickets range from 50 Kč. to 400 Kč. and sell out fast; the box office is open Monday 10–noon and 2–6 and Tuesday–Saturday 2–6. Noted Czech mime Boris Hybner performs nightly at 8 PM at the **Gag Studio** in the New Town (Národní 25, Nové Město, tel. 02/265436). "Bohemian Fantasy," which performs May through October every Monday, Wednesday, Friday, and Saturday evening at the **Lucerna Palace** (Štěpánská ul. 61, tel. 02/235–0909), is a glitzy, Las Vegas-style sendup of

Bohemian history. Tickets cost $30 and can be purchased at the Lucerna box office. For adult stage entertainment (except some nudity) try the **Lucerna Bar** (Štěpánská ul. 61, Nové Město, tel. 02/235–0888) or **Varieté Praga** (Vodičkova ul. 30, Nové Město, tel. 02/235–0861).

Casinos Hard-currency casinos operate nightly in the **Forum, Ambassador, Palace,** and **Jalta** hotels (*see* Lodging, *above*). The action begins around 6 PM and lasts into the wee hours of the morning.

Discos Dance clubs come and go with predictable regularity. The current favorite is **Radost FX** (Bělehradská 120, Prague 2, tel. 02/251210), featuring imported DJs playing the latest dance music and technopop from London. The café on the ground floor is open all night and serves wholesome vegetarian food. Two popular discos for dancing the night away with fellow tourists include **Lavká** (Lavká 1, Staré Město, near the Charles Bridge) and the **Classic Club** (Pařížsá 4, Staré Město, tel. 02/2319473). The former features open-air dancing by the bridge on summer nights. Wenceslas Square is also packed with discos; the best strategy for finding the right place is simply to stroll the square and size up the crowds and the music.

Jazz Clubs Jazz gained notoriety as a subtle form of protest under the Communists, and the city still has some great jazz clubs, featuring everything from swing to blues and modern. **Reduta** (Národní 20, tel. 02/203825) features a full program of local and international musicians. **Agharta** (Krakovská 5, tel. 02/224558) offers a variety of jazz acts in an intimate café/nightclub atmosphere. Music starts around 8 PM, but come earlier to get a seat. Check posters around town or any of the English-language newspapers for current listings.

Rock Clubs Prague's rock scene is thriving. Hard-rock enthusiasts should check out the **Rock Café** (Národní 20, tel. 02/203825) or **Strahov 007** (near Strahov Stadium; take bus No. 218 two stops from Anděl metro station). The trendiest underground spots are **Borát** (Újezd 18, Malá Strana, tel. 02/538362), one of Václav Havel's former hangouts; and **RC Bunkr** (Lodecká 2, Nové Město). The **Malostranska Beseda** (Malostranské nám. 21, tel. 02/539024) and the **Belmondo Revival Club** (Slavíkova 22, Prague 2, tel. 02/7551081) are dependable bets for sometimes bizarre, but always good, musical acts from around the country.

Bohemia

The turbulent history of the Czechs has indelibly marked the gentle rolling landscape of Bohemia. With Prague at its heart, and Germany and the former Austrian empire on its mountainous borders, the kingdom of Bohemia was for centuries buffeted by religious and national conflicts, invasions, and wars. But its position also meant that Bohemia benefited from the cultural wealth and diversity of Central Europe. The result is a glorious array of castles, walled cities, and spa towns, boasting a past that would be difficult to match in any other provincial area of Central Europe.

Southern Bohemia is particularly famous for its involvement in the Hussite religious wars of the 15th century, which revolved around the town of Tábor. But the area also has more than its fair share of well-preserved and stunning walled towns, built up through the ages by generations of the noble families of the day, who left behind layers of Gothic, Renaissance, and Baroque architecture (particularly notable in Český Krumlov). Farther north and an easy drive east of Prague is the old silver-mining town of Kutná Hora, once a rival to Prague for the royal residency.

Western Bohemia was, until World War II, the playground of Central Europe's rich and famous. Its three well-known spas, Karlovy Vary, Mariánské Lázně, and Františkový Lázně (better known by their German names: Karlsbad, Marienbad, and Franzensbad, respectively) were the annual haunts of everybody who was anybody—Johann Wolfgang von Goethe, Ludwig van Beethoven, Karl Marx, and England's King Edward VII, to name but a few. Although strictly "proletarianized" throughout the communist era, the spas still exude a nostalgic aura of a more elegant past and, unlike most of Bohemia, offer a basic tourist infrastructure that makes dining and lodging a pleasure.

Northern Bohemia is a paradox: While much of it was despoiled in the past 40 years by rampant industrialization, here and there you can still find areas of great natural beauty. Rolling hills, perfect for walking, guard the country's northern frontiers with Germany and Poland. Hikers and campers head for the Giant Mountains (Krkonoše) on the Polish border; this range is not so giant, actually, though it is very pretty. As you move toward the west, the interest is more historical, in an area where the influence of Germany was felt in less pleasant ways than in the spas. Most drastically affected was Terezín, better known as the infamous concentration camp Theresienstadt, where the Nazis converted the redbrick fortress town into a Jewish ghetto and prison camp during World War II.

Important Addresses and Numbers

Tourist Information Most major towns have a local or private information office, usually located in the central square and identified by a capital "I" on the facade. These offices are often good sources for maps and historical information and can usually help book hotel and private accommodation. Most are open during normal business hours, with limited hours on Saturdays (until noon), and are closed on Sundays and holidays.

Emergencies Police (tel. 158). Ambulance (tel. 155).

Late-Night Pharmacies Pharmacies take turns staying open late or on Sunday; for the latest information, consult the list posted on the front door of each pharmacy. For after-hours service, ring the bell; you will be served through a little hatch door.

Arriving and Departing by Plane

The only real option is to fly to Prague, from which it is quite easy to travel to any city in Bohemia by car, train, or bus.

Arriving and Departing by Car, Train, and Bus

Major trains from Munich and Nürnberg stop at Cheb and some of the spa towns. It is also an easy drive across the border from Bavaria on the E48 to Cheb, and from there to any of the spas. Several trains a day run from Vienna to Prague; most travel via

Třeboň and Tábor in southern Bohemia, although some make the trip by way of Brno (through Moravia). To drive from Vienna take the E49 from Gmünd. There is also a daily bus from Vienna to Karlovy Vary via Prague.

Getting Around

By Car Car travel affords the greatest ease and flexibility in this region. The major road from Prague south to Tábor and České Budějovice, although often crowded, is in relatively good shape. Exercise caution on smaller roads, many of which are poorly marked and maintained (and always have a good map or auto atlas handy). Most of the towns are very small and, depending on public transportation, may require you to schedule some overnight stays. Driving through Bohemia, motorists are rewarded with a particularly picturesque drive along the Labe (Elbe) River on the way to Střekov.

By Train Good, if slow, train service links all of the major towns west of Prague. The best stretches are from Františkovy Lázně to Plzeň and from Plzeň to Prague. The Prague–Karlovy Vary run takes longer than it should but has its own romantic charm. Note that most trains heading west to Germany (direction Nürnberg) stop at Mariánské Lázně. Most trains leave from Prague's Hlavní nádraží (main station), but be sure to check on the station if in doubt.

Benešov (Konopiště), Tábor, and Třeboň all lie along the major southern line in the direction of Vienna, and train service to these cities from Prague is frequent and comfortable. Good connections also exist from Prague to České Budějovice. For other destinations, you may have to combine the train and bus. Train connections in the north are spotty at best. Regular service connects Prague with Mělník and Ústí nad Labem, but to reach the other towns you'll have to resort to the bus.

By Bus All the major sights are reachable from Prague using ČSAD's dense bus network. Service between the towns, however, is far less frequent and will require some forethought. For information, consult schedules at local bus stations. The small letters or numbers beside the times indicate whether the bus runs on weekdays, holidays, and so on.

Guided Tours

Čedok (tel. 02/231–8255) offers several specialized tours covering the sights listed in the tours below. Tour "G-O" combines a trip to Lidice in northern Bohemia with a visit to the spa town of Karlovy Vary. The trip takes a full day and departs three times weekly. Other tours include visits to České Budějovice, Hluboka castle, Český Krumlov, Třeboň, Kutná Hora, and Český Šternberk. Čedok also offers a full-day excursion to the oldest glassworks in Central Europe, south of Prague. Prague departure points include the Čedok offices at Na Příkopě 20 and Bílkova ul. 6.

Several private companies also offer trips to Lidice and Terezín (Theresienstadt) in northern Bohemia. For the latter, try **Wittmann Tours** (tel. 02/231–2895). Bus tours leave from Prague's Jewish Town Hall (Maislova ul. 18) every Thursday and Sunday at 11 AM, returning at 6 PM (450 Kč. adults, 350 Kč. for students and children).

Highlights for First-Time Visitors

Český Krumlov (*see* Tour 1)
Karlovy Vary (*see* Tour 2)
Konopiště Castle (*see* Tour 1)
Lidice Museum (*see* Tour 3)
Mariánské Lázně (*see* Tour 2)
Mělník Castle (*see* Tour 3)
Rosenberg Castle (*see* Tour 1)
St. Barbara's Cathedral in Kutná Hora (*see* Tour 1)
Tábor (*see* Tour 1)
Terezín (*see* Tour 3)

Exploring Bohemia

Tour 1: *Numbers in the margin correspond to points of interest on the*
Southern Bohemia *Bohemia map.*

At one time Prague's chief rival in Bohemia for wealth and
❶ beauty, **Kutná Hora** lies about 70 kilometers (44 miles) east of
the capital. To get there from Prague, follow the signs along
Route 333 through the city's dusty eastern suburbs and little
resort towns, such as Říčany, on the outskirts. The approach to
Kutná Hora looks much as it has for centuries. The town's long
economic decline spared it the postwar construction that has
blighted the outskirts of so many other Czech cities.

While undeniably beautiful, with an intact collection of Gothic
and Baroque ruins, Kutná Hora can leave one feeling a bit melancholy. The town owes its illustrious past to silver, discovered
here in the 12th century. For some 400 years the mines were
worked with consummate efficiency, the wealth going to support grand projects throughout Bohemia. Charles IV used the
silver to finance his transformation of Prague from a market
town into the worthy capital of the Holy Roman Empire in the
14th century. As the silver began to run out in the 16th and 17th
centuries, however, Kutná Hora's importance faded. What remains is the paradox you see today: poor inhabitants dwarfed
by the splendors of the Middle Ages.

Forget the town center for a moment and walk to the **Chrám
svatej Barbory** (St. Barbara's Cathedral), a 10-minute stroll
from the main Palackého náměstí along Barborská ulice The approach to the cathedral, overlooking the river, is magnificent.
Statues line the road, and the Baroque houses vie for your attention. In the distance, the netted vaulting of the cathedral
resembles a large and magnificent tent more than a religious
center; the effect gives the cathedral a cheerier look than the
dignified Gothic towers of Prague. St. Barbara's is undoubted-
ly Kutná Hora's masterpiece. Built in the 14th and 15th centuries, it drew on the talents of the Peter Parler workshop as well
as other Gothic luminaries, such as Matthias Rejsek and
Benedikt Ried.

St. Barbara is the patron saint of miners, and silver-mining
themes dominate the interior. Gothic frescoes depict angels
carrying shields with mining symbols. The town's other major
occupation, coin production, can be seen in frescoes in the
Mintner's Chapel. A statue of a miner, donning the characteristic smock and dating from 1700, stands proudly in the nave.
But the main attraction of the interior is the vaulting itself, attributed to Ried (also responsible for the fabulous vaulting in

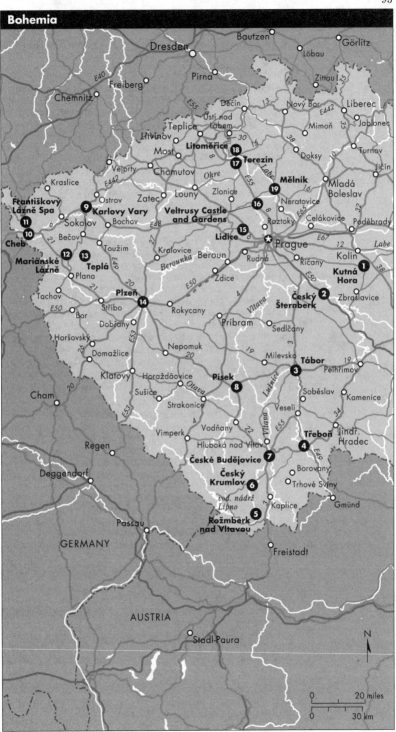

Prague Castle's Vladislav Hall), which carries the eye effortlessly upward. *Barborská ul. Admission: 20 Kč. Open Apr.–Oct., daily 10–4; irregular hours at other times of the year.*

The romantic view over the town from the cathedral area, marked by the 260-foot tower of the St. James Church, is impressive, and few modern buildings intrude. As you descend into town, the **Hradek** (Little Castle), on your right along Barborská ulice, was once part of the town's fortifications and now houses a museum of mining and coin production. *Barborská ul. Admission: 20 Kč. adults, 10 Kč. children. Open Apr.–Oct., daily 8–noon and 1–5.*

Time Out The **Café U Hradků** is a pleasant place to stop for refreshments or a light home-cooked meal. Lamps and furnishings from the 1920s add a period touch. *Barborská ul. 33, tel. 0327/4277. Open Tues.–Sun. 10–7. No credit cards.*

More interesting, however, is the old mint itself, the **Vlašský dvůr** (Italian Court), which you'll find easily by following the signs through town. Coins were first minted here in 1300, struck by Italian artisans brought in from Florence—hence the mint's odd name. It was here that the famed Prague groschen, one of the most widely circulated coins of the Middle Ages, was minted until 1726, and it was here that the Bohemian kings stayed on their frequent visits. Something of the court's former wealth can be glimpsed in the formal Gothic interiors of the chapel and tower rooms. A **coin museum** is open in season where you can see the small silvery groschen being struck and also buy replicas. Small wooden triptychs can be purchased in the chapel. *Havlíčkovo nám. Admission: 10 Kč. adults, 5 Kč. children. Open Apr.–Oct., daily 8–4.*

If the door to the **Chrám svatého Jakuba** (St. James Church) next door is open, peek inside. Originally a Gothic church dating from the early 1400s, the structure was almost entirely transformed into Baroque in the 17th and 18th centuries. The characteristic onion dome on the tower was added in 1737. The paintings on the wall include works of the best Baroque Czech masters; the *Pietà* is by the 17th-century painter Karel Škréta. Pause to admire the simple Gothic beauty of the 12-sided **kamenná kašna** (stone fountain) at the Rejskovo náměstí, just off Husova ulice. This unique work, some 500 years old, is supposedly the creation of Rejsek, one of the architects of St. Barbara's.

Before leaving the city, stop in the nearby suburb of Sedlec for a bone-chilling sight: namely, a chapel decorated with the bones of some 40,000 people. The All Saints' Cemetery Chapel, or "Bone Church," at the site of the former Sedlec Monastery, came into being in the 14th century, when development forced the clearing of a nearby graveyard. Monks of the Cistercian order came up with the bright idea of using the bones for decoration; the most recent creations date from the end of the last century. *Admission: 20 Kč., 10 Kč. children. Open daily 9–noon and 2–4.*

Leave Kutná Hora via Route 337; at Uhlířské Janovice switch to Route 125 and then, a little farther on, to Route 111, which leads through gentle hills and pleasant countryside to the castle at **Český Šternberk**. At night, this 13th-century castle, last renovated in the 17th century, looks positively evil, occupying a forested knoll over the Sázava River. By daylight, the structure is less haunting but still impressive. Although the castle became the property of the Czechoslovak state following the Second World War, Count Šternberk (the former owner) was permitted to occupy it until his death in 1966 as a reward for not cowering to the occupying German forces. In season, you can tour some of the rooms fitted out with period furniture (mostly Rococo); little of the early Gothic has survived the many renovations. *Admission: 20 Kč. adults, 10 Kč. children. Open May–Aug., Tues.–Sun. 8–5; Apr. and Oct., Sat. and Sun. 9–4; Sept., Tues.–Sun. 9–5.*

Given its remote location, Český Šternberk is ill-equipped for a meal or an overnight stay. Instead, continue on to the superior facilities of **Konopiště** (via the industrial town of Benešov) some 24 kilometers (15 miles) away. Konopiště is best known for its 14th-century castle, which served six centuries later as the residence of the former heir to the Austrian crown, Franz Ferdinand d'Este. Scorned by the Austrian nobility for having married a commoner, Franz Ferdinand wanted an impressive summer residence to win back the envy of his peers, and he spared no expense in restoring the castle to its original Gothic form, filling its 82 rooms with outlandish paintings, statues, and curiosities. Franz Ferdinand's dream came to a fateful end in 1914 when he was assassinated at Sarajevo, an event that precipitated World War I. The Austrian defeat in the war ultimately led to the fall of the Habsburgs. Ironically, the destiny of the Austrian empire had been sealed at the castle a month before the assassination, when Austrian kaiser Franz Joseph I met with Germany's kaiser Wilhelm II and agreed to join forces with him in the event of war.

Time Out	The little cabin restaurant **Stodola** (tel. 0301/25071), next to the Konopiště Motel (*see* Lodging, *below*) serves excellent grilled meats, chicken, and fish in a traditional setting. The live folk music in the evenings is romantic rather than obtrusive; the wines and service are excellent.

To visit the castle, start from the Konopiště Motel, located about a kilometer (half-mile) off of Route 3 (in the direction of Tábor; follow the signs), and walk straight for about 2 kilometers (a mile) along the trail through the woods. Before long, the rounded, neo-Gothic towers appear through the trees, and you reach the formal garden with its almost mystical circle of classical statues. Built by the wealthy Beneschau family, the castle dates from around 1300 and for centuries served as a bastion of the nobility in their struggle for power with the king. In what must have been a great affront to royal authority, at the end of the 14th century, Catholic nobles actually captured the weak King Wenceslas (Václav) IV in Prague and held him prisoner in the smaller of the two rounded towers. To this day the tower is known affectionately as the Václavka. Several of the rooms, reflecting the archduke's extravagant taste and lifestyle, are open to the public during the summer months. A valuable collection of weapons from the 16th to 18th century can be seen in the Weapons Hall on the third floor. Less easy to miss are the hundreds of stuffed animals, rather macabre monuments to the archduke's obsession with hunting. *Admission: 20 Kč. adults, 10 Kč. children. Open Apr.–Oct., daily 9–4.*

❸ The next stop, **Tábor,** is an easy 40 kilometers (25 miles) down Route 3. It's hard to believe this dusty Czech town was built to receive Christ on his return to Earth in the Second Coming. But that's what the Hussites intended when they flocked here by the thousands in 1420 to construct a society modeled after the communities of the early Christians. Tábor's fascinating history is unique among Czech towns. It started out not as a mercantile or administrative center but as a combination utopia and fortress.

Following the execution of Jan Hus, a vociferous religious reformer who railed against the Catholic church and nobility, reform priests drawing on the support of poor workers and peasants took to the hills of southern Bohemia. These hilltop congregations soon grew into permanent settlements, wholly outside the feudal order. The most important settlement, located on the Lužnice River, became known in 1420 as Tábor. Tábor quickly evolved into the symbolic and spiritual center of the Hussites (now called Taborites) and, together with Prague, served as the bulwark of the reform movement.

The early 1420s in Tábor were heady days for religious reformers. Private property was denounced, and the many poor who made the pilgrimage to Tábor were required to leave their possessions at the town gates. Some sects rejected the doctrine of transubstantiation (the belief that the Eucharist becomes the body and blood of Christ), making Holy Communion into a bawdy, secular feast of bread and wine. Still other reformers considered themselves superior to Christ—who by dying had shown himself to be merely mortal. Few, however, felt obliged to work for a living, and the Taborites had to rely increasingly on raids on neighboring villages for survival.

War fever in Tábor at the time ran high, and the town became one of the focal points of the ensuing Hussite wars (1419–34), which pitted reformers against an array of foreign crusaders, Catholics, and noblemen. Under the brilliant military leadership of Jan Žižka, the Taborites enjoyed early successes, but the forces of the established church proved too mighty in the end. Žižka was killed in 1424, and the Hussite uprising ended at the rout of Lipany 10 years later. But even after the fall, many of the town's citizens resisted recatholicization. Fittingly, following the Battle of White Mountain in 1620 (the final defeat for the Czech Protestants), Tábor was the last city to succumb to the conquering Habsburgs.

Begin a walking tour of the town at the **Žižkovo náměstí** (Žižka Square), named for the gifted Hussite military leader. A large bronze statue of Žižka from the 19th century dominates the square, serving as a reminder of the town's fiery past. The stone tables in front of the Gothic Town Hall and the house at No. 6 date from the 15th century and were used by the Hussites to give daily Communion to the faithful. Follow the tiny streets around the square, which seemingly lead nowhere. They curve around, branch off, and then stop; few lead back to the main square. The confusing street plan was purposely laid in the 15th century to thwart incoming invasions.

The **Museum of the Hussite Movement,** just behind the Town Hall, documents the history of the reformers. Note the elaborate network of tunnels carved by the Hussites below the Old Town for protection in case of attack. *Křivkova ul. 31. Admis-*

sion: 20 Kč. adults, 10 Kč. children. Open Apr.–Oct., daily 9–4.

Leave the square along **Pražská ulice**, a main route to the newer part of town, and note the beautiful Renaissance facades from the 16th century. Turn right at Divadelní, and head to the Lužnice River to see the remaining walls and fortifications of the 15th century, irrefutable evidence of the town's vital function as a stronghold. The **Kotnov hrad** (Kotnov Castle), rising above the river in the distance to the right, dates from the 13th century and was part of the earliest fortifications. The large pond to the northeast of Tábor was created as a reservoir in 1492; since it was used for baptism, the fervent Taborites named the lake "Jordan."

From Tábor head due south for 26 kilometers (16 miles) along Route 3 to Veselí nad Lužnicí; and then drive 22 kilometers (14 miles) along picturesque Route 150 through a plethora of ponds ❹ to **Třeboň**, another jewel of a town with a far different historical heritage than Tábor's. Třeboň was settled in the 13th century by the Wittkowitzes (later called the Rosenbergs), once Bohemia's noblest family. From 1316 to the end of the 16th century, the dynasty dominated southern Bohemia. Their wealth was based on silver and real estate. Their official residence was 40 kilometers (25 miles) to the southwest, in Český Krumlov, but Třeboň was an important second residence and repository of the family archives.

Thanks to the Rosenberg family, this unlikely landlocked town has become the center of the Czech Republic's fishing industry. In the 15th and 16th centuries, the Rosenbergs peppered the countryside with 6,000 enormous ponds, partly to drain the land and partly to breed fish. Carp breeding is still big business, and if you are in the area in the late autumn you may be lucky enough to witness the great carp harvests, when tens of thousands of the glittering fish are netted. The largest pond, bearing the Rosenberg name, lies just north of Třeboň. The **Rybník Svět** (Svět Pond) is closest to town along the southern edge. Join the locals on a warm afternoon for a stroll along its banks and enjoy the mild breezes.

Begin a walking tour of Třeboň from the park outside the town walls, with the Svět Pond at your back. From here, the simple sgraffito Renaissance exterior of the castle, with its deep turrets, is highly impressive. The intact town walls, built in the 16th century, are some of the best in the Czech Republic. Continue along the park, turning left at the first of the three gates into town. An 18th-century brewery, still producing outstanding beer, is off to the right. Beer enjoys nearly as long a tradition here as in Plzeň or České Budějovice, having been brewed since 1379 as the redbrick tower proudly boasts. Continue straight ahead to arrive at the main square, with its familiar collection of arcaded Renaissance and Baroque houses. Look for the **Bílý Koníček** (Little White Horse), the best-preserved Renaissance house on the square, dating from 1544. The large rectangular gable on the roof is composed of numerous tiny towers.

The entrance to **Třeboň hrad** (Třeboň Castle) lies at the southwest corner of the square. From here, it looks plain and sober with its plain white walls, but the rooms (open to the public) are sumptuous re-creations of 16th-century life. The castle also houses a permanent exhibition of pond building. After passing out of the hands of the Rosenbergs, the castle eventually became the property of the Schwarzenberg family, who built their family tomb in a grand park across the other side of Svět Pond. It is now a monumental neo-Gothic destination for Sunday-afternoon picnickers. *Třeboň Castle. Admission: 20 Kč. adults, 10 Kč. children. Open Apr.–Oct., Tues.–Sun. 10–3:30.*

In the **Augustine monastery,** adjacent to the castle, stop to take a look at the famous **Altar of the Masters of Wittingau,** dating from the late-14th century. The altar was removed from the St. Giles Church (Chrám svatého Jiljí) on Husova třída in 1781. The paintings themselves, the most famous example of Bohemian Gothic art, are now in the National Gallery in Prague.

Time Out Before leaving Třeboň, sample some of the excellent local beer at the **Bílý Koníček** (tel. 0333/2248), now a modest hotel and restaurant on the square. You can also get a variety of nonalcoholic beverages as well as good local dishes at reasonable prices.

Drive south out of Třeboň along Route 155 in the direction of Borovany. From here you can continue straight to busy Route 3, which takes you down to Kaplice. A more scenic but time-consuming drive takes you down Route 157 via Trhové Sviny. The heavily forested countryside, regardless of the road you choose, is some of the most unspoiled in Bohemia. Don't be surprised to see deer grazing, unfazed by passing cars. Once you reach Route 3, proceed in the direction of Linz, turning off to the right just before the border crossing with Austria. Follow the signs in the direction of Vyšší Brod, and turn right at the sign to Rožmberk nad Vltavou.

❺ The little village of **Rožmberk nad Vltavou,** just a few kilometers from the former Iron Curtain, has been forgotten in the postwar years. The atmosphere is akin to that of a ghost town, especially at night with the darkened **Rosenberg hrad** (Rosenberg Castle) keeping lonely vigil atop the hill overlooking the Vltava River. A barely visible German sign, WIRTSCHAFT ZUM GOLDENEN BÄREN, on the battered facade of a beer hall across the bridge, adds to the feeling of abandonment, as if nothing has happened here in decades. Take a moment to enjoy the silence, and walk up the hill to the castle. The slender tower, the Jakobinka, dates from the 13th century, when the Rosenberg family built the original structure. Most of the exterior, however, is neo-Gothic from the last century. In the summer, you can tour some of the rooms, admiring the weapons and Bohemian paintings. From the castle gates, the Romanesque-Gothic church below, standing beside the lone figure of St. Christopher on the bridge, looks especially solemn. *Admission: 20 Kč. adults, 10 Kč. children. Open Apr.–Oct., daily 9–noon and 1–5.*

❻ Continue north along the pretty Vltava River for about 20 kilometers (13 miles) to **Český Krumlov,** the official residence of the Rosenbergs for some 300 years. Český Krumlov is an eye-opener: None of the surrounding towns or villages, with their open squares and mixtures of old and new buildings, will prepare you for the beauty of the Old Town. Here, the Vltava works its wonders as nowhere else but in Prague itself, swirling in a nearly complete circle around the town. Across the river stands the proud castle of the Rosenbergs, rivaling any in the country in size and splendor.

For the moment, Český Krumlov's beauty is still intact. The dilapidated buildings that lend the town its unique atmosphere remain untouched by developers. This, of course, has a negative side. In peak months, when visitors from Austria and Germany pack the streets, the few existing facilities for visitors are woefully overburdened. The town also lacks a decent restaurant (although the **Krumlovská pivnice** serves a tasty goulash). But overlook any minor inconveniences, and enjoy a rare, unspoiled trip through time. (Český Krumlov is also a good place for an overnight stay. The town has lots of private rooms and two older hotels, both rich in atmosphere, that provide a perfect complement to the town's splendors.)

Begin a tour of the Old Town from the main **Svornosti náměstí.** If you've booked a room at the Hotel Krumlov on the square, you can drive up the narrow Latrán and park in the square. Otherwise, park outside the town gates and walk. The square itself is disappointing; the arcades hide the richness of the buildings' architecture. The **Town Hall** at No. 1, built in 1580, is memorable for its Renaissance friezes and Gothic arcades. Tiny alleys fan out from the square in all directions. The **Horní ulice** begins just opposite the Hotel Krumlov. A quick visit to the **Městské Muzeum** (Museum of the City) on this street is a good way to familiarize yourself with the rise and fall of the Rosenberg dynasty. *Horní ul. 152. Admission: 20 Kč. adults, 10 Kč. children. Open Tues.–Fri. 10–noon and 12:30–6.*

Just opposite the museum at No. 154 are the Renaissance facades, complete with lively sgraffiti, of the former **Jesuit School**—now newly renovated as the luxurious Růže Hotel. Český Krumlov owes its abundance of Renaissance detailing to its location on the main trading routes to Italy and Bavaria—a perfect site for absorbing incoming fashions. The tower of the nearby late-Gothic **St. Vitus** church, built in the late 1400s, rises from its position on the Kostelní ulice to offset the larger, older tower of the castle across the river. The view over the Old Town and castle is at its most spectacular from here.

To get to **Krumlov hrad** (Krumlov Castle), make your way from St. Vitus to the main street, the **Radniční**, via either **Masná** or **Kostelní ulice**, both of which form a big ring around the square. Cross the peaceful Vltava and enter at one of two gates along the Latrán. The oldest and most striking part of the castle is the round 12th-century tower, renovated like the rest of the building in the 16th century to look something like a minaret, with its delicately arcaded Renaissance balcony. The tower is part of the old border fortifications, guarding the Bohemian frontiers from Austrian incursion.

As you enter the castle area, look into the old moats, where two playful brown bears now reside—unlikely to be of much help in protecting the castle from attack. In season, the castle rooms are open to the public. The Hall of Masks is the most impressive interior, with its richly detailed 18th-century frescoes. After proceeding through a series of courtyards, you come to a wonderfully romantic elevated passageway, with spectacular views of the huddled houses of the Old Town. The Austrian Expressionist painter Egon Schiele made Český Krumlov his home in the early years of this century and often painted this particular view over the river. He entitled his now famous Krumlov series *The Dead Town*. From the river down below, the elevated passageway is revealed in all its Renaissance glory as part of a network of tall arches, looking like a particularly elaborate Roman viaduct. Up on top runs a narrow three-storied residential block (still inhabited), dressed in gray-and-white Renaissance stripes. At the end of the passageway you come to the luxuriously appointed castle gardens (open only in summer). In the middle is an open-air theater, one of Bohemia's first such theaters and remarkable for its still-intact gold stage. Performances are held here in July and August. *Český Krumlov Castle. Admission: 30 Kč. adults, 20 Kč. children. Open May–Aug., Tues.–Sun. 8–noon and 1–5; Apr. and Oct., Tues.–Sun. 9–noon and 1–4; Sept., Tues.–Sun. 9–noon and 1–5.*

❼ From Český Krumlov, follow Route 159 and then Route 3 up to **České Budějovice,** an easy drive of some 22 kilometers (14 miles). After the glories of Český Krumlov, any other town would be a letdown—and České Budějovice, known as *Budweis* under the Habsburgs and famous primarily for its beer, is no exception. The major attraction of what is basically an industrial town is the enormously proportioned main square, lined with arcaded houses and worth an hour or two of wandering. To get a good view over the city, it's well worth climbing the 360 steps up to the Renaissance gallery of the **Černá Věž** (Black Tower) at the northeast corner of the square next to the St. Nicholas Cathedral. *Admission: 10 Kč. Open Tues.–Sun. 9–5.*

From České Budějovice, follow the signs to **Hluboká nad Vltavou** about 9 kilometers (6 miles) to the north, to one of the Czech Republic's most curious castles. Although the structure dates from the 13th century, what you see is pure 19th-century excess, perpetrated by the wealthy Schwarzenberg family as proof of their good taste. If you think you've seen it somewhere before, you're probably thinking of Windsor Castle near London, on which it was carefully modeled. Take a tour of the inside; 41 of the 140 rooms are open to the public. The rather pompous interior reflects the "no holds barred" tastes of the time, but many individual pieces are interesting in their own right. The wooden Renaissance ceiling in the large dining room was removed by the Schwarzenbergs from the castle at Český Krumlov and brought here in the 19th century. Look also for the beautiful late-Baroque bookshelves of the library, holding some 12,000 books. If your interest in Czech painting wasn't satisfied in Prague, have a look at the **Aleš Art Gallery** in the Riding Hall, featuring the works of southern Bohemian painters from the Middle Ages to the present. The collection is the second largest in Bohemia. *Admission to castle and gallery: 10 Kč. adults, 5 Kč. children. Open Apr.–Oct., daily 9–noon and 1–4 (until 5 PM May–Aug.).*

In summer the castle grounds make a nice place for a stroll or picnic. If you're in the mood for a more strenuous walk, follow the yellow trail signs 2 kilometers (1¼ miles) to the **Ohrada hunting lodge,** which houses a museum of hunting and fishing and also has a small zoo for children. *Open Apr.–Oct., daily 9–noon and 1–4; May–Aug. daily 1–5.*

From Hluboká nad Vltavou drive back in the direction of České Budějovice along Route 105, following the signs at the junction

8 with Route 20 to Vodňany and eventually **Písek**. The 50 kilometers (31 miles) to Písek can be covered comfortably in about an hour. If it weren't for Písek's 700-year-old **Gothic bridge**, peopled with Baroque statues, you could easily bypass the town and continue on to Prague. After the splendors of Český Krumlov or even Třeboň, Písek's main square is admittedly plain, despite its many handsome Renaissance and Baroque houses.

The bridge, a five-minute walk from the main square along Karlovo ulice, was commissioned in 1254 by Přemysl Otakar II, who sought a secure crossing over the difficult Otava River for his salt shipments from nearby Prachatice. Originally one of the five major Hussite strongholds, Písek stood at the center of one of the most important trade routes to the west, linking Prague to Passau and the rest of Bavaria as early as the 9th century. The saintly Baroque statues were not added until the 18th century.

Return to the town square and look for the 240-foot tower of the early Gothic **Mariánský chrám** (Church of Mary). Construction was started at about the time the bridge was built. The tower was completed in 1487 and got its Baroque dome in the mid-18th century. On the inside, look for the *Madonna from Písek*, a 14th-century Gothic altar painting. On a middle pillar is a rare series of early Gothic wall paintings dating from the end of the 13th century.

You can return to Prague from here via Route 20, turning north on Route 4 for the duration. If you've got room for still another castle, take a short detour at Route 121, about 10 kilometers (6 miles) north on Route 4, and head for **Zvíkov**. The castle, at the confluence of the Otava and Vltava rivers, is impressive for its authenticity. Unlike many other castles in Bohemia, Zvíkov survived the 18th and 19th centuries unrenovated and still looks just as it did 500 years ago. The side trip also brings you to the dams and man-made lakes of the Vltava, a major swimming and recreation area that stretches all the way back to Prague.

Tour 2: Western Bohemia From Prague, it's an easy two-hour drive due west on Route 6 to **Karlovy Vary**, better known outside the Czech Republic by **9** its German name, Karlsbad. The most famous Bohemian spa, it is named for Emperor Charles (Karl) IV, who allegedly happened upon the springs in 1358 during a hunting expedition. As the story goes, the emperor's hound—chasing a harried stag—fell into a boiling spring and was scalded. Charles had the water tested and, familiar with spas in Italy, ordered baths to be established in the village of Vary. The spa reached its heyday in the 19th century, when royalty came here from all over Europe for treatment. The long list of those who "took the cure" includes Goethe (no fewer than 13 times, according to a plaque on one house in the Old Town), Schiller, Beethoven, and Chopin. Even Karl Marx, when he wasn't decrying wealth and privilege, spent time at the resort and wrote some of *Das Kapital* here between 1874 and 1876.

The shabby streets of modern Karlovy Vary, though, are vivid reminders that those glory days are long over. Aside from a few superficial changes, the Communists made little new investment in the town for 40 years; many of the buildings are literally falling down behind their beautiful facades. Today, officials face the daunting tasks of financing the town's reconstruction and carving out a new role for Karlovy Vary, in an era when few people can afford to set aside weeks or months at a time for a leisurely cure. To raise some quick cash, many sanatoria have turned to offering short-term accommodations to foreign visitors (at rather expensive rates). It's even possible at some spas to receive "treatment," including carbon-dioxide baths, massage, and the ever-popular gas injections. For most visitors, though, it's enough simply to stroll the streets and parks and allow the eyes to feast awhile on the splendors of the past.

Whether you're arriving by bus, train, or car, your first view of the town on the approach from Prague will be of the ugly new section on the banks of the Ohře River. Don't despair: Continue along the main road—following the signs to the Grandhotel Pupp—until you reach the lovely main street of the older spa area, situated gently astride the banks of the little Teplá River. The walk from the New Town to the spa area is about 20 minutes; take a taxi if you're carrying a heavy load. The **Old Town** is still largely intact. Tall 19th-century houses, boasting decorative and often eccentric facades, line the spa's proud, if dilapidated, streets. Throughout you'll see colonnades full of the healthy and not-so-healthy sipping the spa's hot sulfuric water from odd pipe-shaped drinking cups. At night, the streets fill with steam escaping from cracks in the earth, giving the town a slightly macabre feel.

Karlovy Vary's jarringly modern **Yuri Gagarin Colonnade,** home of the **Vřídlo,** is the town's hottest and most dramatic spring. The Vřídlo is indeed unique, shooting its scalding water to a height of some 40 feet. Walk inside the arcade to watch the hundreds of patients here take the famed Karlsbad drinking cure. You'll recognize them promenading somnambulistically up and down, eyes glazed, clutching a drinking glass filled periodically at one of the five "sources." The waters are said to be especially effective against diseases of the digestive and urinary tract. They're also good for the gout-ridden (which probably explains the spa's former popularity with royals!). If you want to join the crowds and take a sip, you can buy your own cup with a spout at vendors located within the colonnade.

Leave the colonnade and walk in the direction of the New Town, past the wooden **Market Colonnade,** currently undergoing reconstruction. Continue down the winding street until you get to the **Main Colonnade.** This neo-Renaissance pillared hall, built in 1871–81, offers four springs bearing the romantic names of Rusalka, Libussa, Prince Wenceslas, and Millpond. If you continue on down the valley, you'll soon arrive at the very elegant **Park Colonnade,** a white, wrought-iron construction built in 1882 by the Viennese architectural duo of Fellner and Helmer, who sprinkled the Austro-Hungarian empire with many such edifices in the late-19th century and who also designed the town's theater (1886), a Market Colonnade (1883), and one of the old bathhouses (1895), now a casino (*see* Nightlife, *below*).

The 20th century emerges at its most disturbing a little farther along the valley across the river, in the form of the huge bunkerlike **Thermal Hotel,** built in the late 1960s. Although the building is a monstrosity, the view of Karlovy Vary from the rooftop pool is nothing short of spectacular. Even if you don't feel like a swim, it's worth taking the winding road up to the baths for the view. You can't miss the very imposing **Imperial**

Sanatorium in the distance, a perfect example of turn-of-the-century architecture, with its white facade and red-tower roof. The Imperial was once the haunt of Europe's wealthiest financiers. Under the Communists, though, the sanatorium was used to house visiting Soviet dignitaries—a gesture of "friendship" from the Czechoslovak government. The Imperial has recently reopened as a private hotel (*see* Lodging, *below*), but it will be many years before it can again assume its former role.

Return to the Main Colonnade by crossing over the little Gogol Bridge near the Hotel Otova. Here you'll see steps leading behind the colonnade, through a park, and finally emerging onto the steep road **Zámecký vrch.** Walk uphill until you come to the redbrick **Victorian Church,** once used by the local English community. A few blocks farther on, along Petra Velikeho street, you come to a splendiforous Russian Orthodox church, once visited by Czar Peter the Great. Return to the English church and take a sharp right uphill on the redbrick road. Then turn left onto a footpath through the woods, following the signs to **Jeleni Skok** (Stag's Leap). After a while you'll see steps leading up to a bronze statue of a deer towering over the cliffs, the symbol of Karlovy Vary. From here a winding path leads up to a little red **gazebo** (Altán Jeleni Skok), opening onto a fabulous panorama of the town.

Time Out Reward yourself for making the climb with a light meal at the nearby restaurant **Jeleni Skok.** You may have to pay an entrance fee if there is a live band (but you'll also get the opportunity to polka). If you don't want to walk up, you can drive from the church.

Take the steps down to the Marianská and enter the grounds of the **Grandhotel Pupp,** the former favorite of the Central European nobility and longtime rival of the Imperial. The Pupp's reputation was tarnished somewhat during the years of communist rule (the hotel was renamed the Moskva-Pupp), but the hotel's former grandeur is still in evidence. Even if you're not staying here, be sure to stroll around the impressive facilities and have a drink in the elegant cocktail bar.

Diagonally across from the Grandhotel Pupp, behind a little park, is the pompous Fellner and Helmer **Imperial Spa,** now known as **Lázně I** and housing the local casino. As you walk back into town along the river, you'll pass a variety of interesting stores, including the Moser glass store and the Elefant, one of the last of a dying breed of sophisticated coffeehouses in the Czech Republic. Across the river is the Fellner and Helmer theater. Continue on to the right of the Vřídlo, where we began the tour, and walk up the steps to the white **Kostel svatej Maří Magdaleny** (Church of Mary Magdalene). Designed by Kilian Dientzenhofer (architect of the two St. Nicholas churches in Prague), this church is the best of the few Baroque buildings still standing in Karlovy Vary.

Known for centuries by its German name of Eger, the old town ❿ of **Cheb** lies on the border with Germany, an easy 42-kilometer (26-mile) drive from Karlovy Vary along Route 6. The town has been a fixture of Bohemia since 1322 (when the king purchased the area from German merchants), but as you walk around the beautiful medieval square, it's difficult not to think you're in Germany. The tall merchants' houses surrounding the square, with their long, red-tiled sloping roofs dotted with windows like droopy eyelids, are more Germanic in style than anything else in Bohemia. You'll also hear a lot of German on the streets—but more from the many German visitors than the town's residents.

Germany took full possession of the town in 1938 under terms of the notorious Munich Pact. But, following World War II, virtually the entire German population was expelled, and the Czech name of Cheb was officially adopted. A more notorious German connection has emerged in the years following the 1989 revolution. Cheb has quickly become the unofficial center of prostitution for visiting Germans. Don't be startled to see young women, provocatively dressed, lining the highways and bus stops on the roads into town. Prostitution of this sort is illegal, and the police have been known to crack down periodically on the women and their customers.

Begin a tour of the town in the bustling central square, the **Náměstí Krále Jiřího z Poděbrad,** once a large market area but now more a promenade for visiting Germans. The statue in the middle, similar to the Roland statues you see throughout Bohemia and attesting to the town's royal privileges, represents the town hero, Wastel of Eger. Look carefully at his right foot, and you'll see a small man holding a sword and a head—this denotes that the town had its own judge and executioner.

Walk downhill from the square to see two rickety groups of timbered medieval buildings, 11 houses in all, divided by a narrow alley. The houses, forming the area known as the **Špalíček,** date from the 13th century and were home to many Jewish merchants. **Židovská ulice** (Jews' Street), running uphill to the left of the Špalíček, served as the actual center of the ghetto. Note the small alley running off to the left of Židovská. This calm street, seemingly inappropriately named **ulička Zavražděných** (Murderers' Lane), was the scene of an outrageous act of violence in 1350. Pressures had been building for some time between Jews and Christians. Incited by an anti-Semitic bishop, the townspeople finally chased the Jews into the street, closed off both ends, and massacred them. Only the name attests to the slaughter.

Time Out Cheb's main square abounds with cafés and little restaurants, all offering a fairly uniform menu of schnitzels and sauerbratens aimed at the visiting Germans. The **Kaverna Špalíček,** nestled in the Špalíček buildings, is one of the better choices and has the added advantage of a unique architectural setting.

History buffs, particularly those interested in the Habsburgs, will want to visit the **Chebský muzeum** (Cheb Museum) in the Pachelbel House, situated behind the Špalíček on the main square. It was in this house that the great general of the Thirty Years' War, Albrecht von Wallenstein (Valdštejn), was murdered in 1634 on the orders of his own emperor, the Habsburg Ferdinand II. According to legend, Wallenstein was on his way to the Saxon border to enlist support to fight the Swedes when his own officers barged into his room and stabbed him through the heart with a stave. The stark bedroom with its four-poster bed and dark-red velvet curtains has been left as it was in his memory. The museum is also interesting in its own right: It has a section on the history of Cheb and a collection of minerals (including one discovered by Goethe). *Špalíček. Admission: 15 Kč. adults, 10 Kč. children. Open Tues.–Sun. 8–noon and 1–4.*

In the early 1820s, Goethe often stayed in the **Gabler House,** on the corner of the square at the museum. He shared a passionate interest in excavation work with the town executioner, and they both worked on the excavation of the nearby extinct volcano Komorní Hůrka. In 1791 Germany's second most famous playwright, Friedrich Schiller, lived at No. 2, at the top of the square next to the "new" town hall, where he planned his famous *Wallenstein* trilogy.

If you follow the little street on the right side of the square at the Gabler House, you will quickly reach the plain but imposing **Kostel svatého Mikuláše** (St. Nicholas Church). Construction began in 1230, when the church belonged to the Order of the Teutonic Knights. You can still see Romanesque windows under the tower; renovations throughout the centuries added an impressive Gothic portal and a Baroque interior. Just inside the Gothic entrance is a wonderfully faded plaque commemorating the diamond jubilee of Habsburg emperor Franz Josef in 1908.

From here walk down the little alley on to the Kammená, and then turn left on to the Křižovnická. Follow the Hradní road up to the **Chebský hrad** (Cheb Castle), situated on a cliff overlooking the Elbe River. The castle was built in the late-12th century for Holy Roman Emperor Frederick Barbarossa. The square black tower was built with blocks of lava taken from the nearby Komorní Hůrka volcano; the redbrick walls were added in the 15th century. Inside the castle grounds is the carefully restored double-decker chapel, built in the 12th century. The rather dark ground floor, still in Romanesque style, was used by commoners. The bright ornate top floor, with pointed Gothic windows, was reserved for the emperor and his family and has a wooden bridge leading to the royal palace. *Hradní ul. Admission: 15 Kč. adults, 10 Kč. children. Open Apr.–Oct., daily 9–4 (until 6 in summer).*

⑪ From Cheb, it's a short drive to **Františkovy Lázně Spa,** only 6 kilometers (4 miles) away. If you're interested in seeing the **Komorní Hůrka volcano,** take the first left off of Route 21 from Cheb, or follow the red-marked footpath 3½ kilometers (2¼ miles) from Františkovy Lázně. The extinct volcano is now a tree-covered hill, but excavations on one side have laid bare the rock, and one tunnel is still open. Goethe instigated and took part in the excavations, and you can still barely make out a relief of the poet carved into the rock face.

Františkovy Lázně, or Franzensbad, the smallest of the three main Bohemian spas, isn't really in the same league as the other two (Karlovy Vary and Mariánské Lázně). Built on a more modest scale at the start of the 19th century, the town's ubiquitous Kaiser-yellow buildings weathered the communist occupation especially badly. Come here not so much to walk the once lovely gardens or to admire the faded elegance of the gently monumental Empire-style architecture but instead to bear witness to the effects of 40 years of wanton neglect. There is no town to speak of, just **Národní ulice,** the main street, which leads down into the spa park. The waters, whose healing properties were already known in the 16th century, are used primarily for curing infertility—hence the large number of young women wandering the grounds.

The most interesting sight in town may be the small **Spa Museum,** situated just off Národní ulice. There is a wonderful collection of spa antiques, including copper bathtubs and a turn-of-the-century exercise bike called a Velotrab. The guest books (*Kurbuch*) provide an insight into the cosmopolitan world of pre–World War I Central Europe. The book for 1812 contains the entry "Ludwig van Beethoven, composer from Vienna." *Ul. Doktora Pohoreckého 8. Admission: 15 Kč. adults, 10 Kč. children. Open weekends 9–noon and 2–5.*

Exploration of the spa itself should start on Národní ulice. Wander down through the street to the main spring, **Františkuv prameň,** under a little gazebo, filled with brass pipes. The colonnade to the left was decorated with a bust of Lenin that was replaced in 1990 by a memorial to the American liberation of the town in April 1945. Walk along the path to the left until you come to the **Lázeňská poliklinika,** where you can arrange for a day's spa treatment for around 350 Kč. The park surrounding the town is good for aimless wandering, interrupted by empty pedestals for discarded statues of historical figures no longer considered worthy of memorial.

Time Out Františkovy Lázně is blessed with some of Bohemia's best restaurants. For a cut above the average fare, try lunch or dinner in the restaurant of the **Hotel Slovan** (tel. 0166/942841).

---

⑫ Mariánské Lázně, about 40 minutes' drive from Františkový Lázně (via Cheb), best fulfills visitors' expectations of what a spa resort should be. It's far larger and better maintained than Františkovy Lázně and is greener and quieter than Karlovy Vary. This was the spa favored by Britain's Edward VII; Goethe and Chopin, among other luminaries, also repaired here frequently. Mark Twain, on a visit to the spa in 1892, labeled the town a "health factory" and couldn't get over how new everything looked. Indeed, at that time, everything was new. The sanatoria, all built at the middle of the last century in a harmonious neoclassical style, fan out impressively around an oblong, finely groomed park. Cure takers and curiosity seekers alike parade through the two stately colonnades, both placed near the top of the park. Buy a spouted drinking cup (available at the colonnades) and join the rest of the sippers taking the drinking cure. Be forewarned, though: The waters from the Rudolph, Ambrose, and Caroline springs, while harmless, all have a noticeable diuretic effect. For this reason, they're used extensively in treating disorders of the kidney and bladder. Several spa hotels offer more extensive treatment, including baths and massage, to visitors. Prices are usually reckoned in U.S. dollars or German marks. For more information, inquire at the main spa offices at Masarykova 22 (tel. 0165/2170, fax 0165/2982).

A stay in Mariánské Lázně, however, can be healthful even without special treatment. Special walking trails, of all levels of difficulty, surround the resort in all directions. The best advice is simply to put on comfortable shoes, buy a hiking map, and head out. One of the country's few golf courses lies 3 or 4 kilometers (5 or 6 miles) from town to the east. Hotels can also help to arrange special activities, such as tennis and horseback riding. For the less intrepid, a simple stroll around the gardens, with a few deep breaths of the town's famous air, is enough to restore a healthy sense of perspective.

It is worth making the 15-kilometer (10-mile) detour to the little town of **Teplá** and its 800-year-old monastery, which once played an important role in christianizing pagan Central Europe. If you don't have a car, a special bus departs daily in season from Mariánské Lázně (inquire at the information office in front of the Hotel Excelsior). The sprawling monastery, founded by the Premonstratensian order of France in 1193 (the same order that established Prague's Strahov monastery), once controlled the farms and forests in these parts for miles around. The order even owned the spa facilities at Mariánské Lázně and until 1942 used the proceeds from the spas to cover operating expenses. The complex you see before you today, however, betrays none of this earlier prosperity. Over the centuries, the monastery was plundered dozens of times during wars and upheavals, but history reserved its severest blow for the night of April 13, 1950, when security forces employed by the Communists raided the grounds and imprisoned the brothers. The monastery's property was given over to the Czechoslovak army, and for the next 28 years the buildings were used as barracks to house soldiers. In 1991, the government returned the monastery buildings and immediate grounds (but not the original land holdings) to the order, and the brothers began the arduous task of picking up the pieces—physically and spiritually.

The most important building on the grounds from an architectural point of view is the Romanesque **basilica** (1197), with its unique triple nave. The rest of the monastery complex was originally Romanesque, but it was rebuilt in 1720 by Baroque architect K. I. Dientzenhofer. There are several wall and ceiling paintings of interest here, as well as some good sculpture. The most valuable collection is in the **Nová knihovna** (New Library), where you will find illuminated hymnals and rare Czech and foreign manuscripts, including a German translation of the New Testament that predates Luther's by some 100 years. Tours of the church and library are given daily in German at 1 PM (English notes are available). At press time, the monastery was also preparing to offer short-term accommodations to visitors (inquire directly at the monastery offices on the grounds). *Klášter. Admission: 20 Kč. Open daily 9–noon and 1–4.*

The sprawling industrial city of **Plzeň** is hardly a tourist mecca, but it's worth stopping off for an hour or two on the way back to Prague. There are two sights of particular interest to beer fanatics. The first is the **Pilsner-Urquell brewery,** located to the east of the city near the railway station. Group tours of the 19th-century redbrick building are offered daily at 12:30 PM, during which you can taste the valuable brew, exported around the world. The beer was created in 1842 using the excellent Plzeň water, a special malt fermented on the premises, and hops grown in the region around Žatec. *U Prazdroje, tel. 019/2164. Admission: 60 Kč.*

Time Out   You can continue drinking and find some traditional, cheap grub at the large **Na Stilce** beer hall just inside the brewery gates. The pub is open daily from 10 AM to 11 PM.

The second stop on the beer tour is the **Pivovarské muzeum** (Brewery Museum), located in a late-Gothic malthouse one block northeast of the main square. *Veleslavinova ul. 6. Admission: 10 Kč. adults, 5 Kč. children. Open Tues.–Sun. 10–6.*

The city's architectural attractions center on the main square, **náměstí Republiky,** dominated by the enormous Gothic **Chrám svatého Bartoloměja** (Church of St. Bartholemew). Both the square and the church towers hold size records, the former being the largest in Bohemia and the latter, at 102 meters (335 feet), the highest in the Czech Republic. The church was begun in 1297 and completed almost 200 years later. Around the square, mixed in with its good selection of stores, are a variety of other architectural jewels, including the town hall, adorned with sgraffiti and built in Renaissance style by Italian architects during the town's heyday in the 16th century.

Tour 3: Northern Bohemia Nowhere else in the Czech Republic have modern history and postwar industrialization conspired to alter the landscape as severely as in northern Bohemia. The hilly land to the north of Prague, along the Labe (Elbe) River, has always been regarded as border country with Germany, and you needn't drive too far to reach the Sudetenland, the infamous German-speaking border area that was ceded to Hitler in 1938. Indeed, the landscape here is riddled with the tragic remains of the Nazi occupation of the Czech lands from 1939 to 1945.

Leave Prague on Route 7 (the road to Ruzyně Airport), and head in the direction of Slaný. After about 18 kilometers (11 ⑮ miles), turn off at the **Lidice** exit and follow the country road for 3 kilometers (1¾ miles) straight through the little town to the **Lidice museum and monument,** where you'll find a large parking lot. In front of you is the museum area. The empty field to the right, with a large cross at the bottom, is where the town of Lidice stood until 1942, when it was viciously razed by the Nazis in retribution for the assassination of a German leader.

The Lidice story really begins with the notorious Munich Pact of 1938, according to which the leaders of Great Britain and France permitted Hitler to occupy the largely German-speaking border regions of Czechoslovakia (the so-called Sudetenland). Less than a year later, in March 1939, Hitler used his forward position to occupy the whole of Bohemia and Moravia, making the area into a protectorate of the German Reich. To guard his new possessions, Hitler appointed ruthless Nazi Reinhard Heydrich as Reichsprotektor. Heydrich immediately implemented a campaign of terror against Jews and intellectuals while currying favor with average Czechs by raising rations and wages. As a result, the Czechoslovak army-in-exile, based in Great Britain, soon began planning Heydrich's assassination. In the spring of 1942 a small band of parachutists was flown in to carry out the task.

The assassination attempt took place just north of Prague on May 27, 1942, and Heydrich died of injuries on June 4. Hitler immediately ordered that the little mining town of Lidice, west of Prague, be "removed from the face of the earth," since it was alleged (although later found untrue) that some of the assassins had been sheltered by villagers there. On the night of June 9, a Gestapo unit entered Lidice, shot the entire adult male population (199 men), and sent the 196 women to the Ravensbruck concentration camp. The 103 children in the village were sent either to Germany to be "Aryanized" or to death camps. On June 10, the entire village was razed. The assassins and their accomplices were found a week later in the Orthodox Church of Sts. Cyril and Methodius in Prague's New Town, where they committed suicide after a shoot-out with Nazi militia.

The monument to these events is a sober place. The arcades are graphic in their depiction of the deportation and slaughter of the inhabitants. The museum itself is dedicated to those killed, with photographs of each person and a short description of his or her fate. You'll also find reproductions of the German documents ordering the village's destruction, including the Gestapo's chillingly bureaucratic reports on how the massacre was carried out and the peculiar problems encountered in Aryanizing the deported children. The exhibits highlighting the international response (a suburb of Chicago was even renamed for the town) are heartwarming. An absorbing 18-minute film in Czech (worthwhile even for non-Czech speakers) tells the Lidice story. *Ul. 10. června 1942. Admission: 20 Kč. adults, 10 Kč. children and students. Open daily 9–5.*

Lidice was rebuilt after the war on the initiative of a group of miners from Birmingham, England, who called their committee "Lidice Must Live." Between new Lidice and the museum is a rose garden with some 3,000 bushes sent from all over the world. The wooden cross in the field to the right of the museum, starkly decorated with barbed wire, marks the place in old Lidice where the men were executed. Small remains of brick walls are visible here, left over from the Gestapo's dynamite and bulldozer exercise. Still, Lidice is a sad town and not a place to linger.

Leaving Lidice, turn back onto Route 7 in the direction of Prague and take the exit at Tuchoměřice (second exit after Lidice), driving in the direction of Kralupy nad Vltavou. The winding lane takes you through rolling countryside to Route 240, which will bring you, after a further 11 kilometers (7 miles), to Kralupy, an industrial town better left unexplored. Drive through town, cross the Vltava River, and take a right

16 turn after a kilometer to **Veltrusy Castle and Gardens.** The Baroque splendor of Veltrusy Castle, vividly contrasting with Kralupy's ordinariness, is hidden in a carefully laid out English park full of old and rare trees and scattered with 18th-century architectural follies. The castle itself has been turned into a museum of the cosmopolitan lifestyle of the imperial aristocracy, displaying Japanese and Chinese porcelain, English chandeliers, and 16th-century tapestries from Brussels. *Admission: 20 Kč. adults, 10 Kč. children and students. Open May–Oct., Tues.–Sun. 10–5.*

From Veltrusy Castle you can walk the 2½ kilometers (1½ miles) by marked paths to **Nelahozeves,** the birthplace in 1841 of Antonín Dvořák, the Czech Republic's greatest composer. By car, the route is rather more circuitous: Turn right out of Veltrusy onto the highway and over the river, then make a sharp left back along the river to Nelahozeves. Dvořák's pretty corner house on the main road (No. 12), with its tidy windows and arches, has a small memorial museum. In Dvořák's time, the house was an inn run by his parents, and it was here that he learned to play the violin. *Admission free. Open Tues.–Thurs., Sat., and Sun. 9–noon and 2–5.*

For those not enamored of the spirit of Dvořák's youth, the main attraction in town is the brooding Renaissance **castle,** with its black-and-white sgraffito, once the residence of the powerful Lobkowitz family. The castle now houses an excellent collection of modern art. *Admission: 20 Kč. adults, 10 Kč. children and students. Open May–Oct., Tues.–Sun. 10–5.*

17 Drive back to Route 8 and continue north 36 kilometers (22 miles) to the old garrison town of **Terezín,** which gained notoriety under the Nazis as the nefarious Nazi concentration camp **Theresienstadt.** Theresienstadt is difficult to grasp at first. The Czechs have put up few signs to tell you what to see; the town's buildings, parks, and buses resemble those of any of a hundred other unremarkable places, built originally by the Austrians and now inhabited by Czechs. You could easily pass through it and never learn any of the town's dark secrets.

Part of the problem is that **Malá Pevnost** (Small Fortress), the actual prison and death camp, is located 2 kilometers (1¼ mile) south of Terezín. Visitors to the strange redbrick complex see the prison more or less as it was when the Nazis left it in 1945. Over the entrance to the main courtyard stands the cynical motto ARBEIT MACHT FREI (roughly, "Work Liberates"). Take a walk around the various rooms, still housing a sad collection of rusty bedframes, sinks, and shower units. At the far end of the fortress, opposite the main entrance, is the special wing built by the Nazis when space became tight. The windowless cells are horrific; try going into one and closing the door—and then imagine being crammed in with 14 other people. In the center of the fortress is a museum and a room where films are shown. *Admission: 50 Kč. adults, 25 Kč. children and students. Open May–Sept., daily 8–6:30; Oct.–Apr., daily 8–4:30.*

During World War II, Terezín served as a detention center for thousands of Jews and was used by the Nazis as an elaborate prop in a nefarious propaganda ploy. The large barracks buildings around town, once used in the 18th and 19th centuries to house Austrian soldiers, became living quarters for thousands of interred Jews. But in 1942, to placate international public opinion, the Nazis cynically decided to transform the town into a showcase camp—to prove to the world their "benevolent" intentions toward the Jews. To give the place the image of a spa town, the streets were given new names such as Lake Street, Bath Street, and Park Street. Numerous elderly Jews from Germany were taken in by the deception and paid large sums of money to come to the new "retirement village." Just before the International Red Cross inspected the town in early 1944, Nazi authorities began a beautification campaign and painted the buildings, set up stores, laid out a park with benches in front of the Town Hall, and arranged for concerts and sports. The map just off the main square shows the town's street plan as the locations of various buildings between 1941 and 1945. The Jews here were able, with great difficulty, to establish a cultural life of their own under the limited "self-government" that was set up in the camp. The inmates created a library and a theater, and lectures and musical performances were given on a regular basis.

Once it was clear that the war was lost, however, the Nazis dropped any pretense and quickly stepped up transports of Jews to the Auschwitz death camp in Poland. Transports were not new to the ghetto; to keep the population at around 30,000, a train was sent off every few months or so "to the east" to make room for incoming groups. In the fall of 1944, these transports were increased to one every few days. In all, some 87,000 Jews were murdered in this way, and another 35,000 died from starvation or disease. The town's horrific story is told in words and pictures at the **Ghetto Museum,** located just off the central park in town. *Admission: 50 Kč. adults, 25 Kč. children and students. Open May–Sept., daily 8–6:30; Oct.–Apr., daily 8–4:30.*

For all its history, Terezín is no place for an extended stay. Locals have chosen not to highlight the town's role during the Nazi era, and hence little provision has been made for the visitor. Instead, continue the several kilometers along Route 15 to **⑱ Litoměřice.** Although it, too, lacks much in the way of modern facilities, Litoměřice is livelier and its history dates from the far less harrowing 13th, 14th, and 15th centuries.

Given the decrepit state of the houses and streets, it's hard to believe that in the 13th century Litoměřice was considered one of Bohemia's leading towns and a rival to Prague. Bypassed by the railroad and left to drift, the town is largely untouched by modern development. Even today, although the food industry has established several factories in the surrounding area, much of central Litoměřice is like a living museum.

The best way of getting a feel for Litoměřice is to start at the excellent **Městske Muzeum** (City Museum) on the corner of the main square and Dlouhá ulice in the building of the Old Town Hall. The entrance is under the Renaissance arcades. Unfortunately, the exhibits are described in Czech (with written commentary in German available from the ticket seller); but even without understanding the words, you'll find this museum is fascinating. Despite its position near the old border with Germany, Litoměřice was a Czech and Hussite stronghold, and one of the museum's treasures is the brightly colored, illuminated Bible depicting Hus's burning at the stake in Constance. Note also the golden chalice nearby, the old symbol of the Hussites. Farther on you come to an exquisite Renaissance pulpit and altar decorated with painted stone reliefs. On the second floor the most interesting exhibit is from the Nazi era, when Litoměřice became a part of Sudeten Germany and a border town of the German Reich, providing soldiers for nearby Theresienstadt. Although most of the Communist party's exhibits have been removed, this section still boasts a number of posters proclaiming the victory of the working class, unwittingly marking the slide from one totalitarian state to another. *Mirové nám. Admission: 10 Kč. adults, 5 Kč. children and students. Open Tues.–Sun. 10–noon and 1–4.*

After leaving the museum, stroll along the busy but decaying central square, which sports a range of architectural styles from Renaissance arcades to Baroque gables and a Gothic bell tower. The town's trademark, though, is the chalice-shaped tower at No. 7, the **Chalice House,** built in the 1580s for an Utraquist patrician. The Utraquists were moderate Hussites who believed that laymen should receive wine as well as bread in the sacrament of Holy Communion. On the left-hand corner of the Old Town Hall is a replica of a small and unusual Roland statue (the original is in the museum) on a high stone pedestal. These statues, found throughout Bohemia, signify that the town is a "royal free town" and due all of the usual privileges of such a distinction. This particular statue is unique in that, instead of showing the usual handsome knight, it depicts a hairy caveman wielding a club. Even in the 15th century, it seems, Czechs had a sense of humor.

Time Out For an ice cream, a fruit drink, or a cup of coffee, try the little standup **Atropic Cafe** next to the museum on the main square. Good beer and passable Czech food are served up daily in clean surroundings at the **Pivnice Kalich** (Lidická 9), a block from the main square.

The Baroque facade and interior of the **All Saints' Church,** to the right of the Town Hall, and **St. Jacob's Church,** farther down Dlouhá ulice, are the work of the 18th-century Italian master-builder Octavian Broggio. His most beautiful work, though, is the small **Kostel svatého Václava** (St. Wenceslas Chapel), squeezed into an unwieldy square to the north of town on the cathedral hill and now a Russian Orthodox church. **Dom svatého Štěpána** (St. Stephen's Cathedral), farther up the hill, is monumental but uninspired. Its one real treasure is a Lucas Cranach painting of St. Antonius—but unfortunately the cathedral door is often locked. There are also a number of paintings by the famed 17th-century Bohemian artist Karel Škréta.

Follow the Elbe River in the direction of the industrial town of Ústí nad Labem. The best route for views is Route 30 (accessed via Route 8 near Terezín): It passes through a long, unspoiled winding valley, packed in by surrounding hills, and has something of the look of a 16th-century landscape painting. As you near Ústí, your eyes are suddenly assaulted by the towering mass of **Střekov hrad** (Střekov Castle), perched precariously on huge cliffs, rising abruptly over the right bank. The fortress was built in 1319 by King Johann of Luxembourg to control the rebellious nobles of northern Bohemia. In the 16th century, it became the residence of Wenceslas of Lobkowitz, who rebuilt the castle in Renaissance style. The lonely ruins have served to inspire many German artists and poets, including Richard Wagner, who came here on a moonlit night in the summer of 1842. But if you arrive on a dark night, about the only classic that comes to mind is Mary Shelley's *Frankenstein*. Drive up to the castle by taking the first turnoff into Ústí and immediately turning left onto the bridge over the Elbe. Across the bridge, turn right and follow the signs.

From Střekov, continue on Route 261 through the picturesque hills of the Elbe banks back through Litoměřice and on to **Mělník,** 50 kilometers (31 miles) south. Park on the small streets just off the pretty but hard-to-find main square. Mělník is a lively town, known best perhaps as the source of the special "Ludmila" wine, the country's only decent wine not produced in southern Moravia. The town's **zámek,** a smallish castle a few blocks from the main square, majestically guards the confluence of the Elbe River with two arms of the Vltava. The view here is stunning, and the sunny hillsides are covered with vineyards. As the locals tell it, Emperor Charles IV was responsible for bringing wine production to the area. Having a good eye for favorable growing conditions, he encouraged vintners from Burgundy to come here and plant their vines.

So, you're getting away from it all.

Just make sure you can get back.

AT&T Access Numbers
Dial the number of the country you're in to reach AT&T.

*ANDORRA	19◇-0011	GERMANY**	0130-0010	*NETHERLANDS	06◇-022-9111
*AUSTRIA	022-903-011	*GREECE	00-800-1311	*NORWAY	050-12011
*BELGIUM	078-11-0010	*HUNGARY	00◇-800-01111	POLAND¹♦²	0◇010-480-0111
BULGARIA	00-1800-0010	*ICELAND	999-001	PORTUGAL¹	05017-1-288
CROATIA¹♦	99-38-0011	IRELAND	1-800-550-000	ROMANIA	01-800-4288
*CYPRUS	080-90010	ISRAEL	177-100-2727	*RUSSIA¹ (MOSCOW)	155-5042
CZECH REPUBLIC	00-420-00101	*ITALY	172-1011	SLOVAKIA	00-420-00101
*DENMARK	8001-0010	KENYA¹	0800-10	SPAIN	900-99-00-11
*EGYPT¹ (CAIRO)	510-0200	*LIECHTENSTEIN	155-00-11	*SWEDEN	020-795-611
*FINLAND	9800-100-10	LITHUANIA♦	8◇196	*SWITZERLAND	155-00-11
FRANCE	19◇-0011	LUXEMBOURG	0-800-0111	*TURKEY	9◇9-8001-2277
*GAMBIA	00111	*MALTA	0800-890-110	UK	0800-89-0011

Countries in bold face permit country-to-country calling in addition to calls to the U.S. *Public phones require deposit of coin or phone card.
**Western portion. Includes Berlin and Leipzig. ◇Await second dial tone. ¹May not be available from every phone. ♦ Not available from public phones. ²Dial "02" first, outside Cairo. ³Dial 010-480-0111 from major Warsaw hotels. ©1993 AT&T.

Here's a travel tip that will make it easy to call back to the States. Dial the access number for the country you're visiting and connect right to AT&T **USADirect**® Service. It's the quick way to get English-speaking operators and can minimize hotel surcharges.

If all the countries you're visiting aren't listed above, call **1 800 241-5555** before you leave for a free wallet card with all AT&T access numbers. International calling made easy—it's all part of **The *i* Plan.**℠

THE *i* PLAN℠

AT&T

All The Best Trips Start with Fodor's

Fodor's Affordables
Titles in the series: Caribbean, Europe, Florida, France, Germany, Great Britain, Italy, London, Paris.

"Travelers with champagne tastes and beer budgets will welcome this series from Fodor's." — *Hartford Courant*

"These books succeed admirably; easy to follow and use, full of cost-related information, practical advice, and recommendations...maps are clear and easy to use." — *Travel Books Worldwide*

The Berkeley Guides
Titles in the series: California, Central America, Eastern Europe, France, Germany, Great Britain & Ireland, Mexico, The Pacific Northwest, San Francisco.

The best choice for budget travelers, from the Associated Students at the University of California at Berkeley.

"Berkeley's scribes put the funk back in travel." — *Time*

"Hip, blunt and lively." — *Atlanta Journal Constitution*

"Fresh, funny and funky as well as useful." — *The Boston Globe*

Fodor's Bed & Breakfast and Country Inn Guides
Titles in the series: California, Canada, England & Wales, Mid-Atlantic, New England, The Pacific Northwest, The South, The Upper Great Lakes Region, The West Coast.

"In addition to information on each establishment, the books add notes on things to see and do in the vicinity. That alone propels these books to the top of the heap."— *San Diego Union-Tribune*

Exploring Guides
Titles in the series: Australia, California, Caribbean, Florida, France, Germany, Great Britain, Ireland, Italy, London, New York City, Paris, Rome, Singapore & Malaysia, Spain, Thailand.

"Authoritatively written and superbly presented, and makes worthy reading before, during or after a trip." — *The Philadelphia Inquirer*

"A handsome new series of guides, complete with lots of color photos, geared to the independent traveler." — *The Boston Globe*

Visit your local bookstore or call 1-800-533-6478 24 hours a day.
Fodor's The name that means smart travel.

The courtyard's three dominant architectural styles, reflecting alterations to the castle over the years, fairly jump out at you. On the north side, note the typical arcaded Renaissance balconies, decorated with sgraffiti; to the west, a Gothic tract is still easy to make out. The southern wing is clearly Baroque (although also decorated with arcades). Inside the castle at the back, you'll find a vinárna with mediocre food but excellent views over the rivers. On the other side is a museum devoted to wine making and folk crafts. *Museum admission: 20 Kč. adults, 10 Kč. children. Open May–Oct., Tues.–Sun. 10–5.*

To return to Prague, about 30 kilometers (20 miles) from Mělník, follow Route 9 south.

What to See and Do with Children

Children will be fascinated by Český Krumlov; its Old World streets and castle, complete with brown bears, make for a fairy-tale atmosphere. Karlovy Vary's warm open-air pool (on top of the Thermal Hotel) offers the unique experience of swimming comfortably even in the coolest weather. Terezín (Theresienstadt) makes a valuable educational outing for older children.

Off the Beaten Track

If you're not planning to go to the Tatras in Slovakia but nevertheless want a few days in the mountains, head for the Krkonoše range—the so-called Giant Mountains—near the Polish frontier. Here you'll find the most spectacular scenery in Bohemia, although it oversteps linguistic convention to call these rolling hills "giant" (the highest point is 1,602 meters, or 5,256 feet). Not only is the scenery beautiful, but the local architecture is refreshingly rural after all the towns and cities; the steeped-roof timber houses, painted in warm colors, look just right pitched against sunlit pinewoods or snowy pastures.

The principal resorts of the area are Janské Lázně (another spa), Pec pod Sněžkou, and Špindlerův Mlýn, this last being the most sophisticated in its accommodations and facilities. It is attractively placed astride the rippling Labe (Elbe) River, here in its formative stages. To get out and experience the mountains, a good trip is to take a bus from Špindlerův Mlýn via Janské Lázně to Pec pod Sněžkou—a deceptively long journey by road of around 50 kilometers (31 miles). From there, embark on a two-stage chair lift to the top of Sněžka (the area's highest peak), and then walk along a ridge overlooking the Polish countryside, eventually dropping into deep, silent pinewoods and returning to Špindlerův Mlýn. If you walk over the mountain instead of driving around it, the return trip is just 11 kilometers (7 miles)—a comfortable walk of about three to four hours. The path actually takes you into Poland at one point; you won't need a visa, but take your passport along just in case.

The source of the Labe also springs from the heights near the Polish border. From the town of Harrachov, walkers can reach it by a marked trail. The distance is about 10 kilometers (6 miles). From Špindlerův Mlýn, a beautiful but sometimes steep trail follows the Labe valley up to the source near Labská Bouda. Allow about three hours for this walk, and take good shoes and a map.

To get to the Krkonoše area from Prague, take the D11 freeway to Poděbrady and then go through Jičín, Nová Paka, and Vrchlabí, finally reaching Špindlerův Mlýn. Excellent bus connections link Prague with the towns of Špindlerův Mlýn, Vrchlabí, and Pec pod Sněžkou.

Shopping

Bohemia is justly world-famous for the quality of its lead crystal, porcelain, and garnets. Stores offering a stunning array of these items, at excellent prices, can be found in practically any town frequented by tourists. In western Bohemia, Karlovy Vary is best known to glass enthusiasts as home of the **Moser** glass company, one of the world's leading producers of crystal and decorative glassware. In addition to running the flagship store at Na Příkopě 12 in Prague, the company operates an outlet in Karlovy Vary on Stará Louka, next to the Cafe Elefant. A number of outlets for lesser-known, although also high-quality makers of glass and porcelain can also be found along Stará Louka. For excellent buys on porcelain, try the **Pirkenhammer** outlet below the Hotel Atlantic (Tržiště 23). A cheaper but nonetheless unique gift from Karlovy Vary would be a bottle of the ubiquitous bittersweet (and potent) Becherovka, a liqueur produced by the town's own Jan Becher distillery. Always appreciated as gifts are the unique pipe-shaped ceramic drinking cups used to take the drinking cure at spas. Find them at the colonnades in Karlovy Vary and Mariánské Lázně. You can also buy boxes of tasty Oplatky wafers, sometimes covered with chocolate, at shops in all of the spa towns.

The garnet center of the country is in **Turnov,** northern Bohemia. The main producer there, **Granát Turnov,** maintains two outlets in town (at 5 Května ul. 27 and Palackého ul. 188), and one shop in České Budějovice (at Stejskala ul. 9). Bohemian garnets are noted for their hardness and color: deep, deep red. The stone is traditionally set in both silver and gold, with the better pieces reserved for the latter.

Sports and Outdoor Activities

Hiking The **Krkonoše** range near the Polish border is prime hiking and wandering territory. Before setting off, buy the excellent *Soubor Turistických* map No. 15 of the area, available in larger bookstores (try the Melantrich bookstore at Na příkopě 3 in Prague). Wear sturdy shoes, and be prepared for virtually any kind of weather. The Krkonoše range gets some type of precipitation about 200 days out of the year on average.

Skiing All three of the principal resorts in the Krkonoše are good ski bases, with lifts and runs nearby. An excellent cross-country course begins in **Horní Misecky,** and an 8-kilometer (5-mile) course runs through the Labe valley. Ask at the Čedok office in Vrchlabí about ski rentals; otherwise you may have to buy your own equipment at local sporting-goods shops.

Swimming You can swim in most of the larger carp ponds around **Třeboň.** The Svět pond is particularly appealing because of its little sandy beaches, although these are generally crowded in summer.

Dining and Lodging

The major towns of western and southern Bohemia offer some of the best accommodation in the Czech Republic. In northern Bohemia, however, only the Krkonoše (Giant Mountain) region has good hotels. In the area around Terezín and Litoměřice, tourist amenities are practically nonexistent; if you do choose to stay overnight, you'll usually be able to find a room in a primitive inn or a rather unwelcoming modern hotel. Towns with private rooms available are noted below.

In many parts of Bohemia, the only real options for dining are the restaurants and cafés at the larger hotels and resorts.

Highly recommended restaurants and lodgings in a particular price category are indicated by a star ★.

České Budějovice
Dining and Lodging

Gomel. This modern high rise, a 15-minute walk from the main square along the road to Prague, probably is best suited to business travelers. The rooms are plain, but the hotel does offer a reasonable range of facilities, including an English-speaking staff. *Pražská tř. 14, tel. 038/27949. 180 rooms with bath or shower. Facilities: 3 restaurants, café, nightclub, conference hall, parking. Breakfast not included. AE, DC, MC, V. Expensive.*

Zvon. Old-fashioned, well-kept, and comfortable, the Zvon has an ideal location, on the main town square. Don't be put off by the indifferent staff and unpromising public areas—the rooms are bright, and the period bathrooms have large bathtubs. The price is high, however, for the level of facilities. *Nám. Přemysla Otakara II 28, tel. 038/353–6162. 50 rooms, most with bath. Facilities: restaurant. Breakfast not included. No credit cards. Expensive.*

Český Krumlov

Český Krumlov is crammed with pensions and private rooms for let, many priced around $15 per person per night. The best place to look is along the tiny Parkán ulice, which parallels the river just off the main street. A safe bet is the house at Parkán No. 107, blessed with several nice rooms and friendly management (tel. 0337/4396).

Dining and Lodging

Krumlov. At this attractive older hotel located directly on the main square, the ambience is decidedly homey: Wooden staircases and a rambling floor plan add to the effect. The older rooms with bath tend to be larger and nicer. The service is friendly but not overly efficient. *Svornosti nám. 14, tel. 0337/2255, fax 0337/3498. 36 rooms, 13 with bath. Facilities: restaurant. Breakfast included. AE, DC, MC, V. Expensive.*

★ **Růže.** This Renaissance monastery has been newly rennovated and transformed into an excellent luxury hotel, only a five-minute walk from the main square. The rooms are spacious and clean—some also have drop-dead views of the town below, so ask to see several before choosing. The restaurant, too, is top-rate; the elegant dining room is formal without being oppressive, and the menu draws from traditional Czech and international cuisines. *Horní ul. 153, tel. 0337/2245, fax 0337/3881. 110 rooms with bath. Facilities: restaurant, café, snack bar. Breakfast not included. AE, DC, MC, V. Expensive.*

Cheb (Eger)
Dining

Eva. Of the many new private restaurants opened on and around the main square, the Eva is certainly one of the best. A decent array of mostly Czech and German dishes is served in a stylish, contemporary setting that is carefully maintained by a troop of attentive waiters. *Jatečni 4, tel. 0166/22498. Dress: casual. No credit cards. Moderate.*

Lodging Cheb's hotels have failed to keep pace with the times; none offer western standards of cleanliness and all are overpriced. For a short stay, a room in a private home (pension) is a better bet. Owners of an older home at Valdstejnova 21 offer two clean and comfortable rooms (tel. 0166/33088). Several houses along Přemysla Otakara street north of the city have rooms available. Try the house at No. 7 (tel. 0166/22270).

Hradní Dvůr. This somewhat seedy, older hotel is due for a renovation; until then, the plain rooms are kept acceptably clean even if the facilities appear neglected. The hotel's prime asset is location, on a side street that runs parallel to the main square. *Dlouhá ul. 12, tel. 0166/22006. 21 rooms, some with bath. Breakfast not included. No credit cards. Moderate.*

Hvězda. This turn-of-the century hotel was last renovated in the 1970s, which is partly responsible for the Hvězda's present disheveled look. The location at the top of the main square is excellent, but the dilapidated facilities do not justify the prices. *Nám. Krále Jiřího, tel. 0166/22549, fax 0166/22546. 38 rooms, most with bath. Facilities: restaurant. Breakfast included. No credit cards. Moderate.*

Františkovy Lázně
Dining and Lodging

Centrum. Recent renovations have left the rooms clean and well-appointed if a bit sterile. Still, it is by far the best-run hotel in town and only a short walk from the main park and central spas. *Anglická 41, tel. 0166/943156, fax 0166/942843. 30 rooms with bath. Facilities: restaurant, wine bar, TV in rooms. Breakfast included. No credit cards. Expensive.*

★ **Slovan.** This is a quaint and gracious establishment, the perfect complement to this relaxed little town. The eccentricity of the original turn-of-the-century design survived a thorough renovation in the 1970s; the airy rooms are clean and comfortable, and some come with a balcony overlooking the main street. The main-floor restaurant serves above-average Czech dishes; consider a meal here even if you're staying elsewhere. *Národní 5, tel. 0166/942841. 25 rooms, most with bath. Facilities: restaurant, café, wine bar. Breakfast included. No credit cards. Expensive.*

Bajkal. This is an offbeat, older hotel with acceptably clean rooms and a friendly staff. It is located on the far side of the park from the main spas, roughly a 10-minute walk from the city center. The travel agency in the same building also books private accommodations. *Americká ul. 84/4, tel. and fax 0166/942501. 25 rooms, most with bath. Facilities: restaurant, parking. Breakfast not included. No credit cards. Moderate.*

Karlovy Vary
Dining

Embassy. This cozy wine restaurant, conveniently located near the Grandhotel Pupp, serves an innovative range of pastas, seafoods, and meats: Tagliatelle with salmon in cream sauce makes an excellent main course. Highlights of the varied dessert menu include plum dumplings with vanilla sauce. *Nová Louka 21, tel. 017/23049. Reservations advised. AE, DC, MC, V. Expensive.*

★ **Karel IV.** Its location on top of an old castle not far from the main colonnade affords diners the best view in town. Good renditions of traditional Czech standbys—mostly pork and beef entrées—are served in small, reclusive dining areas that are particularly intimate after sunset. *Zámecký vrch 2, tel. 017/*

27255. Reservations advised. Dress: casual but neat. AE, DC, MC, V. Moderate.

Vegetarian. This is a tiny meat-free oasis not far from the Hotel Thermal in the new town. Look for an impressive array of vegetarian standards and nontraditional variations of Czech dishes. *I.P. Pavlova 25, tel. 017/29021. No credit cards. Inexpensive.*

Lodging **Dvořák.** Consider a splurge here if you're longing for Western ★ standards of service and convenience. Opened in late 1990, this Austrian-owned hotel occupies three renovated town houses a five-minute walk from the main spas. The staff is helpful and the rooms are spotlessly clean. If possible, request a room with a bay-window view of the town. *Nová Louka 11, tel. 017/24145, fax 017/22814. 76 rooms with bath. Facilities: restaurant, café, pool, massage, sauna, fitness room, beauty parlor, satellite TV, parking. Breakfast included. AE, DC, MC, V. Very Expensive.*

Grandhotel Pupp. This enormous 300-year-old hotel, perched on the edge of the spa district, is one of Central Europe's most famous resorts. Standards and service slipped under the Communists (when the hotel was known as the Moskva-Pupp), but the present management is working hard to atone for the decades of neglect. Ask for a room furnished in 19th-century period style. The food in the ground-floor restaurant is only passable, but the elegant setting makes the hotel worth a visit. *Mírové nám. 2, tel. 017/209111, fax 017/24032. 350 rooms with bath. Facilities: 2 restaurants, lounge, satellite TV, sauna, fitness room. Breakfast included. AE, DC, MC, V. Very Expensive.*

Atlantic. The Atlantic is a haven for eccentrics who can appreciate the fanciful art-nouveau exterior (especially the comical porcelain figurines lining the roof) and for those who don't mind the lack of modern amenities and so-so service. Ask for a room with a balcony or with a view over the town and colonnade. *Tržiště 23, tel. 017/25251, fax 017/29086. 38 rooms, some with bath or shower. Breakfast not included. AE, DC, MC, V. Expensive.*

Central. True to its name, this hotel is right in the middle of the old spa district immediately across from the theater. The service is good and the lobby and public areas pleasant, but the smallish rooms are merely adequate (ask for one overlooking the town). *Divadelní nám. 17, tel. 017/25251, fax 017/29086. 61 rooms with bath. Facilities: restaurant, disco, parking. Breakfast included. AE, DC, MC, V. Expensive.*

Elwa. Recent renovations successfully integrated modern comforts into this older, elegant spa resort located midway between the old and new towns. Modern features include clean, comfortable rooms (most with televisions) and an on-site fitness center. *Zahradní 29, tel. 017/28472, fax 017/28473. 17 rooms with bath. Facilities: restaurant, bar, beauty parlor, fitness center. Breakfast included. AE, DC, MC, V. Expensive.*

Konopiště **Konopiště Motel.** It has long been a favorite with diplomats in *Dining and Lodging* Prague, who come for the fresh air and horseback riding. The motel is located about 2 kilometers (1 mile) from the Konopiště castle, on a small road about a kilometer from the main Prague–Tabor highway (Route 3). The rooms are small but well appointed (ask for one away from the main road). The castle and gardens are an easy 20-minute walk away through the woods; a campground is nearby. *Jarkovicé, tel. 0301/25071. 40 rooms with bath. Facilities: 2 restaurants, minigolf, horseback* *riding, satellite television, parking. Breakfast included. AE, DC, MC, V. Expensive.*

Kutná Hora
Lodging

Medínek. This is one of the few hotels in town with modern conveniences, so book in advance or risk being squeezed out by German and Austrian tour groups. The location, on the main square, puts you at an easy stroll from the sights, and the ground-floor restaurant offers decent Czech cooking in an atmosphere more pleasant than that found in the local beer halls. Yet, as with many of the hotels built in the 1960s and '70s, the modern architecture blights the surrounding square. *Palackého nám., tel. 0327/2741, fax 0327/2743. 90 rooms, some with bath. Facilities: restaurant, café. Breakfast not included. No credit cards. Expensive.*

U Hrnčíře. This is a picturesque little inn situated next to a potter's shop near the town center. The quaintness doesn't make up for the very standard, plain rooms but the friendly staff gives the hotel a decidedly homey feel. The restaurant in the back garden features a beautiful view over the valley. *Barborska 24, tel. 0327/2113. 6 rooms with bath. Facilities: restaurant, terrace. Breakfast not included. No credit cards. Moderate.*

Litoměřice
Dining
★

Činská Restaurace. At this oasis of well-prepared, spicy Chinese food in an otherwise bleak culinary setting, excellent dumpling and cold chicken appetizers give way to succulent renditions of Chinese classics. Try Chicken Kung-Pao, prepared spicy-hot with peanuts, or the steamed duck in honey sauce. For dessert the fried apple in honey is deservedly popular. *Mirové nám., in the former Rak hotel, tel. 041980/3008. No credit cards. Moderate.*

Lodging

At press time, the Rak, the town's only hotel, was preparing to reopen in 1994, following a one-year renovation. Until then, other accommodation is not readily available.

Mariánské Lázně
Dining

Filip. This bustling wine bar is where locals come to find relief from the sometimes large tourist hoard. A tasty selection of traditional Czech dishes—mainly pork, grilled meats, and steaks—is served by a friendly and efficient staff. *Poštovní 96, tel. 0165/2639. No credit cards. Moderate.*

★

Koliba. This combination hunting lodge and wine tavern, set in the woods roughly 20 minutes by foot from the spas, is an excellent alternative to the hotel restaurants in town. Grilled meats and shish kebabs, plus tankards of Moravian wine (try the cherry-red *Rulandské Červené*), are served up with traditional gusto. *Dusíkova, on the road to Karlovy Vary, tel. 0165/5169. Reservations advised. Dress: casual but neat. No credit cards. Moderate.*

Classic. This small, trendy café on the main drag serves fine sandwiches and light meals throughout the day. Unusual for this part of the world, it also offers a full breakfast menu until 11 AM. *Hlavní tř. 131/50, tel. 0165/2807. No credit cards. Inexpensive.*

Lodging

The best place to look for private lodgings is along Paleckého ulice, south of the main spa area. Private accommodation can also be found in the neighboring villages of Zádub and Závišín, and along roads in the woods to the east of Mariánské Lázně.

Hotel Golf. Book in advance to secure a room at this stately villa situated 3½ kilometers (2 miles) out of town on the road to Karlovy Vary. A major renovation in the 1980s left the large, open rooms with a cheery, modern look. The restaurant on the main floor is excellent, but the big draw is the 18-hole golf course on the premises, one of the few in the Czech Republic. *Zádub 55, Mariánské Lázně 35301, tel. 0165/2651 or 0165/2652, fax 0165/2655. 25 rooms with bath. Facilities: restaurant, satellite TV, golf, tennis, swimming pool. Breakfast included. AE, DC, MC, V. Very Expensive.*

★ **Bohemia.** This renovated spa resort is definitely worth the splurge; beautiful crystal chandeliers in the main hall set the stage for a comfortable and elegant stay. The rooms are well appointed and completely equipped, though you may want to be really decadent and request one of the enormous suites overlooking the park. The efficient staff can arrange spa treatments and horseback riding. *Hlavní tř. 100, tel. 0165/3251, fax 0165/2943. 100 rooms with bath. Facilities: restaurant; TV and phones in rooms; fitness center; swimming; horseback riding. Breakfast included. AE, DC, MC, V. Expensive.*

Excelsior. This lovely older hotel is on the main street and convenient to the spas and colonnade. The renovated rooms are clean and comfortable, and the staff is friendly and helpful. The food in the adjoining restaurant is only average, but the romantic setting provides adequate compensation. *Hlavní tř. 121, tel. 0165/2705, fax 0165/5346. 53 rooms with bath. Facilities: restaurant, café, parking. Breakfast included. AE, DC, MC, V. Expensive.*

Corso. This compact 19th-century hotel, due for a renovation, has the distinction of being the cheapest hotel along the main drag. The rooms and corridors are large and clean; the staff at the reception is helpful. You can dance in the wine bar during the evenings or enjoy above-average Bohemian cuisine in the quiet, elegant restaurant. *Hlavní tř. 61, tel. 0165/3091, fax 0165/3093. 28 rooms, 17 with bath. Facilities: restaurant, bar. Breakfast not included. No credit cards. Moderate.*

Kavkaz. You'll love or hate the heavy-handed 19th-century Empire style of this former spa hotel, located just behind the Main Colonnade area. The rooms are airy and large, and the public areas are still suitably elegant for entertaining past guests such as King Edward VII of England and the illustrious Goethe. Ask for one of the 10 recently renovated rooms. *Goethovo nám. 9, tel. 0165/3141. Facilities: restaurant. Breakfast not included. No credit cards. Moderate.*

Mělník **Ludmila.** Though the hotel looks slightly ragged and is situated
Dining and Lodging 4 kilometers (2½ miles) outside of town, the Ludmila's English-speaking staff keeps the plain but cozy rooms impeccably clean, and the restaurant is better than many you will find in Mělník itself. *Pražská ul., tel. 0206/2578. 73 rooms with shower or bath. Facilities: restaurant, parking, souvenir shop. Breakfast not included. No credit cards. Moderate.*

Písek **Otava.** Originally a music school, this pleasant midsize hotel,
Lodging located a short walk from the city center, was built at the end of the last century; adorning the facade are 11 period frescoes depicting the history of the Czech nation. The gracious restaurant, with characteristic high ceilings and murals, provides a relaxing setting for an evening meal. The rooms, while less grand, are adequate for a short stay. *Komenského 58, tel. 0362/2861. 36 rooms with bath. Facilities: restaurant, café. Breakfast included. No credit cards. Moderate.*

Plzeň
Dining and Lodging

Central. This angular 1960s structure (named the Ural until 1990) is recommendable for its sunny rooms, friendly staff, and great location, right on the main square. Indeed, even such worthies as Czar Alexander of Russia stayed here in the days when the hotel was a charming inn known as the Golden Eagle. *Nám. Republiky 33, tel. 019/226059, fax 019/226064. 84 rooms with shower. Facilities: restaurant, wine bar, café, parking. Breakfast not included. AE, DC, MC, V. Expensive.*

Continental. Situated just five minutes by foot from the main square, the fin-de-siècle Continental remains the best hotel in Pzleň, a relative compliment considering that the hotel is slightly run-down and the rooms, though large, are exceedingly plain. The restaurant, however, serves dependably satisfying traditional Czech dishes. *Zbojnická ul. 5, tel. 019/36477, telex 0154380. 53 rooms, half with bath or shower. Facilities: restaurant, café, parking. Breakfast included. AE, DC, MC, V. Expensive.*

Slovan. While the gracious white facade, sweeping stairways, and large, elegant rooms attest to the Slovan's former grandeur, poor management of late has allowed a marked seediness to creep in. The restaurant still occupies the once beautiful ballroom, but the experience is spoiled by mediocre food and the rock-music accompaniment. The Slovan's best asset may be its location, a short walk from the main square. *Smetanový Sady 1, tel. 019/33551, telex 0154245. 113 rooms, half with bath. Facilities: restaurant, café. Breakfast included. AE, DC, MC, V. Moderate.*

Špindlerův Mlýn
Dining and Lodging

Montana. This "modern" 1970s hotel is ill-suited to the rustic setting, and the rooms are more spartan than luxurious; but the service is attentive, and the staff can offer good advice for planning walks around this popular resort town. *54351 Špindlerův Mlýn, tel. 0438/93551, fax 0438/93556. 70 rooms with bath. Facilities: restaurant, café, bar, TV in rooms. Breakfast included. AE, DC, MC, V. Expensive.*

★ **Savoy.** This Tudor-style chalet, more than 100 years old but thoroughly renovated in the early 1980s, is rich in Alpine atmosphere and very comfortable—its cozy reception area is more typical of a family inn than a large hotel. The rooms, although on the smallish side and sparsely furnished, are immaculately clean. The restaurant serves fine traditional Czech dishes in a comfortably polished setting. *54351 Špindlerův Mlýn, tel. 0438/93521, fax 0438/93641. 50 rooms, most with bath or shower. Facilities: restaurant, bar. Breakfast included. AE, DC, MC, V. Moderate.*

Nechanicky. At this private, older hotel located near the bridge in the center of town, the new management is working hard to improve the hotel's somewhat tarnished appearance. And despite some obvious disadvantages (bathrooms are communal and in the hallway), the rooms are bright, clean, and well-proportioned; front-facing rooms enjoy an excellent view over the town. *54351 Špindlerův Mlýn, tel. 0438/93263, fax 0438/93315. 12 rooms without bath. Facilities: restaurant. Breakfast not included. No credit cards. Inexpensive.*

Tábor
Lodging

The house at No. 189 Hradební 16 (tel. 0361/22109), just behind the square, has two large rooms to let for about $15 per person per night, including breakfast; one room even has a sauna. Otherwise, the private tourist office on Námestí Františka Križíka will help book private accommodation (tel. 0361/23401; open daily 10–noon and 1–6).

Bohemia. Privatization has transformed this sleepy train-station hotel (known formerly as the Slavia) into a pleasant alternative to the stark Palcát. The young staff is cheerful, and the corridors and rooms (many with TV) are bright and clean. The restaurant on the main floor (open nightly until 10:30) is better than many other restaurants in town. *Husovo nám. 591, tel. 0361/22827, fax 0361/63341. 33 rooms, 22 with bath. Facilities: restaurant. Breakfast not included. No credit cards. Moderate.*

Palcát. Located a 10-minute walk from the Old Town square, the slightly run-down Palcát is quite a contrast. The architecture is overwhelmingly drab, but the rooms, though plain, are bright and comfortable; those on the upper floors have a dazzling view of the Old Town. Still, you're probably better off at the Bohemia. *9 Května tř., tel. 0361/22901, fax 0361/22905. 68 rooms with shower. Facilities: restaurant, café, bar, conference hall, parking. Breakfast not included. MC, V. Moderate.*

Třeboň
Dining and Lodging

Svět. A functional 1960s structure that's recommended most for its location, on the banks of the Svět pond (although inconvenient for travelers without a car). The rooms are plain and unimaginative, but all come with a balcony. The adjoining seafood restaurant is a good place to sample the spoils of the fish harvests. *Hliník ul. 750/2, tel. 0333/3147 or 0333/3046. 55 rooms, some with shower. Facilities: restaurant, parking. Breakfast not included. No credit cards. Moderate.*

The Arts and Nightlife

The Arts

Mariánske Lázně sponsors a music festival each June, with numerous concerts featuring Czech and international composers and orchestras. The town's annual Chopin festival each autumn brings in fans of the Polish composer's work from around the world. Karlovy Vary and Františkový Lázně also offer concerts throughout the year. When in Karlovy Vary, pick up a copy of *KAM*, the town's monthly cultural magazine (available at major hotels). **Karlovy Vary** is also the site of a major international film festival, held yearly in the fall. An outdoor Renaissance theater in the castle gardens in **Český Krumlov** is a popular venue for plays and concerts throughout the summer.

Nightlife

Nightlife in the towns and villages of Bohemia revolves around the *pivnice* (beer hall). If you want to see a piece of the real Czech Republic and can take the thick smoke, this is the place to go. The beer, of course, is excellent.

Drinking and dancing until dawn are understandably not part of the daily regimen of serious convalescent centers, especially when patients have to be in bed at 10 PM sharp. Still, the major spas of western Bohemia do offer some lively evening entertainment—if only for the more robust relatives of those receiving treatment. Both **Karlovy Vary** and **Mariánské Lázně** have casinos open until the wee hours of the morning. In Mariánské Lázně, the **Casino Marienbad** is situated at Anglická 336 (open daily 6 AM–2 AM, tel. 0165/2056). In Karlovy Vary, go to the **Lázně I** (open daily 6 AM–2 AM, tel. 017/23100), situated near the Grandhotel Pupp.

For late-night drinks in Mariánské Lázně, try the **Hotel Golf** (*see* Lodging, *above*), which has a good nightclub with dancing in season. In Karlovy Vary, the action centers on the two nightclubs of the **Grandhotel Pupp.** The "little dance hall" is open daily 8 PM–1 AM. The second club is open Wednesday through Sunday 7 PM–3 AM. **Club Propaganda** (Jaltska 7) is Karlovy Vary's best venue for live rock and new music.

Moravia

Lacking the turbulent history of Bohemia to the west or the stark natural beauty of Slovakia farther to the east, Moravia, the eastern-most province of the Czech Republic, is frequently overlooked as a travel destination. Still, though Moravia's cities do not match Prague for beauty, nor do its gentle mountains compare with Slovakia's strikingly rugged Tatras, Moravia's colorful villages and rolling hills certainly do merit a few days of exploration. After you've seen the admittedly superior sights of Bohemia and Slovakia, come here for the good wine, the folk music, the friendly faces, and the languid pace.

What makes Moravia interesting is precisely that it's neither Bohemia nor Slovakia but rather a little of both. Culturally, Moravia is closer to Bohemia. The two were bound together as one kingdom for some 1,000 years, following the fall of the Great Moravian Empire (Moravia's last stab at Slavonic statehood) at the end of the 10th century. All of the cultural and historical movements that swept through Bohemia, including the religious turbulence and long period of Austrian Habsburg rule, were felt strongly here as well.

But, oddly, in many ways Moravia resembles Slovakia more than its cousin to the west. The colors come alive here in a way that is seldom seen in Bohemia: The subdued earthen pinks and yellows in towns such as Telč and Mikulov suddenly erupt into the fiery reds, greens, and purples of the traditional folk costumes farther to the east. Folk music, all but gone in Bohemia, is still very much alive in Moravia. You'll hear it, ranging from foot stomping to tear jerking, sung with pride by young and old alike.

Important Addresses and Numbers

Tourist Information Most major towns have a local or private information office, usually located in the central square and identified by a capital "I" on the facade. These offices are often good sources for maps and historical information and can usually help book hotel and private accommodation. Most are open during normal business hours, with limited hours on Saturdays (until noon) and closed on Sundays and holidays.

Brno also has a helpful **American-Moravian Center** (Radnická ul. 10, tel. 05/25908 or 05/25909), where you can get information on just about everything.

Emergencies **Police** (tel. 158). **Ambulance** (tel. 155).

Late-Night Pharmacy **Brno:** The pharmacy at Kobližná ulice 7 (tel. 05/22275) is open 24 hours.

Arriving and Departing by Plane

ČSA, the national carrier of the Czech Republic, has regular flights to Brno from Prague and Bratislava. The distances between the cities are short, however, and it's ultimately cheaper and quicker to drive or take a bus. During the two large Brno trade fairs, in April and September, foreign carriers also connect the city with Frankfurt and Vienna. These flights are usually crowded with businessmen, so you'll have to book well in advance. For more information on flights, contact ČSA offices in Prague or Brno (tel. 05/671249).

Arriving and Departing by Car, Train, and Bus

By Car Occupying the middle of the country, Moravia is within easy driving distance of Prague, Bratislava, and eastern Slovakia. Jihlava, the starting point for the tour below, is 124 kilometers (78 miles) southeast of Prague along the excellent D1 freeway. Brno, the capital, is 196 kilometers (122 miles) from Prague and 121 kilometers (75 miles) from Bratislava. Moravia is also easily reached by car from Austria. Major border crossings exist at Hate (below Znojmo) and Mikulov. Olomouc lies on the major east–west highway, convenient for returning to Prague or continuing farther east to the Tatras, eastern Slovakia, and Poland.

By Train Several trains daily make the three-hour run from Prague to Brno. Most use Prague's **Hlavní nádraží** (main station), but some depart from and arrive at the suburban station **Holešovice nádraží** (Holešovice Station), or at **Masarykovo nádraží** (Masaryk Station), on Hybernská ulice in the city center. Trains leaving Prague for Budapest and Bucharest (and some Vienna-bound trains) also frequently stop in Brno (check timetables to be sure).

By Bus Bus connections from Prague to Jihlava and Brno are excellent and inexpensive, and, in lieu of a car, the best way to get to Moravia. Moravian destinations are also well-served from Bratislava and other points in Slovakia. Buses also run daily between Vienna and Brno, leaving Vienna's Wien-Mitte station at 7:30 AM, and leaving Brno for the return to Vienna at 5:30 PM. Round-trip tickets cost around AS340 ($27).

Getting Around

By Car Having your own car is the best way to tour Moravia; the roads are generally good, and there is little traffic. Avoid driving at night and in bad weather when possible, as many of the smaller roads are poorly marked.

By Train Train service in Moravia is thin, linking only the major towns. Moreover, sorting out the schedules and buying tickets can be a hassle. In any event, you'll inevitably have to resort to the bus to reach the smaller, out-of-the-way places on the tour below.

By Bus As in the rest of the Czech Republic, the national bus network, ČSAD, operates a dense network of lines in Moravia; with a little advance planning, you'll be able to reach all of the destinations on the tour. The prices are also reasonable. The only drawback is time, as the buses can sometimes be very, very slow. Watch for the little symbols on the timetables, which tell you if the bus runs on weekends and holidays. The Brno bus station is located behind the train station. To find it, simply go to the train station and follow the signs to ČSAD.

Highlights for First-Time Visitors

Brno (*see* Tour 2)
Main square in Telč (*see* Tour 1)
Moravian Caves (*see* Tour 3)
Olomouc (*see* Tour 3)
Vranov Castle (*see* Tour 1)

Exploring Moravia

Numbers in the margin correspond to points of interest on the Moravia map.

The first tour outlined below begins in the west of the province, along the highlands that define the "border" with Bohemia. Here, towns such as Jihlava and Telč are virtually indistinguishable from their Bohemian counterparts. The handsome squares, with their long arcades, bear witness to the prosperity enjoyed by this part of Europe several hundred years ago. The tour then heads south along the frontier with Austria—until recently a heavily fortified expanse of the Iron Curtain. Life is just starting to return to normal in these parts, as the towns and people on both sides of the border seek to reestablish ties going back centuries. One of their common traditions is wine making; and Znojmo, Mikulov, and Valtice are to the Czech Republic what the small towns of the *Weinviertel* on the other side of the border are to Austria.

Tour 2 covers **Brno** (pronounced *burrno*), Moravia's cultural and geographic center. Brno grew rich in the 19th century as the industrial heartland of the Austrian empire and doesn't look or feel like any other Czech or Slovak city. In the early years of this century, the city became home to the best young architects working in the cubist and constructivist styles. And experimentation wasn't restricted to architecture. Leoš Janáček, an important composer of the early modern period, also lived and worked in Brno. The modern tradition continues even today, and the city is considered to have the best theater and performing arts in the country.

Tour 3 covers the area just north of Brno, where you'll find the **Moravian Karst,** a beautiful wilderness area with an extensive network of caves, caverns, and underground rivers. Many caves are open to the public, and some tours even incorporate underground boat rides. Farther to the north lies Moravia's "second capital," **Olomouc,** an industrial but still charming city, with a long history as a center of learning. Paradoxically, despite its location far from the Austrian border, Olomouc remained a bastion of support for the Habsburgs and the empire at a time when cries for independence could be heard throughout Bohemia and Moravia. In 1848, when revolts everywhere threatened to bring the monarchy down, the Habsburg family fled here for safety. Franz Joseph, who went on to personify the stodgy permanence of the empire, was even crowned here as Austrian emperor that same year.

The green foothills of the **Beskydy range** begin just east of Olomouc, perfect for a day or two of walking in the mountains. Farther to the east you'll find the spectacular peaks of the Tatras, and the tour is a good jumping-off point for exploring eastern Slovakia or southern Poland. Similarly, if you're coming from

Slovakia, you could easily begin in Olomouc and conduct the tour in reverse order.

Tour 1:
Southern Moravia
❶ On the Moravian side of the rolling highlands that mark the border between Bohemia and Moravia, and just off the main highway from Prague to Brno, lies the old mining town of **Jihlava,** a good place to begin an exploration of Moravia. If the silver mines here had held out just a few more years, the townspeople claim, Jihlava could have become a great European city—and a household name to foreign visitors. Indeed, in the 13th century, the town's enormous **main square** was one of the largest in Europe, rivaled in size only by those in Cologne and Kraków. But history can be cruel: The mines went bust in the 17th century, and the square today bears witness only to the town's once oversize ambitions.

The **Kostel svatého Ignáce** (St. Ignace Church) in the northwest corner of the square is relatively young for Jihlava, built at the end of the 17th century, but look inside to see a rare Gothic crucifix, created in the 13th century for the early Bohemian king Přemysl Otakar II. The town's most striking structure is the Gothic **Kostel svatého Jakuba** (St. James Church) to the east of the main square, down the Farní ulice. The church's exterior, with its uneven towers, is Gothic; the interior is Baroque; and the font is a masterpiece of the Renaissance, dating from 1599. Note also the Baroque **Chapel of the Holy Virgin,** sandwiched between two late-Gothic chapels, with its oversize 14th-century pietà. Two other Gothic churches worth a look are the **Kostel svatého Kříža** (Church of the Holy Cross), north of the main square, and the **Minoritský kostel** (Minorite Church), to the west of the square. Just next to the latter is the last remaining of the original five medieval town gates.

❷ The little town of **Telč,** about 30 kilometers (19 miles) to the south via Route 406, has an even more impressive main square than Jihlava. But what strikes the eye most here is not its size but the unified style of the buildings. On the lowest levels are beautifully vaulted Gothic halls, just above are Renaissance floors and facades, and all of it is crowned with rich Baroque gables. The square is so perfect that you feel more as if you've entered a film set than a living town. The town allegedly owes its architectural unity to Zacharias of Neuhaus, after whom the main square is now named. In the 16th century, so the story goes, the wealthy Zacharias had the castle—originally a small fort overlooking the Bohemian border with Hungary—rebuilt in Renaissance style. But the contrast between the new castle and the town's rather ordinary buildings was so great that Zacharias had the square rebuilt to match the castle's splendor. Luckily for architecture fans, the Neuhaus dynasty died out shortly thereafter, and succeeding nobles had little interest in refashioning the town according to the vogue of the day.

It's best to approach the main square on foot. If you've come by car, park outside the main walls on the side south of town and walk through the **Big Gate,** part of the original fortifications dating back to the 13th century. The tiny Palackého ulice takes you past the 160-foot Romanesque tower of the **Kostel svatého Ducha** (Church of the Holy Ghost) on your right. This is the oldest standing structure in Telč, dating from the first quarter of the 13th century. As you walk up Palackého ulice, the **square** unfolds nobly in front of you, with the castle at the top and beautiful houses, bathed in pastel reds and golds, gracing both

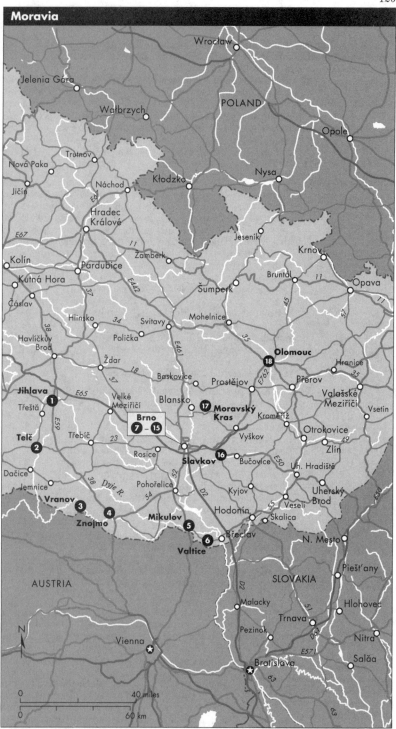

Moravia

sides. If you're a fan of Renaissance reliefs, note the black-and-white sgraffito corner house at No. 15, which dates from the middle of the 16th century. The house at No. 61, across from the Černý Orel hotel, is also noteworthy for its fine detail.

At the northern end of the square, the **Town Castle** forms a complex with the former **Jesuit college** and the **St. James Church.** The castle, originally Gothic, was built in the 14th century, when Telč first gained importance as a border town with the old Hungarian kingdom. It was given its current Renaissance appearance by Italian masters between 1553 and 1568. In season, you can tour the castle and admire the rich Renaissance interiors, equally as impressive as the Italian palaces after which the castle was modeled. Given the reputation of nobles for lively banquets lasting for hours, the sgraffito relief in the dining room depicting gluttony (in addition to the six other deadly sins) seems odd indeed. Other interesting rooms with sgraffiti include the Treasury, the Armory, and the Blue and Gold chambers.

Time Out The restaurant of the **Černý Orel** hotel on the main square is a good place to have coffee or a meal; the hotel itself is a fine place to spend the night. If you're looking for sweets, you can get good homemade cakes at a little private café, **Cukrárna u Matěje,** at Na baště 2.

Leave Telč and continue farther south into the heart of Moravian wine country. Follow the signs first to the picturesque little town of **Dačice,** then along Route 408 through **Jemnice,** and finally to the chain of recreation areas along the man-made lakes of the **Dyje** (Thaya) River. Turn right at Šumná, and follow the signs to the little town of Vranov, nestled snugly between hill and river. In all, the trip from Telč is about 55 kilometers (34 miles).

As a swimming and boating center for southern Moravia, ❸ **Vranov** would be a good place to stop in its own right. But what makes the town truly noteworthy is the enormous and colorful **Vranov castle,** rising 200 feet from a rocky promontory. For nearly 1,000 years, this was the border between Bohemia and Austria and therefore worthy of a fortress of these dimensions. You'll either love or hate this proud mongrel of a building, as its multi-colored Gothic, Renaissance, and Baroque elements vie for your attention. In the foreground, the solemn Renaissance tower rises over some Gothic fortifications. The structure is shored up on its left by a golden Baroque church, with a beautiful pink-and-white Baroque dome to the back. Each unit is spectacular, but the overall effect of so many styles mixed together is jarring.

Take your eyes off the castle's motley exterior and tour its mostly Baroque (and more harmonious) interior. The most impressive room is certainly the 43-foot-high elliptical **Hall of Ancestors,** the work of the Viennese master Johann Bernhard Fischer von Erlach (builder of the Clam-Gallas Palace in Prague and the Hofburg in Vienna). The frescoes, added by the Salzburg painter Johann Michael Rottmayr, depict scenes from Greek mythology. Look inside the **Castle Church** as well. The rotunda, altar, and organ were designed by Fischer von Erlach at the end of the 17th century.

❹ The old border town of **Znojmo** is an easy 20-kilometer (12-mile) drive to the east of Vranov. Follow Route 408, and turn right on the busier Route 38. Znojmo enjoys a long history as an important frontier town between Austria and Bohemia and is the cultural center of southern Moravia. The Přemyslide prince Břetislav I had already built a fortress here in the 11th century, and in 1226 Znojmo became the first Moravian town (ahead of Brno) to receive town rights from the king. But, alas, modern Znojmo, with its many factories and high rises, isn't really a place to linger. Plan on spending no more than a few hours walking through the Old Town, admiring the views over the Dyje River, and visiting the remaining fortifications and churches that stand between the New Town and the river.

Znojmo's tumbledown **main square,** now usually filled with peddlers selling everything from butter to cheap souvenirs, isn't what it used to be when it was crowned by Moravia's most beautiful **town hall.** Unfortunately, the 14th-century building was destroyed in 1945, just before the end of the war, and all that remains of the original structure is the 250-foot Gothic tower you see at the top of the square—looking admittedly forlorn astride the modern department store that now occupies the space.

For a cheerier sight, follow the lovely Zelinářská ulice, which trails from behind the Town Hall Tower to the southwest in the direction of the old town and river. The Gothic **Kostel svatého Mikuláše** (St. Nicholas Church), on the tiny old town square (Staré Město), dates from 1338, but its neo-Gothic tower was not added until the last century, when the original had to be pulled down. If you can get into the church (it's often locked), look for the impressive Sacraments House, which was built around 1500 in late-Gothic style.

Just behind St. Nicholas stands the curious, two-layered **Kostel svatého Václava** (St. Wenceslas Church), built at the end of the 15th century. The upper level of this tiny white church is dedicated to St. Anne, the lower level to St. Martin. Farther to the west, along the medieval ramparts that separate the town from the river, stands the original 11th-century **Rotunda svatej Kateřiny** (St. Catherine's Rotunda), still in remarkably good condition. Step inside to see a rare cycle of restored frescoes from 1134 depicting various members of the early Přemyslide dynasty.

The **Jihomoravské Muzeum** (South Moravian Museum), just across the way in the former town castle, houses an extensive collection of artifacts from the area, dating from the Stone Age to the present. However, unless you're a big fan of museums, there's little point in making a special visit to this one; and unless you can read Czech, you'll have difficulty making sense of the collection. *Přemyslovců ul., no phone. Admission: 10 Kč. adults, 5 Kč. children. Open Tues.–Sun. 9–5.*

Znojmo's other claims to fame have endeared the town to the hearts (and palates) of Czechs everywhere. The first is the Znojmo gherkin, first cultivated in the 16th century. You'll find this tasty accompaniment to meals at restaurants all over the country. Just look for the *Znojmo* prefix—as in *Znojemský guláš,* a tasty stew spiced with pickles. Znojmo's other treat is wine. As the center of the Moravian wine industry, this is an excellent place to pick up a few bottles of your favorite grape at any grocery or beverage store. But don't expect to learn much about a wine from its label: Oddly, you'll search in vain for the vintage or even the name of the vineyard on labels, and about the only information you can gather is the name of the grape and the city in which the wine was bottled. The best towns to look for, in addition to Znojmo, are Mikulov and Valtice (*see below*). Some of the best varieties of grapes are Rulandské and Vavřinecké (for red) and Ryslink and Müller Thurgau (for white).

Leave Znojmo by heading northeast on Route 54 in the direction of Pohořelice. Make a right turn when you see signs to **⑤ Mikulov,** eventually arriving in town along Route 52 after a semicircuitous drive of 54 kilometers (34 miles). Mikulov is known today chiefly as the border crossing on the Vienna–Brno road. If you want to leave the Czech Republic for a day to stock up on Western supplies, this is the place to do it. The nearest Austrian town, Poysdorf, is just 7 kilometers (4½ miles) away.

In many ways, Mikulov is the quintessential Moravian town. The soft pastel pinks and yellows of its buildings look almost mystical in the afternoon sunshine against the greens of the surrounding hills. But aside from the busy wine industry, not much goes on here. The main sight is the striking **castle,** which dominates the tiny main square and surrounding area. The castle started out as the Gothic residence of the noble Liechtenstein family in the 13th century and was given its current Baroque appearance some 400 years later. The most famous resident was Napoleon, who stayed here in 1805 while negotiating peace terms with the Austrians after winning the battle of Austerlitz (Slavkov, near Brno). Sixty-one years later, Bismarck used the castle to sign a peace treaty with Austria. The castle's darkest days came at the end of World War II, when retreating Nazi SS units set the town on fire. In season, take a walk from the main square up around the side of the castle into the **museum** of wine making. The most remarkable exhibit is a wine cask made in 1643 with a capacity of more than 22,000 gallons. This was used for collecting the vintner's obligatory tithe. *Admission: 20 Kč. adults, 10 Kč. children. Open May–Oct., Tues.–Sun. 9–4.*

If you happen to arrive at grape-harvesting time in October, head for one of the many private *sklípeks* (wine cellars), built into the hills surrounding the town. The tradition in these parts is simply to knock on the door; more often than not, you'll be invited in by the owner to taste a recent vintage.

⑥ The small town of **Valtice,** just 9 kilometers (6 miles) to the east of Mikulov along Route 414, would be wholly nondescript except for the fascinating **castle,** just off the main street, built by the Liechtenstein family in the 19th century. Next to the town's dusty streets, with their dilapidated postwar storefronts, the castle looks positively grand, a glorious if slightly overexuberant holdover from a long-lost era. But the best news of all is that you can also spend the night there if you want. Unusual for the country, the left wing of the castle has been converted into a hotel (*see* Lodging, *below*). The rooms aren't luxurious, but the setting is inspiring (especially if the standard high-rise hotels are getting you down). The castle boasts some 365 windows, painted ceilings, and much ornate woodwork. A small museum on the ground floor demonstrates how the town and castle have changed over the years, according to aristocratic and political whim. Even if you're just passing through, enjoy a drink on the terrace behind the hotel, an ideal spot to relax on a warm afternoon. The Valtice winery is situated behind and to the right of the castle, but it is not open to the public. *Castle admission: 10 Kč. adults, 5 Kč. children. Open Tues.–Sun. 9–11:30 and 1–4.*

Time Out The little mountain town Pavlov, a short drive or bus ride from Mikulov or Valtice, has several wine cellars built into the hills and makes for a good refreshment stop. At U **Venuše** (Česká 27, dinner only), be sure to sample some of the owner's wine, which comes from his private *sklípek* across the lake in Strachotín. After dinner, stroll around the village, perched romantically over a man-made lake.

Between Valtice and another aristocratic pile at **Lednice,** 7 kilometers (4 miles) to the northwest, the Liechtenstein family peppered the countryside with neoclassical temples and follies throughout the 19th century as a display of their wealth and taste. An abandoned summer palace lies just to the north of Valtice, not far from the tiny town of **Hlohovec.** In winter, you can walk or skate across the adjoining Hlohovec Pond to the golden yellow building; otherwise follow the tiny lane to Hlohovec, just off Route 422 outside Valtice. Emblazoned across the front of the palace is the German slogan ZWISCHEN ÖSTERREICH UND MÄHREN (Between Austria and Moravia), another reminder of the proximity of the border and the long history that these areas share.

The extravagantly neo-Gothic castle at **Lednice,** while obviously in disrepair, affords stunning views of the surrounding grounds and ponds. Be sure to tour the sumptuous interior; particularly resplendent with the afternoon sunshine streaming through the windows are the blue-and-green silk wallcoverings embossed with the Moravian eagle in the formal dining room and bay-windowed drawing room. The grounds, now a pleasant park open to the public, even boast a 200-foot minaret and a massive greenhouse filled with exotic flora. *Zámek. Admission: 20 Kč. adults, 10 Kč. children. Open May–Sept. daily 9–4; Oct., weekends 9–4.*

From Lednice, follow the Dyje River to the northwest through the villages of Bulhary and Milovice and on to the tiny town of **Dolní Věstonice,** perched alongside another giant artificial lake. Although the town has little going for it today, some 20,000 to 30,000 years ago the area was home to a thriving prehistoric settlement, judging from ivory and graves found here by archaeologists in 1950. Some of the world's earliest ceramics also were discovered, among them a curvaceous figurine of ash and clay that has become known as the Venus of Věstonice. The original is kept in Brno, but you can see replicas, real mammoth bones, and much else of archaeological interest at the excellent **museum** in the center of town along the main road. *Admission: 20 Kč. adults, 10 Kč. children. Open May–Sept., Tues.–Sun. 8–noon and 1–4; Apr. and Oct., weekends 8–noon and 1–4.*

For walking enthusiasts, the **Pavlovské vrchy** (Pavlov Hills), where the settlement was found, offers a challenging climb. Start out by ascending the **Devín Peak** (1,800 feet), located just south of Dolní Věstonice. A series of paths then follows the ridges the 10 kilometers (6 miles) to Mikulov.

Tour 2: Brno *Numbers in the margin correspond to points of interest on the Brno map.*

From Dolní Věstonice, follow Route 420 about 10 kilometers (6 miles) to the D2 freeway. From here it is a quick 23 kilometers ❼ (14 miles) to **Brno,** whose 19th-century buildings show signs of a prosperity that is rare for Czech towns. Beginning with a textiles industry imported from Germany, Holland, and Belgium, Brno became the industrial heartland of the Austrian empire in the 18th and 19th centuries—hence its "Manchester of Moravia" sobriquet. You'll search in vain for an extensive Old Town; you'll also find few of the traditional arcaded storefronts that typify other historical Czech towns. What you will see instead are fine examples of Empire and neoclassical styles, their formal, geometric facades more in keeping with the conservative tastes of the 19th-century middle class.

Begin the walking tour, which should take two or three hours ❽ at a leisurely pace, at the triangular **Náměstí Svobody** (Freedom Square), in the heart of the commercial district. The square itself is architecturally undistinguished, but here and along the adjoining streets you'll find the city's best stores and shopping opportunities.

Walk up the main **Masarykova ulice** toward the train station, and make a right through the little arcade at No. 6. to see the ❾ animated Gothic portal of the **Stará radnice** (Old Town Hall), the oldest secular building in Brno. The door is the work of Anton Pilgram, architect of Vienna's St. Stephen's Cathedral, and was completed in 1510; the building itself is about 200 years older. Look above the door to see a badly bent pinnacle that looks as if it wilted in the afternoon sun. This isn't the work of vandals but was apparently done by Pilgram himself out of revenge against the town. According to legend, Pilgram had been promised an excellent commission for his portal, but when he finished, the mayor and city councillors reneged on their offer. So angry was Pilgram at the duplicity that he purposely bent the pinnacle and left it poised, fittingly, over the statue of justice.

Just inside the door are the remains of two other famous Brno legends, the **Brno Dragon** and the **wagon wheel.** The dragon—a female alligator to be anatomically correct—apparently turned up at the town walls one day in the 17th century and began eating the children and livestock. A young gatekeeper came up with the novel idea of filling a sack with limestone and placing it inside a freshly slaughtered goat. The dragon devoured the goat, swallowing the limestone as well, and went to quench its thirst at a nearby river. The water mixed with the limestone, bursting the dragon's stomach (the scars on the dragon's stomach are still clearly visible). The story of the wagon wheel, on the other hand, concerns a bet placed some 400 years ago that a young wheelwright, Jiří Birk, couldn't chop down a tree, fashion the wood into a wheel, and roll it from his home at Lednice (33 miles away) to the town walls of Brno—all between sunup and sundown. The wheel stands as a lasting tribute to his achievement (the townspeople, however, became convinced that Jiří had enlisted the help of the devil to win the bet, and so

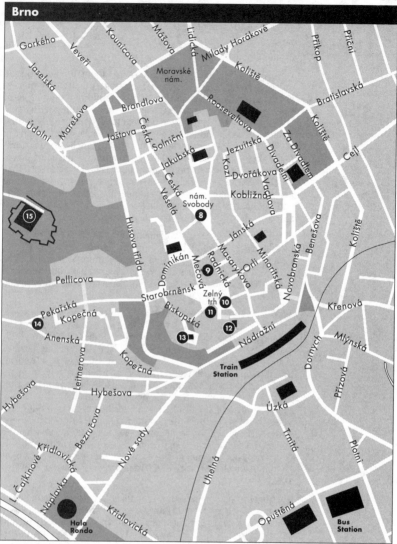

Brno

Dietrichstein
Palace, **11**

Dóm na Petrove, **13**

Kostel Náležení
svatého Kříže, **12**

Monastery of
Staré Brno, **14**

Náměstí Svobody, **8**

Špilberk hrad, **15**

Stará Radnice, **9**

Zelný Třída, **10**

they stopped frequenting his workshop; poor Jiří died penniless).

No longer the seat of the town government, the Old Town Hall holds exhibitions and performances of various kinds. To find out what's on, look for a sign on the door of the exhibition room. The view from the top of the tower is one of the best in Brno, but the climb (five flights) is strenuous. What catches the eye is not so much any one building—although the cathedral does look spectacular—but the combination of old and new that defines modern Brno. In the distance, next to the crooked roofs and Baroque onion domes, a power plant looks startlingly out of place. *Radnická ul. 8. Admission: 10 Kč. adults, 5 Kč. children. Open Tues.–Sun. 9–5.*

⑩ Leave the tower by Pilgram's portal, and turn right into the old **Zelný třída** (Cabbage Market), the only place where Brno begins to look like a typical Czech town. You'll recognize the market immediately, not just for the many stands from which farmers still sell vegetables but also for the unique **Parnassus** fountain that adorns its center. This Baroque pile of rocks (you either love it or hate it) couldn't be more out of place amid the formal elegance of most of the buildings on the square. But when Johann Bernhard Fischer von Erlach created the fountain in the late-17th century, it was important for a striving town like Brno to display its understanding of the classics and of ancient Greece. Thus, Hercules slays a three-headed dragon, while Amphitrite on top awaits the arrival of her lover—all incongruously surrounded by farmers hawking turnips and onions.

⑪ On the far side of the market, dominating the square, stands the severe Renaissance **Dietrichstein Palace** at No. 8. The building was once home to Cardinal Count Franz von Dietrichstein, who led the Catholic counterreformation in Moravia following the Battle of White Mountain in 1620. Today, the palace houses the **Moravské muzeum** (Moravian Museum) with its mundane exhibits of local birds and other wildlife. The museum is undergoing extensive renovation, and some of the more interesting exhibits (such as the ancient Venus of Věstonice) may not be open to the public. To enter the museum, walk through the little gate to the left of the Dietrichstein Palace and then through the lovely Renaissance garden. Note the arcades, the work of 16th-century Italian craftsmen. *Zelný tř 6. Admission: 10 Kč. adults, 5 Kč. students. Open Tues.–Sun. 9–5.*

⑫ From the garden, walk down the stairs to the Baroque **Kostel Náležení svatého Kříže** (Church of the Holy Cross), formerly part of the Capuchin monastery. If you've ever wondered what a mummy looks like without its bandages, then enter the door to the monastery's *hrobka* (crypt). In the basement are the mummified remains of some 200 nobles and monks from the late-17th and 18th centuries, ingeniously preserved by a natural system of air circulating through vents and chimneys. The best-known mummy is Colonel František Trenck, commander of the brutal Pandour regiment of the Austrian army, who spent several years in the dungeons of the Špilberk castle before finding his final rest here in 1749. Even in death the hapless colonel has not found peace—someone made off with his head several years ago. One note of caution about the crypt: The graphic displays may frighten small children, so ask at the admission desk for the small brochure (10 Kč.) with pictures that preview what's to follow. *Kapucínské nám. Admission: 10 Kč. adults, 5 Kč. children. Open Tues.–Sat. 9–11:45 and 2–4:30, Sun. 11–11:45 and 2–4:30.*

🔞 Towering above the church and market is the **Dóm na Petrově** (Cathedral of Sts. Peter and Paul), Brno's main church and a fixture of the skyline. The best way to get to the cathedral is to return to the Cabbage Market (via the little street off the Kapucínské náměstí), make a left at the market, and walk up the narrow Petrská ulice, which begins just to the right of the Dietrichstein Palace. The normally picturesque Petrská is currently undergoing massive reconstruction; if the road is blocked, just follow your instincts up and around to the cathedral. Sadly, Sts. Peter and Paul is one church that probably looks better from a distance. The interior, a blend of Baroque and Gothic, is light and tasteful but hardly overwhelming. Still, the slim neo-Gothic twin spires, added in this century to give the cathedral more of its original Gothic dignity, are a nice touch.

Don't be surprised if you hear the noon bells ringing from the cathedral at 11 o'clock. The practice dates from the Thirty Years' War, when Swedish troops were massing for an attack outside the town walls. Brno's resistance had been fierce, and the Swedish commander decreed that he would give up the fight if the town could not be taken by noon the following day. The bell ringer caught wind of the decision and the next morning, just as the Swedes were preparing a final assault, rang the noon bells—an hour early. The ruse worked and the Swedes decamped. Ever since, the midday bells have been rung an hour early as a show of gratitude.

Before leaving the cathedral area, stroll around the park and grounds. The view from here is pretty and the mood is restful. Continue the tour by walking down the continuation of the Petrská ulice to Biskupská ulice (still more construction). Turn left at the Starobrněnská ulice, and cross the busy Husova třída onto Pekařská ulice, which planners are hoping to transform into a lively area of boutiques and shops someday. At the end of the street is the **Mendelovo náměstí** (Mendel Square) and the

🔞 **Monastery of Staré Brno,** home in the 19th century to Gregor Mendel, the shy monk who became the father of modern genetic research. The uninspiring location seems to confirm the adage that genius can flourish anywhere. If you recall from high school science, it was Mendel's experiments with crossing pea and bean plants and his working out dominant and recessive traits that led to the first formulations of the laws of heredity. A small statue to his memory can be found in the garden behind the monastery.

Continue the tour along the busy and somewhat downtrodden Úvoz ulice in the direction of Špilberk castle. Take the first right and climb the stairs to the calmer residential street of Pellicova. If there's a unique beauty to Brno, it's in neighborhoods such as this one, with their attractive houses, each sporting a different architectural style. Many houses incorporate cubist and geometric elements of the early modern period (1920s and '30s).

🔞 Begin the ascent to **Špilberk hrad** (Špilberk Castle), the fortress–cum–torture chamber that, while long out of business as a prison, still broods over the town from behind its menacing walls. There is no direct path to the castle; just follow your instincts (or a detailed map) upward, and you'll get there. Before you're too far along on the 160-foot climb, however, it's only fair to warn you that the castle is closed for renovation and that no café or restaurant awaits to reward your effort. But push on anyway: You can still get a good look at the castle from the outside, and the views over the city are magnificent. From the top, look over to the west at the gleaming Art Deco pavilions of the Brno **Výstaviště** (Exhibition Grounds) in the distance. The buildings were completed in 1928, in time to hold the first cultural exhibition to celebrate the 10th anniversary of the Czechoslovak state. The grounds are now the site of annual trade fairs.

Špilberk's advantageous location was no secret to the early kings, who moved here in the 13th century from the neighboring Petrov hill. During the Thirty Years' War, Italian builders converted the old castle into a virtually impregnable Baroque fortress. Indeed, it successfully withstood the onslaught of the Swedes and fell only to Napoleon in 1805. But the castle is best known for its gruesome history as a prison and torture chamber for the Austro-Hungarian monarchy and, later, for the Nazis in World War II. After 1994, the public will again be able to tour this Moravian Alcatraz.

Walk down the opposite side of the hill to the east in the direction of the center of town. Sooner or later you'll come to the busy Husova třída again. Cross the street, continue walking straight, and you'll eventually run into the busy pedestrian zone of the **Česká.** Turn to the right along the Česká, and in a couple of minutes you're back at Náměstí Svobody.

Time Out After a long walk and a good climb, what could be better than one of the best beers you'll ever have? The **Stopkova Pivnice** at Česka 5 will set you up with a big one or a small one (or even a soft drink) in clean, comfortable surroundings. If you're hungry, try the house goulash, a tangy mixture of sausage, beef, rice, egg, and dumpling. If you want something more substantial, head for the restaurant on the second floor.

Before leaving Brno, fans of modern architecture will want to see the austere **Tugendhat Haus,** designed by Ludwig Mies van der Rohe and completed in 1930. The white villa, built in Bauhaus style, counts among the most important works of the modern period. The emphasis here is on function and the use of geometric forms, but you be the judge as to whether the house fits the neighborhood or not. Badly damaged during the war, it now houses guests of the city of Brno and is closed to the public. The best way to get there is to take a taxi, or walk 20 minutes northeast of the city center to the area known as Černá Pole.

Tour 3: Northern Moravia *Numbers in the margin correspond to points of interest on the Moravia map.*

Just 20 kilometers (12 miles) east of Brno lies the site of one of ⓰ the great battlefields of European history, **Slavkov,** better known as **Austerlitz,** where the armies of Napoleon met and defeated the combined forces of Austrian emperor Franz II and Czar Alexander I in 1805. If you happen to have a copy of *War and Peace* handy, you will find no better account of it anywhere. Scattered about the rolling agricultural landscapes are a museum, a garden, and the memorial chapel of the impressive **Cairn of Peace.** In the town of Slavkov itself, the Baroque châteu houses more memorabilia about the battle; it's well worth visiting. From Brno, follow the D1 freeway to the east, and turn onto Route 50, following the signs to Slavkov.

If it's scenic tourism you want, however, take a short trip north ⓱ from Brno up the Svitava valley and into the **Moravský Kras** (Moravian Karst), an area of limestone formations, underground stalactite caves, rivers, and tunnels. The most interesting part is near **Blansko** and includes the **Kateřinská** jeskyně (Catherine Cave), **Punkevní jeskyně** (Punkva Cave), and the celebrated **Macocha Abyss,** the deepest drop (more than 400 feet) of the karst. Several caves can be visited: Try the 90-minute Punkva tour, which includes a visit to the Macocha Abyss and a boat trip along an underground river. From Brno, follow Route 43 north in the direction of Svitavy. Turn off at Route 379 to Blansko, and follow Route 380 to the Punkevní jeskyně, about 30 kilometers (19 miles) in all. *Admission: 20 Kč. adults, 10 Kč. students. Open Apr.–Sept., daily 8–3:15 (last tour 2:45 on weekends); Oct.–Mar., daily 7:30–1:45 (until 2:45 on Sun.).*

⓲ To reach **Olomouc** from Brno, drive north on the E462, following the signs all the way. With light traffic, you can cover the 77 kilometers (48 miles) in about an hour. Olomouc is a paradox—so far from Austria yet so supportive of the empire. The Habsburgs always felt at home here, even when they were being violently opposed by Czech nationalists and Protestants throughout the Czech Republic. During the revolutions of 1848, when the middle class from all over the Austrian empire seemed ready to boot the Habsburgs out of their palace, the royal family fled to Olomouc, where they knew they could count on the population for support. The 18-year-old Franz Joseph was even crowned emperor here in 1848 because the situation in Vienna was still too turbulent.

Despite being overshadowed by Brno, Olomouc, with its proud square and prim 19th-century buildings, still retains something of a provincial imperial capital, not unlike similarly sized cities in Austria. The focal point here is the triangular **Horní náměstí** (Upper Square), marked at its center by the bright and almost flippantly colored Renaissance **radnice** (town hall) with its 220-foot tower. The tower was begun in the late-14th century and given its current appearance in 1443; the astronomical clock on the outside was built in 1422, but its inner mechanisms and modern mosaic decorations date from immediately after World War II. Be sure to look inside at the beautiful Renaissance stairway. There's also a large Gothic banquet room in the main building, with scenes from the city's history, and a late-Gothic chapel.

The eccentric **Trinity Column** in the northwest corner of the square, at more than 100 feet, is the largest of its kind in the Czech Republic and houses a tiny chapel. Four Baroque fountains, depicting Hercules (1687), Caesar (1724), Neptune (1695), and Jupiter (1707), dot the main square and the adjacent **Dolní náměstí** (Lower Square) to the south, as if to reassure us that this Moravian town was well versed in the humanities.

Just north of the Horní náměstí, along the small Jana Opletala ulice, stands the **Chrám svatého Mořice** (Church of St. Maurice), the town's best Gothic building. Construction began in 1412, but a fire some 40 years later badly damaged the structure, and its current appearance dates from the middle of the 16th century. The Baroque organ inside, the largest in the Czech Republic, is said to contain some 2,311 pipes.

The most interesting sights in Olomouc are not in the Old Town but about 400 yards to the east in the vicinity of the **Dóm svatého Václava** (Cathedral of St. Wenceslas). If you're approaching from the Horní náměstí, follow the tiny Ostružnícká ulice, turn right onto the busy Denisova ulice, and keep walking straight (beyond yet another Baroque fountain at the náměstí Republiky) until you reach Dómská ulice. As it stands today, the original Gothic cathedral is just another example of the overbearing neo-Gothic enthusiasm of the late-19th century. To the left of the church, however, is the entrance to the **Kostel svatej Anny** (St. Anne's Chapel), now a museum, where you can see early 16th-century wall paintings decorating the Gothic cloisters and, upstairs, a wonderful series of two- and three-arched Romanesque windows. This part of the building was used as a schoolroom some 700 years ago, and you can still make out drawings of animals engraved on the walls by early young vandals. You can get an oddly phrased English pamphlet to help you around the building. *Dómská ul. Admission: 10 Kč. adults, 5 Kč. children. Open Tues.–Sun. 9–12:30 and 1–5.*

The **deacon's house** opposite the cathedral, now part of the Palacký University, has two unusual claims to fame. Here in 1767, the young musical prodigy Wolfgang Amadeus Mozart, age 11, spent six weeks recovering from a mild attack of chicken pox. The 16-year-old King Wenceslas III suffered a much worse fate here in 1306, when he was murdered, putting an end to the Přemyslide dynasty.

What to See and Do with Children

Small children will no doubt be amused by the enormous **alligator** hanging from the ceiling in the Old Town Hall in Brno and by some of the stories associated with how it got there (*see* Tour 2). If you're traveling with older children, head out to the **Moravian Karst** (*see* Tour 3) and take a tour of the caves. Some tours include an exciting boat ride on an underground river. The archaeological museum at **Dolní Věstonice** (*see* Tour 1) has mammoth bones and remains from Stone Age settlements to keep junior scientists occupied for a while. The park at the **Lednice** castle (*see* Tour 1) has plenty of ground for playing on, wandering around, throwing a Frisbee, or kicking a ball. In winter, the frozen ponds here and in the surrounding area are great for ice skating (but you'll have to buy skates, as rentals are impossible to find).

Off the Beaten Track

Fans of dream interpretation and psychoanalysis shouldn't leave Moravia without stopping at the little town of **Příbor,** the birthplace of Sigmund Freud. To find it, drive east out of Olomouc along Route 35, following the signs first to Lipník, then Hranice, Nový Jičín, and finally Příbor—about 50 kilometers (31 miles) in all. Park at the Náměstí Sigmunda Freuda Sigmund Freud Square. The seemingly obvious name for the main square is actually new; the former communist regime was not in favor of Freudians. The comfortable, middle-class house, marked with a plaque where the doctor was born in 1856, is a short walk away along Freudova ulice. At present, the house is still residential, so you can't go inside. *Freudova ul. 117.*

Admirers of art-nouveau meister Alfons Mucha may want to make a short detour to the southern Moravian town of **Moravský Krumlov,** not far from the main highway linking Mikulov and Brno. The town museum is the unlikely home of one of Mucha's most celebrated works, his 20-canvas "Slav Epic." This enormous work, which tells the story of the emergence of the Slav nation, was not well received when it was completed in 1928; painters at the time were more interested in imitating modern movements and considered Mucha's representational art to be old-fashioned. Interest in Mucha's lyrical style has grown in recent years, however, and the museum annually attracts some 15,000 visitors.

Shopping

Moravia produces very attractive folk pottery, painted with bright red, orange, and yellow flower patterns. You can find these products all over Moravia, but some of the most attractive pieces can be found in two tourist centers in Brno: the souvenir shop of the **Hotel International** (Husova ul. 16, tel. 05/213–4111) and the **American-Moravian Center** (Rádnická ul. 10, tel. 05/25908). The latter also sells T-shirts printed with the Brno dragon. You can buy English paperbacks in Brno at the **Zahraniční literatura** shop (nám. Svobody 18). The secret of Moravian wine is only now beginning to extend beyond the country's borders. A vintage bottle from one of the smaller but still excellent vineyards in Bzenec, Velké Pavlovice, or Hodonín would be appreciated by any wine connoisseur.

Sports and Outdoor Activities

For mountain walking or cross-country skiing (if you're not going on to the High Tatras), try the gentle peaks of the **Beskydy Mountains,** about 25 kilometers (16 miles) south of Příbor; follow Route 58 south in the direction of Rožnov. Stay the night at one of the modest but comfortable mountain chalets in the area. You'll find a good one, the **Chata Solan,** along the road between Rožnov and Velké Karlovice (*see* Lodging, *below*). Another place to try is **Tanečnice** (south of Frenštát). But be sure to take along a good map before venturing along the tiny mountain roads. Also, some roads may be closed during the winter.

Dining and Lodging

Don't expect gastronomic delights in Moravia. The food—especially outside of Brno—is reasonably priced, but the choices are usually limited to roast pork, sauerkraut, and dumplings, or fried pork and french fries. Moravia's hotels are only now beginning to recover from 40 years of state ownership, and excellent hotels are few and far between. In many larger towns, private rooms are preferred. In mountainous areas inquire locally about the possibility of staying in a *chata* (cabin). These are abundant and often a pleasant alternative to the faceless modern hotels. Many lack modern amenities, though, so be prepared to rough it.

It's best to avoid Brno at trade-fair time (April and September), when hotel and restaurant facilities are badly strained. If the hotels are booked, Brno's Čedok (Divadlení ul., tel. 05/25466) and ČKM (Česká 11, tel. 05/23641) offices will help you find accommodations.

Highly recommended restaurants and lodgings in a particular price category are indicated by a star ★.

Brno
Dining

Baroko vinárna. This 17th-century wine cellar housed in a Minorite monastery offers excellent cooking in a fun, if touristy, setting. Try the roast beef Slavkov, named for the site of Napoleon's triumph not far from Brno. Mystery of Magdalene is a potato pancake stuffed with pork, liver, mushrooms, and presumably anything else the cook could get his hands on. *Orlí 17, tel. 05/25547. No credit cards. Dinner only. Moderate.*

Modrá Hvězda. Liberal opening hours and a convenient location just to the west of náměstí Svobody make this cheery restaurant a good choice for a quick lunch or off-hours snack. *Šilingrovo nám. 7, tel. 05/27910. No credit cards. Moderate.*

Klub Restaurant Pod Petrovem. This typical Moravian inn, just behind the Zelný třída, serves authentic country cuisine at reasonable prices. Try the delicate Moravian goulash or the hard-to-find poppyseed dumplings, which nicely round off the usually heavy Czech cuisine. *Petrská 2, tel. 05/26474. No credit cards. Inexpensive.*

Motorest Devět Křížů. Believe it or not, you get decent local cooking (pork and dumplings or goulash) at this clean and comfortable roadside restaurant, situated on the main highway to Prague. *D1 freeway (26 km/16 mi west of Brno). No credit cards. Inexpensive.*

Špalíček. This raucous pivnice is for serious beer drinkers only. Nevertheless, it serves hearty, simple beef and pork dishes, and on warm summer evenings the terrace overlooking the Cabbage Market is the best place in town to linger over a drink. *12 Zelný tř., tel. 05/23692. No credit cards. Inexpensive.*

Lodging
★

Grand. Though not really grand, this hotel, built in 1870 and thoroughly remodeled in 1988, is certainly comfortable and the best in Brno. High standards are maintained through the hotel's association with an Austrian chain. The reception and public areas are clean and modern; service is attentive; and the rooms, while small, are well appointed. Ask for a room at the back, overlooking the town, as the hotel is situated on a busy street opposite the railroad station. *Tř. Máje 18–20, tel. 05/23526, fax 05/22426. Facilities: 3 restaurants, minibar, satellite TV, casino, nightclub. Breakfast included. AE, MC, V. Very Expensive.*

International. This 1960s high rise, perched between the central square and Špilberk castle, was Brno's showcase for two decades. It is still elegant, particularly in its lavish cafés and restaurants; but the dark corridors and small, functional rooms are more reminiscent of a dormitory than a luxury hotel. *Husova ul. 16, tel. 05/213–4111, fax 05/23051. 280 rooms with bath. Facilities: 2 restaurants, snack bar, nightclub, parking garage, minibars, satellite TV. Breakfast included. AE, MC, V. Very Expensive.*

Continental. Situated along a major artery heading out of the city center, this modern edifice exudes a 1960s optimism yet can't quite overcome the institutional feel. However, the standards of service are high, and the rooms are functional and clean. The terrace at the front is a good place to sit and watch one day fade into the next. *Konicová ul. 6, tel. 05/753121, telex 62350. 228 rooms, most with bath. Facilities: restaurant, bar. Breakfast included. AE, DC, MC, V. Expensive.*

Slavia. The century-old Slavia, located just off the main Česká ulice, was thoroughly renovated in 1987, giving the public areas an efficient, up-to-date look and leaving the rooms plain but clean. The café, with adjacent terrace, is a good place to enjoy a cool drink on a warm afternoon. *Solniční 15–17, tel. 05/23711, fax 05/24179. 81 rooms with shower or bath. Facilities: restaurant, café, minibars, parking. Breakfast included. AE, DC, MC, V. Expensive.*

Jihlava
Dining and Lodging

Zlatá Hvězda. Centrally located on the main square, this reconstructed old hotel in a beautiful Renaissance house is comfortable and surprisingly elegant. You're a short walk from Jihlava's restaurants and shops, though the on-site café and wine bar are among the best in town. *Nám. Míru 32, tel. 066/29421. 18 rooms. Facilities: restaurant, wine bar, café. Breakfast included. No credit cards. Moderate.*

Mikulov
Lodging

Rohatý Krokodýl. This is a prim, newly renovated hotel on a quaint street in the Old Town. The standards and facilities are the best in Mikulov, particularly the ground-floor restaurant, which serves a typical but delicately prepared selection of traditional Czech dishes. *Husova 8, tel. 0625/2692. 15 rooms with bath. Facilities: restaurant, terrace. Breakfast included. No credit cards. Expensive.*

Olomouc
Dining and Lodging

Flora. Don't expect luxury at this 1960s cookie-cutter high rise, located about a 15-minute walk from the town square. To its credit, the staff is attentive (English is spoken), and the pleasant if anonymous rooms are certainly adequate for a short stay. *Krapkova ul. 34, tel. 068/23241, fax 068/25449. 175 rooms, most with bath or shower. Facilities: restaurant, parking. Breakfast not included. AE, DC, MC, V. Expensive.*

Národní Dům. Built in 1885 and located a block from the main square, this is a better choice than the Flora for evoking a little of Olomouc's 19th-century history. The handsome building recalls the era's industriousness, as does the large, gracious café on the main floor. Standards have slipped in the intervening years, though, and signs of decline are evident. *Ul. 8. května 21, tel. 068/24806. 63 rooms, most with bath or shower. Facilities: restaurant, café, snack bar. Breakfast not included. No credit cards. Moderate.*

Morava. This traditional hotel located a block from the main square is strictly low budget. Still, don't be put off by the cramped, musty reception area; the rooms themselves are quite clean. *Riegrova ul. 16, tel. 068/29671. 50 rooms, some with shower. Breakfast not included. No credit cards. Inexpensive.*

Telč
Dining and Lodging
★

Černý Orel. Here you'll get a very rare treat: an older, refined hotel that combines modern amenities in a traditional setting. The public areas are functional but elegant, and the inviting rooms are well balanced and comfortably furnished. The hotel, with its Baroque facade, is a perfect foil to the handsome main square outside; ask for a room overlooking it. Even if you don't stay here, take a meal at the hotel restaurant, the best in town. *Nám. Zachariase z Hradce 7, tel. 066/962221. 30 rooms, most* with bath. *Facilities: restaurant. Breakfast not included. AE, DC, MC, V. Moderate.*

Valtice **Hubertus.** This comfortable hotel, tucked away in one wing of a
Dining and Lodging neo-Renaissance palace, is not hard to find. Just look for the
★ only palace in town; the hotel is on the left-hand side. While the
rooms are neither palatial nor furnished in period style, they
are nevertheless generously proportioned and comfortable.
The restaurant, with garden terrace, serves reasonable Moravian cooking and good wine. Book ahead in summer, as the
hotel is popular with Austrians who like to slip across the border for an impromptu holiday. *Zámek, tel. 0627/94537. Facilities: restaurant, wine bar. Breakfast not included. No credit
cards. Moderate.*

Velké Karlovice **Chata Solan.** This tiny lodge is perched amid the hills and trees
Dining and Lodging of the Beskydy range. Follow the road from Rožnov in the
direction of Velké Karlovice for about 10 kilometers (6 miles);
the lodge is the small wooden building on the left. Don't expect
many amenities (you may have to share a room), but the standards of comfort and cleanliness are very high. A good breakfast is served in the rustic restaurant on the first floor. *Velké
Karlovice, tel. 0657/94365. 5 rooms share a bath. No credit
cards. Inexpensive.*

Znojmo **Dukla.** There are no surprises at this fairly modernized hotel
Dining and Lodging set on the road to Vienna about 7 kilometers (4 miles) south of
town. The staff is competent, and the corridors and small
rooms are dreary but clean. The restaurant serves good Czech
dishes in a relaxed atmosphere. *Antonína Zápotockého 5, tel.
0624/76320. 110 rooms with bath or shower. Facilities: restaurant, parking. Breakfast not included. AE, DC, MC, V. Moderate.*
Pension Inka. Rather than stay in a hotel, you might consider
staying in this tiny, family-run pension not far from the center
of town. The facilities are modest, but the rooms are bright and
well kept. The kitchen is available for the use of guests.
*Jarošova ul. 27, tel. 0624/4059. 3 rooms without bath. Break-
fast not included. No credit cards. Inexpensive.*

The Arts and Nightlife

The Arts **Brno** is renowned throughout the Czech Republic for its theater and performing arts. The two main locales for cultural
events are the **Mahen theater** (for drama) and the modern **Janáček theater** (for opera and ballet). Both are located just to the
northwest of the center of town, just off Rooseveltova ul. Don't
miss an opportunity to attend a concert here. Check the schedule at the theater or pick up a copy of *KAM*, Brno's monthly
bulletin of cultural events. Buy tickets directly at the theater
box office 30 minutes before showtime.

Nightlife Nightlife in **Brno** revolves around the local pivnice or vinárna.
Several good places can be found along **Česká ulice.** If it's a
warm evening, head for the **Spaliček** pivnice (12 Zelný tř., tel.
05/23692), invariably packed but with a great terrace overlooking the central Cabbage Market.

More sophisticated entertainment can be found at the **casinos**
at the **Grand** and **International** hotels (*see* Lodging, *above*); the
tables usually stay open until 3 or 4 AM. Both hotels also have
bars that serve drinks until the wee hours of the morning.

3 Slovakia

By Mark Baker

Despite more than 70 years of common statehood with the Czechs (which ended in 1993), Slovakia *(Slovensko)* differs from the Czech Republic in a great many aspects. Its mountains are higher and more rugged, its veneer less sophisticated, its people more carefree. Observers of the two regions like to link the Czech Republic geographically and culturally with the orderly Germans, while they put Slovakia with the Ukraine and Russia firmly in the east. This is a simplification, yet it contains more than a little bit of truth.

Although they speak a language closely related to Czech, the Slovaks managed to maintain a strong sense of national identity throughout the period of common statehood. Indeed, the two Slavic groups developed quite separately: Though united in the 9th century as part of the Great Moravian Empire, the Slovaks were conquered a century later by the Magyars and remained under Hungarian or Habsburg rule until 1918. Following the Tartar invasions in the 13th century, many Saxons were invited to resettle the land and develop the economy, including the rich mineral resources. In the 15th and 16th centuries, Romanian shepherds migrated from Wallachia through the Carpathians into Slovakia, and the merging of these varied groups with the resident Slavs bequeathed to the region a rich folk culture and some unique forms of architecture, especially in the east.

In the end, it was this very different history that split the Slovaks from the Czechs, ending the most successful experiment in nation-building to follow World War I.

For many Slovaks, the 1989 revolution provided for the first time an opportunity not only to bring down the Communists, but also to establish a fully independent state—thus ending what many Slovaks saw as a millennium of subjugation by Hungary and the Hapsburgs, Nazi Germany, Prague's communist regimes, and ultimately the Czechs. Although few Slovaks harbored any real resentment toward the Czechs, Slovak politicians were quick to recognize and exploit the deep, inchoate longing for independence. Slovak nationalist parties won more than 50% of the vote in the crucial 1992 Czechoslovak elections, and once the results were in, the end came quickly: on January 1, 1993, Slovakia became the youngest country in Europe.

The outside world witnessed the demise of the Czechoslovak federation in 1993 with some sadness; the split seemed just another piece of evidence to confirm that tribalism and nationalism continue to play the deciding role in European affairs. Yet there is something hopeful to be seen in the fact that the separation took place peacefully. Despite lingering differences on dividing the federation's assets, no Czechs or Slovaks have yet died in nationalistic squabbles. For the visitor, the changes may in fact be positive. The Slovaks have been long overshadowed by their cousins to the west; now they have the unfettered opportunity to tell their story to the world.

Most visitors to Slovakia head first for the great peaks of the High Tatras. The smallest alpine range in the world, the Tatras rise magnificently from the foothills of northern Slovakia. The tourist infrastructure here is very good, catering especially to hikers and skiers. Visitors who come to admire the peaks, however, often overlook the exquisite medieval towns of Spiš in the plains and valleys below the High Tatras and the beautiful

18th-century country churches farther east. (Away from main centers, these areas are short on tourist amenities, so if creature comforts are important to you, stick to the High Tatras.)

Bratislava, the capital of Slovakia, is a disappointment to many visitors. The last 40 years of communism left a clear mark on the city, hiding its ancient beauty with hulking, and now dilapidated, futurist structures. Yet despite its gloomy appearance, Bratislava tries hard to project the cosmopolitanism of a European capital, bolstered by the fact that it is filled with good restaurants and wine bars, opera and art.

Before You Go

Government Tourist Offices

Čedok, the official travel bureau for both the Czech Republic and Slovakia, is a travel agent rather than a tourist information office. As such, it will supply you with hotel and tour information, and book air, rail, and bus tickets, but do not expect much in the way of general information.

In the United States: 10 E. 40th St., New York, NY 10016, tel. 212/689–9720. **In the United Kingdom:** 17–18 Old Bond St., London W1X 4RB, tel. 071/629–6058.

Tour Groups

U.S. Tour Operators Although there are no U.S.-based operators that specialize in tours to Slovakia and Bratislava, **General Tours** (245 5th Ave., New York, NY 10016, tel. 212/685–1800 or 800/221–2216) arranges excursions through Slovakia in conjunction with some of its East European packages. For information about other operators that include Slovakia on their East European itineraries, *see* Before You Go in Chapter 1.

U.K. Tour Operators **Čedok Tours and Holidays** (17–18 Old Bond St., London W1X 4RB, tel. 071/629–6058) offers packages to Prague and the Czech Republic with optional sightseeing excursions to Slovakia. Čedok also has packages to Bratislava's music festival.

Danube Travel Ltd. (6 Conduit St.1, London W1R 9TG, tel. 071/493–0263) offers a variety of packages that include a few nights' stay in Bratislava.

When to Go

Slovakia, with its four full seasons, is beautiful throughout the year. The High Tatras come into their own in winter (January–March), when skiers by the thousand descend on the major resorts. A smaller summer season in the mountains attracts mostly walkers and hikers looking to escape the heat and noise of the cities. Because of the snow, many of the hiking trails, especially those that cross the peaks, are open only between June and October.

Bratislava is best visited in the temperate months of spring and autumn. July and August, while not especially crowded, can be unbearably hot. In winter, when many tourist attractions are closed, expect lots of rain and snow in the capital. Note that, year-round, temperatures are much cooler in mountainous are-

519 M.P.H.

190 M.P.H.

75 M.P.H.

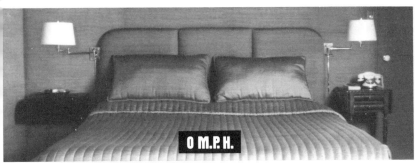

0 M.P.H.

WE LET YOU SEE EUROPE AT YOUR OWN PACE.

Regardless of your personal speed limits, Rail Europe offers everything to get you over, around and through anywhere you want in Europe. For more information, call your travel agent or 1-800-4-EURAIL.

OFFICIAL DISTRIBUTOR
Rail Europe
OF THE EURAIL PASS

We can wire money to every major city in Europe almost as fast as you can say, "Zut alors! J'ai perdu mes valises".

How fast? We can send money in 10 minutes or less, to 13,500 locations in over 68 countries worldwide. That's faster than any other international money transfer service. And when you're *sans* luggage, every minute counts.

MoneyGram from American Express® is available throughout Europe. For more information please contact your local American Express Travel Service Office or call: 44-71-839-7541 in England; 33-1-47777000 in France; or 49-69-21050 in Germany. In the U.S. call 1-800-MONEYGRAM.

MoneyGram
INTERNATIONAL MONEY TRANSFERS.

Ten-minute delivery subject to local agent hours of operation. Local send/receive facilities may also vary. ©1993 First Data Corporation.

as. Even in summer, expect to wear a sweater or jacket in the High Tatras.

Festivals and Seasonal Events

For the moment, Slovakia's only major festival is the **Bratislava Music Festival,** which attracts national and international musicians to venues throughout the capital in late October.

Many towns and villages host annual folklore festivals, usually on a weekend in late summer or early fall. These frequently take place in the town center and are accompanied by lots of singing, dancing, and drinking. Information is hard to come by, which makes planning difficult. Čedok promises to compile and publish a list of regional Slovakian festivals sometimes in 1994; keep an eye out for it.

What to Pack

As is the case throughout Eastern Europe, many consumer items are still in short supply in Slovakia. Be certain to pack any special medications, as well as any special toiletries or hygienic materials you may require (i.e., special soaps, shampoos, contact-lens solution, nonaspirin pain relievers). You will need an electrical adapter for small appliances; the voltage is 220, with 50 cycles. If you plan to hike in the mountains, a sturdy pair of shoes or boots is a must.

Slovak Currency

The unit of currency in Slovakia is the crown (Sk.), which is divided into 100 halers. There are (little used) coins of 10, 20, and 50 halers; coins of 1, 2, 5, 10, and 20 Sk., and notes of 10, 20, 50, 100, 500, and 1,000 Sk. The 100-Sk. notes are by far the most useful. The 1,000-Sk. note won't always be accepted for small purchases, because the proprietor may not have enough change. Also note: Czech money is no longer accepted as legal tender in Slovakia. If you're headed for the Czech Republic, exchange your Slovakian crowns for Czech crowns before crossing the border.

Try to avoid exchanging money at hotels or private exchange booths. They routinely take commissions of 8%–10%. The best places to exchange are banks, where the commissions average 1%–3%. Although the Slovak crown is more or less convertible, you will still encounter difficulty in exchanging your money when you leave. To facilitate this process, keep your original exchange receipts so no one will think you bought your crowns on the black market. It is technically illegal to buy crowns abroad and bring them into Slovakia (or to take them out when you leave), although this is not strictly controlled. At press time (summer 1993) the official exchange rate was around 29 Sk. to the U.S. dollar and 43 Sk. to the pound sterling. There is no longer a special exchange rate for tourists.

What It Will Cost

Slovakia is a bargain by Western standards, particularly in the outlying areas and off the beaten track. The exception is the price of accommodation in Bratislava, where hotel rates often meet or exceed the U.S. and Western European average. Accommodations outside of the capital, with the exception of the High Tatras resorts, are significantly lower. Tourists can now legally pay for hotel rooms in Slovakian crowns, although some hotels will still insist on payment in "hard" (i.e., Western) currency.

Sample Costs A cup of coffee, 15 Sk.; museum entrance, 10 Sk.–20 Sk.; a good theater seat, up to 100 Sk.; a cinema seat, 25 Sk.–30 Sk.; a half liter (pint) of beer, 15 Sk.; a 1-mile taxi ride, 60 Sk.; a bottle of Slovak wine in a good restaurant, 100 Sk.–150 Sk.; a glass (2 deciliters, or 7 ounces) of wine, 25 Sk.

Passports and Visas

American and British citizens do not need a visa to enter Slovakia. A valid passport is sufficient for stays of up to 30 days. Questions should be directed to the Slovakian embassy (3900 Linnean Ave. NW, Washington, DC, tel. 202/363–6315). Canadian citizens must obtain a visa (C$50) before entering the country; for applications and information contact the Slovakian embassy (50 Rideau Terrace, Ottawa, Ontario K1M 2A1, tel. 613/749–4442).

Customs and Duties

You may import duty-free into Slovakia 250 cigarettes or the equivalent in tobacco, one liter of spirits, two liters of wine, and ½ liter of perfume. You are also permitted to import duty-free up to 1,000 Sk. worth of gifts and souvenirs.

As with the Czech Republic, if you take into Slovakia any valuables or foreign-made equipment from home, such as cameras, it's wise to carry the original receipts with you or register the items with U.S. Customs before you leave (Form 4457). Otherwise you could end up paying duty on your return.

Language

Slovak, a western-Slavic language closely related to both Czech and Polish, is the official language of Slovakia. Czech and Slovak are mutually comprehensible; if you speak Czech, you'll have little problem in Slovakia. Learning English is popular among young people, but German is still the most useful language for tourists. Don't be surprised if you get a response in German to a question asked in English.

Staying Healthy

Slovakia poses no great risk to health for the short-term visitor. As is the case throughout Eastern Europe, vegetarians and those on special diets will have trouble adjusting to Slovakia's pork- and beef-based cuisine. Fresh fruits and vegetables are bountiful during summer and fall, but not during winter.

Car Rentals

There are no special requirements for renting a car in Slovakia, but be sure to shop around, as prices can differ greatly. **Avis** and **Hertz** offer Western makes for as much as $500 per week. Smaller local companies, on the other hand, can rent local cars for as low as $130 per week. The following agencies are located in Bratislava:

Avis, Hviezdoslavovo nám. 14, tel. 07/333201
Europcar/National, Bratislava airport, tel. 07/220285; Hotel Danube, tel. 07/340841
Hertz, Bratislava airport, tel. 07/226770; Hotel Forum, tel. 07/348155
Recar, Stefanikova 1, tel. 07/333420

Rail Passes

The **European East Pass** is good for unlimited first-class travel on the national railroads of Austria, the Czech Republic, Slovakia, Hungary, and Poland. The pass allows five days of travel within a 15-day period ($169) or 10 days of travel within a 30-day period ($275). Apply through your travel agent or through **Rail Europe** (226–230 Westchester Ave., White Plains, NY 10604, tel. 914/682–2999 or 800/848–7245).

The **EurailPass** and **Eurail Youthpass** are not valid for travel within Slovakia. The **InterRail Pass,** available to European citizens only through local student or budget travel offices, is valid for unlimited train travel in Slovakia and the other countries covered in this book. For more information, *see* Before You Go in Chapter 1.

Student and Youth Travel

ČKM is the center for student and youth discounts; it will also help book spaces in hostels and cheaper hotels (Hviezdoslavovo nám. 19, Bratislava, tel. 07/331607). For general information about student identity cards, work abroad programs, and youth hostelling, *see* Before You Go in Chapter 1.

Further Reading

Slovak writers have long been overshadowed in the West by their Bohemian counterparts, hence little of Slovakia's literature is available to the English reader. Given the 74-year political union of Czechs and Slovaks, however, many Czech authors (*see* Before You Go in Chapter 2), including Milan Kundera, Josef Skvorecký, and Václav Havel, addressed themes of relevance to Slovakia. In addition, many of the general books on Eastern Europe listed in Chapter 1 contain chapters and background information on Slovakia.

Arriving and Departing

From North America by Plane

Airports and Airlines At press time, few international airlines provided direct service to Bratislava, hence the best airports for traveling to Slovakia remain Prague's Ruzyně Airport and Vienna's Schwechat Airport. **ČSA,** the Czech and Slovak national carrier (in U.S. tel. 718/656–8439), offers regular service to Prague from New York's JFK, Chicago, Los Angeles, and Montreal. Many of these flights have direct connections from Prague to Bratislava ($60–$75 each way); the trip takes about an hour. ČSA also offers regular air service between Prague and the High Tatras

(Poprad) and Košice. Vienna's Schwechat Airport lies a mere 50 kilometers (30 miles) to the west of Bratislava. Four buses a day stop at Schwechat en route to Bratislava; the journey takes just over an hour. Numerous trains and buses also run daily between Vienna and Bratislava.

Flying Time From New York, a flight to Bratislava (with a stopover in Prague) takes 11–12 hours. From Montreal it is 8½ hours; from Los Angeles, 17 hours.

From the United Kingdom by Plane, Bus, Car, and Train

By Plane British Airways (in U.K., tel. 071/897–4000) has daily nonstop service to Prague from London; ČSA (in U.K., tel. 071/255–1898) flies five times a week nonstop from London. The flight takes about three hours. Numerous airlines offer service between London and Vienna. **Tatra Air,** a private airline based in Bratislava (tel. 07/292306), does not service London but does provide frequent flights between the Slovak capital and Zurich, Geneva, Munich, Stuttgart, and Frankfurt.

By Bus There is no direct bus service from the United Kingdom to Slovakia; the closest you can get is Vienna. **International Express** (Coach Travel Center, 13 Lower Regent St., London SW1Y 4LR, tel. 071/439–9368) operates daily in summer.

By Car Hoek van Holland and Ostend are the most convenient ferry ports for Bratislava. From either, drive to Cologne (Köln) and then through Dresden or Frankfurt to reach Bratislava.

By Train There are no direct trains from London. You can take a direct train from Paris via Frankfurt to Vienna (and connect to another train or bus), or from Berlin via Dresden and Prague (en route to Budapest). Vienna is a good starting point for Bratislava. There are several trains that make the 70-minute run daily from Vienna's Südbahnhof.

Staying in Slovakia

Getting Around

By Plane Despite the splintering of the Czechoslovak federation, ČSA (Czechoslovak Airlines) maintains a remarkably good internal air service within Slovakia, linking Bratislava with Poprad (Tatras), Piešt'any, and Košice. The flights, by jet or turboprop aircraft, are relatively cheap and frequent. Reservations can be made through Čedok offices abroad or ČSA in Bratislava (tel. 07/331230).

By Train Trains come in a variety of speeds, but it's not really worth taking anything less than an "express" train, marked in red on the timetable. Tickets are relatively cheap; first class is considerably more spacious and comfortable and well worth the 50% more than you'll pay for standard tickets. If you don't specify "express" when you buy your ticket, you may have to pay a supplement on the train. If you haven't bought a ticket in advance at the station, it's easy to buy one on the train for a small extra charge. On timetables, departures appear on a yellow background; arrivals are on white. It is possible to book *couchettes* (sleepers) on most overnight trains, but don't expect much in the way of comfort. The European East Pass and InterRail Pass are valid for all rail travel within Slovakia (*see* Rail Passes, *above*).

By Bus ČSAD (Bratislava, tel. 07/63213), the national bus carrier for the Czech Republic and Slovakia, maintains a comprehensive network in both countries. Buses are usually much quicker than the normal trains and more frequent than express trains, though prices are comparable with train fares. Buy your tickets from the ticket window at the bus station or directly from the driver on the bus. Long-distance buses can be full, so you might want to book a seat in advance; any Čedok office will help you do this. The only drawback to traveling by bus is figuring out the timetables. They are easy to read, but beware of the small letters denoting exceptions to the time given.

By Car Slovakia has few multi-lane highways, but the secondary road network is in reasonably good shape, and traffic is usually light. Roads are poorly marked, however, so an essential purchase is the *Auto Atlas ČSFR* or the larger-scale *Velký Autoatlas Československá* (which also shows locations of lead-free gas pumps). Both are multilingual, inexpensive, and available at bookstores throughout Slovakia and the Czech Republic.

Slovakia follows the usual Continental rules of the road. A right turn on red is permitted only when indicated by a green arrow. Signposts with yellow diamonds indicate a main road where drivers have the right of way. The speed limit is 110 kph (70 mph) on four-lane highways; 90 kph (55 mph) on open roads; and 60 kph (40 mph) in built-up areas. The fine for speeding is roughly 300 Sk., payable on the spot. Seat belts are compulsory, and drinking before driving is prohibited.

To report an accident, call the emergency number (tel. 155). In case of an auto breakdown, in Bratislava contact the 24-hour towing service (tel. 07/363711). The *Auto Atlas ČSFR* has a list of emergency road-repair numbers in various towns.

Telephones

Local Calls A local call costs 1 Sk., and coin-operated telephones take either 1-Sk. coins exclusively, or any combination of 1-, 2-, and 5-Sk. coins. To make a call, lift the receiver and listen for the dial tone (a series of long buzzes), then dial the number. Public phones are often out of order, however; try asking in a hotel if you're stuck.

International Calls Dial tel. 00–420–00101 (AT&T) or tel. 00–420–00112 (MCI) to reach an English-speaking operator who can effortlessly connect your direct, collect, or credit card call to the United States. Otherwise, you can make a more time-consuming and expensive international call from Bratislava's main post office (Námestie SNP 36), or, for an even larger fee, at major hotels throughout the country.

Mail

Postal Rates Postcards to the United States cost 6 Sk.; letters, 11 Sk. Postcards to Great Britain cost 4 Sk.; a letter, 6 Sk. Prices are due for an increase in 1994, so check with your hotel for current rates. You can buy stamps at post offices, hotels, and many shops that sell postcards.

Receiving Mail If you don't know where you'll be staying, you can have mail held *poste restante* at post offices in major towns, but the letters should be marked *Pošta 1* to designate a city's main post office. You will be asked for identification when you collect mail. The *poste restante* window in Bratislava is at Námestie SNP 35.

Tipping

To reward good service in a restaurant, round up the bill to the nearest multiple of 10 (if the bill comes to 86 Sk., for example, give the waiter 90 Sk.). A tip of 10% is considered appropriate on very large tabs. If you have difficulty communicating the amount to the waiter, just leave the money on the table. Tip porters who bring bags to your rooms 20 Sk. For room service, a 20-Sk. tip is sufficient. In taxis, round up the bill by 10%. Give tour guides and helpful concierges 20 Sk.–30 Sk.

Opening and Closing Times

Banks Bank hours vary, but most are open weekdays 8–3:30, with a one-hour lunch break.

Museums Museums are usually open daily 9–5 except Monday and sometimes Tuesday. Some tourist sights, including many castles, are open only May through October.

Stores Stores generally are open weekdays 9–6. Some grocery stores open at 6 AM, and some department stores often stay open until 7 PM. On Saturday, most shops close at noon. Nearly all stores are closed on Sunday.

National Holidays

January 1; Easter Monday; May 1 (Labor Day); May 8 (Liberation); July 5 (Sts. Cyril and Methodius); October 28 (Independence); and December 24, 25, and 26.

Shopping

The best buys in Slovakia are folk-art products sold at stands along the roads and in **Slovart** stores in most major towns. Among the most interesting finds are batik-painted Easter eggs, cornhusk figures, delicate woven table mats, hand-knitted sweaters, and folk pottery. The local brands of firewater— *slivovice* (plum brandy) and *borovička* (a spirit made from juniper berries)—also make for excellent buys.

Sports and Outdoor Activities

Bicycling Slovaks are avid cyclists, and the flatter areas to the south and east of Bratislava and along the Danube are ideal for biking. Outside of the larger towns, quieter roads stretch out for many kilometers. A special bike trail links Bratislava and Vienna, paralleling the Danube for much of its 40-kilometer (25-mile) length. Not many places rent bikes, however; inquire at Čedok or at your hotel for rental information.

Boating and Sailing Slovaks with boats head to the man-made lakes of Zemplínska Šírava (*see* Eastern Slovakia, *below*) or Orava (northwest of the Tatras near the Polish border). River rafting has been hampered in recent years by dry weather, which also has reduced river levels. However, raft rides still are given in summer at Červený Kláštor, north of Kežmarok (*see* Eastern Slovakia, *below*).

Camping There are hundreds of camping sites for tents and trailers throughout Slovakia, but most are open only in summer (May to mid-September). You can get a map of all the sites, with addresses, opening times, and facilities, from Čedok; auto atlases also identify campsites. Camping outside of official sites is prohibited. Some camping grounds also offer bungalows. Campsites are divided into categories A and B according to facilities, but both have hot water and toilets.

Fishing There are hundreds of lakes and rivers suitable for fishing in Slovakia, but because rental equipment is scarce, you should bring your own tackle or be prepared to buy it locally. To legally cast a line you must have a fishing license (valid for one year) plus a fishing permit (valid for a day, week, month, or year for the particular body of water you plan to fish on). Both are available from Čedok offices.

Hiking Slovakia is a hiker's paradise, with more than 20,000 kilometers (15,000 miles) of well-kept, marked, and signposted trails in both the mountainous regions and the rural countryside. You'll find the colored markings denoting trails on trees, fences, walls, rocks, and elsewhere. The colors correspond to the path-marking on the large-scale *Soubor turistickych* maps available at many bookshops and tobacconists. The main paths are marked in red, others in blue and green; the least important trails are marked in yellow. The best areas for ambitious mountain walkers are the Small Carpathians (near Bratislava), the Fatra range in western Slovakia, and the High Tatras to the north.

Skiing The two main skiing areas in Slovakia are the Low Tatras (Nízke Tatry) and the High Tatras (Vysoké Tatry). The latter offers more reliable conditions (good snow throughout winter) and superior facilities. Lifts in both regions generally operate from January through March, though cross-country skiing is a popular alternative. In both areas you will find a number of organizations that rent limited equipment.

Tennis Larger hotels and resorts sometimes can arrange for tennis courts if they don't have them in-house. In larger towns, ask at the Čedok office or in hotels for the address of the nearest public tennis courts.

Dining

Slovak food is an amalgam of its neighbors' cuisines. As in Bohemia and Moravia, the emphasis is on meat, particularly pork and beef. But seldom will you find the Czechs' traditional (and often bland) roast pork and dumplings on the menu. The Slovaks, betraying their long link to Hungary, prefer to spice things up a bit, usually with paprika and red peppers. Roast potatoes or french fries are often served in place of dumplings, although occasionally you'll find a side dish of tasty *halušky* (noodles similar to Italian gnocchi or German spaetzle) on the menu. No primer on Slovak eating would be complete without mention of *Bryndzové halušky*, the country's unofficial national dish, a tasty and filling mix of halušky, sheep's cheese, and a little bacon fat for flavor (it seldom makes it onto the menu at elegant restaurants, so look for it instead at roadside restaurants and snack bars). For dessert, the emphasis comes from upriver, in Vienna: pancakes, fruit dumplings (if you're lucky), poppy-seed dumplings, and strudel.

Eating out is still not a popular pastime amongst Slovaks, particularly since prices in the last few years have risen markedly. As a result, you will find relatively few restaurants about; and those that do exist cater most often to foreigners. Restaurants known as *vináreň* specialize in serving wines, although you can order beer virtually anywhere. The Slovaks, however, do not have an equivalent to the Czech *pivnice* (beer hall).

Slovaks pride themselves on their wines, and to an extent they have a point. Do not expect much subtlety, for what you most often find are hearty, sometimes heavy, but always very drinkable wines that complement the region's filling and spicy food. This is especially true of the reds. The most popular is *Frankovka*, which is fiery and slightly acidic. *Vavrinecké*, a relatively new arrival, is dark and semisweet and stands up well to red meats. Slovakia's few white wines are similar in character to the Moravian wines and, on the whole, are unexceptional.

Mealtimes Lunch, usually eaten between noon and 2, is the main meal for Slovaks and offers the best deal for tourists. Many restaurants put out a special luncheon menu, with more appetizing selections at better prices. Dinner is usually served from 5 until 9 or 10, but don't wait too long to eat. Cooks frequently knock off early on slow nights. The dinner menu does not differ substantially from lunch offerings, except that the prices are higher.

Ratings

Category	Cost*
Very Expensive	over $20
Expensive	$15–$20
Moderate	$7–$15
Inexpensive	under $7

*per person for 3-course meal, excluding wine and tip

Highly recommended restaurants are indicated by a star ★.

Lodging

Slovakia's hotel industry has been slow to react to the political and economic changes that have taken place since 1989. Few new hotels have been built, and many of the older hotels are still majority-owned by the state. As a result, there has been little appreciable increase in quality outside of the major tourist centers: The facilities in the Tatras remain good, and Bratislava added a new hotel in 1993, but elsewhere things have been fairly quiet.

In general, hotels divide up into two categories: edifices built in the 1960s or '70s that offer modern amenities but not much character; and older, more central establishments that are heavy on personality but may lack basic conveniences. Hostels are understood to mean cheap dormitory rooms and are probably best avoided. In the mountainous areas, you can often find little *chata* (chalets), where pleasant surroundings compensate for a lack of basic amenities. *Autokempink* (campsites) generally have a few bungalows available for visitors.

Slovakia's official hotel classification, based on letters (Deluxe, A*, B*, B, C), is gradually being changed over to the international star system, although it will be some time before the old system is completely replaced. These ratings correspond closely to our categories as follows: Deluxe or five-star (Very Expensive); A* or four-star (Expensive); B* or three-star (Moderate); and B or two-star (Inexpensive). We've included C hotels, some with cold water only, in our listings where accommodations are scarce. Nevertheless, prices in the upper ranges are difficult to predict, since hotels are free to set their own prices. As a rule, always ask the price before taking a room.

Ratings The prices quoted below are for double rooms, generally not including breakfast. Prices at the lower end of the scale apply to low season. At certain periods, such as Easter or during festivals, there may be an increase of 15%–25%.

Category	Cost*
Very Expensive	over $100
Expensive	$50–$100
Moderate	$15–$50
Inexpensive	under $15

*All prices are for a standard double room, including tax and service.

Bratislava

Many visitors are disappointed when they see Europe's newest capital city, Bratislava. Expecting a Slovak version of Prague or Vienna, they discover instead a rather shabby city that seems to embody the Communists' blind faith in modernity rather than the stormy history of this once Hungarian and now Slovak capital. The problem, of course, is that Bratislava has more than its fair share of high-rise housing projects, faded supermodern structures, and less-than-inspiring monuments to carefully chosen acts of heroism. Even the handsome castle on the hill and the winding streets of the Old Town look decidedly secondary in their crumbling beauty. Despite its new stature, Bratislava is definitely an inhabited city and not a living, lively museum or a repository of past glories.

The jumble of modern Bratislava masks a long and regal history that rivals Prague's in terms of importance and complexity. Settled by a variety of Celts and Romans, the city became part of the Great Moravian Empire around the year 900 under Prince Břetislav. After a short period under the Bohemian Přemysl princes, Bratislava was brought into the Hungarian kingdom by Stephan I at the end of the 10th century and was given royal privileges in 1217. Following the Tatar invasion in 1241, the Hungarian kings brought in German colonists to repopulate the town. The Hungarians called the town Pozsony;

the German settlers referred to it as Pressburg; and the original Slovaks called it Bratislava after Prince Břetislav.

When Pest and Buda were occupied by the Turks, in 1526 and 1541, respectively, the Hungarian kings moved their seat to Bratislava, which remained the Hungarian capital until 1784, and the coronation center until 1835. At this time, with a population of almost 27,000, it was the largest Hungarian city. Only in 1919, when Bratislava became part of the first Czechoslovak Republic, did the city regain its Slovak identity. In 1939 Bratislava infamously exerted its yearnings for independence by becoming the capital of the puppet Slovak state, under the fascist leader Jozef Tiso. In 1945 it became the provincial capital of Slovakia, still straining under the powerful hand of Prague (Slovakia's German and Hungarian minorities were either expelled or repressed). In the run-up to the 1989 revolution, Bratislava was the site of numerous anticommunist demonstrations; many of these were carried out by supporters of the Catholic Church, long repressed by the regime then in power. Following the "Velvet Revolution" in 1989, Bratislava gained importance as the capital of the Slovak republic within the new Czech and Slovak federal state, but rivalries with Prague persisted. It was only following the breakup of Czechoslovakia on January 1, 1993, that the city once again became a capital in its own right. But don't come to Bratislava expecting the beauty of Prague or the bustle of Budapest. Instead, plan on spending no more than a day or two leisurely sightseeing before setting off for Slovakia's superior natural splendors.

Important Addresses and Numbers

Tourist Information
Bratislava's tourist information service, **Bratislavská informačná a propagačná služba (BIPS)** (Panská 18, tel. 07/333715), is a good source for maps and basic information. The office is open weekdays 8–4:30 (until 6 in summer) and Saturday 8–1. The city's large **Čedok** office (Jesenského 5, tel. 07/52624; open weekdays 9–6, Sat. 9–noon) can help with finding hotel and private accommodations and will provide information on Bratislava and surrounding areas.

Embassies
U.S. Embassy, Hviezdoslavovo 4, tel. 07/335932. **British Embassy,** Panská 17, tel. 07/335922.

Emergencies
Police (tel. 158). **Ambulance** (tel. 155).

English-Language Bookstores
Several Slovak bookstores stock English-language titles. Try **Mestská Knižnica** at Obchodná 2. Another possibility is the beautiful second-hand bookstore **Antikvariat Steiner** (Venturská ul. 20, tel. 07/52834). The newsstand at Laurinská 2 is a good source for English-language newspapers and periodicals. The well-stocked reading room of the U.S. embassy (*see above*) is open to the general public (Tues.–Fri. 9–2, Mon. noon–5). Bring a passport.

Late-Night Pharmacies
The pharmacy at Špitálska 3, near the Old Town, maintains 24-hour service; other pharmacies hold late hours on a rotating basis.

Travel Agencies
At press time, neither American Express nor Thomas Cook had offices in the Slovak capital, although this is likely to change. **Čedok** (*see above*) can provide basic travel agency services, such as changing traveler's checks and booking bus and train tickets to outside destinations. **Tatratur** (Bajkalská 25,

tel. 07/68877, fax 07/212722) is another dependable local travel agency that can help arrange sightseeing tours throughout Slovakia.

Arriving and Departing by Plane

Although few international airlines provide direct service to Bratislava, ČSA (tel. 07/331230), the Czech and Slovak national carrier, offers frequent and convenient connections to Bratislava via Prague. Another possibility is to fly into Vienna's Schwechat Airport, about 50 kilometers (30 miles) to the west of Bratislava, and finish the hour-long journey by bus or train.

Arriving and Departing by Car, Train, Bus, and Boat

By Car There are good freeways from Prague to Bratislava via Brno (D1 and D2); the 325-kilometer (203-mile) journey takes about 3½ hours. From Vienna, take the A4 and then Route 8 to Bratislava, just across the border. Depending on the traffic at the border, the 60-kilometer (37-mile) journey should take about 1½ hours.

By Train Reasonably efficient train service regularly connects Prague and Bratislava. Trains leave from Prague's Hlavní nádraží (main station) or from Holešovice station, and the journey takes five hours. From Vienna, four trains daily make the one-hour trek to Bratislava. Bratislava's train station, **Hlavná Stanica,** is situated about 2 kilometers (one mile) from the city center; to travel downtown from the station, take streetcar No. 1 or No. 13 to Poštová ulica; or jump in a taxi.

By Bus There are numerous buses from Prague to Bratislava; the five-hour journey costs less than 250 Sk. From Vienna, there are four buses a day from Autobusbahnhof Wien Mitte. The journey takes 1½–2 hours and costs about AS150. Bratislava's main bus terminal, **Autobus Stanica,** is roughly 2 kilometers (one mile) from the city center; to get downtown, take trolley (*trolej*) No. 217 to Mierové námestie or bus No. 107 to the castle (*hrad*); or flag down a taxi.

By Boat Hydrofoils travel the Danube between Vienna and Bratislava from April to December. Boats depart in the morning from Bratislava, on the eastern bank of the Danube just down from the Devin Hotel, and return from Vienna in the evening. Tickets cost $40–$70 per person and should be booked in advance; in Bratislava contact ČSPD (tel. 07/59518).

Getting Around

Bratislava is compact, and most sights can be covered easily on foot. Taxis are cheap and easy to hail; at night, they are the best option for returning home from wine cellars and clubs.

By Bus and Tram Buses and trams in Bratislava run frequently and connect the city center with outlying sights. Tickets cost 5 Sk. and are available from large hotels, news agents, and tobacconists. Validate the tickets on board the bus or tram (watch how the locals do it). The fine for riding without a ticket is 200 Sk., payable on the spot.

By Taxi Meters start at 8 Sk. and jump 10 Sk. per kilometer (half-mile). The number of dishonest cabbies, sadly, is on the rise; to avoid being ripped off, watch to see that the driver engages the meter. If the meter is broken, negotiate a price with the driver before even getting in the cab. Taxis are hailable on the street, or call 07/311311.

Guided Tours

The best tours of Bratislava are offered by **BIPS** (*see* Tourist Information, *above*), although during the off-season tours are conducted only in German and only on weekends. Tours typically last two hours and cost 270 Sk. per person. **Čedok** (*see* Tourist Information, *above*) also offers tours of the capital from May through September. You can sometimes combine these with an afternoon excursion through the Small Carpathian mountains, including dinner at the Zochová chata.

Highlights for First-Time Visitors

Bratislava Castle
Červený Kameň (*see* Excursions from Bratislava)
Kapitulská ulica
Old Town Hall

Exploring Bratislava

Numbers in the margin correspond to points of interest on the Bratislava map.

❶ Begin your tour of the city at the modern **Námestie SNP** square; SNP is an abbreviation for *Slovenské Národné Povstanie* (Slovak National Uprising), common addendums to street names, squares, bridges, and posters throughout Slovakia. (The uprising was actually a protracted anti-Nazi resistance movement, involving partisan fighting, which began in the central part of the country in the final years of World War II.) In the middle of the square, formerly known as Stalinovo námestie (Stalin Square), are three larger-than-life statues: a dour partisan with two strong, sad women in peasant clothing. This was formerly the center for demonstrations in support of Slovak independence, and even now you will occasionally see the Slovak flag (red, blue, and white with a double cross) flying from the partisan's gun.

From here walk up toward **Hurbanovo námestie.** The golden-❷ yellow Baroque **Kostol svätej Trojice** (Church of the Holy Trinity) is worth visiting—if the doors are open, which they often are not—for the almost three-dimensional, space-expanding frescoes on the ceiling, the work of Antonio Galli Bibiena in the early 18th century.

Across the road, unobtrusively located between a shoe store and a bookshop, is the enchanting entrance to the **Old Town.** A small bridge, decorated with wrought-iron railings and statues of St. John of Nepomuk and St. Michael, takes you over the old moat, now blossoming with trees and fountains, into the intricate barbican, a set of gates and houses that composed Bratislava's medieval fortifications. After going through the first archway, you come to the narrow **Michalská ulica;** in front ❸ of you is the **Michalská brána** (Michael's Gate), the last remain-

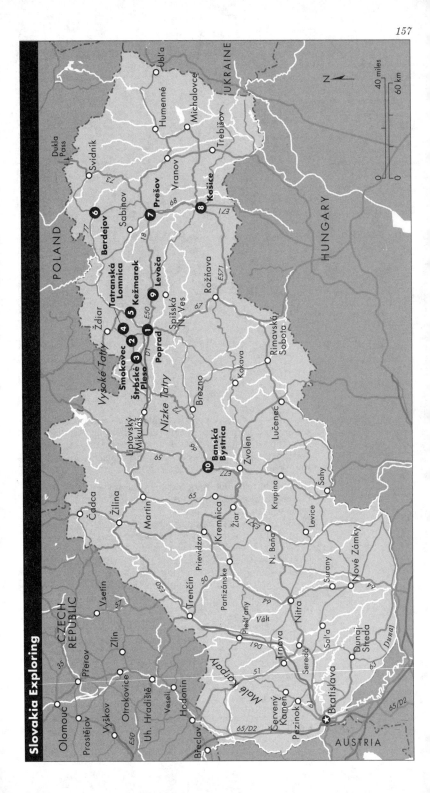

Slovakia Exploring

Dóm Sv. Martina, **7**

Františkánsky
Kostol, **13**

Hrad, **9**

Jezuitské Kolégium, **6**

Jezuitský Kostol, **15**

Klariský Kostol, **5**

Kostol Kapucínov, **12**

Kostol Sv. Trojice, **2**

Michalská Brána, **3**

Mirbachov Palác, **14**

Most SNP, **8**

Múzeum Umeleckých
Remesiel/ Múzeum
Bratislavských
Historických
Hodín, **10**

Námestie SNP, **1**

Palác Uhorskej
Kráľovskej Komory, **4**

Primaciálny Palác, **17**

Reduta, **19**

Slovenská Národná
Galéria, **20**

Slovenské Národné
Divadlo, **18**

Stará Radnica, **16**

Židovská Ulica, **11**

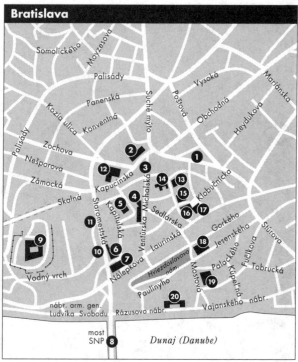

ing of the city's three original gates. The bottom part of the tower, built in the 14th century, retains its original Gothic design; the octagonal section was added in the early 16th century; and the flamboyant copper onion tower, topped with a statue of St. Michael, is an addition from the 18th century.

On your left, before going through the tower, you'll find the **Farmaceutické múzeum** (Pharmaceutical Museum). Housed in the barbican wall, on the site of the former Pharmacy of the Red Crab, this small museum is worth visiting if only to see the beautifully carved wooden shelves and imaginative pharmaceutical receptacles. Next to the museum, a small arched gateway topped with the symbol of a crab leads down through an apartment building to the moatside garden, which affords good views of the looming fortifications. *Michalská ul. 26. Admission: 10 Sk. adults, 5 Sk. children and students. Open Tues.– Sun. 10–4:30.*

Through the Michalská brána, in a door to the left, is the entrance to the **Múzeum zbraní a mestského opevnenia** (Museum of Weapons and Fortifications), built into the tower. The museum itself is not really worth a lot of time, but the *veža* (tower) affords a good view over the city. *Michalská veža, Michalská ul. 24. Admission: 5 Sk. adults, 2 Sk. children. Open Wed.– Mon. 10–5.*

Continue down Michalská ulica. Many of the more interesting buildings along the street are undergoing renovation, but notice the eerie blue **Kaplnka svätej Kataríny** (Chapel of St. Catherine) at No. 6 on the left, built in 1311 but now graced with a sober classical facade. Opposite, at No. 7, is the Renaissance **Segnerova kúria** (Segner House), built for a wealthy merchant in 1648.

❹ A little farther down on the right is the **Palác Uhorskej král'ovskej komory** (Hungarian Royal Chamber), a Baroque palace that housed the Hungarian nobles' parliament from 1802 until 1848; it is now used as the University Library. Go through the arched passageway at the back of the building, and you'll emerge in a tiny square dominated by the **Church and Convent of the Poor Clares** (Kostol Klarisiek); the convent is now the Slovak Pedagogical Library.

❺ The 14th-century **Klarisky kostol** (church), stretched along Farská ulica ahead of you, is simple but inspiring with a wonderfully peaceful early Gothic interior. Unfortunately, the church is now a concert hall—and usually locked, but you may be able to get in for a concert or during rehearsals. The small High Gothic steeple was added in an unusually secondary position at the back of the church in the 15th century; as a mendicant order, the Poor Clares were forbidden to build a steeple onto the church, so they sidestepped the rules and built it on a side wall.

Follow Farská ulica up to the corner, and turn left on **Kapitulská ulica** (noticing the ground stone depicting two kissing lizards). This street could be the most beautiful in Bratislava, but its array of Gothic, Renaissance, and Baroque buildings is in such disrepair that the effect is almost lost. Renovation has now begun, and you can see on No. 15 that the remains of a wall painting have been uncovered from a stone facade. At the bottom of the street on the right is the late-Renaissance **Jezuitské kolégium** (Jesuit College), a theological seminary since 1936; every few minutes, young men in black rush out of the door, cross the road, and disappear into the luxurious garden of the former Provost's Palace.

❼ Ahead of you is the side wall of the **Dóm svätého Martina** (St. Martin's Cathedral). Construction of this massive Gothic church, with its 280-foot steeple twinkling beneath a layer of golden trim, began in the 14th century. The cathedral finally was consecrated in 1452, and between the 16th and 19th centuries it hosted the coronation of 17 Hungarian royals. Numerous additions over the centuries were unfortunately removed in the 19th century, when the church was re-Gothicized; nowadays the three equal-size naves give an impression of space and light, but the uplifting glory found in Bohemia's Gothic cathedrals is definitely missing. The peace is further disturbed by the noise of traffic zooming by on an elevated freeway built in the 1970s across the front entrance, which nearly reduces the church to an irrelevant religious relic.

❽ As you leave the church and walk around to the front, the freeway leading to the futuristic spaceship bridge, **Most SNP,** is the first thing you see. The road was built at the cost of destroying a row of old houses and a synagogue in the former Jewish quarter, outside of the city walls. The only good thing to be said for the road is that its construction led to the discovery of remains of the city's original walls, which have been partially restored and now line the freeway on the right. Follow the steps under the passageway and up the other side in the direction of the castle.

Time Out Walk across the pedestrian lane on the **Most SNP** bridge to have a drink at the café—reached via speedy glass-faced elevators for a minimal charge—perched on top of the pylons. One of Prague's English-language newspapers, *Prognosis*, recently dubbed the café's retro-Socialist interior "*Starship Enterprise*-gone-cocktail lounge." However you may feel about the architecture, it's not a bad place for a reasonable snack and an excellent view of the city.

---

9 Continue up the steps, through a Gothic arched gateway built in 1480, until you reach the **hrad** (castle) area. From the top, there are views over the Danube to the endless apartment blocks on the Petržalka side of the river. On a good day, you can see over to Austria to the right.

Bratislava's castle has been continually rebuilt since its establishment in the 9th century. The Hungarian kings expanded it into a large royal residence, and the Habsburgs further developed its fortifications, turning it into a very successful defense against the Turks. Its current design, square with four corner towers, stems from the 17th century, although the existing castle had to be completely rebuilt after a disastrous fire in 1811. In the castle, you'll find the **Slovenské národné múzeum** (Slovak National Museum), with exhibits that cover glass making, medieval warfare, and coin making. The layout is a little confusing, so unless you're an expert in one of these fields, it's difficult to get very much out of this museum. *Hrad, Zámocká ul. Admission: 40 Sk. adults, 10 Sk. children and students. Open Tues.–Sun. 10–5.*

10 Leave the castle by the same route, but instead of climbing the last stairs by the Arkadia restaurant, continue down the Old World Beblavého ulica. At the bottom of the street, on the right, is the **Múzeum umeleckých remesiel** (Museum of Artistic Handicrafts, Beblavého ul. 1); in front, in the tall and thin Rococo **Dom U dobrého pastiera** (House at the Good Shepherd), look for the **Múzeum bratislavských historických hodín** (Museum of Clocks, Židovská ul. 1). Neither museum is a must, but both are housed in attractive buildings, particularly the latter. *Admission to each museum: 10 Sk. adults, 5 Sk. children. Open Wed.–Mon. 10–5.*

Time Out Snuggle up to a mug of beer or glass of wine at **Judy's Gallery Bar** (Beblavého ul. 4) and contemplate the offbeat local art hanging from the walls.

---

11 Go around the House at the Good Shepherd and continue along **Židovská ulica,** marred by the freeway and dominated by a rash of buildings under construction. (The street name, Jews' Street, marks this area as the former Jewish ghetto.) Continue on Židovská until you come to a thin concrete bridge that connects with the reconstructed city walls across the freeway. Standing in the middle of this bridge, looking toward the river, you get one of the best views of the incongruous and contradictory jumble of buildings that makes up Bratislava. Directly to the south is the Most SNP bridge, surrounded by housing blocks; to the east (left) are the city walls, leading into St. Martin's Cathedral; to the west (right), the little Rococo house backed by construction and the towers of the castle.

If you turn left and walk along the city walls, you will come, after negotiating a series of steps, to the main road, **Kapucínska ulica.** Across the road on the left is the small, golden yellow **⑫ Kostol kapucínov** (Capuchin Chapel), in front of which is a pillar of Mary, commemorating the plague. The Baroque chapel, dating from 1717, is of little artistic interest, but its peaceful interior is always filled with worshipers—something not often seen in Slovakia.

Across the road are steps leading down into the Old Town. Turn left at the bottom to access little Baštová ulica. Go through the arch at the end, and you'll find yourself back at Michael's Gate. Continue straight along Zámočnícka ulica, which turns right heading in the direction of **Františkánske námestie.** To the left is the oldest preserved building in Bratislava, the **⑬ Františkánsky kostol** (Franciscan Church), consecrated in 1297 and funded by the Hungarian king László IV to celebrate his victory over the Bohemian king Přemysl Otakar II at the Battle of the Marchfeld, near Vienna. Only its presbytery is still in early Gothic style, the rest having been destroyed in an earthquake in the 17th century and rebuilt in a mixture of Baroque and Gothic.

Just around the corner, built onto the church, is another quite different and much more stunning Gothic building, the 14th-century **Chapel of St. John the Evangelist,** the burial chapel for Mayor Jakub. Art historians believe that Peter Parler, architect of Prague's Charles Bridge and St. Vitus Cathedral, may have worked on this Gothic gem.

Across from the Franciscan church is the beautifully detailed **⑭** Rococo **Mirbachov palác** (Mirbach Palace), built in 1770 for a brewery owner. Nowadays the palace houses the **Municipal Gallery,** which contains a reasonable collection of European art from the 18th and 19th centuries. *Františkánske nám. Admission: 10 Sk. adults, 5 Sk. children and students. Open Tues.–Sun. 10–7.*

Go through the Františkánske námestie, with its statues of little-known Slovak World War II heroes, onto the adjoining square, **Hlavné námestie.** This square is lined with old houses and palaces, representing the spectrum of architectural styles from Gothic (No. 2), through Baroque (No. 4) and Rococo (No. 7), to a wonderfully decorative example of art-nouveau at No. 10. To your immediate left as you come into the square is **⑮** richly decorated **Jezuitský kostol** (Jesuit Church), originally built by Protestants who in 1636 were granted an imperial concession to build a place of worship on the strict condition that it have no tower. The Jesuits took over the tower-less church in 1672 and, to compensate for its external simplicity, went wild with Baroque detailing on the inside.

Next to the Jesuit church is the colorful agglomeration of old **⑯** bits and pieces that makes up the **Stará radnica** (Old Town Hall). The building as it stands today developed gradually over the 13th and 14th centuries out of a number of burgher's houses. The imaginative roofing stems from the end of the 15th century, and the wall paintings from the 16th century. The strangely out-of-place Baroque onion tower was a revision of the original tower. Walk through the arched passageway, still with its early Gothic ribbing, into a wonderfully cheery Renaissance courtyard with romantic arcades and gables. During the summer, concerts are held here. Toward the back of the courtyard, you'll find the entrance to the **Mestské múzeum** (City Museum), which documents Bratislava's varied past. *Primaciálne nám. Admission: 10 Sk. adults, 5 Sk. children and students. Open Tues.–Sun. 10–5.*

Leaving the back entrance of the Old Town Hall, you come to the **Primaciálne námestie** (Primates' Square), dominated by ❶ the glorious pale-pink **Primaciálny palác** (Primates' Palace). If the building is open, make your way to the dazzling Hall of Mirrors with its six English tapestries depicting the legend of the lovers Hero and Leander. In this room, Napoleon and Habsburg emperor Franz I signed the Bratislava Peace of 1805, following Napoleon's victory at the Battle of Austerlitz. In the revolutionary year of 1848, when the citizens of the Habsburg lands revolted against the imperial dominance of Vienna, the rebel Hungarians had their headquarters in the palace; ironically, following the failed uprising, the Habsburg general Hainau signed the rebels' death sentences in the very same room.

Walk down Uršulínska ulica, and turn right at the bottom onto Laurinská ulica. If you continue to the left down Rybárska brána, you emerge into the more modern part of the Old Town, with business and hotels stretched out along the rectangular **Hviezdoslavovo námestie** (Hviezdoslav Square). To your right is ❶ the **Slovenské národné divadlo** (Slovak National Theater), Bratislava's excellent opera house. The theater was built in the 1880s by the famous Central European architectural duo of Hermann Helmer and Ferdinand Fellner. If you get a feeling of déjà vu looking at the voluptuous neo-Baroque curves, it's not surprising: The two men built opera houses in Vienna, Prague, and Karlovy Vary, to name but a few.

Across the square, on the corner of Mostová ulica and Palackého ulica, is Bratislava's second musical center, the ❶ **Reduta,** home of the Slovak Philharmonic Orchestra. Also built in neo-Baroque style but dating from 1914, the Reduta is richly decorated. If you can't make it to a concert, try to sneak a peek inside. You can get tickets for concerts or the opera at the ticket offices directly before the performance; for advance reservations inquire at BIPS (*see* Tourist Information, *above*).

Continue down Mostová ulica to the banks of the Danube. To ❷ the right is the **Slovenská národná galéria** (Slovak National Gallery), a conspicuously modern restoration of an old 18th-century barracks. However you feel about the strange additions to the old building, the museum itself has an interesting collection of Slovak Gothic, Baroque, and contemporary art, along with a small number of European masters. *Rázusovo nábrežie. Admission: 10 Sk. adults, 5 Sk. children and students. Open Tues.–Sun. 10–5.*

What to See and Do with Children

On a balmy summer's day, you can take a pleasant 10-kilometer (6-mile) ride up the **Danube River,** or a short ferry across to the **Petržalka gardens** on the far shore. The ferry operates between April and October and costs 10 Sk.; the ferry offices are on Fajnorovo nábrežie near the Slovak National Museum.

Off the Beaten Track

You can get a dose of communist Bratislava by walking up to the **Slavín Memorial**. This group of socialist-realist statues is a monument to the 6,000 who died during the Soviet liberation of Bratislava in 1945. Even if you're not interested in the sculpture, the monument gives fine views over Bratislava. Take a taxi for about 200 Sk.; or ride bus No. 27, 43, 47, or 104 to Puškinová, where you can climb the long series of steps to the top.

Just west of the city is the ruined castle of **Devín,** beautifully located atop a hill overlooking both the Danube and Morava rivers. Take bus No. 29 from under the Most SNP bridge to Devín, and follow the marked path up the hill to the castle.

Shopping

Bratislava is an excellent place to find Slovak arts and crafts of all types. **Folk Folk** has an excellent collection at its centrally located shop (Rybárska brána 2, tel. 07/334874). **Antikvariat Steiner** (Venturská ul. 20, tel. 07/52834) stocks beautiful old books, maps, and graphics and posters. For original pieces of art and pottery, try the **Gremium Café** (Gorkého 11, tel. 07/51818).

Dining

Prague may have its Slovak rival beat when it comes to architecture, but when it's time to eat, you can thank those lucky red stars you still see around town that you're in Bratislava. The long-shared history with Hungary gives Slovak cuisine an extra fire that Czech cooking admittedly lacks. Geographic proximity to Vienna, moreover, has lent something of grace and charm to the city's eateries. What it adds up to is that you'll seldom see pork and dumplings on the menu. Instead, prepare for a variety of shish kebabs, grilled meats, steaks, and pork dishes, all spiced to enliven the palette and served (if you're lucky) with those special noodles Slovaks call *halušky.* Wash it all down with a glass or two of red wine from nearby Modra or Pezinok.

A price-conscious alternative to restaurant dining is the city's many street stands. In addition to the ubiquitous hot dogs and hamburgers (no relation to their American namesakes), try some *langoš*—flat, deep-fried, and delicious pieces of dough, usually seasoned with garlic. Another budget option is Slovakia's unofficial national dish, *Bryndzové halušky,* little noodles served with bacon and slightly sour sheep's cheese (don't knock it until you've tried it). One place certain to serve it is **Café Blankyt** (Obchodná 48, tel. 07/332248), which, despite the dingy surroundings, is quite respectable.

Highly recommended restaurants in each price category are indicated by a star ★.

Very Expensive **Arkadia.** The elegant setting, at the threshold to the castle, sets the tone for a luxurious evening. There are several dining rooms to choose from, ranging from the intimate to the more boisterous, all decorated with period 19th-century furnishings. A standard repertoire of Slovak and international dishes, which include shish kebabs and steaks, is prepared to satisfaction. It is a 15-minute walk from the town center; take a taxi here and enjoy the mostly downhill walk back into town. *Zámocké schody, tel. 07/335650. Reservations advised. Jacket and tie required. AE, DC, MC, V.*

Rybársky cech. The name means Fisherman's Guild, and fish is the unchallenged specialty at this refined but comfortable eatery set on a quiet street by the Danube. Freshwater fish is served upstairs, with pricier saltwater varieties offered on the ground floor. *Žižkova 1, tel. 07/313049. Reservations advised. Dress: casual but neat. AE, DC, MC, V.*

Expensive **Kláštorná vináreň.** Located in the wine cellar of a former
★ monastery, this restaurant with its wine-barrel–shaped booths is pleasantly dark and intimate. The Hungarian-influenced spiciness of traditional Slovak cooking comes alive in dishes such as *Cíkos tóken*, a fiery mixture of pork, onions, and peppers; or try the milder *Bravcové Ražnicí*, a tender pork shish kebab served with fried potatoes. *Frantíškanská ul., tel. 07/330430. Reservations advised. Dress: casual. No credit cards. Closed Sun.*

Velkí Františkáni. This popular wine cellar has a menu and an atmosphere similar to that at Kláštorná. However, the Velkí's expansive dining area nurtures a more raucous, giddy clientele. *Františkánske nám. 10, tel. 07/333073. Reservations advised. Dress: casual. No credit cards.*

Moderate **Korzo.** Here you'll find delicious Slovak specialties—try a shish kebab or spicy grilled steak—served in a clean, cozy cellar setting. After dinner take a stroll along the Danube, right next door. The Korzo's ground-floor café is a great spot for people-watching or writing postcards. *Hviezdoslavovo nám. 11, tel. 07/334974. Reservations advised. Dress: casual. No credit cards.*

Modra Hviezda. The first of a new breed of small, privately owned wine cellars, this popular eatery eschews the international standards in favor of regional Slovak fare; try the sheep-cheese pie (*Bryndzové halušky*) or the fiery goulash. *Beblavého 14, tel. 07/332747. Reservations advised. Dress: casual. No credit cards.*

Inexpensive **Gremium.** This trendy restaurant caters to the coffee-and-cigarette crowd and to anyone in search of an uncomplicated light meal; choose from a small menu of pastries and sandwiches. Regulars consist of students and, because of the adjoining ceramics gallery, Bratislava's self-styled art crowd. *Gorkého 11, tel. 07/51818. No credit cards.*

Micháelska. This light and airy luncheon restaurant with an adjacent stand-up buffet is situated conveniently in the Old Town. Soup, *halušky* (boiled dumplings), and salad make a budget meal fit for a king. *Michálská 1, tel. 07/332389. No credit cards.*

Pizza. Come here for tasty local renditions of the international favorite, served in a clean, casual setting. The location, a couple of blocks from the Forum Hotel, makes it a convenient stop for lunch. *Obchodná 45. No phone. No credit cards.*

★ **Stará Sladovňa.** To Bratislavans, this gargantuan beer hall is known lovingly, and fittingly, as *mamut* (mammoth). Locals come here for the Bohemian brews on tap, but it is also possible to get an inexpensive and filling meal. *Cintorínska 32, tel. 07/51101. No credit cards.*

Lodging

The lodging situation in Bratislava is poor and not improving very quickly. The few decent hotels that do exist are very expensive; the cheaper hotels tend to be run-down and utterly depressing. The problem is compounded by the general lack of private rooms to rent, though Čedok (*see* Tourist Information, *above*) can assist you in locating whatever private accommodation is available.

Highly recommended lodgings in a particular price category are indicated by a star ★.

Very Expensive **Danube.** Opened in 1992 as the Forum's principal rival, the
★ Danube lacks the Forum's grace but, at approximately two-thirds the price, is better value for the money. The Danube also wins hands down on location, fittingly alongside the Danube River with a stunning view of the castle from the front entrance. *Rybné Nám. 1, tel. 07/55355, fax 07/50218. 280 rooms with bath. Facilities: 2 restaurants, nightclub, sauna, pool, solarium, health club, conference facilities. AE, DC, MC, V.*

Forum. Bratislava's most expensive hotel, built in 1987 right in the center of town, offers a complete array of services and facilities. It is the perfect choice for a business trip; the staff is efficient and friendly, and the functional rooms are pleasantly, if innocuously, decorated. If creature comforts are an important factor, the Forum is for you. *Mierové nám. 2, 81625, tel. 07/348111, fax 07/314645. 219 rooms with bath. Facilities: 2 restaurants, 2 cafés, 2 bars, nightclub, casino, fitness center with pool and sauna, beauty salon. Breakfast not included. AE, DC, MC, V.*

Expensive **Devín.** This boxy 1950s hotel set on the banks of the Danube has managed to create an air of elegance in its reception area that doesn't translate into much else, despite its five-star status. The rooms are small and badly organized, and service is on the gruff side. Nevertheless, the hotel is clean and offers a good selection of services, with a variety of restaurants and cafés that serve dependably satisfying food. *Riečna ul. 4, 81102, tel. 07/330852, fax 07/330682. 98 rooms with bath. Facilities: 3 restaurants, café, 2 bars. Breakfast included. AE, DC, MC, V.*

Kjev. True to its Soviet-inspired name, this 1970s high rise, located on a concrete-dominated square close to the Old Town, embodies the communist aesthetic for luxury hotels: functional but bluntly impersonal decor. Still, the rooms are large, bright, and clean, and the service is reasonably polite. *Rajská ul. 2, 81448, tel. 07/52041, fax 07/56820. 199 rooms with bath. Facilities: restaurant, café, 3 bars, nightclub, sauna. Breakfast included. AE, DC, MC, V.*

Moderate **Bratislava.** This bland but suitably clean cement-block hotel, situated in the suburb of Ružinov, has well-appointed rooms each equipped with a television and private bathroom. It offers few facilities beyond a standard restaurant and lounge, though there is a large department store nearby where you can stock up on supplies. From the city center take bus No. 34 or tram No. 8. *Urxova ul. 9, tel. 07/239000, fax 07/236420. 344 rooms with bath. Facilities: restaurant, snack bar, lounge. Breakfast included. AE, DC, MC, V.*

★ **Zochová Chata.** If you have your own transportation, this attractive 1920s-style hunting chalet, located near Modra 32 kilometers (20 miles) outside Bratislava, is a comfortable alternative to the latter's large luxury hotels. The rooms here are small but very comfortable, and the food served in the adjoining tavern a few doors down is top-rate. *90001 Modra-Piesky, tel. 0704/922991. 10 rooms with bath. Facilities: restaurant, wine tavern. Breakfast not included. No credit cards.*

Inexpensive **Palace.** Run-down and due for a face-lift, this venerable downtown hotel, situated just behind the Forum hotel, is a passable alternative if everything else is booked and you can not find a private room. The furnished rooms are clean, but do not expect much in the way of creature comforts; the bathrooms, for a start, are down the corridor. And be sure to ask for a room far away from noisy Poštová ulica. *Poštová ul. 1, tel. 07/333656, fax 07/333200. 50 rooms without bath. Facilities: restaurant, café. Breakfast not included. No credit cards.*

The Arts and Nightlife

The Arts Bratislava has a thriving arts scene. The celebrated **Slovak Philharmonic Orchestra** plays regularly throughout the year, and chamber-music concerts are held at irregular intervals in the stunning Gothic **Church of the Poor Clares.** In summer, the Renaissance courtyard of the **Old Town Hall** also is used for concerts. Call BIPS or Čedok for program details and tickets. Other good sources of information include the English-language *Prague Post* and *Prognosis*, two Prague-based newspapers with regular features on Bratislava's cultural life.

Concerts The **Slovak Philharmonic Orchestra** plays a full program, featuring Czech and Slovak composers as well as European masters, at its home in the Reduta (Medená 3, tel. 07/333351). Buy tickets at the theater box office (open weekdays 1–5).

Film Most new releases are shown in their original language with Slovak subtitles. **Charlie Centrum** (Špitálska 4, tel. 07/53678) regularly shows American classics, in English, in a friendly, artsy environment.

Opera and Ballet The **Slovenské národné divadlo** (Slovak National Theater) at Hviezdoslavovo námestie 1 (tel. 07/51146) is the place for high-quality opera and ballet in season. Buy tickets at the theater office on the corner of Jesenského and Komenského streets (open weekdays noon–6) or at the theater 30 minutes before showtime.

Theater Traditional theater is usually performed in Slovak and hence incomprehensible to most visitors. For non-Slovak speakers, the **Stoka Theater** blends nontraditional theater with performance art in a provocative and entertaining way. For details contact the theater box office (Pribinova 1, tel. 07/68016).

Nightlife
Bars and Lounges Bratislava doesn't offer much in the way of bars and lounges; after-dinner drinking takes place mostly in wine cellars and beer halls. For the former, try **Kláštorná vináreň** or **Veľkí Františkáni** (*see* Dining, *above*), both located in vaulted, medieval cellars. For beer swilling, the only real address in town is the mammoth **Stará Sladovňa** (*see* Dining, *above*).

Jazz Clubs Bratislava hosts an annual jazz festival in the fall, but the city lacks a good venue for regular jazz gigs. That said, **Mefisto Club** (Panenska 24, no phone) occasionally features local jazz acts.

Rock Clubs Bratislava's live-music and club scene is exploding; new bands, running the spectrum from folk and rock to rap, are constantly turning up. The venues are changing just as rapidly; check the *Prague Post* or *Prognosis* for the lowdown on the latest clubs. Dependable hot spots include **Rock Fabrik Danubius** (Komanárska ul. 3, no phone), featuring loud and sweaty Czech and Slovak acts nightly; and the **New Model Club** (Obchodná 2, no phone), where hard-core rock can be a gad of fun if you're into that sort of thing.

Excursions from Bratislava

The Wine Country Much of the country's best wine is produced within a 30-minute drive of Bratislava, in a lovely mountainous region that offers a respite from the noise and grime of the capital. Two towns, Pezinok and Modra, vie for the distinction of being Slovakia's wine capital.

Pezinok, the larger of the two, is home to the Small Carpathian vineyards, the country's largest wine producer. In this quaint, red-roofed town you can find enough to keep you busy for an entire day without ever stepping off its busy main street, **Stefanika ulica.** Take in the wine-making exhibits at the **Malokarpatské muzeum** (Small Carpathian Museum, Stefanika ul., closed Monday), and then head next door to the outstanding bakery. Leave some room for lunch at the Zámocka wine cellar (open daily 11–11), situated in the town's castle at the end of the street. The castle also serves as a winery; around the side you will find a sales counter offering a variety of locally produced wines.

Modra is a typical one-horse town, with some pretty folk architecture and a few comfortable wine gardens scattered about town. Combine a visit here with a night at the nearby Zochová Chata (*see* Lodging, *above*). A favorite hiking destination from the Zochová chalet is the Renaissance castle **Červený Kameň** (Red Rock). On the prettier yellow-marked trail, the walk takes upwards of 2½ hours; on the more plain blue-and-green trail, around 1½ hours. Although renovations to the castle are not expected to be finished until 1995, visitors can still go to the most fascinating parts of the structure with a guide (who unfortunately is likely to speak only Slovak and German): the vast storage and wine cellars, with their movable floors and high arched ceilings; and the bastions, completed with an intricate ventilation system and hidden pathways in the middle of the thick slate walls. *Castle admission: 10 Sk. adults, 5 Sk. children. Open daily 11–3 (closed Mon. Nov.–Apr.). Tours on the hour.*

Getting There Infrequent buses link Bratislava with Modra and Pezinok; most leave early in the morning, so contact ČSAD (Bratislava, tel. 07/63213), the national bus carrier, at least a day in advance. By car from Bratislava, take Route 502 4 kilometers (2½ miles) past the village of Jur pri Bratislave, and turn right down a smaller road in the direction of the villages Slovenský Grob and Viničné. At the latter, turn left onto Route 503 to reach Pezinok, a few kilometers beyond. Modra lies 4 kilometers (2½ miles) farther along the same road.

Trnava **Trnava,** with its silhouette of spires and towers, is the oldest town in Slovakia, having received royal town rights in 1238. Trnava was the main seat of the Hungarian archbishop until 1821 and a principal Hungarian university center in the 17th and 18th centuries, until Marie Theresa shifted the scholarly crowd to Budapest. That Trnava's "golden age" coincided with the Baroque period is readily apparent in its architecture, beneath the neglected facades and pervasive industrial decay. Look for the enormous **University Church of John the Baptist,** designed by Italian Baroque architects, with fabulous carved-wood altars. The renowned, 18th-century, Viennese architect Franz Anton Hillebrandt was responsible for the central chapel of **St. Nicholas Cathedral,** which dominates the town with its large onion towers.

Getting There   Bratislava and Trnava are connected by frequent bus and train service. By car, it's an easy 45-kilometer (28-mile) drive from Bratislava on the D61 highway.

The High Tatras

The *Vysoké Tatry* (High Tatras) alone would make a trip to Slovakia worthwhile. Although the range is relatively small as mountains go (just 32 kilometers, or 20 miles, from end to end), its peaks seem wilder and more starkly beautiful than even those of Europe's other great range, the Alps. Some 20 Tatras peaks exceed 8,000 feet, the highest being **Gerlachovský Štít** at 8,710 feet. The 35 mountain lakes are remote and clear and, according to legend, can impart the ability to see through doors and walls to anyone who bathes in them, but take care before diving in: They are also very cold and sometimes eerily deep.

Man is a relative latecomer to the Tatras. The region's first town, Schmecks (today Starý Smokovec), was founded in the late-18th century, and regular visitors began coming here only after 1871 with the construction of a mountain railroad linking the resort to the bustling junction town of Poprad. In the late-19th and early 20th centuries, with the founding of Štrbské pleso and Tatranská Lomnica, the Tatras finally came into their own as an elegant playground for Europe's elite.

But the post–World War II communist era was hard on the Tatras. Almost overnight, the area became a mass resort for the mountain-starved, fenced-in peoples of the Eastern bloc, prompting much development and commercialization. Yet don't despair: The faded elegance of these mountain retreats and spa resorts remains intact, despite the sometimes heavy summertime crowds.

Important Addresses and Numbers

Tourist   The Čedok office in **Starý Smokovec** (tel. 0969/2417) is the best
Information   source for general information; it can change money, dispense hiking and driving maps, and assist in booking hotels (but not private rooms). For more in-depth information on hiking and skiing conditions, inquire next door at the **Mountain Rescue Service** (Horška služba, tel. 0969/2820). **Slovakoturist** (tel. 0969/2827), situated ½ kilometer east of Starý Smokovec in Horný Smokovec, can help arrange private accommodation, including stays in mountain cottages. In **Poprad** there is a Čedok office at Námestie Dukelských hrdinov 60 (tel. 092/23262).

Few books or pamphlets on the Tatras are available in English. One good overview of the area, including a list of services, hotels, and restaurants, is provided in the hard-to-find booklet *Everyman's Guide to the Tatras.* Look for it at hotel gift shops.

Emergencies Police (tel. 158). **Medical emergencies** (tel. 2444). **Car repair** (tel. 2704).

Late-Night Pharmacies (*lekárna*) are located in all three major resorts and
Pharmacies in the neighboring town of Ždiar (*see* Off the Beaten Track, *below*). The pharmacy in Nový Smokovec maintains late hours (tel. 0969/2577).

Arriving and Departing by Plane

ČSA, the Czech and Slovak national carrier, offers regular service to the Tatra city of Poprad from Prague and Bratislava. The flight from Prague takes a little over an hour. On arrival, take a taxi to your hotel or to the Poprad train station, from where you can catch an electric railroad to the Tatras resorts.

Arriving and Departing by Car, Train, and Bus

By Car Poprad, the gateway to the Tatras, lies on the main east–west highway about 560 kilometers (350 miles) from Prague in the direction of Hradec Králové. The eight-hour drive from Prague is relatively comfortable and can be broken up easily with an overnight stay in Olomouc, in the Czech Republic province of Moravia. The road is well marked, with some four-lane stretches. The drive to Poprad from Bratislava is 328 kilometers (205 miles), with a four-lane stretch between Bratislava and Trenčín, and a well-marked, two-lane highway thereafter.

By Train Regular rail service connects both Prague and Bratislava with Poprad, but book ahead, as the trains are often impossibly crowded, especially in August and during the skiing season. The journey from Prague to Poprad takes about 10 hours; several night trains depart from Prague's Hlavní nádraží (main station) and Holešovice station.

By Bus Daily bus service connects Prague and Bratislava with Poprad, but on this run, trains tend to be quicker and more comfortable. From Prague the journey will take 10 hours or longer, depending on the route.

Getting Around

By Car It's more of a hindrance than help to have a car if you're just going to the High Tatras. Traveling the electric railway is much quicker than taking the winding roads that connect the resorts, and hotel parking fees can add up quickly. However, if you plan to tour the region's smaller towns and villages, or if you are continuing on to eastern Slovakia, a car will prove nearly indispensable.

By Train An efficient electric rail connects Poprad with the High Tatras resorts, and the resorts with one another. If you're going just to the Tatras, you won't need any other kind of transportation.

By Bus ČSAD's bus network links all of the towns covered on the following tour; but budget a few extra days to compensate for connections and the sometimes infrequent service between smaller towns.

Guided Tours

From Poprad airport, **Slovair** offers a novel biplane flight over
the Tatras region; contact the Čedok office in Poprad (tel. 092/
23262). The Čedok office in Starý Smokovec (tel. 0969/2417) also
is helpful in arranging tours of the Tatras and surrounding
area.

Highlights for First-Time Visitors

Cable-car ride to Lomnický štít (*see* Walking Tour 1)
Magistrale trail (*see* Walking Tour 1)
Museum of the Tatras National Park (*see below*)

Exploring the High Tatras

*Numbers in the margin correspond to points of interest on the
Slovakia Exploring map.*

Most of the tourist facilities in the High Tatras are concen-
trated in three towns: Štrbské pleso to the west, Smokovec in
the middle, and Tatranská Lomnica to the east. All can be
accessed by car or the electric railroad, though each is slightly
different in terms of convenience and atmosphere.

The best way to see these beautiful mountains is on foot. Three
of the best Tatras walks (three to five hours each) are outlined
below, arranged according to difficulty (with the easiest and
prettiest first), although a reasonably fit person of any age will
have little trouble with any of the three. Yet, even though the
trails are well marked, it is very important to buy a walking
map of the area—the detailed *Vysoké Tatry, Letná Turistická
Mapa* is available for around 20 Sk. at newspaper kiosks. Another good source of information is the Mountain Rescue Service (*see* Tourist Information, *above*), next to Starý Smokovec's
Čedok office. If you're planning to take any of the higher-level
walks, be sure to wear proper shoes with good ankle support.
Also use extreme caution in early spring, when melting snow
can turn the trails into icy rivers. And don't forget drinking water, sunglasses, and sunscreen.

❶ Poprad, the gateway to the Tatras, is a good place to begin exploring the region. But don't expect a beautiful mountain village. Poprad fell victim to some of the most insensitive
communist planning perpetrated in the country after the war,
and mostly what you see today is row after row of apartment
blocks, interspersed with factories and power plants. There's
no need to linger here. Instead, drive or take the electric railroad to the superior sights and facilities of the more rugged resorts just over 30 kilometers (20 miles) to the north.

The first town you come to by road or rail from Poprad is
❷ Smokovec, the undisputed center of the Slovak Tatras resorts
and the major beneficiary of postwar development. Smokovec is
divided into two prinicpal areas, **Starý Smokovec** (Old
Smokovec) and **Nový Smokovec** (New Smokovec), which are
within a stone's throw of one another. Stay in Starý Smokovec if
you want to be near grocery stores, bars, and the local Čedok
office. The town is also a good starting point for many mountain
excursions (from here, for example, a funicular can take you the
4,144 feet to Hrebienok and its many marked trails).

❸ **Štrbské pleso,** which lies 18 kilometers (11 miles) west of Smokovec, is the main center for active sports. As such, Štrbské pleso is best suited for skiers, and for those who thrive on crowds and commotion. The Tatras' best ski slopes are not far away, and the fine mountain lake is a perfect backdrop for a leisurely stroll. Štrbské pleso is also good for walkers, and many excellent trails are within easy reach. As for facilities, the town boasts not only the most modern hotels but also the most jarringly modern hotel architecture. This large resort also presides over the finest panoramas in the Tatras. For a breathtaking view over the valley and mountains, head for the lawn of the town's sanitorium.

❹ **Tatranská Lomnica,** on the eastern end of the electric rail line, offers a near-perfect combination of peace, convenience, and atmosphere. Spread out and relatively remote, the town is frequently overlooked by the masses of students and merrymakers, so it has been more successful in retaining a feel of "exclusivity" without being any more expensive than the other towns. Moreover, the lift behind the Grandhotel Praha brings some of the best walks in the Tatras to within 10 minutes or so of your hotel door.

If you want to brush up on the area's varied flora and fauna, visit Tatranská Lomnica's fascinating **Museum of the Tatras National Park (Tatranská Museum).** The museum is especially well suited to children, who will love the startlingly realistic stuffed animals on the first floor. Each animal is marked with a symbol: A red square denotes a common species, a blue triangle means the animal is native to the Tatras, and a yellow circle signals a rare or endangered species. The upper floor documents the life of local peasants, who still wear vibrantly colored traditional dress in many villages. *Tel. 0969/967951. Admission: 10 Sk. adults, 5 Sk. children. Open weekdays 8:30–1 and 2–5, Sat. and Sun. 8–noon.*

Walking Tour 1: Tatranská Lomnica to Starý Smokovec

The **Magistrale,** a 24-kilometer (15-mile) walking trail that skirts the peaks just above the tree line, offers some of the best views for the least amount of exertion. A particularly stunning stretch of the route—which is marked by red signposts— begins in Tatranská Lomnica and ends 5 kilometers (3 miles) away in Starý Smokovec. Total walking time is three or four hours.

To start the walk, take the aerial gondola located behind the Grandhotel Praha in Tatranská Lomnica to Skalnaté pleso—a 10-minute proposition. From here you can access the trial immediately; or, if you are really adventurous, consider a 30-minute detour via cable car (25 Sk.) to the top of Lomnický Štít (8,635 feet), the second-highest peak in the range. Because of the harsh temperatures (be sure to dress warmly, even in summer) you're permitted to linger at the top for only 30 minutes, after which you take the cable car back down.

Return to the cable-car station at Skalnaté pleso and follow the red markers of the Magistrale trail to the right (as you stand facing Tatranská Lomnica below). The first section of the trail cuts sharply across the face of the Lomnický mountain just above the tree line. Note the little dwarf pines to the right and left of the trail. The trail then bends around to the right and again to the left through a series of small valleys, each view more outstanding than the last. Finally, you begin a small descent into the woods. Continue by following the signs to Hrebienok.

Time Out Don't pass up the chance to have a snack and a hot or cold drink at the rustic **Bilková Chata** situated in a little clearing just before you reach Hrebienok. This cozy cabin is a veritable oasis after the long walk.

From Hrebienok, take the funicular down to Starý Smokovec. The funicular runs at 45-minute intervals beginning at 6:30 AM and ending at 7:45 PM, but check the schedule posted at the Bilková Chata for any schedule changes. The funicular drops you off in the center of Starý Smokovec, just behind the Grand Hotel and convenient to shops and the electric rail.

Walking Tour 2:
Starý Smokovec
to Tery Chata

Starý Smokovec is the starting point for the second trek, which parallels a cascading waterfall for much of its three-hour length. From Starý Smokovec, walk out along the main road in the direction of **Tatranská Lomnica** for roughly 1 kilometer (½ mile). In **Tatranská Lesná,** follow the yellow-marked path that winds gently uphill through the pines and alongside a swift-running stream. In winter, the walk is particularly lovely; the occasional burst of sunshine warms your cheeks and transforms the cold running water to a tropical blue-green.

Farther along there are red markers leading to the funicular at Hrebienok, which returns you to the relative comforts of Starý Smokovec. However, if you're in good physical shape and if there is *plenty* of daylight left, consider extending your hike by four hours. (The extension is striking, but avoid it during winter, when you may find yourself neck-deep in snow). Just before the Bilková chata turn right along the green path and then follow the blue, red, and then green trails in the direction of windswept **Tery chata,** a turn-of-the-century chalet perched amid five lonely alpine lakes. The scenery is a few notches above dazzling. Once you reach the chalet after two fairly strenuous hours of hiking, backtrack to Bilková chata and follow the signs to the funicular at Hrebienok.

Walking Tour 3:
Starý Smokovec
to Sliezsky Dom

A more adventurous and rigorous five-hour walk starts in Starý Smokovec behind and to the west of the Grand Hotel. Begin by ascending to the tree line along the blue path. Thirty minutes of uphill hiking brings you to the Magistrale trail; follow the trail to the left, and after 20 minutes or so of moderately strenuous climbing, the trees thin out—leaving nothing but dwarf pines, the rocks, and the breathtaking peaks.

Sliezsky Dom, a 1960s cookie-cutter prefab (surely Slovakia's highest-elevation housing project), lies an hour down the trail. Forgive the building's architectural sins and head inside for a cup of tea and a bite to eat. The descent to Starý Smokovec along the green and then yellow trails is long and peaceful: Nothing breaks the silence save for the snapping of twigs or, in winter, the crunch of snow underfoot.

What to See and Do with Children

If it's rainy or too cold for a stroll through the mountains, younger children will enjoy the stuffed animals and other exhibits at the **Museum of the Tatras National Park** in Tatranská Lomnica (*see* Exploring the High Tatras, *above*).

If there's snow on the ground and the children are too young to ski, you'll find a good sledding slope at **Hrebienok,** just above Starý Smokovec. To get there, take the funicular from behind the Grand Hotel. There is an even gentler slope at the Hotel Fis in **Štrbské pleso.** You can rent sleds from the Ski Service near the Grand Hotel in Starý Smokovec or purchase them for 200 Sk.–300 Sk. from local sporting-goods stores.

Off the Beaten Track

Ždiar, about 24 kilometers (15 miles) north of the Tatras range along the road to the Polish border, and its twin **Javorina** are noted for their unique folk architecture—mostly enchanting, vibrantly painted wood houses built in traditional peasant designs. The population of Ždiar is Polish in origin (the Polish border is less than 16 kilometers [10 miles] away), but the people have long considered themselves Slovak. To reach either village, leave Tatranská Lomnica heading east on Route 537, and turn left at Route 67.

Shopping

The Tatras resorts are short on places to shop. Still, you'll find good-quality, reasonably priced hiking and camping equipment at several sporting-goods stores. You can buy skis and equipment, plus a thousand other things, in the department store **Prior** at Štrbské pleso and at the **Mladosť** store in Starý Smokovec. The outlying towns around Ždiar are good sources for lace and other types of folk arts and crafts.

Sports and Outdoor Activities

Hiking and Climbing
The Tatras are tailor-made for hikers of all levels; and since the whole area is a national park, the trails are well marked in different colors. Newspaper kiosks sell a reasonable and cheap walking map, which includes all the marked paths. For more detailed information on routes, mountain chalets, and weather conditions, contact the **Mountain Rescue Service** (Horská služba) in Starý Smokovec (tel. 0969/2820). This office can also provide guides for the more difficult routes for around 500 Sk. per day. Mountain climbers who do not want a guide have to be members of a climbing club (this also provides you with free mountain rescue). There are climbs of all difficulties (although grade-1 climbs may be used only as a starting point), the best being the west wall of **Lomnický Štít,** the north wall of the **Kežmarský Štít,** and the **Široká veža.**

Paragliding
Local sports shops offer instruction and provide equipment for many newer sports, including paragliding and paraskiing. The rates, surprisingly, are very reasonable. For information, consult the sporting-goods store in Horný Smokovec (a 10-minute walk along the highway to the east of Starý Smokovec).

Skiing
Moderately challenging slopes are found at the **Skalnaté pleso,** above Tatranská Lomnica; and around **Štrbské pleso.** Ždiar (*see* Off the Beaten Track, *above*), toward the Polish border, has a good ski area for beginners. The whole region is crisscrossed with paths ideal for cross-country skiing. You can buy a special ski map at newspaper kiosks. The season lasts from December through April, though the best months are traditionally January and February. Take your own equipment if you can, as not

many places rent. However, one place that does rent a limited selection of equipment is the Ski Service in the **Švajčiarský Dom,** next to the Grand Hotel in Starý Smokovec (open 8–noon, 12:30–4). Arrive early to get the right-size skis; the equipment rents quickly when it snows. The **Sport Centrum** (tel. 0969/ 2953) in Horný Smokovec and the **Hotel Patria** in Štrbské pleso also rent skis. You can buy skis and equipment at low prices in the department store **Prior** at Štrbské pleso and at the **Mladost'** store in Starý Smokovec.

Swimming   Swimming is not permitted in the cold glacier lakes of the Tatras. Indoor pools can be found at the **Bellevue** and **Grand** hotels in Starý Smokovec and the **Hotel Patria** in Štrbské pleso.

Dining and Lodging

Despite the steady influx of visitors, finding a satisfying meal in the Tatras is about as tough as making the 1,000-foot climb from Starý Smokovec to Hrebienok. The best option is eating in one of the hotels; both the Grand Hotel in Starý Smokovec and the Grandhotel Praha in Tatranská Lomnica have decent restaurants that make up in style what they might lack in culinary excellence. An alternative to the restaurants are local grocery stores—try the one in Starý Smokovec—which stock basic sandwich fixings.

If you are looking to splurge on accommodation, you will find no better place than the Tatras. Several hotels—including the Grand and Bellevue in Smokovec and the Patria in Štrbské pleso—feature indoor swimming pools; and at the Grand, you can combine a trip to the pool with a massage and sauna. In older hotels, ask to see several rooms before selecting one, as room interiors can be quite quirky. Also note that prices fluctuate wildly between seasons. Prices are highest in January and February, when there is snow on the ground. Prices are lower during the off-season (late fall and early spring), and the mountains are just as beautiful.

Highly recommended restaurants and lodgings in a particular price category are indicated by a star ★.

Poprad   **Gerlach.** If the Europa is full (*see below*), try this modern struc-
Dining and Lodging   ture located a couple of blocks away from the station. Be forewarned: The Gerlach is as dreary as Poprad itself. The rooms are cheerier than the public areas, but the bathrooms are only just acceptable. If you're not satisfied with your room, ask to see an apartment (about double the standard room price). One is attractively, if incongruously, decorated with antique furniture. *Hviezdoslavova ul. 3, tel. 092/33759, fax 092/63663. 120 rooms, most with bath. Facilities: restaurant, café, hairdresser, parking. Breakfast not included. No credit cards. Moderate.*
Europa. If you have to stay in Poprad, you could do far worse than this cozy little hotel just next to the train station. From the reception area to the modest, old-fashioned (but bathroomless!) rooms, the place exudes a faint elegance. In season, the bar and restaurant on the ground floor buzz with activity in the evenings. *Volkerová ul., tel. 092/32744. 73 rooms without bath. Facilities: restaurant, bar; no TV or telephone in rooms. Breakfast not included. AE, DC, MC, V. Inexpensive.*

Smokovec **Tatranská Kuria.** This modest restaurant situated just down
Dining   the street from Čedok and the train station is the only place for
miles that offers genuine *halušky* (noodles) with *bryndza*
(sheep's cheese). Note the early 8 PM closing hours. *Starý
Smokovec, tel. 0969/2806. No credit cards. Moderate.*

Lodging   **Bellevue.** This modern hotel, just outside of Starý Smokovec
along the road to Tatranská Lomnica, lacks the atmosphere of
the Grand but nevertheless offers top services and clean,
functional rooms. However, you are a good 15-minute walk
away from Starý Smokovec's grocers and bars. For skiers and
sports enthusiasts, a sporting-goods rental shop is right next
door. *Starý Smokovec, tel. 0969/2941, fax 0969/2719. 110 rooms
with bath. Facilities: restaurant, pool. Breakfast included.
AE, DC, MC, V. Expensive.*

★ **Grand Hotel.** Along with its sister hotel in Tatranská Lomnica,
this hotel epitomizes Tatra luxury at its turn-of-the-century
best. The hotel's golden Tudor facade rises majestically over
the town of Starý Smokovec, with the peaks of the Tatras looming in the background. The location, at the commercial and
sports center of the region, is a mixed blessing, however. In
season, skiers and hikers crowd the reception area, and the
hallways are filled with guests and visitors alike. The rooms
themselves are quieter, and many come furnished in period
style. *Starý Smokovec, tel. 0969/2154, fax 0969/2157. 83 rooms
with bath. Facilities: restaurant, café, souvenir shop, pool,
sauna. Breakfast included. AE, DC, MC, V. Expensive.*

Tatra. Centrally located in Starý Smokovec, the Tatra, known
until recently as the Úderník, is a cheaper alternative to the
Grand or Bellevue. Its informal atmosphere is popular with
students and skiers who don't mind the noise and lack of amenities. The hallways and public areas are dark; the rooms functional and clean but uninviting. *Starý Smokovec, tel. 0969/
2458. 37 rooms without bath. No credit cards. Moderate.*

★ **Villa Dr. Szontagh.** Away from the action in Nový Smokovec,
this be-steepled little chalet, formerly known as the Tokajík, offers mostly peace and quiet. The darkly furnished rooms and
public areas are well maintained, and the courtly staff goes out
of its way to please. The decent restaurant has an extensive
wine cellar that's open only during summer and winter. *Nový
Smokovec, tel. 0969/2061. 11 rooms with bath. Facilities: restaurant, wine cellar. Breakfast not included. No credit cards.
Moderate.*

Štrbské Pleso **Panoráma.** The architects of Štrbské pleso must have had a ball
Dining and Lodging   designing hotels. This one, built in the 1960s, resembles an up-
side-down staircase. The rooms are small and plain, with newly
renovated bathrooms. What is special, though, is the truly
panoramic view of the High and Low Tatras. Nevertheless, the
public areas are unimpressive, and the hotel is too expensive for
what it offers. *Štrbské pleso, across from bus and rail station,
tel. 0969/92111, fax 0969/92810. 96 rooms with bath. Facilities:
restaurant, bar, parking. Breakfast not included. AE, DC,
MC, V. Expensive.*

★ **Patria.** This modern, slanting pyramid on the shores of a mountain lake has two obvious advantages: location and view. Ask
for a room on a higher floor; those overlooking the lake have balconies, and the other side opens onto the mountains. The rooms
are functional, bright, and clean. Sadly, the hotel managers
have opted for darker interiors in the public areas and for facilities (except for the top-floor restaurant) that block out the mar-

velous view. Don't bother trying the Slovenka tavern on the side of the hotel—both the food and atmosphere are abominable. *Štrbské pleso, tel. 0969/92591, fax 0969/92590. 150 rooms with bath. Facilities: 3 restaurants, café, souvenir shop, parking. Breakfast included. AE, DC, MC, V. Expensive.*

Fis. Located right next to the ski jump, within easy reach of several slopes, the Fis is for young, athletic types. It has no pretense to elegance, preferring a busy jumble of track suits, families with young children, and teenagers on the make. The rooms, each with a balcony, are pleasant if a little institutional. The hotel also has bungalows for rent. *Štrbské pleso, tel. 0969/92221, fax 0969/92422. Facilities: 2 restaurants, sauna, pool, fitness center. No credit cards. Moderate.*

Tatranská Lomnica
Dining

Zbojnická Koliba. This stylish cottage restaurant, situated near the Grandhotel Praha, serves up tasty shish kebab in a romantic setting, though the portions are snack-size. Stock up on the tasty bread and cheese appetizers. *Tatranská Lomnica, tel. 0969/967630. Reservations advised. Dress: casual. No credit cards. Closed Sun. Moderate.*

Lodging
★

Grandhotel Praha. This large, multiturreted mansion, dating from the turn of the century and resting at the foothills of the Lomnický Štít mountain, is one of the wonders of the Tatras. Although no longer filled with the rich and famous, the hotel has managed to retain an air of relaxed elegance. The staff is polite and attentive. The rooms are large and well appointed, some with period furniture—ask for a large corner room with a view of the mountains. Since the hotel is far from the action, the price remains reasonable for what's offered. Be sure to have a meal in the well-run restaurant, though arrive well before the 9 PM closing or you'll be hustled out the door. As an added compensation, the cable car to the peak is only a five-minute walk away. *Tatranská Lomnica, tel. 0969/967941, fax 0969/967891. Facilities: restaurant, bar, fitness center, sauna. AE, MC, V. Expensive.*

The Arts and Nightlife

Despite the crowds, nightlife in the Tatras is usually little more than a good meal and an evening stroll before bed. For discos, check out the **Patria** and **Panorama** hotels in **Štrbské pleso,** or the **Park Hotel** in **Nový Smokovec.** For a more sophisticated evening out, there's live dance music in the **Grandhotel Praha** nightclub, as well as a floor show (admission 30 Sk.).

Eastern Slovakia

To the east of the High Tatras lies an expanse of Slovakia that seldom appears on tourist itineraries. Here, the High Tatras mountains become hills that gently stretch to the Ukrainian border, with few "musts" for visitors in between. For 1,000 years, eastern Slovakia was isolated from the West; much of the region was regarded simply as the hinterland of Greater Hungary. The great movements of European history—the Reformation and the Renaissance—made their impact here as elsewhere on the continent, but in an insulated and diluted form.

Isolation can have its advantages, however, and therein may lie the special charm of this area for the visitor. The Baroque and

© MCI International Inc. 1993

> Spend your vacation touring castles. Not train stations.

Vacation Cars. Vacation Prices. Wherever your destination in Europe, there is sure to be one of more than 1,000 Budget locations nearby. Budget offers considerable values on a wide variety of quality cars, and if you book before you leave the U.S., you'll save even more with a special rate package from the Budget World Travel Plan.℠ For information and reservations, contact your travel consultant or call Budget in the U.S. at **800-472-3325.** Or, while traveling abroad, call a Budget reservation center.

THE SMART MONEY IS ON BUDGET.®

We feature Ford and other fine cars.   *A system of corporate and licensee owned locations.*

Renaissance facades that dominate the towns of Bohemia and Moravia make an appearance in eastern Slovakia as well, but early artisans working in the region often eschewed the stone and marble preferred by their western counterparts in favor of wood and other local materials. Look especially for the wooden altars in Levoča and other towns.

The relative isolation also fostered development of a whole civilization in medieval times, the Spiš, with no counterpart in the Czech Republic or even elsewhere in Slovakia. The kingdom of the Spiš eventually came to encompass 24 towns within Greater Hungary. The group had its own hierarchies and laws, which were quite different from those brought in by Magyar or Saxon settlers. Although the last Spiš town lost its independence 100 years ago, much of the group's architectural legacy remains—again, thankfully, to another by-product of isolation, namely economic stagnation. Spiš towns are predominantly Gothic beneath their graceful Renaissance overlays. Their steep shingled roofs, high timber-framed gables, and brick-arched doorways have survived in a remarkable state of preservation. Gothic churches with imposing Renaissance bell towers are other major features of the area, as are some quite stunning altar triptychs and exquisite wood carvings. Needless to say, Spiš towns are worth seeking out when you see them on a map; look for the prefix "Spišsky" preceding a town name.

Farther to the northeast, the influences of Byzantium are strongly felt, most noticeably in the form of the simple wooden churches that dominate the villages along the Slovak frontier with Poland and Ukraine. This area marks a border in Europe that has stood for a thousand years: the ancient line between Rome and Constantinople, between Western Christianity and the Byzantine Empire. Many of the churches here were built by members of the Uniat Church, Christians who acknowledge the supremacy of the Pope but retain their own organization and liturgy.

The busy industrial cities of Prešov and Košice, with their belching factories and rows of housing projects, quickly bring you back to the 20th century. Although these cities do bear signs of the region's historical complexity, come here instead for a taste of modern Slovakia, of a relatively poor country that is just beginning to shed a long legacy of foreign domination.

Important Addresses and Numbers

Tourist Information The Čedok offices in eastern Slovakia are the best—and often the only—places to come for basic assistance and information, but don't expect too much in the way of service. You've done very well if they exchange your currency and offer to book you a room at an uncle's or cousin's house. There are branch offices in the following towns: **Banská Bystrica** (Tř. SNP 4, tel. 088/242575), **Košice** (Rooseveltová ul. 1, tel. 095/23123), **Prešov** (Hlavná ul. 1, tel. 091/24042), and **Žilina** (Hodzová ul. 9, tel. 089/46532).

Emergencies **Police** (tel. 158). **Ambulance** (tel. 155).

Late-Night Pharmacies *Lekárna* (Pharmacies) take turns staying open late or on Sunday. Look for the list posted on the front door of each pharmacy. For after-hours service, ring the bell; you will be served through a little hatch-door.

Arriving and Departing by Plane

The Tatras town of Poprad is well served by ČSA from Prague and Bratislava. ČSA also offers regular flights from Prague and Bratislava to Košice.

Arriving and Departing by Car, Train, and Bus

By Car Poprad, the starting point for the tour, lies on Slovakia's main east–west highway about 560 kilometers (350 miles) from Prague in the direction of Hradec Králové. The seven- to eight-hour drive from Prague can be broken up easily with an overnight in Olomouc. The drive from Bratislava to Poprad is 328 kilometers (205 miles), with a four-lane stretch from Bratislava to Trenčín and a well-marked two-lane highway thereafter.

By Train Trains regularly connect Poprad with Prague (10 hrs) and Bratislava (5 hrs), but book in advance to ensure a seat on these sometimes crowded routes. Several night trains make the run between Poprad and Prague's main station (Hlavní nádraží).

By Bus Daily bus service connects Prague and Bratislava with Poprad, but on this run, trains tend to be quicker and more comfortable. There's also daily bus service between Bratislava and Košice.

Getting Around

By Car A car is essential for reaching some of the smaller towns along the tour. Roads are of variable quality. Try to avoid driving at night, due to poor sign-posting. A good four-lane highway links Prešov with Košice.

By Train Regular trains link Poprad with Košice and some of the other larger towns, but you'll have to resort to the bus to reach smaller villages along the tour.

By Bus Most of the tour is reachable via ČSAD's extensive bus network. The only exceptions are some of the smaller towns in northeastern Slovakia. Most buses run only on weekdays; plan carefully or you may end up getting stuck in a small town that is ill-equipped for visitors.

Highlights for First-Time Visitors

St. Giles Church, Bardejov
Šaris Icon Museum, Bardejov
Spiš Castle, near Levoča
Wood Churches near the Dukla Pass

Exploring Eastern Slovakia

Numbers in the margin correspond to points of interest on the Slovakia Exploring map.

A kilometer and a half (1 mile) or so northeast of the High Tatras town of Poprad is the medieval hamlet of **Spišská Sobota,** now a suburb of Poprad but formerly one of the main centers of the historic Spiš empire. Sobota's lovely old square features a Romanesque church, rebuilt in Gothic style in the early 16th century, with an ornate altar carved by master Pavol of Levoča. The Renaissance belfry dates from the end of the 16th century. The square itself is a nearly perfect ensemble of Renaissance houses. But what impresses most of all is the setting, a 16th-century oasis amid the desert of socialist realism.

The history of the Spiš is an interesting one. The territory of the kingdom, which spreads out to the east and south of the High Tatras, was originally settled by Slavonic, and later by German, immigrants who came here in medieval times to work the mines and defend the western kingdoms against an invasion from the East. No one really knows where the "Spiš" name came from. Some believe the word derives from the Latin word *saepes* ("fence"); others think the origin is Slovak for "collecting tithes." Some 24 towns in all eventually came to join the Spiš group, functioning as a minikingdom within the Hungarian kingdom. They enjoyed many privileges denied to other cities and could choose their own count to represent them before the Hungarian king.

As the mines thrived, Spiš power and influence reached their height. But the confederation also had its bad times. In 1412, the Holy Roman Emperor Sigismund, king of Hungary, decided to sell 13 of the towns to his brother-in-law, the king of Poland, in order to finance a war with Venice. The split lasted until 1769, when the towns were reunited with one another. In 1876, the last of the Spiš towns lost its privileges, and the German-speakers in the area were forced to learn Hungarian or emigrate—mainly to the United States. In 1919, when Slovakia became part of the new Czechoslovak state, the German-speakers were again allowed to establish German schools, but in 1945 almost all of them were forced to leave the country for real or suspected collaboration with the Nazis.

❺ Return to Poprad and drive northeast via Route 67 to **Kežmarok**, the once great "second town" of the Spiš region. Kežmarok was founded by German settlers in the 12th century and for years waged an ultimately unsuccessful competition with Levoča to become the capital of this minikingdom. The main sights of Kežmarok today, however, have less to do with the Spiš tradition than with the town's later role within the greater Hungarian kingdom. The chief sight is the enormous Gothic-Renaissance **Tokolyho hrad** (Tököly Palace), situated east of the main square. It was from here in the late-17th century that Count Imre Tököly launched his unsuccessful uprising against the Habsburgs to form an independent Hungarian state in "Upper Hungary" (present-day Slovakia). The count initially enjoyed great success and soon united all of Upper Hungary, but he made the fateful decision of depending on the Ottoman Empire for support in his war. When the Turks were finally defeated by the Habsburgs in 1683 at the city walls of Vienna, the Habsburgs had the count condemned to death. Tököly escaped to Turkey, where he died in exile in 1705.

In the 19th century, the structure served as a barracks and was even used for a time as a textile factory. Today, it houses a small museum of the town's history, with a cozy wine cellar in the basement. *Palace admission: 10 Sk. adults, 5 Sk. children. Open Tues.–Sun. 8–noon and 12:30–5.*

Walk from the Tököly Palace down Nová ulica to the **Kostol svätého kríža** (Church of the Holy Cross), a Gothic structure dating from the beginning of the 15th century, with impressive netted vaulting. The designs on the 16th-century bell tower, with its tin crown, are characteristic of the so-called Spiš

Renaissance style. The large and handsome main square, be-fitting Kežmarok's history as a leader among the Spiš towns, is just a couple of minutes' walk from the church. *Nová ul. Admission free. Open weekdays 9–noon and 2–5.*

The other great sight in Kežmarok is the wooden **Protestant Church,** which stands just outside the former city walls a few blocks west of the main square. The church owes its existence to a congress held in 1681 in Sopron, Hungary, where it was de-cided that Protestants living on then-Hungarian lands could have their own churches only if the churches were located out-side the town boundaries and were constructed completely of wood (without even iron nails or stone foundations). In 1717, Kežmarok's Protestants lovingly built this structure from red pine and yew, fashioning its gracious vaulting from clay. The church could accommodate some 1,000 worshipers. But the once idyllic setting has long since yielded to urban sprawl, and the church itself has been covered over in stone to protect the interior, so what you see today is something of a letdown. Still, next to the pompous pink-and-green Evangelical Church next door, built at the end of the last century in neo-Arabian Nights style, the church's elegant simplicity is still affecting. *Hlavné nám. Admission free. Open daily 8–noon and 1–5.*

❻ The journey to **Bardejov** takes you along the Poprad River val-ley for 22 kilometers (14 miles), with the Tatras slowly dis-appearing behind, and then across another mountain range along the Polish border. Bardejov is a great surprise, tucked away in this remote corner of Slovakia yet boasting one of the nation's most enchanting squares. Indeed, Bardejov owes its splendors precisely to its location astride the ancient trade routes to Poland and Russia. It's hard to put your finger on ex-actly why the square is so captivating. Maybe it's the lack of ar-cades in front of the houses, which, while impressive, can sometimes overburden the squares of Bohemian and Moravian towns. It could also be the pointed roofs of the houses, which impart a lighter, almost comic effect.

The chief sight in town is certainly the **Kostol svätého Egídia** (St. Egidius [Giles] Church), situated on the northern edge of the square. The exterior of this Gothic structure, built in stages in the 15th century, is undeniably handsome, but take a walk inside for the real treasure. The main aisle is lined with 11 priceless Gothic side altars, all carved between 1460 and 1510 and perfectly preserved. Here you get pure Gothic, with no Renaissance or Baroque details to dampen the effect. A short commentary on the altars in several languages including German and French (but unfortunately no English) can be found on a pillar near the church entrance.

The most famous side altar is to the left of the main altar (look for the number 1 on the side). The intricate work of Stefan Tarner, it depicts the birth of Christ and dates from the 1480s. Other noteworthy altars include the figure of St. Barbara and the *Vir dolorum*, both on the right-hand side of the main altar. All of the altars, however, with their vivid detailing, reward close inspection. The rest of the church is also strikingly beau-tiful. The Gothic pulpit, just off the main aisle, is as old as the church itself. The early Baroque pews, with their sensuous curves, must have caused quite a sensation when they were added in about 1600.

Stroll around the square after leaving the church. The modest building in the center is the **Town Hall** (Radnice), sporting late-Gothic portals and Renaissance detailing. Next to the dark and imposing Gothic of the town halls in Bohemia and Moravia, this smaller, more playful structure is a breath of fresh air.

Make your way over to the pink **Šariš Icon Museum** on the southern side of the main square to view its collection of 16th-century icons and paintings, taken from the area's numerous Russian Orthodox churches. The museum affords a fascinating look at the religious motifs of the surrounding area from between the 16th and 19th centuries. Pick up the short but interesting commentary in English (5 Sk.) when you buy your ticket. Many of the icons feature the story of St. George slaying the dragon (for the key to the princess's chastity belt!). The legend of St. George, which probably originated in pre-Christian mythology, was often used to attract the peasants of the area to the more abstemious myths of Christianity. Take a close look at the icon of the Last Judgment on the second floor for what it reveals of this area's practices and fashions in the 16th century. The complex morality of the subject matter reflects quite sophisticated beliefs. Also on the second floor are models of the wood churches that dot the surrounding countryside and from which many of these icons and paintings were taken. *Nám. Osloboditel'ov 27. Admission: 10 Sk. adults, 5 Sk. children. Open Tues.–Sat. 8:30–11:30 and 12:30–4:30.*

The **Rhody House,** just across the Rhodyho ulica from the museum, is Bardejov's best remaining example of Renaissance relief work. The house, essentially Gothic with the reliefs added in the 16th century, was one of the few structures in the city center that survived the great fire of 1878. Continue down the Rhodyho to Na Hradbach to see the **town walls,** built in the middle of the 14th century. Some eight of the 23 original bastions are still standing, mostly along the south and east walls.

Just 6½ kilometers (4 miles) to the north of Bardejov, off Route 77, lies the old spa town of **Bardejovské Kúpele.** While no longer the favorite haunt of Hungarian counts, the spa is still a pleasant enough place to stroll around and take in the fresh air from the surrounding hills. Don't expect lots of beautiful architecture unless you're a fan of "postwar modern." The town was built up rapidly after the war to serve as a retreat for the proletariat, and little of its aristocratic heritage remains. Be sure to walk behind the space-age colonnade to view a lovely wooden Russian Orthodox church from the 18th century along with some older wooden houses that form an open-air museum. The church was brought here in 1932 as a specimen of the "primitive" age. Ironically, the 225-year-old structure is holding up markedly better than the 20-year-old buildings from the "advanced" culture surrounding it.

Leave the Bardejov area along Route 77, heading north and east in the direction of Svidník. This is really where *eastern* Slovakia, with its strong Byzantine influence, begins. The colors seem wilder here; the villages also look poorer, reflecting the area's physical—and cultural—insularity. Both the Orthodox and Uniat faiths are strong in these parts, echoing the work of Byzantine missionaries more than a millennium ago.

The area's great delight is doubtless the old wood churches in their original village settings and still in use. The first church lies in the small village of **Jedlinka,** about 13 kilometers (8 miles) north of Bardejov along the road to Svidník. Most of the wooden churches, this one included, date from the 18th and 19th centuries and combine architectural elements from the Byzantine and Baroque styles. The three steeples, each dotted with a wooden Baroque onion, rise characteristically to the west. On the inside, the north, east, and south walls are painted with scenes from the Old and New Testaments, with the west wall reserved for icons (many of which hang in the icon museum in Bardejov). The churches are usually locked, and you'll need some luck to see the inside. If you happen across a villager, ask him or her (with appropriate key-turning gesticulations) to let you in. More often than not, someone will turn up with a key, and you'll have your own guided tour. If you see a collection plate inside, make a small donation—though there is no pressure to do so.

There are about a score of Uniat churches in the countryside north of Svidník, itself an uninteresting town destroyed in World War II and completely rebuilt in the 1960s. Some recommendations are churches in the villages of **Ladomirová,** **Hunkovce,** and **Nižný Komárnik.** Venture off the main road to see more churches at **Bodružal, Mirol'a, Príkra,** and **Šemetkovce**—but be sure to take along a good map.

World War II buffs will want to complete the drive north of Svidník to the **Dukelský Priesmyk** (Dukla Pass) on the Polish border. It was here in late 1944 that Soviet troops, along with detachments of Czech and Slovak resistance fighters, finally made their long-awaited advance to liberate Czechoslovakia from the Nazis. Most of the fighting took place between the town of Krajná Pol'ana and the border. Alongside the many war monuments, which are in odd juxtaposition to the tranquil loveliness of the wood churches, you'll find bunkers, trenches, and watchtowers. The Germans mustered far more resistance than expected during the battle, and the number of dead on both sides grew to more than 100,000. Near the top of the pass, a great monument and cemetery commemorate the fallen Slovaks; their leader, General Ludvík Svoboda, went on to become president of the reborn Czechoslovak state.

7 Return to Svidník via the same road, and continue on in the direction of **Prešov,** a lively town and the center of Ukrainian culture in Slovakia. Its other claim to fame is a little controversial now that the Communists have been ousted from power. It was here in 1919, from the black wrought-iron balcony at Hlavná ulica 73, that enthusiastic Communists first established their own Slovak Soviet Republic in 1919, just 17 months after the Bolshevik Revolution in Russia (this early attempt at communism lasted only three weeks, however). The balcony is still ceremoniously lit up at night, but the square's former name, Slovak Soviet Republic (SSR for short), was quickly changed back to Main Street in 1990.

8 In **Košice,** you leave rural Slovakia behind. Traffic picks up, the smog settles in, and the high-rise apartment buildings of the suburbs suddenly seem to stretch out for miles. Košice is a sprawling, modern city, the second largest in Slovakia after Bratislava, and the capital of the province of East Slovakia. Situated along the main trade route between Hungary and Poland, the city was the second-largest in the Hungarian empire (after Buda) during the Middle Ages. With the Turkish occupation of the Hungarian homeland in the 16th and 17th centuries, the town became a safe haven for the Hungarian nobility from which to oppose the Turks. Inevitably, however, it fell into economic decline as trade with Hungary came to a standstill. Relief did not come until 1861 with the advent of the railroad.

In this century, the city has been shuttled between Hungary, Czechoslovakia, and now Slovakia. Sadly, Slovak efforts after World War II to eliminate Hungarian influence in Košice were remarkably successful. As you walk around, you'll be hardpressed to find evidence that this was once a great Hungarian city—even with the Hungarian frontier just 20 kilometers (12 miles) away.

You won't see many Westerners strolling Košice's enormous medieval square, the **Hlavná ulica**; most of the tourists here are Hungarians on a day trip to shop and sightsee. The square is dominated on its southern flank by the huge Gothic tower of the **Dóm svätej Alžbety** (Cathedral of St. Elizabeth). Built throughout the 15th century and finally completed in 1508, the cathedral is the largest in Slovakia. First walk over to the north side of the cathedral (facing the square) to look at the famed "golden door." The reputed friend of the sick and aged, the Holy Elizabeth, after whom the cathedral is named, stands in the middle of the door. The reliefs above her depict her good works. Inside the church is one of Europe's largest Gothic altars, the 35-foot Altar of the Holy Elizabeth. The altar is a monumental piece of medieval wood carving attributed to the master Erhard of Ulm. Although generally open to worshipers, the church is under renovation, and you may not be able to roam around at will.

Next door to the cathedral is the **Urbanová veža** (Urbans' Tower), a 14th-century bell tower remodeled in Renaissance style in 1612. But much of what you see today doesn't go back much further than 1966, when the tower caught fire and had to be almost completely rebuilt, brick by brick. It now houses a permanent exhibition of bell making, but don't waste your time climbing to the top unless you're interested in forging and casting techniques. The view is disappointing and can't compensate for the eight floors of bell and iron exhibits you have to look at to get there. *Hlavná ul. Admission: 5 Sk. adults, 2 Sk. children. Open Tues.–Sat. 9–5, Sun. 9–1.*

On the other side of the cathedral is the even older **Kaplnka svätého Michala** (St. Michael's Chapel), which dates from around 1260. A relief on the portal shows the archangel Michael weighing the souls of the dead. Just across from the chapel, on the east side of the square, is the **Dom Košického vládneho programu** (House of the Košice Government Program), which played an important role in Czechoslovakia's history in the final days of World War II. It was from here that the "Košice Program" was proclaimed on April 5, 1945, announcing the reunion of the Czech lands and Slovakia into one national state.

The center of the square is dominated by the **Štátne Divadlo** (State Theater), a mishmash of neo-Renaissance and neo-Baroque elements, built at the end of the last century. This conscious imitation of architectural styles was all the rage in the Habsburg lands at the time; indeed, the building would be equally at home on Vienna's Ringstrasse. To the right of the

State Theater, the impressive Rococo palace at Hlavná ulica 59, which once housed the city's wealthiest nobility, was the unlikely site of a Slovak Soviet Republic congress in 1919, just a week before the revolutionary movement was aborted. The relief on the house has nothing to do with communism but recalls the stay here of the Russian commander Mikhail Kutuzov, who in 1805 led the combined Russian-Austrian forces in battle against Napoleon at Austerlitz.

Time Out To feel as though you've really stepped into turn-of-the-century Vienna, have a cup of coffee or a cold drink within the elegant Jugendstil confines of the **Café Slavia** at Hlavná ulica 63.

A little farther up the square, take a right at **E. Adyho ulica,** and continue to the end of the street to the town walls. In the 16th and 17th centuries, these bastions—which date from the 13th century—helped secure Košice as a safe haven for the Hungarian nobility; it was from here that they launched their attacks on the Turks occupying the Hungarian motherland.

The **Miklusova väznica** (Nicholas Prison), an old Gothic building used as a prison and torture chamber until 1909, now houses an excellent museum with exhibits on the history of Košice. *E. Adyho ul. (at Hrnčiarská ul.). Admission: 10 Sk. adults, 5 Sk. children. Open Tues.–Sat. 9–5, Sun. 9–1.*

An interesting day trip from Košice is to drive the 30 kilometers (20 miles) to the **Herl'any geyser.** Follow Route 50 east out of the city, making a right at Route 576 and following the signs. The geyser has an eruption interval of 32 to 36 hours. The display, with water shooting up nearly 130 feet, lasts for about 20 minutes. Check with the Čedok office in Košice (Rooseveltová ul. 1, tel. 095/23123) for the expected eruption times.

Leave Košice via Route 547, following the signs in the direction of **Spišská Nová Ves.** The road quickly turns hilly, offering beautiful panoramas over several central Slovak ranges. Continue on Route 547 to **Spišské Podhradie,** turning left on Route 18 in **❾** the direction of **Levoča,** the center of the Spiš kingdom and the quintessential Spiš town.

You enter Levoča from Route 18 through the Košice Gate, emerging after a few hundred yards into the large and beautiful main square, surrounded by colorful Renaissance facades. Some are in appalling disrepair, and others are undergoing renovation, but this detracts little from the honest Old World feel. The main sights are in the middle of the square. The **Mestská radnica** (town hall), with its fine example of whitewashed Renaissance arcades, gables and clock tower, was built in 1551 after the great fire of 1550 destroyed the old Gothic building along with much of the town. The clock tower, which was added in 1656, now houses the excellent **Spiš Museum,** with exhibits of guild flags and a good collection of paintings and wood carvings. A ticket for the museum will also get you in to the exquisite interior of St. Jacob's Church next door. *Hlavné nám. Admission: 10 Sk. adults, 5 Sk. children. Open Mon.–Sat. 10–5.*

The nearby **Kostol svätého Jakuba** (St. James Church) is a huge Gothic construction, begun originally in the early 14th century but finished in its present form a century later. The interior is a breathtaking concentration of Gothic religious art. It was here in the early 16th century that the greatest Spiš artist, Pavol of Levoča, created his most unforgettable pieces. The carved-wood high altar, said to be the world's largest and incorporating a truly magnificent carving of *The Last Supper* in limewood, is his most famous work. The 12 disciples are, in fact, portraits of Levoča merchants. Two of the Gothic side altars are also the work of master Pavol. The wall paintings on the left wall are fascinating in their detail and imagination; one depicts the seven deadly sins, each riding a different animal into hell.

Several houses on the square are worth a closer look. The house at No. 20 is the former residence of Pavol of Levoča. Farther up, at No. 7, is the golden sgraffiti-decorated **Thurzo House,** named for the powerful mining family. The wonderfully ornate gables are from the 17th century, though the sgraffiti was a 19th-century addition. At the top of the square is the **Small Committee House** (No. 60), the former administrative center of the Spiš region. Over the doorway in sgraffito style, is the coat of arms of the Spiš towns. The monumental classicist building next door, the **Large Committee House,** was built in the early 19th century by Anton Povolný, also responsible for the Evangelical Church at the bottom of the square.

From Levoča, it's worth taking a short 16-kilometer (10 mile) detour east along Route 18 to the magnificent **Spišský hrad** (Spiš Castle), a former administrative center of the kingdom and now the largest castle in Slovakia (and one of the largest in Europe). Spiš overlords occupied this site since 1209; the castle soon proved its military value by surviving the onslaught of the Mongol hordes in the 13th century. The castle later came under the domination of the Hungarians. Now, however, it's firmly in Slovak hands and in season is open to the general public. The museum has a good collection of torture devices, and the castle affords a beautiful view of the surrounding hills and town. *Spišský hrad. Admission: 10 Sk. adults, 5 Sk. children. Open May—Oct., Tues.–Sun. 8–4.*

From Levoča, head south on Route 533 through Spišská Nová Ves, continuing along the twisting roads to the junction with Route 535. Turn right onto Route 535, following the signs to Mlynky and beyond, through the tiny villages and breathtaking countryside of the **Slovensky Raj** (*see* Off the Beaten Track, *below*), the national park whose name means "Slovak Paradise." When you finally reach Route 67, turn in the direction of Poprad until you cross Route 66 and see the signs for Banská Bystrica.

❿ Next to the medieval grandeur of the Spiš towns, **Banská Bystrica**'s provincial prosperity—with its prim white-and-yellow houses—looks admittedly bland. Even the hills and mountains that enfold the town are tame next to the splendors of eastern Slovakia proper. Still, the Lux Hotel (*see* Dining and Lodging, *below*) on the edge of town is a good place to pause on the return trip to Bratislava, and the town itself has enough interesting sights to justify a short stay.

Although it has been around since the 13th century, growing wealthy from the nearby copper mines, Banská Bystrica is known throughout Slovakia for its role in more recent history, namely as the center of the Slovak National Uprising during World War II. It was from here that the underground Slovak National Council called the uprising into existence on August

29, 1944. For some two months, thousands of Slovaks valiantly rose up against their Nazi oppressors, forcing the Germans to divert critically needed troops and equipment from the front lines. The Germans eventually quashed the uprising on October 27, but the costly operation is credited with accelerating the Allied victory.

You'll find reminders of the uprising (known in Slovak by its initials, SNP) just about everywhere. The mecca for fans is the **Múzeum Slovenského Národného Povstania** (Museum of the Slovak National Uprising), which stands in a large field just outside the center of town, between Horný ulica and ulica Dukelských Hrdinov. No matter where you stay in Banská Bystrica, you won't be able to miss the monument's massive concrete wings—surprisingly evocative of a captive people rising up to freedom. The effect is particularly striking at night. The museum itself isn't of much interest, however. The commentary is heavily biased toward a communist perspective, and you can't help but feel as you look at the maps and photographs that you're getting half-truths. More telling, perhaps, is the absence of Slovak visitors; since the locals are no longer required to visit, the corridors are often empty. *Admission: 10 Sk. adults, 5 Sk. children. Open Tues.–Sun. 8–4.*

If you're partial to less-recent history, head for the main square, the **Námestie SNP,** with its cheery collection of Renaissance and Baroque houses. The most impressive is the **Thurzo house,** an amalgamation of two late-Gothic structures built in 1495 by the wealthy Thurzo family. The genuine Renaissance sgraffiti on the outside were added in the 16th century, when the family's wealth was at its height. Today the building houses the **City Museum,** which is more interesting for the chance to see inside the house than for its artifacts. *Nám. SNP. Admission: 10 Sk. adults, 5 Sk. children. Open weekdays 8–noon and 1–4, Sun. 9–noon and 1–4.*

Cross the main square in front of the 16th-century **Hodinová veža** (Clock Tower), and venture up the Jána Bakoša ulica to see the **Parish Church,** situated near the town walls. The church dates from 1255 and forms a unit with the other surviving structures of the former castle complex: the Gothic **Royal Palace** and the **Praetorium** (the former city hall). Inside the church, in **St. Barbara's Chapel,** you'll find a beautiful late-Gothic altar, another wooden masterpiece from Pavol of Levoča.

Off the Beaten Track

South of Levoča lies a wild and romantic area of cliffs and gorges, caves and waterfalls known as **Slovenský Raj** (Slovak Paradise). Once the refuge for Spiš villagers during the Tatar invasion of 1241–42 and now a national park, the area is perfect for adventurous hikers. The gorges are accessible by narrow but secure iron ladders. The main tourist centers are **Čingov** in the north and **Dedinky** in the south.

The sleepy border town of **Medzilaborce,** east of Svidník, is fast becoming the unlikely mecca for fans of pop-art guru Andy Warhol. It was here in 1991, near the birthplace of Warhol's parents, that the country's cultural authorities, in conjunction with the Andy Warhol Foundation for Visual Arts in New York, opened the **Warhol Family Museum of Modern Art.** In all, the museum holds 17 original Warhol silk screens, including two from the famous Campbell's Soup series, and portraits of Lenin and singer Billie Holiday. The Russian Orthodox church across the street from the museum lends a suitably surreal element to the setting. *Admission: 10 Sk. adults, 5 Sk. for children. Open daily 10–5.*

Sports and Outdoor Activities

Hiking and Walking Eastern Slovakia is a hiker's paradise. In addition to the offerings at **Slovensky Raj** (*see* Off the Beaten Track, *above*), trails fan out in all directions in the area known as Spišská Magura, to the north and east of Kežmarok.

Swimming Good outdoor swimming can be found in lakes in Slovenský Raj and in Michalovce, east of Košice.

Dining and Lodging

The dining revolution in evidence in the Czech Republic and the rest of Slovakia has been slow in coming to eastern Slovakia. You'll look in vain for truly innovative restaurants; the best bet, especially in smaller cities and towns, remains the hotel restaurant.

In eastern Slovakia, the term "hotel" often refers to a less-than-cozy high rise, situated somewhere on the outskirts of town. Although they typically are overpriced for the level of comfort offered, they often are the only option available. Many towns will have some private rooms available; ask at Čedok for information.

Highly recommended restaurants and lodgings in a particular price category are indicated by a star ★.

Banská Bystrica
Dining and Lodging **Lux.** Located on the edge of town, the Lux is one of the few successful high-rise hotels in Slovakia, managing to combine modernity with some semblance of style. The rooms (especially on the upper floors facing town) have a magnificent view over the mountains, enlivened at night by the Museum of the Slovak National Uprising glowing in the foreground. The restaurant is elegant and serves a good range of Slovak specialties. A leisurely breakfast is served in the café. *Nové nám. 2, tel. 088/24141. 120 rooms with bath. Facilities: restaurant, café, bar, parking. Breakfast included. AE, DC, MC, V. Moderate.*

Národný dom. This plain, older hotel, just off the main square, is a cheaper alternative to the Lux. The staff is friendly and the rooms are clean, but the corridors have a stale air about them. *Národná ul., tel. 088/24331. 42 rooms, most with shower. Facilities: restaurant. Breakfast not included. No credit cards. Moderate.*

Urpin. Similar to the neighboring Národný dom above, the Urpin offers clean rooms in an older, somewhat neglected hotel a block away from the city center. *Ul. Jána Cikkera 5, tel. 088/24556. 45 rooms, some with shower. Breakfast included. No credit cards. Moderate.*

Lodging **Motel Ul'anka.** Located 6 kilometers (4 miles) outside of town on the road to Ružomberok, this inexpensive motel is a good alternative for budget-minded travelers with a car. The surrounding mountain scenery is magnificent, but the rooms are only adequate, and the motel's strict rules are reminiscent of a youth hostel. *Ul'anská cesta, tel. 088/53657. 50 rooms without bath. Breakfast not included. No credit cards. Inexpensive.*

Bardejov
Dining and Lodging

Dukla. This depressing socialist-realist structure is an acceptable alternative for travelers without a car and no easy access to the Mineral (*see below*). The hallways are cluttered with mismatched furniture; and the rooms, while clean, show a similar lack of forethought. The big advantage is location: A couple of steps and you're in Bardejov's beautiful medieval square. *Nám. Osloboditel'ov, tel. 0935/2721. 30 rooms, some with shower. Facilities: restaurant. Breakfast not included. No credit cards. Inexpensive.*

Mineral. Despite its location in a 19th-century spa town (the former haunt of the Hungarian aristocracy), this aging 1970s structure is fairly charmless. Yet as Bardejov lacks decent hotels, you may not have a real choice. The rooms, some with a nice view over the spa area, are acceptably clean, and the restaurant on the first floor serves a good breakfast. Follow Route 77 north about 5 kilometers (3 miles) out of town, turning at the sign to Bardejovské Kúpele. *Bardejovské Kúpele, tel. 0935/ 4162. Facilities: restaurant, nightclub. Breakfast not included. No credit cards. Inexpensive.*

Kežmarok
Dining and Lodging

Lipa. This functional 1960s structure, located on a main road away from the town square, remains the best choice in town. But don't expect more in atmosphere or services than a clean place to sleep. *Toporecova ul., tel. 0968/2037–9. 78 rooms, most with bath or shower. Facilities: bar. Breakfast not included. No credit cards. Inexpensive.*

Košice
Dining and Lodging

Slovan. This unsightly high rise surprisingly does many things well. The English-speaking staff is attentive, and the decor is contemporary but tasteful. Choose a room on one of the upper floors for a beautiful view of Košice's main square, just a few minutes' walk from the hotel. *Hlavná ul. 1, tel. 095/27378. 212 rooms with bath. Facilities: restaurant, café, minibars, video-camera rental. Breakfast not included. AE, DC, MC, V. Expensive.*

Imperial. The gracious proportions of this older hotel, situated just off the main square, are marred somewhat by peeling wallpaper and other obvious signs of neglect. Nevertheless, as a cheaper alternative to the Slovan, it's fine for an overnight stay. The restaurant is bright and serves passable food. *Ul. Hrnčiarska 1, tel. 095/22146–7. 45 rooms, half with bath. Facilities: restaurant, café. Breakfast not included. No credit cards. Moderate.*

Prešov
Dining and Lodging

Dukla. Just down the main road from the center of town and right next to the new theater, this hotel is a modern structure that works. The staff is friendly; the rooms, while nothing special, are comfortable and clean, with very immaculate bathrooms. Some rooms have a balcony. *Nám. Legionárov 2, 08001, tel. 091/22741–2. 89 rooms with bath. Facilities: restaurant, snack bar. Moderate.*

Šariš. Though it is a little removed from the city center, the Šariš has facilities—including bike rentals—that you do not often find at a budget hotel. The staff is friendly and helpful, and the rooms, though small, are equipped with refrigerators. The bathrooms, however, are a bit on the old and worn side. *Sabinovská ul. 1, 08001, tel. 091/46351. 110 rooms. Facilities: restaurant, bar. No credit cards. Inexpensive.*

Žilina
Dining and Lodging

Slovakia. This modern megastructure is made human by the friendly staff (English is spoken) and cheerful rooms. The location is excellent for a stopover: a five-minute walk from the town center but convenient to major roads. The restaurant serves good Slovak specialties at very reasonable prices. *Nám. L'udovita Štúra, 01000, tel. 089/46572. 140 rooms with bath. Facilities: restaurant, snack bar, sauna, pool. Breakfast included. AE, DC, MC, V. Moderate.*

Vocabulary

Czech Vocabulary

	English	Czech	Pronunciation
Basics	Please.	Prosím.	**pro**-seem
	Thank you.	Děkuji.	**dyek**-oo-yee
	Thank you very much.	Děkuji pěkně.	**dyek**-oo-yee **pyek**-nyeh
	You're welcome (it's nothing).	Není zač.	**neh**-nee **zahtch**
	Yes, thank you.	Ano, děkuji.	**ah**-no **dyek**-oo-yee
	Nice to meet you.	Těší mě.	**tye**-shee myeh
	Pardon me.	Pardon.	**par**-don
	Pardon me (formal)	Promiňte.	**pro**-meen-teh
	I'm sorry.	Je mi líto.	yeh mee **lee**-to
	I don't understand.	Nerozumím.	**neh**-rohz-oom-eem
	I don't speak Czech very well.	Mluvim česky jen trochu.	**mloo**-vim **ches**-ky yen **tro**-khoo
	Do you speak English?	Mluvte anglicky?	**mloo**-vit-eh ahng-**glit**-ski
	Yes/No	Ano/ne	**ah**-no/neh
	Speak slowly, please.	Mluvíte pomalu, prosím.	**mloo**v-teh poh-**mah**-lo **pro**-seem
	Repeat, please.	Opakujte, prosím.	**oh**-pahk-ooey-teh **pro**-seem
	I don't know.	Nevím.	**neh**-veem
Questions	What . . . What is this?	Co . . . Co je to?	**tso** yeh toh
	When . . . When will it be ready?	Kdy . . . Kdy to bude hotové?	**g'dih** toh **boo**-deh **hoh**-toh-veh
	Why . . . Why is the pastry shop closed?	Proč . . . Proč je cukrárna zavřená?	**protch** yeh tsu-**krar**-na za-v'zhe-nah
	Who . . . Who is your friend?	Kdo . . . Kdo je váš přítel?	**g'doh** yeh vahsh **pshee**-tel

This material is adapted from the Living Language® Fast & Easy *series (Crown Publishers, Inc.). Fast & Easy "survival" courses are available in 15 different languages, including Czech, Hungarian, Polish, and Russian. Each interactive 60-minute cassette teaches more than 300 essential phrases for travelers. Available in bookstores, or call 800/733–3000 to order.*

How . . . How do you say this in Czech?	Jak . . . Jak se to řekne česky?	yak seh toh **zhek**-neh **ches**-kee
Which . . . Which train goes to Bratislava?	Který . . . Který vlak jede do Bratislavy?	k'**tair**-ee vlahk **yeh**-deh doh **bratislavee**
What do you want to do?	Co chcete dělat?	tso kh'**tseh**-teh **dyeh**-laht
Where are you going?	Kam jdete?	kahm **dyeh**-teh
What is today's date?	Kolikátého je dnes?	**ko**-li-kah-**teh**-ho yeh d'nes
May I?/I'd like permission (to do something)	S dovolením, prosím.	s'**doh**-voh-leh-**neem pro**-seem
May I . . . ?	Smím . . . ?	smeem
May I take this?	Smím si to vžít?	**smeem** see toh v'**zheet**
May I enter?	Smím vstoupit?	smeem v'**sto**-pit
May I take a photo?	Smím fotografovat?	smeem **fo**-to-gra-fo-vaht
May I smoke?	Smím kouřit?	smeem **ko**-zhit

Numbers	Zero	Nula	**noo**-la
	One	Jeden, jedna, jedno	ye-**den**, **yed**-nah, **yed**-no
	Two	Dva, dvě	dvah, dvyeh
	Three	Tři	tshree
	Four	Čtyři	ch'**ti**-zhee
	Five	Pět	pyet
	Six	Šest	shest
	Seven	Sedm	**sed**-oom
	Eight	Osm	**oh**-soom
	Nine	Devět	**deh**-vyet
	Ten	Deset	**deh**-set
	Eleven	Jedenáct	yeh-deh-**nahtst**
	Twelve	Dvanáct	dvah-**nahtst**
	Thirteen	Třináct	tshree-**nahtst**
	Fourteen	Čtyrnáct	ch't'r-**nahtst**
	Fifteen	Patnáct	paht-**nahtst**
	Sixteen	Šestnáct	shest-**nahtst**
	Seventeen	Sedmnáct	sed-oom-**nahtst**
	Eighteen	Osmnáct	oh-soom-**nahtst**
	Nineteen	Devatenáct	deh-vah-teh-**nahtst**
	Twenty	Dvacet	**dvaht**-set
	Twenty-one	Dvacet jedna	**dvaht**-set **yed**-nah
	Twenty-two	Dvacet dva	**dvaht**-set dvah
	Twennty-three	Dvacet tři	**dvaht**-set tshree
	Thirty	Třicet	**tshree**-tset
	Forty	Čtyřicet	ch'**ti**-zhee-tset
	Fifty	Padesát	**pah**-deh-**saht**
	Sixty	Šedesát	**sheh**-deh-saht
	Seventy	Sedmdesát	**sed**-oom-deh-saht
	Eighty	Osmdesát	**oh**-soom-deh-saht
	Ninty	Devadesát	deh-**vah**-deh-saht

	100	Sto	sto
	1,000	Tisíc	**tee**-seets
Common Greetings	Hello/Good morning.	Dobrý den.	**dob**-ree den
	Good evening.	Dobrý večer.	**dob**-ree **ve**-chair
	Goodbye.	Na shledanou.	Na **sled**-ah-noh
	Title for married woman (or unmarried older woman)	Paní	**pah**-nee
	Title for young and unmarried woman	Slečno	**sletch**-noh
	Title for man	Pané	**pan**-eh
	How do you do?	Jak se vám daří?	yak seh vahm **dah**-zhee
	Fine, thanks. And you?	Děkuji, dobře. A vám?	**dyek**-oo-yee **dobe**-zheh a vahm
	How do you do? (informal)	Jak se máte?	yak se **mah**-teh
	Fine, thanks. And you?	Děkuji, dobře. A vy?	**dyek**-oo-yee **dobe**-zheh ah vee
	What is your name?	Jak se jmenujete?	yak se **men**-weh-teh
	My name is . . .	Jmenuji se . . .	**ymen**-weh-seh
	I'll see you later.	Na shledanou brzo.	na **sled**-ah-noh **b'r**-zo
	Good luck!	Mnoho štěstí!	m'**no**-ho **shtyes**-tee
Directions	Where is	Kde je	g'deh yeh
	Excuse me. Where is the . . . ?	Promiňte, prosím. Kde je . . . ?	**pro**-meen-teh **pro**-seem g'deh yeh
	Excuse me. Where is Wencaslas Square?	Promiňte, prosím. Kde je Václavské náměstí?	**pro**-meen-teh **pro**-seem g'deh yeh **vat**-slav-skeh **nahm**-yes-tee
	Where is the bus stop?	Kde je autobusová zastávka?	g'deh yeh **ow**-to-boos-oh-vah zah-**stahv**-kah
	Where is the subway station, please?	Kde je stanice metra, prosím?	g'deh je **stah**-nit-seh **meh**-trah **pro**-seem
	Where is the rest room?	Kde jsou toalety, prosím?	g'deh so twa-**leh**-tee **pro**-seem
	Go	Jděte	**dye**-teh
	On the right	Napravo	**na**-pra-vo

One the left	Nalevo	**na**-leh-vo
Straight ahead	Rovně	**rohv**-nyeh
At (go to) the end of the street	Jděte na konec ulici	**dye**-teh na **ko**-nets **oo**-lit-si
The first left	První ulice nalevo	**per**-vnee **oo**-lit-seh **na**-leh-vo
Near	Blízko	**bleez**-ko
It's near here.	Je to blízko.	yeh to **bleez**-ko
Turn	Zahnete	**zah**-hneh-teh
Go back.	Jděte zpátky.	**dye**-teh z'**paht**-ky
Next to	Vedle	ved-**leh**
It's very simple.	To je velmí jednoduché.	to yeh **vel**-mee **yed**-no-doo-kheh

Shopping Money	Peníze	pen-**ee**-zeh
Where is the bank?	Kde je banka?	g'deh yeh **bahn**-ka
I would like to change some money.	Chtěla bych si vyměnit peníze.	kh'**tyel**-ah bikh see vih-myen-it pen-**ee**-zeh
140 crowns	Sto čtyřicet korun	sto ch'**ti**-zhee-tset koh-**roon**
17 crowns	Sedmnáct korun	sed-oom-**nahtst** koh-**roon**
1,100 crowns	Tisíc sto korun	**tee**-seets sto koh-**roon**
3,000 crowns	Tři tisíce korun	tshree **tee**-see-tse koh-**roon**
Please write it down.	Napište to, prosím.	**nah**-peesh-tye toh **pro**-sim
What would you like?	Co si přejete?	tso see **pshay**-eh-teh
I would like this.	Chtěl bych tohle.	kh'**tyel** bikh **toh**-hleh
Here it is.	Tady to je.	**tah**-dee toh yeh
Is that all?	To je všechno?	toh yeh **vshekh**-no
Thanks, that's all.	Děkuji. To je všechno.	**dyek**-oo-yee toh yeh **vshekh**-no
Do you accept traveler's cheques?	Přijímáte cestovni šeky?	**pshee**-yee-**mah**-teh **tses**-tohv-nee **shek**-ee
Credit cards?	Kredit Karty?	**cre**-dit **kar**-tee
How much?	Kolik?	**ko**-lik
Department store	Obchodní dům	**ohb**-khod-nee **doom**
Grocery store	Potraviny	**poh**-trah-**vin**-ee
Pastry shop	Cukrárna	tsoo-**krar**-na

Dairy products shop	Mlekárna	mleh-**kar**-na
The butcher	Řeznictví	**zhez**-nitst-vee
I would like a loaf of bread and rolls.	Chtěla bych chléb a rohlíky.	kh'**tyel**-ah bikh khleb ah **roh**-hleck-ee
Milk	Mléko	**mleh**-koh
A half kilo of this salami	Půl kilo tohoto salámu	**pool kee**-lo **toh**-ho-toh sah-**lah**-moo
This cheese	Tento sýr	**ten**-toh seer
A kilo of apples	Kilo jablek	**kee**-lo **yah**-blek
Give me six cucumbers.	Dejte mi šest okurek.	**day**-teh mee shest **oh**-koo-rek
Three kilos of pears.	Tři kila hrušek.	tshree **kee**-la h'**roo**-shek
Clothing	Oděvy	**oh**-dyeh-vee
Women's clothing	Dámské odévy	**dahm**-skeh **oh**-dyeh-vee
Men's clothing	Pánské odévy	**pahn**-skeh **oh**-dyeh-vee
Souvenirs	Upomínkové předměty	**oo**-poh-**meen**-koh-veh pshed-**myeh**-tee
Toys and gifts	Hračky a dárky	h'**rahtch**-kee ah **dar**-ky
Jewelry and perfume	Bižutérie a voňavky	**bizh**-oo-teh-ree-yeh ah **voh**-nyahv-kee
At the Hotel Room	Pokoj	**poh**-koy
I would like . . .	Chtěl (Chtěla) bych . . .	kh'**tyel** (kh'**tyel**-ah) bikh
I would like a room.	Chtěl (Chtěla) bych pokoj.	kh'**tyel** (kh'**tyel**-ah) bikh **poh**-koy
For one person	Pro jednu osobu	pro **yed**-noo **oh**-so-boo
For two people	Pro dvě osoby	pro dveh **oh**-so-bee
For how many nights?	Na kolik nocí?	na **ko**-lik **note**-see
For tonight	Na dnešní noc	na **dnesh**-nee notes
For two nights	Na dvě noci	na dveh **note**-see
For a week	Na týden	na **tee**-den
Do you have a different room?	Máte jiný pokoj?	**ma**-teh **yee**-nee **poh**-koy
With a bath	S koupelnou	s'**ko**-pel-noh
With a shower	Se sprchou	seh **sp'r**-kho
With a toilet	S toaletou	s'twa-**leh**-to

The key, please.	Klíč, prosím.	kleech **pro**-seem
How much is it?	Kolik to stojí?	**ko**-lik toh **stoy**-ee
One hundred crowns	Sto korun	sto ko-**roon**
Seven hundred crowns	Sedm set korun	**seh**-doom set ko-**roon**
My bill, please.	Účet, prosím.	**oo**-chet **pro**-seem

Dining Out

Café	Kavárna	ka-**vahr**-na
Restaurant	Restaurace	res-toh-**vrat**-seh
A table for two	Stůl pro dva	stool pro dvah
Waiter, the menu, please.	Pane vrchní! Jídelní lístek, prosím.	**pah**-neh **verkh**-nee **yee**-dell-nee **lis**-tek **pro**-seem
The wine list, please.	Líst vin, prosím. (or, vinny listek).	leest vin **pro**-seem **vin**-nee **lis**-tek
The main course	Hlavní jídlo	**hlav**-nee **yid**-lo
What would you like?	Co si přejete?	tso see **psheh**-yeh-teh
What would you like to drink?	Co se přejete k pití?	tso seh **psheh**-yeh-teh k'**pit**-ee
Can you recommend a good wine?	Můžete doporučit dobré víno?	**moo**-zheh-teh **doh**-por-oo-cheet **dohb**-zheh **vi**-noh
Wine, please.	Víno, prosim.	**vi**-noh **pro**-seem
Pilsner beer	Plzeňské pivo	**pil**-zen-skeh **piv**-oh
What's the specialty of the day?	Jaká je dnešní specialitá?	**ya**-ka yeh **dnesh**-nee spet-sya-lih-**tah**
Do you have strawberry ice cream?	Máte jáhodovou zmrzlinu?	**ma**-teh **ya**-ho-doh-voh zmer-**zlee**-noo
I didn't order this.	Tohle jsem neobjednal.	**toh**-hleh sem **neh**-ob-yed-nahl
That's all, thanks.	Děkuji, to je všechno.	**dyek**-oo-yee to yeh **vsheh**-khno
The check, please.	Účet, prosím.	**oo**-chet **pro**-seem
Is the tip included?	Je záhrnuto zpropítně?	yeh **za**-her-noo-toh **zpro**-peet-nyeh
Enjoy your meal.	Dobrou chuť.	**doh**-broh khoot
To your health!	Na zdraví!	**na** zdrah-vee
Fork	Vidlička	**vid**-litch-ka
Knife	Nůž	noozh
Spoon	Lžíce	l'**zheet**-seh

Napkin	Ubrousek	**oo**-bro-sek
A cup of tea	Šálek čaje	**shah**-lek **tcha**-yeh
A bottle of wine	Láhev vína	**lah**-hev **vi**-nah
One beer	Jedno pivo	**yed**-noh **piv**-oh
Two beers, please.	Dvě piva, prosím.	dveh **piv**-ah **pro**-seem
Salt and pepper	Sůl a pepř	sool ah pepsh
Sugar	Cukr	**tsook**-rr
Bread, rolls, and butter	Chléb, rohlíky a máslo	khleb **roh**-hlee-ky ah **mah**-slo
Black coffee	Černá káva	**chair**-na **kah**-va
Coffee with milk	Káva s mlékem (or, Bílá káva)	**kah**-va s **mleh**-kem **bee**-la **kah**-va
Tea with lemon	Čaj se citrónem	**tchai** se **tsi**-tro-nem
Orange juice	Pomerančový džus	po-mair-**ahn**-cho-vee dzhoos
Another (masc., fem., neuter)	Ještě jeden (ještě jednu, ještě jedno)	yesh-**tyeh** ye-**den** (yesh-**tyeh** yed-**nu**, yesh-**tyeh** yed-no)
More	Ještě	yesh-**tyeh**
I'd like more mineral water.	Chtěl bych ještě minerálku.	kh'**tyel** bikh yesh-**tyeh** min-eh-**rahl**-ku
Another napkin, please.	Ještě jeden ubrousek, prosím.	yesh-**tyeh** jeh-**den** **oo**-bro-sek, **pro**-seem
More bread and butter	Ještě chléb a máslo	yesh-**tyeh** khleb ah **mah**-slo
Not too spicy	Ne příliš ostré	neh **pshee**-leesh **oh**-streh
I like the meat well done.	Chci maso dobře upečené (or, Chci propečené).	kh'tsee **mah**-so **dobe**-zheh **oo**-petch-en-eh kh'tsee **pro**-petch-en-eh
One beer. Cold, please.	Jedno pivo. Chlazené, prosím.	**yed**-no **piv**-oh **khlah**-ze-ne **pro**-seem
May I exchange this for . . .	Mohl bych tohle vyměnit za . . .	**mole** bikh **to**-hleh **vee**-myen-it zah
Telling Time What time is it?	Kolik je hodin?	**ko**-lik yeh **ho**-din
Midnight	Půlnoc	**pool**-nohts
It is noon.	Je poledne.	yeh **po**-led-neh
Morning	Ráno, dopoledne	**rah**-no, **doh**-po-led-**neh**

Afternoon	Odpoledne	**ohd**-po-led-**neh**
Evening	Večer	**veh**-chair
Night	Noc	nohts
It is 9:00 AM.	Je deset hodin dopoledne.	yeh **deh**-set **ho**-din **doh**-po-led-neh
It is 1:00 PM.	Je jedna hodina odpoledne.	yeh yed-**na ho**-din-ah **ohd**-po-led-**neh**
It is 3 o'clock.	Jsou tři hodiny.	so tshree **ho**-din-y
It is 5 o'clock.	Je pět hodin.	yeh pyet **ho**-din
5:15	Pět patnáct	pyet paht-**nahtst**
7:30	Sedm třicet	**sed**-oom **tshree**-tset
9:45	Devět čtyřicet pět	**deh**-vyet **ch'ti**-zhee-tset **pyet**
Now	Ted'	tedj
Later	Později	poh-**zdyay**-ee
Immediately	Hned	h'ned
Soon	Brzo	b'**r**-zo
Days of the Week Monday	Pondělí	**pon**-dye-lee
Tuesday	Úterý	**oo**-teh-ree
Wednesday	Středa	**stshreh**-da
Thursday	Čtvrtek	ch't'v'**r**-tek
Friday	Pátek	**pah**-tek
Saturday	Sobota	**so**-boh-ta
Sunday	Neděle	**neh**-dyeh-leh
Months January	Leden	**leh**-den
February	Únor	**oo**-nor
March	Březen	b'**zhe**-zen
April	Duben	**doo**-ben
May	Květen	k'**vyet**-en
June	Červen	**chair**-ven
July	Červenec	**chair**-ven-ets
August	Srpen	s'**r**-pen
September	Září	**zah**-zhee
October	Říjen	**zhee**-yen
November	Listopad	**list**-o-pahd
December	Prosinec	**pro**-sin-ets
At the Airport Airport	Letiště	**leh**-tish-tyeh
Where is customs?	Kde je celnice?	g'deh yeh **tsel**-nit-seh
Where is the passport control?	Kde je pasová kontrola?	g'deh je **pah**-so-vah kon-**trol**-ah
The baggage claim	Zavazadla	**zah**-vah-**zahd**-lah
Where are the international departures?	Kde jsou mezinárodní odlety?	g'deh soh **meh**-zee-**nah**-rohd-nee **ohd**-leh-tee
Arrivals	Přílety	**pshee**-leh-tee

Where are the taxis?	Kde jsou taxíky?	g'deh so **tak**-seek-ee
Where is the exit?	Kde je východ?	g'deh yeh **vee**-khohd
Is there a subway?	Je tady metro?	yeh **tah**-dee **meh**-tro
Is there a bus?	Je tady autobus?	yeh **tah**-dee **out**-oh-boos
Stop here, please!	Zastavte tady, prosím!	**zah**-stahv-teh **tah**-dee **pro**-seem
What is the fare to downtown?	Kolik to stojí do středu města?	**ko**-lik toh **stoy**-ee doh st'**shreh**-doo **myes**-tah
Have a good trip!	Šť'astnou cestu!	sht'**shast**-no **tsest**-oo

<table>
<tr><td rowspan="20">At the Train Station</td><td>Train station</td><td>Nádraží</td><td>nah-drah-zhee</td></tr>
<tr><td>I'd like a ticket, please.</td><td>Chtěl bych lístek, prosím.</td><td>kh'tyel bikh list-ek pro-seem</td></tr>
<tr><td>A one-way ticket</td><td>Jednoduchý lístek</td><td>yed-no-dookh-nee list-ek</td></tr>
<tr><td>A return ticket</td><td>Zpáteční lístek</td><td>zpah-tetch-nee list-ek</td></tr>
<tr><td>A local train</td><td>Osobní vlak</td><td>oh-sobe-nee vlahk</td></tr>
<tr><td>An express train</td><td>Rychlík</td><td>rikh-leek</td></tr>
<tr><td>Do you have a timetable?</td><td>Máte jízdní řád?</td><td>mah-teh yeezd-nee zhahd</td></tr>
<tr><td>Is there a dining car?</td><td>Je ve vlaku jídelní vůz?</td><td>yeh veh vlah-koo yee-dell-nee vooz</td></tr>
<tr><td>A sleeping car</td><td>Spací vůz</td><td>spa-tsee vooz</td></tr>
<tr><td>Where is this train going?</td><td>Kam jede tenhle vlak?</td><td>kahm jeh-deh ten-h-leh vlahk</td></tr>
<tr><td>What time does the train leave for . . . ?</td><td>V kolik hodin odjíždí vlak do . . . ?</td><td>v'ko-lik ho-din ohd-yeezh-dee vlahk doh</td></tr>
<tr><td>What time does the train arrive from . . . ?</td><td>V kolik hodin přijíždí vlak z . . . ?</td><td>v-ko-lik ho-din pshee-yeezh-dee vlahk z</td></tr>
<tr><td>From what platform does the train leave?</td><td>Z kterého nástupiště vlak odjíždí?</td><td>z'k'tair-ay-ho nah-stoo-pish-tyeh vlahk ohd-yeezh-dee</td></tr>
<tr><td>The train arrives at 2:00 PM.</td><td>Vlak přijíždí ve čtyrnact hodin.</td><td>vlahk pshee-yeezh-dee veh ch'tr-nahtst ho-din</td></tr>
<tr><td>The train is late.</td><td>Vlak ma zpoždění.</td><td>vlahk mah z'poh-zhdyeh-nee</td></tr>
</table>

Can you help me, please?	Mohl byste mi pomoci, prosím?	**mole** bis-teh mee **poh**-moh-tsee **pro**-seem
Can you tell me, please?	Mohl byste mi říci, prosím?	**mole** bis-teh mee **zhee**-tsee **pro**-seem
I've lost my bags.	Ztratila jsem zavazadla.	z'**tra**-tih-lah sem **zah**-vah-zahd-lah
My money	Peníze	**peh**-nee-zeh
My passport	Pas	pahss
I've missed my train.	Zmeškal jsem vlak.	z'**mesh**-kahl sem vlahk

At the Post Office

Post office	Pošta	**po**-shta
Stamps, please.	Známky, prosím.	**znahm**-kee **pro**-seem
For letters or for postcards?	Na dopisy nebo na pohlednice?	na **doh**-pis-ee **neh**-bo poh-**hled**-nit-seh
To where are you mailing the letters?	Kam posíláte dopisy?	kahm poh-see-**lah**-teh **doh**-pis-ee
To the United States	Do Spojených Států	doh **spoy**-en ikh **stah**-too
Airmail	Letecky	**leh**-tet-skee
The telephone directory	Telefonní seznam	te-le-**fon**-nee **sez**-nahm
Where can I go to make a telephone call?	Odkud mohu telefonavat?	**ohd**-kood **moh**-hoo te-le-**fo**-no-**vaht**
A telephone call	Telefonní rozhovor	te-le-**fon**-nee **rohz**-ho-vor
A collect call	Hovor na účet volaného	**ho**-vor na **oo**-chet voh-lah-**neh**-ho
What number, please?	Jaké číslo, prosím?	yah -keh **chee**-slo **pro**-seem
May I speak to Mrs. Newton, please.	Mohl bych ja mluvit s paní Newtonovou, prosím.	**mole** bikh ya **mloo**-vit **spah**-nee **new**-ton-oh-voh **pro**-seem
The line is busy.	Je obsázeno.	yeh ob-**sah**-zen-**oh**
There's no answer.	Nehlásí se.	**neh**-hlah-see seh
Try again later.	Zkuste to poszději.	**zkoo**-steh toh po-**zdyay**-ee
May I leave a message, please?	Mohla bych nechát vzkaz, prosím?	**moh**-hla **bikh** **neh**-khaht v'**zkahz** **pro**-seem

Index

Ales Art Gallery, *100*
All Saints Chapel (Prague), *74*
All Saints' Church (Litoměřice), *112*
Altar of the Masters of Wittingau, *98*
American Hospitality Center, *45*
Antiques shops Prague, *77–78*
Arcibiskupský palác, *68*
Art galleries and museums
Bohemia, *100*
Bratislava, *161*, *162*
Eastern Slovakia, *186–187*
Prague, *68*, *74*
Astronomical Clock, *56*
Augustine monastery, *98*
Austerlitz, *135–136*

Baby-sitting services, *18*
Banská Bystrica, *185–186*, *187–188*
Bardejov, *180–181*, *188*
Bardejovské Kúpele, *181*
Bazilika svatého Jiří, *74*
Beskydy mountains, *124–125*, *138*
Betlémská kaple, *58*
Bicycling
Czech Republic, *40*
Slovakia, *151*
Bílý Koníček, *97*
Black Tower, *100*
Boating and sailing
Czech Republic, *40*
Slovakia, *151*
Bohemia, *89–90*
the arts, *121*
children, attractions for, *113*
emergencies, *90*
guided tours, *91*
hotels, *115–121*
nightlife, *121–122*

Northern region, *108–114*
pharmacies, *90*
restaurants, *94*, *95*, *98*, *103*, *104*, *106*, *107*, *112*, *115–121*
shopping, *114*
sightseeing, *92–114*
Southern region, *92–101*
sports, *114*
tourist information, *90*
transportation in, *91*
transportation to, *90–91*
Western region, *101–108*
Bohemian Chancellery, *73*
Book shops
Prague, *45*, *78*
Books on the Czech Republic, *35–36*
Books on Czechoslovakia, *20–21*
Books on Slovakia, *147*
Bratislava, *153–154*
the arts, *166*
children, attractions for, *162*
climate, *4*
embassies, *154*
emergencies, *154*
English-language bookstores, *154*
guided tours, *156*
hotels, *165–166*
nightlife, *166–167*
pharmacies, *154*
restaurants, *160*, *163–164*
shopping, *163*
sightseeing, *156*, *158–163*
tourist information, *154*
transportation in, *155–156*
transportation to, *155*
travel agencies, *154*
Bretfeld Palace, *63*
Breweries
Bohemia, *107*

Bridges
Bohemia, *101*
Prague, *61–62*
Brno, *124*
the arts, *141*
hotels, *139–140*
nightlife, *141*
restaurants, *135*, *139*
sightseeing, *131–135*
tourist information, *122*
transportation, *122–123*
Business hours
Czech Republic, *39*
Slovakia, *150*
Bus travel, *25*
Bohemia, *90–91*
Bratislava, *155*
Czech Republic, *37*, *38*
Eastern Slovakia, *178*
High Tatras, *169*
Moravia, *123*
Prague, *47*
Slovakia, *148*, *149*
from U.K., *24*, *37*

Cage of shame, *171*
Cairn of Peace, *136*
Camcorders, travel with, *10–11*
Cameras, travel with, *10*
Camping
Czech Republic, *40*
Slovakia, *151*
Capuchin Chapel, *161*
Car rentals, *14–15*
Czech Republic, *35*
Slovakia, *146–147*
Car travel, *25–26*
accidents, *26*
Bohemia, *90–91*
Bratislava, *155*
Czech Republic, *38*
Eastern Slovakia, *178*
gasoline, *26*
High Tatras, *169*
Moravia, *123*
Prague, *46*
Slovakia, *148*, *149*
from U.K., *24*, *37*, *148*
Cash machines, *7*

Casinos
Bohemia, *121*
Prague, *89*
Castle Gallery, *69*, *71*
Castles
Bohemia, *94*, *95*, *97*, *98*, *99*, *100*, *101*, *105*, *109*, *110*, *112*
Bratislava, *160*
Modra, *167*
Moravia, *127*, *129*, *130*, *134–135*
Prague, *69*, *71–75*
Cathedral of St. Elizabeth, *183*
Cathedral of Sts. Peter and Paul, *134*
Cathedral of St. Wenceslas, *137*
Catherine Cave, *136*
Čedok (Czechoslovak travel bureau), *2*, *31*, *44*
Cemeteries
Prague, *59*
Ceremony Hall, *60*
Černá Věž, *100*
Červený Kameň, *167*
Česká kancelář, *73–74*
Ceska Národní banka, *53*
České Budějovice, *100*, *115*
Český Krumlov, *98–100*, *113*, *115*, *121*
Český Šternberk Castle, *94–95*
Chalice House, *111–112*
Chapel of St. Catherine, *158–159*
Chapel of St. John the Evangelist (Bratislava), *161*
Chapel of St. Wenceslas, *71–72*
Chapel of the Holy Cross, *71*
Chapel of the Holy Virgin, *125*
Charles Bridge, *61–62*

Cheb, *103–105,* *115–116*
Cheb museum, *104–105*
Chebský hrad, *105*
Children, attractions for
Bohemia, *113*
Bratislava, *162*
High Tatras, *172–173*
Moravia, *137*
Prague, *75–76*
Children, traveling with, *17–18*
Chrám svatého Bartoloměja, *108*
Chrám svatého Jakuba, *94*
Chrám svatého Mikuláše, *62–63*
Chrám svatého Mořice, *136–137*
Chram svatého Víta, *71–73*
Chrám svatej Barbory, *92, 94*
Church and Convent of the Poor Clares, *159*
Churches
Bohemia, *92, 94, 99, 101, 103, 105, 108, 112*
Bratislava, *158, 159, 161*
Eastern Slovakia, *179, 180, 182, 184, 186*
Moravia, *125, 127, 128, 133, 134, 136, 137*
Prague, *54–55, 56, 57, 58, 62–63, 64, 67, 68, 71–73, 74, 76*
Trvana, *168*
wood churches, *182*
Church of Mary, *101*
Church of Mary Magdelene, *103*
Church of Our Lady of Perpetual Help at the Theatines, *64*
Church of Our Lady of Victories, *64*
Church of St. Bartholemew, *108*
Church of St. John Nepomuk, *68*
Church of St. Maurice, *136–137*

Church of St. Procopius, *64*
Church of the Holy Cross (Brno), *133–134*
Church of the Holy Cross (Jihlava), *125*
Church of the Holy Cross (Kežmarok), *179–180*
Church of the Holy Ghost, *125*
Church of the Holy Trinity, *156*
Church of the Most Sacred Heart, *76*
City Museum (Banská Bystrica), *186*
Clam-Gallas-palota, *57*
Climate, *4*
Clock Museum, *160*
Clock towers
Eastern Slovakia, *186*
Prague, *56*
Clothing for the trip, *4–5*
Czech Republic, *33*
Slovakia, *145*
Coin museum, *94*
Colleges and universities
Bratislava, *159*
Concentration camps, *110–111*
Convents
Prague, *74*
Costs of the trip, *8*
Czech Republic, *33–34*
Slovakia, *145–146*
Council Chamber, *74*
Crown Chamber, *72*
Crypts
Brno, *133–134*
Crystal and porcelain shops
Prague, *78*
ČSA (Czechoslovak Airlines), *25, 37, 46*
ČSAD (bus service), *25, 38, 47*
Currency exchange, *6*
Customs, *9–10*
Czech Republic, *34*
Slovakia, *146*
Czech currency, *33*
Czech language, *34*
Czech National

Bank, *53*
Czech National Gallery, *74*
Czech National Museum, *52*
Czech Republic, *30–31*
car rentals, *35*
costs, *33–34*
currency, *33*
hotels, *42–43*
language, *34*
mail, *39*
restaurants, *41–42*
shopping, *40*
sports, *40–41*
student and youth travel, *35*
tourist information, *31*
transportation in, *37–38*
transportation to, *36–37*
Dačice, *127*
Dance
Bratislava, *166*
Prague, *88*
Danube River, *162*
Deacon's house, *137*
Devin Peak, *130–131*
Dietrichstein Palace, *133*
Disabled travelers, hints for, *18–19*
Dolní Věstonice, *130*
Dom Košického vládneho programu, *183*
Dóm na Petrove, *134*
Dóm svätého Martina, *159*
Dom svatého Štěpána, *112*
Dom svatého Václava, *137*
Dóm svätej Alžbety, *183*
'Dragon' of Brno, *131, 133*
Druhé Nádvorí (Second Courtyard), *69*
Dukla Pass, *182*
Duties, *9–10*
Czech Republic, *34*
Slovakia, *146*
Dvořák, Antonín, *109*
Dvořák Birthplace, *109*

Eastern Slovakia, *176–177*
hotels, *187–189*
pharmacies, *177*
restaurants, *184, 187–189*
sightseeing, *178–187*
sports, *187*
tourist information, *177*
transportation in, *178*
transportation to, *178*
Eger. *See* Cheb
Elderhostel program, *20*
Electricity, *5*
Embassies
Bratislava, *154*
Prague, *45*
Emergencies
Bohemia, *90*
Bratislava, *154*
Eastern Slovakia, *177*
High Tatras, *169*
Moravia, *122*
Prague, *45*

Farmaceutické múzeum, *158*
Festivals and seasonal events,
Czech Republic, *32–33*
Slovakia, *145*
Film
Bratislava, *166*
Prague, *87*
Fishing
Czech Republic, *40*
Slovakia, *151*
Food shops
Prague, *78*
Fountains
Brno, *133*
Kutná Hora, *94*
Olomouc, *136*
Františkánsky kostol, *161*
Františkovy Lázně, *105–106, 116*
Františkuv prameň, *106*
Franz Ferdinand d'Este, Archduke, *94*
Freud, Sigmund, *137–138*

Gabler House, *105*
Gardens
Bohemia, *109*
Prague, *65, 66, 76*

Geysers, *184*
Ghetto Museum, *111*
Goethe, J. W. von, *105*
Golf
Czech Republic, *40*
Prague, *79*
Gothic bridge, *101*
Grandhotel Pupp, *103*

Hall of Ancestors, *127*
Harrachov, *113*
Hašek, Jaroslav, *21, 36*
Havel, Vaclav, *21, 36*
Health and fitness clubs
Prague, *79*
Health concerns, *11–12*
Czech Republic, *34–35*
Slovakia, *146*
Health insurance, *12–13*
Herl'any geyser, *184*
Heydrich, Reinhard, *108*
High Tatras, *168*
arts, *176*
children, attractions for, *172–173*
guided tours, *170*
hotels, *174–176*
nightlife, *176*
pharmacies, *169*
restaurants, *172, 174–176*
shopping, *173*
sightseeing, *170–173*
sports, *173–174*
tourist information, *168*
transportation in, *169*
transportation to, *169*
Hiking
Bohemia, *114*
Czech Republic, *40–41*
Eastern Slovakia, *187*
Slovakia, *151*
Hlohovec, *130*
Hluboká nad Vlatavou, *100*
Holidays
Czech Republic, *39*
Slovakia, *150*
Home exchange, *27–28*
Hotel Europa, *52*

Hotels, *27–28. See also under cities and areas*
children, accommodations for, *18*
Czech Republic, *42–43*
Slovakia, *152–153*
Hot springs
Bohemia, *101, 105, 106*
House of the Košice Government Program, *183*
Hradek, *94*
Hradní galérie, *69, 71*
Hungarian Royal Chamber, *159*
Hus, Jan, *55, 96*
Hussite movement, *96–97*
Hydrofoil rides, *155*

Imperial Sanatorium, *102–103*
Imperial Spa, *103*
Insurance, *12–14*
Italian Court, *94*

Jan Hus monument, *55*
Janské Lázně, *113*
Jedlinka, *182*
Jeleni příkop, *71*
Jeleni Skok, *103*
Jemnice, *127*
Jesuit Church, *161*
Jesuit College, *159*
Jesuit School, *99*
Jewelry shops
Prague, *78*
Jewish ghetto (Prague), *58–60*
Jewish Town Hall, *59*
Jezuitské kolégium, *159*
Jezuitský kostol, *161*
Jihlava, *125, 140*
Jihomorauské Muzeum, *128*
John Nepomuk, St., *72*

Kafka, Franz, *21, 36*
birthplace, *57*
grave, *76*
Kamenná kašna, *94*
Kampa Gardens, *65*
Kampa Island, *65*
Kapinka svätej

Kataríny, *158–159*
Kaple svatého Kříže, *71*
Kaplnka svätého Michala, *183*
Kapucínsky Klášter, *136*
Karlovy Vary
the arts, *121*
children, attractions for, *113*
hotels, *117*
nightlife, *121–122*
restaurants, *103, 116–117*
shopping, *114*
sightseeing, *101–103*
tourist information, *90*
Karlsbad. *See* Karlovy Vary
Karlův most, *61–62*
Kateřinská jeskyně, *136*
Kežmarok, *179–180, 188*
Kinský Palace, *55*
Klariský kostol, *159*
Klášter svatého Jiří, *74*
Komorní Hůrka volcano, *105*
Konopiště, *95, 117–118*
Košice, *182–183, 188*
Kostel Najsvětějšího Srdca Pana, *76*
Kostel Náležení svatého Kříže, *133–134*
Kostel Panny Marie ustavičné pomoci u Kajetánů, *64*
Kostel Panny Marie Vítězné, *64*
Kostel svatého Ducha, *125*
Kostol svätého Egídia, *180*
Kostel svatého Ignáce, *125*
Kostel svatého Jakuba (Jihlava), *125*
Kostol svätého Jakuba (Lavoča), *184–185*
Kostel svatého Jana Nepomuckého, *68*
Kostel svatého Jiljí, *57–58*

Kostel svatého Kříža (Jihlava), *125*
Kostol svätého križa (Kežmarok), *179–180*
Kostel svatého Martina ve zdi, *58*
Kostel svatého Mikuláše (Cheba), *105*
Kostel svatého Mikuláše (Prague), *56–57*
Kostel svatého Mikuláše (Znojmo), *128*
Kostel svatého Václava (Litoměřice), *112*
Kostel svatého Václava (Znojmo), *128*
Kostel svatej Anny, *137*
Kostel svatej Maří Magdaleny, *103*
Kostol kapucínov, *161*
Kostol svätej Trojice, *156*
Kotnov castle, *97*
Královský palác, *73–74*
Krkonoše range, *113, 114*
Krumlov castle, *99–100*
Kundera, Milan, *20–21, 35–36, 61*
Kutná Hora, *92, 94, 118*

Labská Bouda, *113*
Laptops, travel with, *10*
Large Committee House, *185*
Lázeňská poliklinika, *106*
Lednice, *130*
Lennon Peace Wall, *65*
Letenské sady, *76*
Letna Gardens, *76*
Levoča, *184*
Libraries
Bohemia, *100, 107*
Prague, *67*
Lidice, *108–109*
Litoměřice, *111–112, 118*

Little White Horse (house), *97*
Lobkovický palác, *75*
Loreto Church, *67*
Luggage
airline rules on, *5–6*
insurance for, *13*
Macocha abyss, *136*
Magistrale Trail, *171–172*
Mail
Czech Republic, *39*
Slovakia, *149–150*
Maislova synagóga, *60*
Malá Pevnost, *110*
Malá Strana Bridge Towers, *62*
Malokarpatské muzeum, *167*
Mariánské Lázně
the arts, *121*
hotels, *118–119*
nightlife, *121*
restaurants, *118*
sightseeing, *106–107*
tourist information, *90*
Mariánský chram, *101*
Market Colonnade, *102*
Martinický palác, *68*
Matthias Gate, *69*
Matyášova brána, *69*
Medical services. *See* emergencies *under cities and areas*
Medzilaborce, *186–187*
Mělník, *112–113, 119*
Mendel, Gregor, *134*
Merchant Bank, *53*
Mestská radnica, *184*
Metzké Muzeum (Bratislava), *162*
Metzké Muzeum (Ceský Krumlov), *99*
Metzké Muzeum (Litomerice), *111*
Michalska brana (Michael's Gate), *156, 158*
Miklusova väznica, *184*
Mikulov, *129, 140*
Military Museum, *68*
Minorite Church, *125*
Minoritský kostel, *125*

Mintner's Chapel, *92, 94*
Mirbachov palác, *161*
Modra, *167*
Monasteries
Bohemia, *98, 107*
Moravia, *133, 134*
Prague, *67*
Slovakia, *171*
Monastery of Staré Brno, *134*
Money, *6–8*
Moravia, *122. See also* Brno
the arts, *141*
children, attractions for, *137*
emergencies, *122*
hotels, *139–141*
nightlife, *141*
Northern region, *135–137*
pharmacies, *122*
restaurants, *127, 135, 138–141*
shopping, *138*
sightseeing, *124–138*
Southern region, *125–131*
sports, *138*
tourist information, *122*
transportation in, *123*
transportation to, *122–123*
Moravian Karst, *124*
Moravské muzeum, *133*
Moravský Kras, *136*
Moravský Krumlov, *138*
Morzin Palace, *63*
Mostecká Věž, *62*
Mountain sightseeing
Bohemia, *113*
High Tatras, *170–173*
Moravia, *130–131, 138*
Mozart, Wolfgang A., *77*
Mummified remains, *133–134*
Municipal Gallery (Bratislava), *161*
Municipal House (Prague), *53*
Museum of Artistic Handicrafts, *160*
Museum of National Literature, *67*
Museum of the City

(Český Krumlov), *99*
Museum of the Hussite Movement, *96–97*
Museum of the Tatra National Park, *171*
Museum of Weapons and Fortifications, *158*
Museums. *See also* Art galleries and museums
archaeology, *130*
Bohemia, *94, 96–97, 99, 100, 104–105, 106, 108–109, 110, 111, 113*
Bratislava, *158, 160, 161, 162*
breweries, *108*
clocks, *160*
coins, *94*
Dvořák, *109*
Eastern Slovakia, *181, 184, 186*
handicrafts, *160*
High Tatras, *171*
history, *52, 104–105, 128, 133, 160, 184*
hunting and fishing, *100*
Hussite movement, *96–97*
Jewish history, *59*
literature, *67*
military, *68, 158*
Moravia, *128, 129, 133*
natural history, *171*
pharmaceuticals, *158*
Prague, *52, 59, 67, 68*
religious icons, *181*
Slovakia, *167*
spa antiques, *106*
winemaking, *113, 129*
World War II, *108–109, 110–111, 186*
Music, classical
Bratislava, *166*
Prague, *87–88*
Music, popular
Bratislava, *166*
Prague, *89*
Musical instrument shops, *78*
Múzeum bratislavských historických hodín, *160*

Múzeum Slovenského Národného Povstania, *186*
Múzeum umeleckých remesiel, *160*
Múzeum zbraní a mestského opevnenia, *158*
Národní galérie, *68*
Národní Muzeum, *52*
National Gallery, *68*
Nazi occupation, *108–109, 110–111, 182, 186–187*
Nelahozeves, *109*
Nicholas Prison, *184*
Nová knihovna, *107*
Obecní dům, *53*
Obřadní síň, *60*
Ohrada hunting lodge, *100*
Old Bohemian Art Collection, *74*
Old Castle Steps, *75*
Older travelers, hints for, *19–20*
Old Jewish Cemetery, *59–60*
Old Town Bridge Tower, *61*
Old Town Hall (Bratislava), *161–162*
Old Town Hall (Brno), *131*
Old Town Hall (Prague), *56*
Olomouc, *124, 136–137, 140*
Opera
Bratislava, *166*
Prague, *88*
Package deals for independent travelers, *3–4*
Palaces
Bratislava, *159, 161*
Eastern Slovakia, *179*
Moravia, *133*
Prague, *55, 57, 63, 64, 67, 68, 73–74, 75*
Palác Kinských, *55*
Palác Uhorskej král'ovskej komory, *159*
Parish Church, *186*
Park Colonnade, *102*

Parks, national, *185,*
186
Parnassus fountain,
133
Passports, *8*
Czech Republic, *34*
Slovakia, *146*
Pavlovské Vrchy,
130–131
Pec pod Sněžkou, *113*
Petřín tower, *76–77*
Pezinok, *167*
Pharmaceutical
Museum, *158*
Philosophical Hall,
67
Pilsner-Urquell
brewery, *107*
Pinkasova synagóga,
60
Písek, *101, 119*
Pivovarské muzeum,
108
Plane travel
airports and airlines,
22, 36–37, 46
Bohemia, *90*
Bratislava, *155*
charter flights, *23*
with children, *17–18*
Czech Republic, *37*
discount flights, *22–24*
Eastern Slovakia, *178*
flying times, *22*
High Tatras, *169*
insurance for, *13*
luggage rules, *5–6*
Moravia, *122–123*
Prague, *46*
Slovakia, *147–148*
smoking, *24*
tips on, *24*
from U.K., *24, 37,*
*148*Plzeň, *107, 120*
Poprad, *170, 174–175*
Powder Tower, *53*
Praetorium, *186*
Prague, *43–44*
the arts, *87–88*
bus and streetcar
network, *47*
Castle District, *66–68*
children, attractions
for, *75–76*
climate, *4*
embassies, *45*
emergencies, *45*
English-language
bookstores, *45*
guided tours, *48*

hotels, *84–87*
Hradčanské náměstí
(Hradčany Square),
68
Hradčany area, *66–68*
Jewish ghetto, *58–60*
Karlova ulice, *57*
Malá Strana (Little
Town), *60–66*
Malé náměstí (Small
Square), *57*
Malostranské náměstí
(Lesser Quarter
Square), *62*
Maltézské náměstí
(Maltese Square),
64–65
Náměstí Republiky,
53
Na příkopě, *52*
Nerudova ulice, *63*
nightlife, *88–89*
Novy Svět, *68*
Old Town, *49, 52–58*
parks, *65*
personal guides, *48*
pharmacies, *45*
Pohořelec (Scene of
Fire) Square, *67*
restaurants, *54, 58,*
60, 63, 65, 67, 79–84
shopping, *77–78*
sightseeing, *49–77*
sports, *79*
Staroměstské náměstí,
54
subway system, *47*
taxis, *46, 47*
tourist information,
44–45
transportation in,
46–47
transportation to,
45–46
travel agencies, *45*
Václavské náměsti
(Wenceslas Square),
49, 52
Velkopřevorské
náměstí (Grand
Priory Square), *65*
Vojanovy sady, *65–66*
Zlatá ulička, *74–75*
Prague Castle, *69–75*
Prašná brána, *53*
Pražský hrad, *69–75*
Prešov, *182, 188*
Pribor, *137–138*
Primaciálny palác,
162

Prisons, *184*
Protestant Church
(Kežmarok), *180*
První Nádvorí (First
Courtyard), *69*
Punkevní jeskyně,
136
Puppet theaters
Prague, *76*

Rail passes, *15–16*
Czech Republic, *35*
Slovakia, *147*
Restaurants, *26–27.*
See also under cities
and areas
Czech Republic, *41–42*
Slovakia, *151–152*
Rhody House, *181*
Riders' Staircase, *74*
Rosenberg Castle, *98*
Rotunda svatej
Kateřiny, *128*
Royal Mausoleum,
72
Royal Oratory, *72*
Royal Palace
(Prague), *73–74*
Royal Palace (Banská
Bystrica), *186*
Rožmberk nad
Vltavou, *98*
Running and jogging
Prague, *79*
Ruzyně Airport, *22,*
36, 46
Rybnik Svět, *97*

St. Anne's Chapel,
137
St. Barbara
Cathedral, *92, 94*
St. Catherine's
Rotunda, *128*
St. Egidius Church,
180
St. Elizabeth's
Church, *172–173*
St. George's Basilica,
74
St. George's Convent,
74
St. Ignace Church,
125
St. Jacob's Church,
112
St. James Church
(Jihlava), *125*
St. James Church
(Kutná Hora), *94*

St. James Church
(Levoča), *184–185*
St.
Martin-in-the-Wall
church, *58*
St. Martin's
Cathedral, *159*
St. Michael's Chapel,
183
St. Nicholas
Cathedral (Trvana),
168
St. Nicholas Church
(Cheb), *105*
St. Nicholas Church
(Prague), *62–63*
St. Nicholas Church
(Znojmo), *128*
St. Stephen's
Cathedral, *112*
St. Vitus Cathedral
(Prague), *71–73*
St. Vitus church
(Český Krumlov), *99*
St. Wenceslas, statue
of, *49, 52*
St. Wenceslas Chapel
(Litoměřice), *112*
St. Wenceslas Church
(Znojmo), *128*
Sanatoriums,
102–103
Šariš Museum, *181*
Schönbornský palác,
64
Schwarzenberg-
palota, *68*
Shopping. See also
under cities and
areas
Sixt House, *54*
Skiing
Bohemia, *114*
Czech Republic, *41*
Slovakia, *151*
Škvorecký, Josef, *21,*
36
Slavín Memorial, *163*
Slavkov, *135–136*
Sliezsky Dom, *172*
Slovak currency, *145*
Slovakia, *143–144*
car rentals, *146–147*
costs, *145–146*
currency, *145*
hotels, *152–153*
language, *146*
mail, *149–150*
restaurants, *151–152*
shopping, *150*

Slovakia (*continued*)
sports, *150–151*
student and youth
travel, *147*
tourist information,
144
transportation in,
148–149
transportation to,
147–148
Slovak language,
146
**Slovak National
Gallery,** *162*
**Slovak National
Museum,** *160*
**Slovak National
Theater,** *162*
**Slovenská národná
galéria,** *162*
**Slovenské národné
divadlo,** *162*
**Slovenské národné
múzeum,** *160*
Slovenský Raj, *185,
186*
**Small Carpathian
Museum,** *167*
**Small Committee
House,** *185*
Smokovec, *170, 172,
175*
Sněžka, *113*
Soccer
Prague, *79*
**South Moravian
Museum,** *128*
Spa Museum, *106*
Špilberk Castle,
134–135
Špindlerův Mlýn,
113, 120
Spiš Castle, *185*
Spiš Museum, *184*
Spišská Sobota,
178–179
Spiš towns, *178–179*
Sports. *See also
specific sports;
under cities and
areas*
Sports shops
Prague, *78*
Stag Moat, *71*
Stag's Leap, *103*
Stará radnica
(Bratislava), *161*
Stará radnice (Brno),
131
Stará sněmovna, *74*

**Staré zámecké
schody,** *75*
Staroměstská radnice
(Prague), *56*
Staronová synagóga,
59
**Starý židovský
hřbitov,** *59–60*
**State Jewish
Museum,** *59*
Štátne Divadlo,
183–184
**Státní Židovské
muzeum,** *59*
Stavovské Divadlo
(Estates Theater),
52–53
Strahov Library, *67*
Strahovský klášter,
67
Štrbské Pleso, *171,
175–176*
Střekov castle, *112*
**Student and youth
travel,** *16–17*
Czech Republic, *35*
Slovakia, *147*
Svět pond, *97*
Swimming
Bohemia, *114*
Eastern Slovakia, *187*
Prague, *79*
Synagogues
Prague, *59, 60*

Tábor, *96–97,
120–121*
Tanečnice, *138*
Tatranska Lesná,
172
Tatranská Lomnica,
171, 176
Tatras Mountains,
168–176
Telč, *125, 127, 140*
Telephones, *26*
Czech Republic, *38–39*
Slovakia, *149*
Tennis
Czech Republic, *41*
Prague, *79*
Slovakia, *151*
Teplá, *107*
**Terezín
concentration camp,**
110–111
Tery chata, *172*
Theater
Bratislava, *166*
Prague, *88*

Theater buildings
Bratislava, *162*
Košice, *183–184*
Prague, *52–53*
Theresienstadt. *See*
Terezín
concentration camp
Thermal Hotel, *102*
**Thun-Hohenstein
Palace,** *63*
Thurzo House
(Banská Bystrica),
186
Thurzo House
(Levoca), *185*
Timing the visit, *4*
Czech Republic, *32*
Slovakia, *144–145*
Tipping
Czech Republic, *39*
Slovakia, *150*
Tokolyho hrad, *179*
Tour groups, *2–4*
Czech Republic, *31–32*
Slovakia, *144*
Tourist information,
*2. See also under
cities and areas*
Town Castle (Telč),
127
Town Hall tower
(Prague), *56*
Train travel, *25*
Bohemia, *90–91*
Bratislava, *155*
Czech Republic, *37–38*
Eastern Slovakia, *178*
High Tatras, *169*
Moravia, *123*
Prague, *46*
rail passes, *15–16*
Slovakia, *148–149*
from U.K., *24, 37,
148*
Traveler's checks, *6*
Třeboň Castle, *97–98*
Tretí nádvorí (Third
Courtyard), *71*
Trinity Column, *136*
Trnava, *167–168*
Tugendhat Haus, *135*
Týn Church, *54–55*

U červeného orla, *63*
U Minuty house, *56*
**University Church of
John the Baptist,**
168
Urbanová veža, *183*
U tří housliček, *63*

U Zvonů House, *55*

Valkoun House, *63*
Valtice, *129–130, 141*
Velké Karlovice, *141*
**Veltrusy Castle and
Gardens,** *109*
Victorian Church,
103
Villa Bertramka, *77*
Visas, *8*
Czech Republic, *34*
Slovakia, *146*
Vladislavský sál, *73*
Vlašský dvůr, *94*
Vojenské muzeum, *68*
Volcanoes, *105*
Vranov castle, *127*
Vřídlo, *102*
Vrtbovský palác, *64*
Vysoká synagóga, *59*

**Wagon wheel of
Brno,** *131–133*
Waldstein Gardens,
66
Wallenstein chapel,
72
**Warhol Family
Museum of Art,**
186–187
Weather information,
4
Wenceslas, St., *71*
Wenceslas Square,
49, 52
Western Union, *7*
Wineries
Bohemia, *112*
Moravia, *128–129*

Youth hostels, *17*
**Yuri Gagarin
Colonnade,** *102*

**Zahrada
Valdštejnského
paláca,** *66*
Židovská radnice,
59
Žilina, *189*
Živnostenská banka,
53
Znojmo, *128–129,
141*
Zoos
Bohemia, *100*
Prague, *75*
Zvíkov, *101*

Fodor's Travel Guides

Available at bookstores everywhere, or call 1–800–533–6478, 24 hours a day.

U.S. Guides

Alaska

Arizona

Boston

California

Cape Cod, Martha's Vineyard, Nantucket

The Carolinas & the Georgia Coast

Chicago

Colorado

Florida

Hawaii

Las Vegas, Reno, Tahoe

Los Angeles

Maine, Vermont, New Hampshire

Maui

Miami & the Keys

New England

New Orleans

New York City

Pacific North Coast

Philadelphia & the Pennsylvania Dutch Country

The Rockies

San Diego

San Francisco

Santa Fe, Taos, Albuquerque

Seattle & Vancouver

The South

The U.S. & British Virgin Islands

The Upper Great Lakes Region

USA

Vacations in New York State

Vacations on the Jersey Shore

Virginia & Maryland

Waikiki

Walt Disney World and the Orlando Area

Washington, D.C.

Foreign Guides

Acapulco, Ixtapa, Zihuatanejo

Australia & New Zealand

Austria

The Bahamas

Baja & Mexico's Pacific Coast Resorts

Barbados

Berlin

Bermuda

Brazil

Brittany & Normandy

Budapest

Canada

Cancun, Cozumel, Yucatan Peninsula

Caribbean

China

Costa Rica, Belize, Guatemala

The Czech Republic & Slovakia

Eastern Europe

Egypt

Euro Disney

Europe

Europe's Great Cities

Florence & Tuscany

France

Germany

Great Britain

Greece

The Himalayan Countries

Hong Kong

India

Ireland

Israel

Italy

Japan

Kenya & Tanzania

Korea

London

Madrid & Barcelona

Mexico

Montreal & Quebec City

Morocco

Moscow & St. Petersburg

The Netherlands, Belgium & Luxembourg

New Zealand

Norway

Nova Scotia, Prince Edward Island & New Brunswick

Paris

Portugal

Provence & the Riviera

Rome

Russia & the Baltic Countries

Scandinavia

Scotland

Singapore

South America

Southeast Asia

Spain

Sweden

Switzerland

Thailand

Tokyo

Toronto

Turkey

Vienna & the Danube Valley

Yugoslavia

Special Series

Fodor's Affordables

Caribbean

Europe

Florida

France

Germany

Great Britain

London

Italy

Paris

**Fodor's Bed &
Breakfast and
Country Inns Guides**

Canada's Great
Country Inns

California

Cottages, B&Bs and
Country Inns of
England and Wales

Mid-Atlantic Region

New England

The Pacific
Northwest

The South

The Southwest

The Upper Great
Lakes Region

The West Coast

The Berkeley Guides

California

Central America

Eastern Europe

France

Germany

Great Britain &
Ireland

Mexico

Pacific Northwest &
Alaska

San Francisco

**Fodor's Exploring
Guides**

Australia

Britain

California

The Caribbean

Florida

France

Germany

Ireland

Italy

London

New York City

Paris

Rome

Singapore & Malaysia

Spain

Thailand

Fodor's Flashmaps

New York

Washington, D.C.

Fodor's Pocket Guides

Bahamas

Barbados

Jamaica

London

New York City

Paris

Puerto Rico

San Francisco

Washington, D.C.

Fodor's Sports

Cycling

Hiking

Running

Sailing

The Insider's Guide
to the Best Canadian
Skiing

Skiing in the USA
& Canada

**Fodor's Three-In-Ones
(guidebook, language
cassette, and phrase
book)**

France

Germany

Italy

Mexico

Spain

**Fodor's
Special-Interest
Guides**

Accessible USA

Cruises and Ports
of Call

Euro Disney

Halliday's New
England Food
Explorer

Healthy Escapes

London Companion

Shadow Traffic's New
York Shortcuts and
Traffic Tips

Sunday in New York

Walt Disney World
and the Orlando Area

Walt Disney World
for Adults

**Fodor's Touring
Guides**

Touring Europe

Touring USA:
Eastern Edition

**Fodor's Vacation
Planners**

Great American
Vacations

National Parks
of the East

National Parks
of the West

**The Wall Street
Journal Guides to
Business Travel**

Europe

International Cities

Pacific Rim

USA & Canada

WHEREVER YOU TRAVEL, *H*ELP IS NEVER FAR AWAY.

From planning your trip to providing travel assistance along the way, American Express® Travel Service Offices* are always there to help.

Czech Republic

PRAGUE
American Express Czechoslovakia Ltd.
Vaclavske Namesti 56
42-2-267528

Slovakia

BRATISLAVA
Tatratour
Frantiskanske Nam. 3
42-7-335852

PIEŠTANY
Tatratour
Winterova 28
42-838-25305

KOŠICE
Tatratour
Alzbetina 6
42-95-24872 or 21334

POPRAD
Tatratour
Nam. Sv. Egidia 9
42-92-63712

ŽILINA
Tatratour
Marianske Nam. 21
42-89-47529